RENAISSANCE VEGETARIANISM
THE PHILOSOPHICAL AFTERLIVES OF
PORPHYRY'S *ON ABSTINENCE*

LEGENDA

LEGENDA is the Modern Humanities Research Association's book imprint for new research in the Humanities. Founded in 1995 by Malcolm Bowie and others within the University of Oxford, Legenda has always been a collaborative publishing enterprise, directly governed by scholars. The Modern Humanities Research Association (MHRA) joined this collaboration in 1998, became half-owner in 2004, in partnership with Maney Publishing and then Routledge, and has since 2016 been sole owner. Titles range from medieval texts to contemporary cinema and form a widely comparative view of the modern humanities, including works on Arabic, Catalan, English, French, German, Greek, Italian, Portuguese, Russian, Spanish, and Yiddish literature. Editorial boards and committees of more than 60 leading academic specialists work in collaboration with bodies such as the Society for French Studies, the British Comparative Literature Association and the Association of Hispanists of Great Britain & Ireland.

The MHRA encourages and promotes advanced study and research in the field of the modern humanities, especially modern European languages and literature, including English, and also cinema. It aims to break down the barriers between scholars working in different disciplines and to maintain the unity of humanistic scholarship. The Association fulfils this purpose through the publication of journals, bibliographies, monographs, critical editions, and the MHRA Style Guide, and by making grants in support of research. Membership is open to all who work in the Humanities, whether independent or in a University post, and the participation of younger colleagues entering the field is especially welcomed.

ALSO PUBLISHED BY THE ASSOCIATION

Critical Texts
Tudor and Stuart Translations • *New Translations* • *European Translations*
MHRA Library of Medieval Welsh Literature

MHRA Bibliographies
Publications of the Modern Humanities Research Association

The Annual Bibliography of English Language & Literature
Austrian Studies
Modern Language Review
Portuguese Studies
The Slavonic and East European Review
Working Papers in the Humanities
The Yearbook of English Studies

www.mhra.org.uk
www.legendabooks.com

ITALIAN PERSPECTIVES

In the light of growing academic interest in Italy and the reorganization of many university courses in Italian along interdisciplinary lines, this book series, founded by Maney Publishing under the imprint of the Northern Universities Press and now continuing under the Legenda imprint, aims to bring together different scholarly perspectives on Italy and its culture. *Italian Perspectives* publishes books and collections of essays on any period of Italian literature, language, history, culture, politics, art, and media, as well as studies which take an interdisciplinary approach and are methodologically innovative.

APPEARING IN THIS SERIES

Managing Editor
Dr Graham Nelson, 41 Wellington Square, Oxford OX1 2JF, UK
www.legendabooks.com

Renaissance Vegetarianism

The Philosophical Afterlives of
Porphyry's On Abstinence

❖

CECILIA MURATORI

l

LEGENDA

Italian Perspectives 46
Modern Humanities Research Association
2020

Published by Legenda
an imprint of the Modern Humanities Research Association
Salisbury House, Station Road, Cambridge CB1 2LA

ISBN 978-1-78188-338-9 (HB)
ISBN 978-1-78188-341-9 (PB)

First published 2020

Copy-Editor: Charlotte Brown

CONTENTS

❖

For James and Amanda

ACKNOWLEDGEMENTS

❖

The idea for this book developed during my years at LMU Munich (2009–13). I gratefully acknowledge the support of the LMU Fellowships programme for the publication of this book, as well as for the excellent working conditions I enjoyed when I was Research Fellow at the *Seminar für Geistesgeschichte und Philosophie der Renaissance*. The project did not start as an investigation of Renaissance animal ethics: that it took this turn, and I had the courage to venture into a largely unexplored area was thanks to Thomas Ricklin. It was he who suggested that I look into the ethical consequences of the debates on the psychological human-animal difference that I was studying at the time. Eventually, the unexpectedly large amount of material that I found on this topic led my research in directions that I had not envisaged. For this, for his encouragement to study what he thought interested me most, and for sharing his knowledge and curiosity with me, I will always remain deeply grateful to him. I also warmly thank my friends and colleagues at LMU, especially Kathrin Schlierkamp and Annika Willer.

Before I embarked on the project of writing a book on Renaissance vegetarianism, Burkhard Dohm and I tested out methodological ideas on researching pre-Cartesian animal ethics: we organised a conference, which gave rise to the edited collection *Ethical Perspectives on Animals in the Renaissance and Early Modern Period* (Micrologus' Library 2013). Exchange with him was instrumental in the early development of my research on this topic, and I am grateful for his support and for his great enthusiasm for the subject.

Chapter 2 ('Health') was mostly developed when I was Frances Yates Fellow at the Warburg Institute, University of London (2015); Chapter 3 ('Otherness') was conceived during the year I spent at Villa I Tatti, The Harvard University Center for Italian Renaissance Studies (2013–14). I am grateful to both institutions, and to the many friends and colleagues with whom I had the pleasure of discussing the unfolding of my book, especially Karen-edis Barzman, Kate Bentz, Robert Black, Angela Matilde Capodivacca, Alberto Frigo, Guy Gelter, Guido Giglioni, John Henderson, Giordano Mastrocola, Eugenio Refini, and Neslihan Şenocak. I also thank Stefano Gensini, Eva del Soldato, and Sara Miglietti for advice regarding, respectively, Girolamo Fabrici D'Acquapendente, Basil Bessarion, and Giovanni Botero.

The book was completed during my fellowship at the University of Warwick within the ERC Starting Grant Project 2013-335949, 'Aristotle in the Italian Vernacular: Rethinking Renaissance and Early-Modern Intellectual History (c. 1400-c. 1650)'. The great support of David Lines and Simon Gilson has been key in finishing this project, and especially in deepening my understanding of Renaissance

Aristotelianism, which plays an important role in Chapter 4 ('Rationality'). I warmly thank Maude Vanhaelen for sharing with me her profound knowledge of Renaissance Platonism, and for her comments on a draft of Chapter 1 ('Sacrifice'). Daniele Conti generously shared his work and his expertise on Ficino with me, also helping me to polish Chapter 1. Exchange with Alessandra Aloisi and Alessio Cotugno, and the many conversations with Amber Carpenter over the years, have often made me doubt, and think again — for which I am very grateful to them.

I had the opportunity of presenting my work in progress at several conferences and workshops. In particular, I would like to thank Gianni Paganini, who invited me to present sections of Chapter 1 at the Università del Piemonte Orientale (Vercelli), and who pointed out the importance of Jacques Boulduc for my research; Francesco Coniglione for his invitation to give a seminar on Porphyry and philosophical vegetarianism at the Università di Catania; Eugenio Canone, who kindly asked me to present at a workshop of the Istituto per il Lessico Intellettuale Europeo e Storia delle Idee; Catherine König-Pralong, Mario Meliadò, and Zornitsa Radeva for the useful exchange we had in Freiburg on diet and religious discipline; and Isabel Iribarren for the invitation to talk about animal eschatology and carnivorism in Strasbourg, and for the very stimulating conversations we had.

I wish to thank my parents for their trust. That I was able complete this project is thanks to my husband's unwavering support through many years of research and travelling. James Vigus was this book's first reader, and his interest nurtured my writing. This book is for him, and for our Amanda, as she starts to think about food, and learns to live with animals.

C.M., June 2020

NOTES

❖

1. Terminology

I have preferred the use of 'human being' to 'man' whenever the context made a generic reference (man and woman) possible. Nevertheless, it is to be noted that in many of the sources quoted in the book, the reference would have been implicitly to men specifically. This is notably the case in Porphyry's conception of the (male) philosopher.

I have used 'human' and 'animal', rather than 'human animal' and 'non-human animal'. This is mainly for concision and readability, but I believe that clarity is not affected. How Renaissance philosophers conceived the difference between the human animal and all other animals is made clear in each specific case considered in the book.

2. Transcriptions

I have applied the following criteria when transcribing Latin and Italian passages: punctuation was modernised whenever necessary to enable better understanding of the text; accents, apostrophes, and capital letters were made uniform according to modern usage; *u* and *v* have been conformed to modern usage; & > *et* (Latin) / *e* (Italian); *ß* > ss. In Italian, *h* has been deleted in occurrences of *cho/cha/chu* and *gho/ gha/ghu* (e.g. *anchora* > *ancora*) but retained when etymologically relevant (e.g. *humore* > *humore*). Abbreviations have been tacitly expanded.

3. Quotations

Main quotations from Renaissance sources in Latin and Italian, in the body of the text, are always given both in the original version and English translation. This allows the reader to appreciate the terminology used in each case, and any continuities or significant variations in the vocabulary employed. Also, some of the texts translated are hardly known to Anglophone readers due to the lack of translations: by including English translations of the most significant passages, it is hoped that this will contribute to making the texts known. Translations are always my own unless stated otherwise.

4. Abbreviations

a) Editions of On Abstinence

OA: Passages from *On Abstinence* are referred to as *OA*, followed by book, chapter, and paragraph number, as in the Budé edition (Porphyry, *De l'abstinence*, ed. by Jean Bouffartique and others, 3 vols (Paris: Les Belles Lettres, 1977–95)), followed by the page number from the English translation (Porphyry, *On Abstinence from Killing Animals*, ed. by Gillian Clark (London: Bloomsbury, 2014)): e.g. *OA* 1.21.1; p. 38.

b) Other Abbreviations

ASD: *Opera omnia Desiderii Erasmi Roterodami*, ed. by C. Augustijn, 9 vols (Amsterdam: Brill, 1982)

DCD: Augustine, *De civitate Dei*, in *Corpus scriptorum ecclesiasticorum latinorum*, ed. by Emanuel Hoffman (Prague, Vienna, & Leipzig: Tempsky & Freytag, 1899–1900), XL.1–2

ICP: Basil Bessarion, *In calumniatorem Platonis*, in *Kardinal Bessarion als Theologe, Humanist und Staatsman*, ed. by Ludwig Mohler, 3 vols (Paderborn: Schöningh, 1927; repr. 1967), II

LMF: *The Letters of Marsilio Ficino*, ed. and trans. by The Language Department of the School of Economic Science, 10 vols to date (London: Shepheard-Walwyn, 1975–)

OGC: Girolamo Cardano, *Opera omnia*, ed. by Charles Spon, 10 vols (Lyon: Jean-Antoine Huguetan and Marc-Antoine Ravaud, 1663; repr. Stuttgart-Bad Cannstatt: Frommann-Holzboog, 1966)

OMF: Marsilio Ficino, *Opera omnia* (Basel: Petri, 1576; reprint Turin: Bottega D'Erasmo, 1959)

INTRODUCTION

❖

'Old Battles Fought Over Again'

1. Renaissance Abstinence

The word 'vegetarianism' was first coined not long before the foundation of the first vegetarian society in England, in 1847.[1] But while the word did not exist in the Renaissance, the philosophical foundation of the diet that excludes meat had been passionately discussed by Renaissance philosophers. 'Vegetarianism' is a useful catch-all term to embrace historical discussions of this topic, since the older vocabulary to describe it was varied. Renaissance philosophers often employed a very versatile term to define a meat-less diet: 'abstinence' (*abstinentia*). Abstinence could reflect religious, medical, or philosophical views. It evokes the practice of monks and the refraining from certain foods on religious occasions. It did not always refer specifically to avoiding meat, but was applied to a whole series of behaviours, extending to hygienic practices as well. As abstinence, vegetarianism is characterized by the sense of renouncing a type of food, and all the practices related to this choice. It is therefore defined by what it excludes, rather than by what it includes.

Abstinentia also features in the Latin title of the most comprehensive philosophical discussion of vegetarianism, written by the Neoplatonist Porphyry around AD 270: *Perí apochés empsúchon*, literally 'On Refraining from Ensouled Creatures', but known in the Latin West as *De abstinentia ab esu carnium*, or 'On Abstaining from Eating Meat'.[2] For Porphyry, the philosopher should practice complete abstinence from eating animals: he calls this the 'fleshless diet', which as such is a form of renunciation, aimed at preparing the body and mind for spiritual exercise.[3] Terminology is important to the question of what 'vegetarianism' meant for Porphyry and for the later philosophers discussed in this book. As we will see, what philosophers in the past termed 'abstinence' is often closer to what is now called 'veganism' (abstinence from all animal products) than to 'vegetarianism' (abstinence from all meat).[4] A study of the transmission of philosophical vegetarianism from antiquity to the Renaissance will thus require both terminological awareness and the use of suitable approximations — especially the term 'vegetarianism' — to gain an accurate sense of the coherent development of a set of ideas.

In the form of an appeal to a friend, Firmus Castricius, who had gone back to eating meat after a period of abstinent vegetarianism, Porphyry's text answers the question: should a philosopher — that is to say, someone whose actions are led by reason — be a vegetarian?[5] In answering in the affirmative, Porphyry presents a wide range of arguments, involving psychological, religious, medical, and even cultural anthropological considerations. His main tenet is that a philosopher should nourish his intellect: the contemplation of the divine is best accompanied and supported by following a vegetarian diet.[6] Porphyry often delineates his arguments in implicit conversation with philosophical schools that did not view the vegetarian diet as a requirement for philosophers, especially the Stoics and the Aristotelians.[7]

In the form in which it has been transmitted to us, *On Abstinence* is not complete. Indeed, it has been termed as one of the most notable 'literary shipwrecks' of antiquity, since what is lost was most likely substantial and influential.[8] In any case, the work became an essential point of reference for the Neoplatonic school and beyond. Divided into four books, it functioned as a channel through which ancient philosophical theories on diet were transmitted and discussed. For instance, extracts by Plutarch, or by Aristotle's successor Theophrastus, are interspersed in the text. Porphyry's position on diet is uniquely well-defined in the panorama of ancient philosophy: he does not advocate moderation in meat eating, but complete abstinence, and develops a variety of arguments to support this view. Even within the Neoplatonic school, vegetarianism was far from being the standard dietetic practice. In *On Abstinence*, Porphyry never mentions the diet of his master, Plotinus, even if in his *Life of Plotinus* he suggests that Plotinus also abstained from animal flesh, because he would not swallow medication containing animal products.[9] On the other hand, Iamblichus, disciple of Porphyry and major figure of Postplotinian Platonism, supported the use of animals, including in sacrificial practice.[10] The addressee of Porphyry's *On Abstinence*, Firmus Castricius, himself a follower of Plotinus, seems to have sided rather with eating (moderate) quantities of meat than with complete vegetarianism.

The philosophical trajectory of what later came to be called 'vegetarianism' is deeply intertwined with the fortune of Porphyry's work. Interest in the philosophical foundations of vegetarianism underwent a powerful revival in the Renaissance due in large measure to the rediscovery of ancient sources on diet, including, but not limited to, *On Abstinence*. Plutarch's essays on animal rationality (*Bruta animantia ratione uti* [Animals Use Reason]) and against the consumption meat (*De esu carnium* [On Meat-eating]) were published in the first edition of his *Moralia* (1509).[11] The diffusion of Diogenes Laertius's *Lives of Eminent Philosophers* from the early fifteenth century onwards, especially thanks to the Latin translation by Ambrogio Traversari, contributed substantially to shaping the reputation of sages like Pythagoras, known for his frugal, abstinent diet. Epicurus, too, is portrayed by Diogenes Laertius as having led a very simple life, as in his letters he claimed to be satisfied with water and cooked bread.[12] Dietetic and medical theories involving meat also circulated through editions of the works of Hippocrates and Galen.[13] Yet, no other source had the same profound impact on Renaissance philosophical debates on the vegetable diet as *On Abstinence*. While Renaissance readers would often intertwine references to Porphyry and Plutarch, or recur to the example of Pythagoras (vegetarianism was sometimes called 'Pythagorean diet', or *diaeta pythagorica*), Porphyry's defence of vegetarianism was a unique source. The breadth and depth of the philosophical material presented in *On Abstinence* is unrivalled by any other ancient text on vegetarianism. A key example is Porphyry's detailed, original treatment of the connection between religion (in particular the issue of sacrifice) and diet, which had a remarkable impact on Renaissance readers, beginning with the author of the first published translation of *On Abstinence*, Marsilio Ficino.[14] Furthermore, Porphyry's thesis — that the philosopher should be vegetarian — was unequivocal, compared to the blurred positions of other ancient philosophers. This ambiguity appears, for instance, in the case of the Pythagoreans, sometimes deemed to have been vegetarians, and sometimes to have eaten small quantities of meat.[15] In *On Abstinence* Renaissance philosophers found a wealth of arguments that resonated and could interact with current debates. Especially after the first Latin translations and editions, dating from the end of the fifteenth to the mid-sixteenth century, *On Abstinence* circulated broadly, as shown by the large quantity of references to it in Renaissance philosophical literature. These range from marginal notes directing the reader to a particular argument in *On Abstinence*, to substantial comments and also critiques of Porphyry's view of the philosophical diet.

The present book considers for the first time how *On Abstinence* became a point of reference for Renaissance philosophers debating the advantages and disadvantages of choosing an abstinent, vegetable diet. In this study, engagement with *On Abstinence* is the *fil rouge* that helps to recover the richness of Renaissance debates on vegetarianism. This is not simply a reception history, and as such does not attempt to provide an account of the full diffusion of the text and the reactions to it. At the centre of the investigation are instead the philosophical arguments of Porphyry's appeal, and especially their Renaissance afterlives. The book reconstructs the history not of a dietetic practice, but of a philosophical position. Therefore the vast Renaissance literature on dietary regimens and cookery is referred to only tangentially when it forms useful context. The aim of this book is to excavate the philosophical arguments that connect Porphyry with his Renaissance readers, admirers, and critics.[16]

In tracking philosophical engagements with *On Abstinence*, *Renaissance Vegetarianism* presents an in-depth analysis of the theoretical background of vegetarian, and also anti-vegetarian, theories in the Renaissance. It shows how Porphyry's positions on the topic were reconsidered and his arguments reassessed within new cultural and philosophical settings. By tracing the rekindling of interest in *On Abstinence*, the book shows how Porphyry's key tenets are developed in new directions, stimulating a debate in the Renaissance over the philosophical foundations of vegetarianism. Porphyry's view of vegetarianism was holistic, as he envisioned the vegetable diet as concerning both body and soul, and the way to balance them in a philosophical life. Renaissance philosophers, too, often crossed the line between medical, religious, and strictly philosophical propositions, when answering the question whether humans should eat animals. Yet, certain key topics crystallized in specific contexts and periods, giving rise to fresh controversies.

Renaissance Vegetarianism systematically organizes the philosophical engagement with vegetarianism into four core topics, devoting a chapter to each. These are central in *On Abstinence*, and Renaissance philosophers reconsidered them, often with direct reference to Porphyry, though they viewed them from new perspectives. The first is the link between sacrificing and eating animals ('Sacrifice'); the second is the question of whether a vegetable diet promotes or endangers health ('Health'); the third is the comparison between the diets of different populations, and the conclusions to be drawn from observing their dietary habits and their level of intelligence and civilization ('Otherness'); the fourth is the question whether maintaining that animals are rational supports vegetarianism or rather makes it impossible ('Rationality').

Should a philosopher abstaining from meat abstain from religious practice (animal sacrifice) as well? Porphyry devotes a substantial section of Book 2 of *On Abstinence* to this issue. He seeks to demonstrate that a vegetarian philosopher can still be pious, even if he does not participate in eating the sacrificial animal. Chapter 1, 'Sacrifice', in the present book investigates why animal sacrifice was still a philosophical problem in the late fifteenth and early sixteenth century, and why it provoked the Renaissance revival of *On Abstinence*. To Renaissance readers, Porphyry's stance on blood sacrifices offers a Neoplatonic view that can be combined with the Christian rejection of pagan rites, despite Porphyry's notorious anti-Christian invective: this is an aspect which recurs in the controversy between Basil Bessarion (1403–72) and George of Trebizond (1395–1472/73), as well as in the work of Marsilio Ficino (1433–99). The chapter has a main focus on Ficino's translation-paraphrase of *On Abstinence*, which laid the foundation for further discussions of the issue of animal sacrifice in the Renaissance. This trajectory then leads from Giovanni Pico della Mirandola's (1463–94) reflections on the symbolic meaning of animal sacrifice to Francesco Zorzi's (1466–1540) assertion of the religious foundation of vegetarianism in his influential *De harmonia mundi* [On the Harmony of the World].

Is eating meat beneficial or harmful for health? How does eating meat affect the body — and the soul? According to Porphyry, a vegetarian diet can only benefit the activities of philosophical speculation; a carnivorous diet, on the other hand, might be indicated for athletes and people who need heavier nutrition. Chapter 2, 'Health', explores the connections between Porphyry's discussion of the effects of a vegetarian diet and the Renaissance reception of medical literature, especially the works of Hippocrates and Galen in which dietary choices are presented as a major aspect in promoting health. The starting point is a contemporary question about religious vegetarianism: do monks who follow a vegetarian, or semi-vegetarian, diet endanger their health? Erasmus (1467?–1536) dealt with this question in his dialogue between a Carthusian monk and a soldier (in his *Colloquia*), as well as in *De esu carnium* [On Meat-eating], but another source for this debate is *De esu carnium* by Arnaldus de Villanova (*c.* 1240–1311). The most extensive discussion of the benefits and dangers of vegetarianism to health is provided by Girolamo Cardano (1501–76), who combined references to Porphyry's *On Abstinence* with contemporary discussion of dietetics, especially that of Alvise Cornaro (*c.* 1484–1566). The chapter ends with an analysis of the critical reply of Julius Caesar Scaliger (1484–1558) to Cardano's stance on the effects of diet, and of vegetarianism in particular, on the nature of a creature.

What do the dietary habits of other people reveal with regard to their level of intelligence? Porphyry had used the examples of the vegetarian Indian Brahmans and of the carnivorous, nomad Scyths to show how the choice of nutrition has an impact on the development of entire populations, promoting contemplation or brutishness respectively. The comparison between different dietary habits gains currency in the aftermath of Renaissance geographical expansion. The figure of the wise, vegetarian Brahmans, already portrayed in *On Abstinence*, is contrasted especially with the savage man-eaters 'discovered' in the Americas. The debates on cannibals, as opposed to the vegetarian Brahmans, demonstrate the key role of diet in defining humanity. The controversy between Cardano and Scaliger turned partly on the link between food and a creature's intelligence: are herbivores cleverer than carnivores or not? This question was applied to the case of different human groups, too. Chapter 3, 'Otherness', examines the Renaissance fascination with two opposite diets: the vegetarian diet of the Brahmans and Gymnosophists of antiquity, and the extreme form of carnivorism of the contemporary American cannibals. Among others, the accounts of Cardano in *Theonoston* [Divine Knowledge] and of Antonio Persio (1543–1612) in *Trattato dell'ingegno dell'huomo* [Treatise on Human Intellection] focus on the ideal of a vegetarian sage and its practical applicability. Such writers contrasted this view of the Brahmans with the image of the anthropophagi, not only as the ultimate example of ferocity or of human perversity, in accordance with portrayals in antiquity, but also, and more problematically, as the embodiment of an ideal of long-lived, healthy populations, living in a fertile, earthly paradise. The chapter shows that out of the contrast between Brahmans and cannibals there emerged in the Renaissance a new understanding of the human-animal border, and thus a new approach to the topic of eating animal flesh.

If animals are rational, is it still legitimate to kill and eat them? And if plants are sentient, is there ethical concern about eating them? Porphyry's vegetarian stance was founded on the belief that animal rationality is an argument against carnivorism: we do not eat creatures which we consider to be rational. On the other hand, Porphyry viewed plants as lacking a soul, and not partaking in the least either in sensation or in rationality. Since abstinence (*apoché*) should be practiced, for Porphyry, only from creatures who possess a soul, the philosopher may eat plants. The topic of animal rationality is ubiquitous in Renaissance texts, and it was also the main issue at stake in the later developments of the debate on the animal soul, as this turned into the seventeenth-century *querelle de l'âme des bêtes*. Chapter 4, 'Rationality', therefore considers the afterlives of Porphyry's basic question about the legitimacy of eating rational creatures, by underlining the persistence and re-elaborations of this issue from the sixteenth to the seventeenth centuries, as the debate on the faculties of the animal soul developed into the controversy on animal automatism. For instance, the question whether animals possess language — answered in the affirmative by thinkers like Girolamo Fabrici D'Acquapendente (1533–1619) and Michel de Montaigne (1533–1592) — resurfaces in the aftermath of Descartes's thesis of the animal-machine. Yet, the ethical implications of animal rationality were debated before the *querelle* fully gained currency in the second half of the seventeenth century.[17] Tommaso Campanella (1568–1639), a contemporary of René Descartes (1596–1650), drew striking ethical consequences from siding with Porphyry on the issue of animal rationality. Since Campanella viewed the universe as permeated by sensation, he argued, against Porphyry, that plants can feel: this fact, in his view, renders vegetarianism impossible. The chapter ends with a consideration of the Porphyrian appeal in favour of vegetarianism by Pierre Gassendi (1592–1655): despite the macroscopic differences between Campanella's attack of vegetarianism and Gassendi's support of Porphyry, the line between abstinence and moderation appears blurred in both cases.

The sections of the book are organized thematically around the four topics just outlined. Taken as a whole, they also unfold chronologically, embracing the period from the mid-fifteenth to the mid-seventeenth century. Despite the fact that these topics are naturally intertwined, there was also a tendency for each of them to receive special attention in a particular phase of the Renaissance reception of *On Abstinence*. The problem of animal sacrifice is discussed especially during the early phase of the rediscovery of Neoplatonic sources through Marsilio Ficino, Basil Bessarion, and Giovanni Pico della Mirandola, while the assessment of vegetarianism within the comparison with the diets of other people becomes central in the first half of the sixteenth century, in the aftermath of the discovery of the Americas. Moreover, the question about the plants' sensibility becomes particularly compelling in the context of late Renaissance theories of pansensism and panpsychism (e.g. in Tommaso Campanella's idea that the entire world is a living creature).

These four topics are clearly interrelated. For instance, considerations about health are also directly relevant when assessing the diet of other people; the definition of rationality plays a crucial role also in understanding the human practice of sacrificing animals; and the question regarding the diet of other peoples is deeply connected to the definition of the human–animal border, and thus to animal rationality. Therefore central argumentative tenets are intertwined throughout the book, and the same philosopher is sometimes treated in more than one section. Nevertheless, the division into main topics has been preferred over a linear structure (whether simply chronological, or proceeding by author) in order to place the arguments in their complex historical-philosophical context. For each section, further case studies could have been added. The choice was directed, however, by the intention of providing coherent and systematic overviews. These, it is hoped, may guide readers to their own further investigations. The goal is not an encyclopedic treatment of the subject. Instead, the reconstruction of selected debates opens up a way of treating Renaissance philosophical animal ethics without placing it in the shadow of later, more well-known discussions, while reflecting its polyphonic character.

2. The Development of 'Vegetarianism'

In *La Vie de Monsieur Des-Cartes* (1691), Adrien Baillet remarked on the fact that the philosopher preferred a diet based on fruits and roots, rather than one which included animal flesh, explaining that he considered a vegetable diet to be more beneficial than a carnivorous one. Descartes praised a plant diet as better suited to extending one's lifespan — even if he did include in his own diet certain types of meat.[18] He surely did not consider it morally wrong to kill animals, however. In a letter to Marin Mersenne, he recounts his regular visits to the butcher to see pigs being slaughtered; this, he explains, is to satisfy his scientific curiosity ('it is not a crime to be curious about anatomy').[19] Even more telling is a passage from a letter to Henry More in which he states that his theory of animal automatism was not cruel towards the animals: rather it was liberating for humans, who were now freed from all concern when killing an animal.[20] But Baillet's remark is more than anecdotal: it reflects the 'common knowledge' that a plant-based diet is beneficial on various levels, and that a carnivorous one can endanger human health. The vegetable diet appreciated by Descartes has a long tradition, associated with the philosophers' wish to preserve at one and the same time the health of the body and the sharpness of the mind.

While Descartes's position with regard to the nature of animals and the legitimacy of their use has been analysed,[21] the wider Renaissance and early modern debates on the topic of eating animals remain until now completely unexplored.[22] The main reason is the historiographical tradition that sees in Descartes's theory of animal automatism a turning point in the history of human approach to animals: the accompanying assumption is that concerns about eating animals did not emerge before the mid-seventeenth century.[23] In analysing debates prior to the publication of Descartes's *Discours de la méthode* (1637), as well as in the years immediately following, this book (especially Chapter 4) will challenge the historiographical bias underpinning many studies of the so-called *querelle de l'âme des bêtes* that was sparked by the ethical consequences of Descartes's automata-theory. It will become clear that there are significant elements of continuity, and not merely radical difference, between the pre- and the post-Cartesian debates on the treatment of animals, especially when viewed as a source of food. *Renaissance Vegetarianism* overturns the assumption of Cartesian uniqueness by demonstrating that the Renaissance was a rich formative period for the conceptual history of vegetarianism. It thus fills a gap which until now has remained invisible.

By following the engagement of Renaissance readers with the philosophical idea(l) of a vegetarian diet, then, this book challenges the preconception that ethical questions involving animals were not discussed before the early modern period.[24] It is not just 'retrospective illusions', to use Renan Larue's apt expression, that make us see discussions on vegetarianism in the Renaissance: philosophically valuable debates on the foundations of vegetarianism took place in the period, and they deserve to be rediscovered.[25] Like Larue (and others before him, notably Haussleiter), I believe that the term 'vegetarianism' can and should be applied to periods before the coinage of the word in the nineteenth century.[26] While other anachronisms — such as the seventeenth-century term 'cosmology' applied to theories of ancient philosophers — have been accepted by historians of philosophy and are regularly used, there appears to be some resistance to the use of 'vegetarianism' to describe pre-modern approaches. This reflects the belief that our modern sensibility to the issue cannot be compared to historical accounts, but it may also result from lack of in-depth studies on the subject, and especially neglect of the main source for philosophical discussions of vegetarianism from late antiquity onwards: Porphyry's *On Abstinence*.[27]

This book provides ample material for a philosophical appreciation both of Renaissance debates on vegetarianism, and of Porphyry's work as their main inspiration. The chronological focus on the period from the mid-fifteenth to the mid-seventeenth century shows the development of the debates on vegetarianism within a framework of continuity from the Renaissance to early modernity. Descartes himself, and the ethical replies to his theory of animal automatism, are only tangentially mentioned — this is both because there already exists literature on the place of animals in these later discussions, and because the main aim of this book is to bring attention to the earlier debates and texts on animal ethics, that have been so far neglected.[28] This framework thus avoids a strict historiographical construction of the kind that opposes the Renaissance to early modernity, a contrast which is often not simply intended as a chronological division, but as a judgment on the method of philosophical investigation, supposedly less systematic and more literary during the Renaissance, and more strictly philosophical and 'scientifically' structured in early modernity.[29] This book offers instead a variety of paths through the complexity of Renaissance animal ethics in relation to diet, showing how main strands of the debate evolved prior to seventeenth-century disputes about animal automatism.

Adopting this perspective brings to light a certain circularity of the arguments adduced for and against vegetarianism, appreciating the difference in historical scenarios and also the theoretical continuities. On a macroscopic level, the context of the first Latin translations of Porphyry (and especially of Ficino's interest in Porphyry's connection of sacrifice, eating meat, and daemonology) and the mid-seventeenth century discussion of pansensism and moderation in meat eating (with which the volume ends) are worlds apart. But by looking into the fabric of the arguments, the presence of the same sources — Porphyry above all — reveals the line of continuity. Vegetarianism is discussed throughout the period, with the emphasis being placed on different aspects, as philosophical interests shift: this book attends to the different voices and traces the variations.

Although the focus is on the historical period just outlined, several of the arguments considered in this book have remained topical well beyond the Renaissance, and into contemporary ethics as well. Such links between current concern and historical reconstruction have been until now partially established only within so-called 'eco-critical studies' in the field of literary criticism.[30] Yet the reappraisal of vegetarianism is a main example of the persistence and change of a philosophical position from the Renaissance onwards. This book thus contributes an historical dimension to the development of ideas that are now in the limelight. For instance, the question whether it is just to eat a creature with sensation, or whether the attribution of rationality marks the ethical line between creatures that can and those that should not be eaten, remains a live one.[31] The definition of rationality, and its relation to sensation, is fundamental in the criticism of Aristotelian psychology by Renaissance philosophers like Telesio and Campanella, who claim that animals do partake in the kind of rationality that is directly embedded in sensation. From this, the latter draws distinct conclusions with regard to animal ethics. When, over a century later, Jeremy Bentham insisted that with regard to animals 'the question is not, Can they *reason*? nor, Can they *talk*? but, Can they *suffer*?', the relation between 'animal ethics' and 'animal minds' was still central, but was reformulated by laying all the emphasis on the animals' capability to feel.[32] This issue has remained at the forefront of ethical debates ever since — even if, as a recent publication has claimed, the 'institutional distinction between theoretical and practical philosophy' has caused the separation of these two interrelated fields of animal ethics and of the philosophy of (animal) mind.[33]

There are also arguments that have significantly shifted due to scientific advancements. The meaning of 'sensation' is one such example. Present-day philosophers are unlikely to support a pansensistic view similar to that of Campanella. Yet, the question whether those who spare animals can justify why they choose to eat plants, is one that vegetarians are still asked to answer — at least by argumentative friends at the dinner table. A modern-day vegetarian is likely to use a Porphyrian answer to this question, referring to the fact that animals feel, and suffer when they are slaughtered, while plants, to the best of our knowledge do not, at least not in the same way.[34] To this, Campanella would object that to a plant its life is as dear as the life of an animal is to the animal in question, even if plants show this attachment in different ways from animals. In contemporary ethics, while plants are generally not considered to be capable of feeling in the same way as animals,[35] the limits of animal sentience, on the other hand, are still debated.[36]

Finally, certain arguments disputed fervently in the Renaissance now have solely historical-philosophical value, as they have been superseded by new knowledge. This is the case with the fear that practising vegetarianism could endanger health and even lead to death, a fear that was still felt by some Renaissance sympathizers of the vegetable diet (as discussed in Chapter 2). Already in the mid-nineteenth century readers of the journal *The Vegetarian Messenger* were reassured that

> 'You will kill yourself', is amusing to the apprehension of the practical Vegetarian, who feels that he has made life more lively and better and bestowed a pleasure over all his physical existence which he did not know before. [...] 'You will die', does not accord with the experience of Vegetarianism; for the most of those who join the movement are out of health.[37]

The article containing this quotation is entitled: 'Old Battles Fought Over Again'. And indeed, in the objectives of *The Vegetarian Messenger*, programmatically printed directly under the title, it is possible to recognize some of the issues debated not only by Porphyry but also some of his Renaissance readers: 'advocating total abstinence from the flesh of animals, and the adoption of vegetarian habits of diet, as prescribed by the nature of the human constitution, and consequently most conducive to the full development and healthful exercise of physical, intellectual, and moral powers'.[38]

The sense of the debate, of 'battles fought over again', is what this book seeks to convey. Not all Renaissance readers of Porphyry were ultimately convinced by his claims in favour of vegetarianism: an approach of careful moderation in meat consumption often appears to be favoured over total abstinence. The Renaissance of vegetarianism is a diffused and complex phenomenon, and Porphyry's argumentative battle against his friend's relapse into carnivorism is its most long-lived, philosophical core.

Notes to the Introduction

1. James Gregory, *Of Victorians and Vegetarians: The Vegetarian Movement in Nineteenth-century Britain* (London & New York: Tauris Academic Studies, 2007), p. 1. See the use of the adjective 'vegetarian' in [Charles Lane], 'Flesh Diet (The Editor's Answer to Barbara's Letter)', Part 1: *The Healthian*, 5.1 (April 1842), 33–35; Part 2: *The Healthian*, 6.1 (May 1842), 42–44. In the anonymous piece 'Vegetarian Intelligence', *The Vegetarian Advocate*, 5 (December 1848), 60–64 (especially 61 & 67), the noun 'vegetarianism' appears as completely established: here 'vegetarianism' is presented as a movement, and Porphyry as a main philosopher in the vegetarian tradition.

2. On the dating of *On Abstinence* see Jean Bouffartigue and Michel Patillon, 'Introduction', in Porphyry, *De l'abstinence*, ed. by Jean Bouffartigue and others, 3 vols (Paris: Les Belles Lettres, 1977–95), I, xi-lxxxiv (p. xix).

3. *OA*, 1.1–2 (p. 31). On this see Pierre Hadot, *Philosophy as a Way of Life: Spiritual Exercises from Socrates to Foucault*, ed. by Arnold I. Davidson, trans. by Michael Chase (Oxford: Blackwell, 1995), p. 100.

4. On refraining from using any animal products — milk, honey, eggs, wool etc. — see *OA*, 1.21.1–2 (p. 38).

5. On Firmus Castricius, see Joseph Bidez, *Vie de Porphyre, le philosophe néo-platonicien* (Ghent & Leipzig: van Goethe & Teuber, 1913), pp. 98–99. According to Bidez, Firmus did not practice 'strict observance' of vegetarianism; Bouffartigue and Patillon counter-argue that it is not correct to view one dietary regimen as the standard for all members of a philosophical school ('Introduction', pp. xix–xx). See also Porphyry, *Vie de Plotin: travaux préliminaires et index grec complet*, ed. by Luc Brisson and others, 2 vols (Paris: Vrin, 1982), I, 89–90.

6. Ibid., p. 2; Bouffartigue and Patillon, 'Introduction', p. liii: 'Pour Porphyry l'abstinence est un moyen non suffisant mais indispensable pour parvenir au salut'. See on Porphyry's asceticism, Gillian Clark, 'Fattening the Soul: Christian Asceticism and Porphyry's *On Abstinence*', *Studia Patristica*, 35 (2001), 41–51. Gillian Clark, 'Introduction', pp. 1–28 (p. 18), states that there is 'no suggestion that the philosopher might be female'.

7. On this see below, Chapter 4.1: 'The Renaissance Roots of the *querelle de l'âme des bêtes*'.

8. See Bouffartigue and Patillon, 'Introduction', p. xiii.

9. Porphyry, *The Life of Plotinus and the Order of His Books*, in Plotinus, *Enneads*, vol. 1, ed. by A. H. Armstrong (Cambridge, MA: Harvard University Press, 1969), pp. 1–87 (p. 5; § 2): 'He refused also to take medicines containing the flesh of wild beasts, giving as his reason that he did not approve of eating the flesh even of domestic animals'. See also Clark, 'Introduction', p. 5.

10. Yet, as Emma Clarke has pointed out, 'it is possible that Iamblichus' respect for the Pythagorean lifestyle as well as for the Platonic ascetic ideal may have encouraged him to favour moderation in sacrifice' (*Iamblichus' 'De Mysteriis': A Manifesto of the Miraculous* (Aldershot: Ashgate 2011), p. 51). See also Iamblichus, *On the Pythagorean Life*, ed. by Gillian Clark (Liverpool: Liverpool University Press, 1989), pp. 28–30, on Pythagoras's purificatory regime.

11. On Plutarch in the Renaissance see Marianne Pade, 'The Reception of Plutarch from Antiquity to the Italian Renaissance', in *A Companion to Plutarch*, ed. by Mark Beck (Oxford: Blackwell, 2014), pp. 531–43.

12. See Diogenes Laertius, *Lives of Eminent Philosophers*, ed. by Tiziano Dorandi (Cambridge: Cambridge University Press, 2013); *Lives of Eminent Philosophers*, trans. by R. D. Hicks, 2 vols (Cambridge, MA, & London: Harvard University Press & Heinemann, 1925), Book x.11. See on the reception of Diogenes Laertius in the Renaissance: Christian Kaiser, *Das Leben der Anderen im Gemenge der Weisheitswege: Diogenes Laertios und der Diskurs um die philosophische*

Lebensform zwischen Spätantike und Früher Neuzeit (Berlin: De Gruyter, 2013). On Pythagoras in the Renaissance see Christiane L. Joost-Gaugier, *Pythagoras and Renaissance Europe: Finding Heaven* (Cambridge: Cambridge University Press, 2009); and Michael J. B. Allen, 'Pythagoras in the Early Renaissance', in *A History of Pythagoreanism*, ed. by Carl A. Huffman (Cambridge: Cambridge University Press, 2014), pp. 532–43.

13. Richard J. Durling, 'Galen in the Renaissance: A Chronological Census of Renaissance Editions and Translations of Galen,' *Journal of the Warburg and Courtauld Institutes*, 24.3–4 (1961), 230–305.

14. On Porphyry's theory of sacrifice see Bidez, *Vie de Porphyre*, pp. 99–101.

15. See M. Laura Gemelli Marciano, 'The Pythagorean Way of Life and Pythagorean Ethics', in *A History of Pythagoreanism*, ed. by Huffman, pp. 131–48 (p. 140). Christoph Riedweg, *Pythagoras. Leben — Lehre — Nachwirkung: eine Einführung* (Munich: Beck, 2007), pp. 49 & 93.

16. Key works on these aspects include: Sandra Cavallo & Tessa Storey, *Healthy Living in Late Renaissance Italy* (Oxford & New York: Oxford University Press, 2013); Jennifer Richards, 'Useful Books: Reading Vernacular Regimens in Sixteenth-century England', *Journal of the History of Ideas*, 73.2 (2012), 247–71; Ken Albala, *Eating Right in the Renaissance* (Berkeley, Los Angeles, & London: University of California Press, 2002); and *Renaissance Food from Rabelais to Shakespeare: Culinary Readings and Culinary Histories*, ed. by Joan Fitzpatrick (London & New York: Routledge, 2016).

17. I discuss sixteenth-century debates on animal automatism in 'Animali automatici precartesiani: due argomenti a partire da Aristotele', in *La voce e il logos. Filosofie dell'animalità nella storia delle idee*, ed. by Stefano Gensini (Pisa: ETS, 2020), pp. 111–37.

18. Adrien Baillet, *La Vie de Monsieur Des-Cartes*, 2 vols (Paris: Horthemels, 1691), II, 448: 'mais il falloit, selui luy, que ce fût avec des choses qui donnassent peu de nourriture, telles que sont les racines & le fruits qu'il recommandoit comme beaucoup plus propres à prolonger la vie de l'homme, que la chair des animaux'. See also p. 130: 'Pour lui qui avoit appris de bonne heure à se gouverner dans son régime de vivre, qui beuvoit tres-peu, & qui ne pronoit ordinairement que des viandes grossiéres & peu nourrissantes, il ne s'étoit point mal précautionné contre la malignité du climat'.

19. René Descartes, letter to Mersenne (13 November 1639), in René Descartes, *Œuvres*, ed. by Charles Adam and Paul Tannery, 12 vols (Paris: Cerf, 1897–1913), II (*Correspondance, Mars 1638-Décembre 1639*), 621: 'ce n'est pas un crime d'estre curieux de l'Anatomie'.

20. René Descartes, letter to Henry More (5 February 1649), in Descartes, *Œuvres*, ed. by Adam & Tannery, V (*Correspondance, Mai 1647-Février 1650*), 278–79: 'Sicque haec mea opinio non tam crudelis est erga belluas, quam pia erga homines'.

21. See especially John Cottingham, '"A Brute to the Brutes?"': Descartes' Treatment of Animals', *Philosophy*, 53.206 (1978), 551–59; Katherine Morris, 'Bêtes-machines', in *Descartes' Natural Philosophy*, ed. by Stephen Gaukroger and others (London & New York: Routledge, 2000), pp. 401–19; Dennis Des Chene, *Spirits and Clocks: Machine and Organism in Descartes* (Ithaca, NY: Cornell University Press, 2001).

22. The existing studies on philosophical vegetarianism do not consider the Renaissance period at all. On the other hand, the studies on Renaissance animals focus only marginally on ethical issues. The essay collection *Ethical Perspectives on Animals in the Renaissance and Early Modern Period*, ed. by Burkhard Dohm & Cecilia Muratori, Micrologus' Library, 55 (Florence: SISMEL, Edizioni del Galluzzo, 2013) proposed methodological strategies to identify ethical concern for animals in Renaissance philosophical texts, and presented a first survey of topics and authors.

23. Renaissance authors are either absent from or play a minor role in: Gary Steiner, *Anthropomorphism and its Discontents: The Moral Status of Animals in the History of Western Philosophy* (Pittsburgh, PA: University of Pittsburgh Press, 2005); *Ethical Vegetarianism: From Pythagoras to Peter Singer*, ed. by Kerry S. Walters & Lisa Portmess (Albany: State University of New York Press, 1999); Erica Joy Mannucci, *La cena di Pitagora: storia del vegetarianesimo dall'antica Grecia a internet* (Rome: Carocci, 2008). Colin Spencer's *Vegetarianism: A History* (London: Grub Street, 2000) contains a short overview of some Renaissance authors who generically engaged with the topic of animals, without in-depth discussions of the philosophical foundations. On the reasons for studying Renaissance animal ethics see Burkhard Dohm and Cecilia Muratori, 'Introduction', in

Ethical Perspectives on Animals in the Renaissance and Early Modern Period, ed. by Dohm & Muratori, pp. 3–19.

24. Exemplarily for this approach, Dombrowski even claims that after Porphyry interest in vegetarianism 'curiously died out for almost seventeen hundred years until the present day' (Daniel Dombrowski, *The Philosophy of Vegetarianism* (Amherst: University of Massachusetts Press, 1984), p. 2). This was evidently not the case.

25. Renan Larue, *Le Végétarisme des Lumières: l'abstinence de viande dans la France du XVIIIe siècle* (Paris: Garnier, 2019), p. 11.

26. Ibid., pp. 11–12. Johannes Haussleiter, *Der Vegetarismus in der Antike* (Berlin: Töpelmann, 1935).

27. This is a point raised by Larue, *Le Végétarisme des Lumières*, p. 12.

28. Gary Steiner, 'Descartes on the Moral Status of Animals', *Archiv für Geschichte der Philosophie*, 80.3 (1998), 268–91; Maria Teresa Marcialis, *Filosofia e psicologia animale: da Rorario a Leroy* (Cagliari: STEF, 1982).

29. This approach is theorized in Cecilia Muratori and Gianni Paganini, 'Renaissance and Early Modern Philosophy: Mobile Frontiers and Established Outposts', in *Early Modern Philosophers and the Renaissance Legacy*, ed. by Cecilia Muratori & Gianni Paganini (Berlin: Springer, 2016), pp. 1–18.

30. Examples are Todd A. Borlik, *Ecocriticism and Early Modern English Literature: Green Pastures* (London & New York: Routledge, 2011); and *Renaissance Ecology: Imagining Eden in Milton's England*, ed. by Ken Hiltner (Pittsburgh, PA: Duquesne University Press, 2008).

31. As popularly evident in Jonathan Safran Foer, *Eating Animals* (New York: Little, Brown & Co., 2009).

32. Jeremy Bentham, *An Introduction to the Principles of Morals and Legislation*, ed. by J. H. Burns & H. J. A. Hart (Oxford & New York: Oxford University Press, 1996), p. 283. It is worth remembering that this famous series of questions appears in a footnote, not in the main text. The long footnote compares human slaves to animals: just as it has gradually become abominable to treat fellow humans as slaves, so 'the day *may* come, when the rest of the animal creation may acquire those rights which never could have been withholden from them but by the hand of tyranny' (ibid.).

33. Klaus Petrus and Markus Wild, 'Introduction', in *Animal Minds and Animal Ethics: Connecting Two Separate Fields*, ed. by Klaus Petrus & Markus Wild (Bielefeld: Transcript Verlag, 2014), pp. 7–12 (p. 8).

34. See Galen Strawson's interpretation of panpsychism: Galen Strawson, 'Realistic Monism: Why Physicalism Entails Panpsychism', in *Consciousness and Its Place in Nature: Does Physicalism Entail Panpsychism?*, ed. by Anthony Freeman (Exeter: Imprint Academic, 2006), p. 26: 'Panpsychism certainly does not require one to hold the view that things like stones and tables are subjects of experience — I don't believe this for a moment, and it receives no support from the current line of thought — but we will need to address William James's well known objection to the idea that many subjects of experience can somehow constitute a single "larger" subject of experience'.

35. See exemplarily Dieter Birnbacher, *Naturalness: Is the 'Natural' Preferable to the 'Artificial'?*, trans. by David Carus (Lanham, MD: University Press of America, 2014), pp. 20–21, who writes that plants are 'often zoomorphized by ascribing them terms such as "interest", which have their exclusive sense when applied to beings endowed with consciousness'. Birnbacher considers this an 'overreaction to the contempt of nature in the main tradition of Western philosophy'.

36. *The Animal Ethics Reader*, ed. by Susan J. Armstrong, & Richard G. Botzler, 3rd edn (Abingdon: Routledge, 2017), esp. James Rachels, 'The Basic Argument for Vegetarianism', pp. 274–79: the line drawn by Gary Verner between animals who feel pain and those who do not is (approximately) the line between vertebrates and invertebrates. However, research constantly moves forwards, and the tendency is to extend the number of animals that might be able to suffer, not decrease it.

37. [Anon.], 'Old Battles Fought Over Again', *The Vegetarian Messenger*, 3.41 (March 1853), 15–20 (pp. 18–19). The issue considers also another topic discussed in the Renaissance, namely the relation between diet and longevity, applied to the comparison between animals and plants ([Anon.], 'The Life of Plants', pp. 20–22, abridged version of an article reviewing two books

by J. M. Schleiden, Professor of Botany in Jena (*Principles of Scientific Botany*, and *The Plant, a Biography*); [Anon.], 'The Life of Plants', *British Quarterly Review*, 11.22 (Feb-May 1850), 336–55 (p. 346): 'The longevity of plants exceeds even that of the longest-lived animals. The elephant, and some of the larger graminivorae, are supposed to live about a century [...]. But a tree will endure ten times as long'). See the discussion of this issue below, Chapter 2.6.

38. See, for example, the title page of *The Vegetarian Messenger*, 3.41 (March 1853).

CHAPTER 1

❖

Sacrifice

1.1. Introduction: Animals on the Altar and Animals on the Plate

Is it legitimate for a vegetarian philosopher to sacrifice animals? Or does the choice not to kill animals for food lead by necessity to opposing all pagan rites that involve slaughtering animals?[1] When Porphyry comes to discuss these questions, at the beginning of Book 2 of *On Abstinence*, his approach indicates that he realizes what is at stake with the issue of sacrifice, namely the possibility of presenting vegetarianism to Firmus as a viable option at all. Indeed, if the vegetarian philosopher considers himself to be necessarily outside the territory of religious practice, then vegetarianism would appear as an implicit critique of religious piety. In this sense, Porphyry's answer to the questions on sacrifice might even be seen as the cornerstone of his entire argumentation: it is a particularly difficult terrain, and Porphyry ventures upon it with the intent to present a position which will be both truthful and 'please the gods'.[2]

The connection between sacrificing and eating animals had been at the centre of one of the most embarrassing stories regarding the choice of a fleshless diet: Pythagoras's sacrifice on the occasion of discovering the famous Pythagorean Theorem.[3] If Pythagoras did perform the sacrifice, then he effectively, at least on one occasion, failed to follow his own precept of not killing animals. Yet, different, conflicting versions of this 'incident' exist, sometimes attributing to the vegetarian sage the sacrifice of one ox, sometimes of an entire hecatomb.[4] Porphyry himself provides different accounts in *On Abstinence* and in his *Life of Pythagoras*, oscillating between both versions,[5] but also adding a third option, the only one that appears truly compatible with his dietary choices: that Pythagoras offered to the gods only inanimate things, as Diogenes Laertius had already reported.[6] The conflict between different reports on Pythagoras's general rule about not killing animals is so strong that Diogenes even mentions the possibility that the biographical details might derive from the lives of two different people named 'Pythagoras': one who allowed killing (in particular for special dietary purposes),[7] and another, the philosopher, who neither ate nor sacrificed animals. Given that Porphyry, in the opening lines of *On Abstinence*, reminds Firmus that his decision to eat meat contrasts with the teaching of those philosophers he used to admire, Pythagoras and Empedocles, it is clear that Porphyry's approach to sacrifice is crucial for his arguments. Porphyry repeatedly returns to the problem of the connection between diet and sacrifice, carefully suggesting that sacrifice does not stand in the way of a philosopher's commitment to vegetarianism.[8]

One of Porphyry's main strategies in the attempt to recruit Firmus (and more generally those interested in leading a philosophical life) back to vegetarianism, consists in separating sacrifice from eating animals, thus avoiding assimilating these two acts of killing: 'it does not follow from killing animals that one must necessarily also eat them: by conceding one of the two, I mean slaughter, one does not thereby postulate eating'.[9] Porphyry thus intends to indicate to Firmus that the connection between vegetarianism and the practice of sacrificing is not as direct as might be assumed at first sight: the vegetarian philosopher does not actually oppose the practice of sacrificing altogether, for, at least in theory, it is possible to sacrifice animals while still refraining from eating them. This means that the dietary restriction with regard to animals does not place the philosopher outside the practice of piety. To clarify this argument, Porphyry even adds that sometimes animals are sacrificed which nobody would eat (with a possible hint at human sacrifice).[10] In any case, the point remains that killing does not involve eating, and the ritual killing of some animals does not involve the legitimacy of killing all for food, regardless of the circumstances.

Porphyry's sharp specification is necessary because the link between sacrificing and eating animals was especially prominent from the point of view of a philosopher writing in the third century AD. In antiquity eating the victim was an essential part of the ritual,[11] and from an anthropological perspective it has even been argued that eating meat coincided entirely with the sacrificial practice: the act of slaughtering an animal finds its completion in the sharing and eating of its flesh.[12] Therefore, eating meat is justified by a religious rite.[13] In *Homo necans* Walter Burkert has argued that the connection between eating and ritual offering can be traced back even to the practice of hunting animals, an activity through which the hunter (the human) mirrors himself in the hunted (the animal). According to Burkert, the sense of rituality is thus inscribed in the killing during hunting, which naturally leads to consuming the flesh, whereby the hunter literally assimilates the hunted.[14] From an anthropological point of view, sacrificing an animal and eating its meat are interpreted as being so strictly connected to the point of becoming the same action.[15]

Porphyry tries to disentangle the two because he is aware that their juxtaposition is key to arguing that the philosopher can choose not to sacrifice animals *and* not to eat them. On the one hand, Porphyry seems to safeguard religious piety by distinguishing the issue of eating animals from that of (occasionally) sacrificing (some of) them. But on the other, he recurs to the very same parallelism of eating and sacrificing when he points out that the ancients neither used animals for food, nor sacrificed them.[16] Porphyry thus suggests that both the sacrificing and the eating of animate creatures are customs which resulted from a betrayal of the original practice. He supports this view by repeatedly quoting Aristotle's disciple Theophrastus, author of a lost treatise *On Piety*[17] in which — as far it is possible to reconstruct from surviving references like those in Porphyry's work — he had argued in favour of returning to the practice of sacrificing solely crops and fruit.[18] The act of slaughtering animals on the altar is therefore presented as the result of a process of corruption, of a fall into unlawful, violent killing.[19] Once again, Porphyry stresses how the two main aims behind animal slaughter — nutrition and religious piety — appear to have developed historically in parallel: driven primarily by famine, humans started to both sacrifice and eat animals at the same time, abandoning the exclusive use of vegetables both on the altar and on the plate.[20] The dietary and the religious choices thus maintain a strong connection. Hence clarifying the position of the vegetarian philosopher with regard to sacrifice is essential in the frame of Porphyry's work.[21]

Given this outline, it might appear at first surprising to discover that the topic of animal sacrifice not only features among the interests of early Renaissance readers of *On Abstinence*, but that it was decisive in catalysing their attention. Out of all the arguments that Porphyry employs in the text to argue in favour of vegetarianism, this particular one — the compatibility between sacrifice and vegetarianism — might be mistakenly assumed to be the least appealing one to Renaissance readers, who after all, unlike the pagans of Porphyry's age, did not sacrifice animals on the altar. Yet, the topic was discussed fervently in the fifteenth and sixteenth centuries, and this for at least two general reasons, which will be discussed throughout the present chapter.

First of all, the question of animal sacrifice finds a place within the fifteenth-century reappraisal of (Neo)Platonism simply because it was crucial in the Neoplatonic tradition, especially in Porphyry and Iamblichus.[22] For Renaissance philosophers interested in certain Neoplatonic authors and ideas 'everything becomes ritual and sacred'.[23] The question whether or not rituals, and those involving slaughter in particular, can have an influence on the gods is at the core of a major controversy within the Neoplatonic tradition on the role and value of theurgy, that is to say the use of various practices and rituals to attract and direct supernatural powers. Porphyry had addressed this issue in a text known as *Letter to Anebo* (c. 263–68),[24] which remains extant only in quotations from other sources, mainly in Iamblichus's reply, written under the pseudonym of 'Abamon', and known as *De mysteriis* [On the Mysteries], and from Eusebius (c. 260–c. 339) and Augustine (354–430).[25] The pun on the name ('Abamon' can be interpreted as 'Father of Amon', that is to say 'Father of God', or *theurgós*) is one indication of Iamblichus's wish to defend the importance of (animal) sacrifice.[26] Porphyry's critical stance might have been stronger in the lost *Letter* than it appears in *On Abstinence*; but what is important is the fact that in *On Abstinence* sacrifice is by no means an issue detached from eating animals.[27] This connection must be borne in mind when considering the Renaissance afterlife of this controversy, which reopens as two of the main texts on which it was based — Porphyry's *On Abstinence* and Iamblichus's *On the Mysteries* — become available again, thanks to Latin translations and the first editions of the Greek original texts.[28]

The second main reason why *On Abstinence* became a point of reference within the fifteenth-century Neoplatonic revival, with special regard to the topic of animal sacrifice, is that sacrifice is integral to the fundamental question regarding the compatibility of Platonism and Christianity. This point is closely linked to the previous one, as it amounts to an enquiry as to which type of (Neo)Platonism is most compatible with Christianity: the version which is in favour of theurgic rituals involving animals, or rather the version which presents in a positive light the simple offering of fruit and cereals? This question is crucial for understanding the context in which different Neoplatonic stances on animal sacrifice are rediscovered and discussed in the Renaissance.

How, then, did Renaissance readers deal with Porphyry's main argument regarding sacrifice, namely that it is crucial for the discussion on diet? When Porphyry examines the legitimacy of sacrifice in *On Abstinence*, he is mainly interested in convincing the addressee of the work to choose the vegetarian diet: since sacrifice, and religious piety in general, do not stand in conflict with this diet, the philosopher can legitimately sacrifice and abstain from eating meat. But are the animals on the altar still in any way contiguous to the animals on the plate in the Renaissance debate, as was the case in Porphyry's text?

The connection of sacrifice and diet represents the guiding thread linking together various authors who dealt more or less deeply with *On Abstinence* during the first phase of Renaissance engagement. This chapter will analyse at the same time the interest of these readers in the specific problem of animal sacrifice and emphasize the consequences that they drew with regard to diet — consequences that were Porphyry's main concern. As we will see, these were largely displaced but not absent in the Renaissance reception. Beginning with Basil Bessarion's references to *On Abstinence* in his *In calumniatorem Platonis* [Against the Slanderer of Plato], the next section will consider Porphyry's specific place in the debate on the compatibility of Platonism and Christianity, showing why his stance on animal sacrifice played the key role in this context. Close analysis of Marsilio Ficino's translations from *On Abstinence* will then (sections 3–6 below) further highlight how a certain presentation of Porphyry's philosophy was created for Renaissance readers, focusing on selected topics within the Platonic tradition. Ficino frames animal sacrifice within a general discussion of Platonic daemonology, and the dietetic conclusions are largely overshadowed by the the role of daemons during sacrificial practice. The latter aspect is also crucial in Giovanni Pico della Mirandola's *Conclusiones* [Conclusions], where he considers the symbolism of sacrifice. In the last section of this chapter, the influence of Ficino's translations and of Pico's emphasis on the meaning of sacrifice come together in a discussion of Francesco Zorzi's *De harmonia mundi* [On the Harmony of the World] and of a series of commentaries on Pico's *Conclusiones* which originated from Zorzi himself. The interpretation of sacrifice and the question whether eating animals is lawful are connected in Zorzi's discussion. This conclusion, and the entire reception leading to it, is a testimony to the rich afterlife of one of Porphyry's central arguments: that sacrifice is a crucial form of religious devotion, and yet animals can, and should, be spared.

1.2. Bessarion's Use of Porphyry

In 1626 the Capuchin friar Jacques Boulduc published a theological work dedicated to the origins of the church and of ecclesiastical rituals from the beginning up to Moses, entitled *De ecclesia ante legem* [The Church Before the Law].[29] The book begins with a discussion of the role and meaning of sacrifice, claiming that God had already taught Adam the cult of the divine. Adam was therefore the first to offer sacrifices to God.[30] In the second edition of the book, four years later, Boulduc inserted a reference to Porphyry's *On Abstinence*: he notes that according to Porphyry the first men to perform sacrifices were not accustomed to slaughtering animals, but rather offered solely the fruits of the earth on the altar. Indeed, killing animals was considered impious and also unnecessary, since what was held to be central to sacrifice (understood as an act of veneration, of thanksgiving, and of protection against misfortune) was nothing other than spiritual prayer.[31] Boulduc also mentions Pythagoras as an example of this non-violent approach to sacrifice, evidently following the tradition that Pythagoras neither ate nor killed animals for other purposes.

The points of view of Porphyry and Pythagoras are thus woven together by Boulduc in a discussion of sacrifice which relies heavily on the Scriptures and the Church Fathers. This association might appear surprising at first: Boulduc even implicitly links Porphyry to one of the key conflicts in the Old Testament, that is between Cain, who offered fruits to God, and Abel the shepherd, who offered animals.[32] In this way Porphyry appears to side with Cain in choosing the non-violent offer.[33] Furthermore, Porphyry's discussion of the origin of sacrifice as a progressive corruption of the non-violent custom of offering vegetables is congruent with Boulduc's argument that idolatry only started after the flood[34] (and he notes that Noah offered an animal sacrifice to God upon setting foot on dry land).[35]

Boulduc thus associates Porphyry and the Bible with regard to the notion that the original practice of sacrifice did not involve slaughter. Not only is the problem of choosing between animal sacrifice and a 'non-violent', vegetable offering thus presented as inherent to Christianity, but the opinion of a Neoplatonist who was critical of early Christians is recalled on this crucial issue. Boulduc thus indicates a connection between a certain Neoplatonic approach and the Christian concern about the meaning of sacrifice.

The early reception of *On Abstinence* reveals the roots of this convergence. When Boulduc wrote his *De ecclesia ante legem*, the parallel between pagan sources such as Porphyry and the Christian question about the development of sacrificial practice was no longer new. But it had been a matter of fervent debate when the sources of (Neo)Platonism were first rediscovered and started to circulate in the Latin West, confronting readers with conflicting Neoplatonic views on the issue.

The problem of dealing with different Neoplatonic interpretations of sacrifice was part of the broader fifteenth-century debate on the opposition or conciliation of Platonism and Aristotelianism, and on their relationship to Christianity.[36] The controversy was sparked by George Gemistos Plethon's *De differentiis Platonis et Aristotelis* [On the Differences Between Plato and Aristotle], in which the author defended Plato against Aristotle: if one follows Aristotle, Plethon claimed, it is impossible to view God as a creator, and even the immortality of the soul becomes doubtful.[37] But it is in the aftermath of this debate that Porphyry and Iamblichus came to play a decisive role.

In his reply to Plethon, George of Trebizond used the topic of sacrifice in order to give a rather different view of Platonism. In *Comparatio philosophorum Aristotelis et Platonis* [Comparison of the Philosophers Aristotle and Plato] he presents Neo-platonic paganism as a source of embarrassment.[38] The Platonists worship various gods, including natural bodies, such as the sun and the moon, a whole series of fictional deities, similar to those 'invented by the poets', and especially daemons.[39] Therefore they are hopelessly far from the cult of the one God, which is the essence of Christianity: a defender of Plato's supposed piety would by necessity become an enemy of Christianity altogether. The 'ars sacerdotalis' characteristic of Platonism consists in sacrifices and invocations, all practices that rely on the working of daemons, beings whose nature is between the divine and the human.[40] For Trebizond, the Platonic cult of worship, and the practice of sacrifice that goes with it, is irreconcilable with the Christian worship of the one God.

George of Trebizond's strategy is to insist on the fact that paganism is so deeply rooted in Platonism as to make a Christian Platonic doctrine unthinkable.[41] This accusation of incompatibility may be the main reason behind Bessarion's lengthy defence — a defence, therefore, not just of Plato, but of the justification of a Christian Platonism detached from neopagan traits.[42] But in his reply to the *Comparatio*, published eleven years later, Bessarion dedicated a large section to the problem of sacrifice, with the intention of showing the shortcomings in George's interpretation of the Platonic cult. First of all, Bessarion raises a conceptual difficulty: it is not self-evident that it should be possible to compare the understanding of worship and sacrifice before Christ (especially according to Plato and Aristotle) and after Christ. Just as with other terms, such as 'angel' (*angelus*), the meanings of 'cult' and 'worship' have shifted over time.[43] Bessarion explains that if one were thus to compare the pagan sacrifices to the worship of God, called *latría* by the theologians, it must be asked what the function of such sacrifices was, and what they actually meant for the Greeks. Quite simply, 'the names of "sacrifice" and of "worship" (*latría*), for which the adversary reproaches Plato', did not mean the same thing in Plato's time and now.[44] Sacrifice, including animal sacrifice, was part of popular devotion in Plato's time, and while Plato himself did not support at all the practice of blood offerings to the gods, he did not wish to (or rather, could not) break with such an established tradition either.[45] Bessarion states that Aristotle did just the same.[46] By underlining that pagan devotion must be understood in its historically specific timeframe, Bessarion thus draws three important conclusions: that pagan sacrifices are not essential to Platonism, just as they are not essential to Aristotelianism; that Plato distinguished between such popular forms of cult and more elevated ones, which did not involve bloodshed; and finally that sacrifice does not hinder a possible convergence of Platonism and Christianity.

It is at this point in the argument that Porphyry comes to play a key role. Bessarion refers to Book 2 of *On Abstinence* in order to claim that by distinguishing popular religion from Platonic divine worship proper, the compatibility with Christianity emerges very clearly. Such a rebuttal of George of Trebizond's accusation is made possible by considering Platonic devotion through the lens of Porphyry's interpretation:

> Quodsi scrutari diligentius velimus ea, quae ille de sacrificiis, et huiusmodi cultu deorum scripserit, videbitur certe, non ex suo iudicio sanguine coli praecipere deum, sed ex usu vulgari, et consuetudine longae aetatis coactus sic agere ne solitam religionem tollere videatur, quod idem quoque Aristotelem fecisse apertum est. Nam quid ipse Plato hac de re senserit explicat satis, cum in Epinomide dicat: 'Ita diis summum exhibemus honorem, si ea de illis sentimus, quae optima, rectaque habeantur'. Et Porphyrius in secundo de abstinentia animatorum: 'Colamus, inquit, deum silentio puro, religione, puris verisque de eo opinionibus assimilarique ei atque coniungi conemur, vitaeque nostrae sanctimoniam pro sacrificio offerre idque deo sacrum accommodare'. Non ergo ille sua sententia diis honorem sanguine nidoreque vituli describit, sed verbis aliis idem significat, quod nostrae sacrosanctae litterae censent spiritum esse deum, et 'spiritu veritateque' eum adorari oportere.[47]

> [If we want to examine more carefully those things which he [Plato] wrote about sacrifices and such cult of the gods, it will appear that the prescription to honour god with blood did not come from his opinion, but rather Plato was forced to act like this by the common custom and a long established habit, so that he would not appear as wanting to abolish ordinary religion. It is evident that Aristotle did the same. Indeed what Plato himself had thought of this is sufficiently disclosed by the fact that in *Epinomis* he says: 'We offer to the gods the highest honour when we think about them what is considered excellent and proper'. And Porphyry says in the second book of *On Abstinence from Living Beings*: 'Let us honour God with pure silence, with religion, and let us seek to be made like him and to be united with him with pure and true opinions about him, and to offer the sanctity of our life as a sacrifice and to devote this worship to God'. Therefore he himself did not assign with his words the honour to the gods [offered] with blood and the smell of the burning calf, but with other words he means the same thing that our sacred Scriptures express, that God is spirit and it is necessary to adore him 'in spirit and truth'.]

Bessarion here quotes Porphyry's rejection of animal sacrifice in support of the argument that Platonism does not necessarily involve cruel, sanguinary rituals. Porphyry's interpretation of sacrifice is the proof that the Platonic tradition can treat sacrifice as a sublimated act and a fully interior offer: this approach is not only close to scripture but even exemplifies the actual overcoming of pagan tendencies, best represented by the smoke arising from an animal sacrifice. From this perspective, Porphyry's Platonism does not stand in obvious contrast with Christianity. Once again, Bessarion is careful to state that there is no contradiction with Aristotelianism on this point either, further presenting Porphyry as a figure to reconcile Platonism with Aristotelian philosophy.[48]

Bessarion, who owned a manuscript of *De mysteriis*,[49] here prefers Porphyry's non-cruel offerings over Iamblichus's theurgic sacrifices, establishing a direct connection between the former and the true Platonic doctrine.[50] Not only is it 'a Neoplatonic Plato' whom Bessarion 'reconciled to the Church':[51] Bessarion's interpretation of the meaning and role of sacrifice shows that he attributed a very specific strand of Neoplatonism to Plato in order to shorten the distance from Christian worship — and that strand is Porphyry's philosophy. What Bessarion finds particularly appealing in *On Abstinence* is Porphyry's acknowledgment of the important role of ritual, including popular forms, alongside the suggestion that the true value of worship does not depend on material offers of any kind. Quoting once again from Book 2 of *On Abstinence*, Bessarion writes:

'Sacrificemus, inquit, ergo nos etiam, sed ut convenit, deo quidem summo et primo, ut quidam vir doctus censuit, nihil vel immolando vel sufficiendo vel nominando. Nulla res enim materialis non illico impura sit excreto illi immaterialique numini'. Quod in eodem quoque repetit et plane confirmat idem auctor, ubi 'sacrificia facta ex sanguine non diis, sed geniis reddi censuisse eos, qui potestates universi perceperant'. Scribit et alio loco idem auctor, sanguinem diis non placere ullo pacto, declarans haec dicens: 'Quamquam veteres non ita agendum censuerant, sed frugibus numina coli voluerunt', in quibus natura omnisque sensus integer delectaretur.[52]

['We shall sacrifice, too,' he says, 'but as is appropriate to the highest and first God, as a wise man decided, without immolating, offering or invoking anything. Indeed there is no material thing which will not be immediately impure to that separate, immaterial deity'. And the same author repeats this and clearly reinforces it in the same book, where he says that 'those who had grasped the powers of the universe decided to offer blood sacrifices not to the gods, but to the spirits'. In another passage the same author says that the gods do not like blood under any circumstances, explaining this as follows: 'Indeed the ancients did not believe it appropriate to do this, but rather preferred the gods to be honoured by offers of fruit', in which nature and all sense would rejoice in a pure way.]

Bessarion then recalls the inscription on the altar of Delos, to which Porphyry refers as well: 'no animal is immolated there, and for this reason the altar is called pious'.[53] Further, Bessarion uses quotations from Porphyry to draw direct conclusions about Plato's approach to sacrifices. In so doing, he not only invests Porphyry with the important role of having presented in clear terms Plato's position on sacrifice, but he even relies heavily on *On Abstinence* for saving Platonism from accusations of impiety. This operation nevertheless requires careful selection of passages from Porphyry's text.

Such an interpretation might at first sight seem paradoxical, given Porphyry's notorious opposition to Christianity. Although his *Against the Christians* is extant only in fragments, quotations and references by other authors make clear that his attack on Christianity had a particular focus on the issue of sacrifice. One of the main sources for reconstructing Porphyry's argument on this aspect is Augustine's *The City of God*, in which Porphyry is presented as 'the most intelligent of philosophers, although the most bitter opponent of the Christians'.[54] According to Augustine, Porphyry 'despised Christ because of the flesh itself which he assumed that he might offer a sacrifice for our purification — a great mystery unintelligible to Porphyry's pride which that true and noble redeemer brought low by his humility'.[55] In Augustine's view this can be explained only by assuming that

Porphyry's opinion was influenced by evil powers, akin to the daemons summoned through the practice of sacrifice.[56] It is therefore all the more noteworthy that Bessarion should even use a passage from *The City of God* in order to support the theory that there is a strong harmony between the Christian Trinity and the Platonic conception of a triad of substances, for instance as presented by Porphyry.[57] While Augustine had been more cautious in suggesting a Christian interpretation of Plato and Porphyry, claiming that only taken together would they reveal the accord with Christianity, Bessarion on the other hand insists on the fact that later Platonists, who lived after Christ, brought to light those aspects of Platonism that are compatible with Christianity, including the doctrine of the Trinity.[58]

Yet Porphyry's critique of the sacrifice of Christ and his emphasis on the ancient practice of sacrificing inanimate things are instrumental to his suggestion that it would be possible to *go back* to that custom. Therefore Porphyry regards with suspicion the shifts in sacrificial practice from vegetable offering to animal sacrifice and ultimately to the sacrifice of a human within Christianity. His statement about the importance of silent, interior worship, quoted by Bessarion, must be considered in the context of Porphyry's aversion not only to animal sacrifice, but also to Christian worship: the implication is that offering animate creatures, animal or human, is in any case a perversion of the early practice, which did not involve bloodshed of any kind. Indeed, from the point of view of Porphyry, Christ's offer of his own body is a further step away from the original non-violent offer. This is the context of Augustine's claim about Porphyry's disgust towards Christ's sacrifice: a man is offered on the altar in the place of an animal, a violent sacrifice which is the result of the corruption of sacrificial practice. Therefore it seems that Porphyry and the Christian doctrine of sacrifice only converge on one aspect: the conviction that the pagan slaughter of animals on the altar is unnecessary and should be superseded. But while Porphyry looks back to the non-violent origins of sacrifice, Christianity looks beyond, to the most radical sacrifice of a living creature — a human being.[59]

Both Porphyry and Bessarion mention Pythagoras as a source of inspiration for the overcoming of animal sacrifice: the Pythagoreans are a role model for the idea that sacrifice can be fully intellectual. Their offer derives from the study of numbers, writes Porphyry;[60] and Bessarion quotes Dionysus of Halicarnassus's report of their choice of an immaterial sacrifice.[61] Yet, as Porphyry emphasizes, the Pythagoreans honour different deities, not one God only. Indeed Porphyry himself, in the passage quoted by Bessarion about the internal, silent sacrifice, claims that different types of offer are appropriate for various powers: silence is thus the fitting offer only for the 'God who rules over all', and who is beyond both internal and external *lógos*.[62] George of Trebizond had remarked on the adoration of various deities within the Platonic tradition, including daemonic powers as well. While daemons — as we will see in analysing Ficino's engagement with Porphyry — are an essential focal point of the Neoplatonic discussion on sacrificing animals, Bessarion for his part carefully selects a passage from *On Abstinence* in which Porphyry addresses specifically the appropriate offer to the highest divinity, emphasizing the tradition of striving towards the divine in silence and contemplation.[63]

Furthermore, Porphyry applies to the topic of sacrifice an approach which characterizes the argument of *On Abstinence* in general. He attempts to distinguish between forms of behaviour that are suitable to different people. A question at the core of *On Abstinence* is: who should abstain from animal flesh? Similarly, Porphyry asks also who should abstain from animal sacrifices, and answers with a reference to Plato, according to whom the philosopher should never be involved in 'bad customs'.[64] The emphasis both on the different sacrifice due to the respective divine powers, and on the different human beings performing the sacrificial action, has the effect of setting clear boundaries to Porphyry's rejection of animal sacrifice. Given the divergent aim of Bessarion's argument, the non-violent sacrifice suggested in *On Abstinence* becomes rather the epitome of a religious Platonism freed from certain pagan traits, such as slaughter on the altar.[65]

The main aspect of Porphyry's argumentation which Bessarion leaves unmentioned is the fact that the discussion of sacrifice in *On Abstinence* is fully integrated within the discourse on the philosopher's abstinence from animal flesh. Elsewhere Bessarion discusses the topic of eating in relation to the Eucharistic sacrifice, but animals are not of concern there either.[66] The connection between sacrificing and eating animals resurfaces in Ficino's engagement with Neoplatonic sources, alongside a reconciliatory tendency which bears some similarities to Bessarion's own.

1.3. To Sacrifice or Not to Sacrifice? Ficino's Translations

On 13 September 1469 Bessarion writes to Marsilio Ficino, announcing that he is sending him a copy of *In caluminatorem Platonis*.[67] Ficino replies by expressing his enthusiasm for Bessarion's approach to Platonism in a letter dedicated to the praise of the followers of Plato (*De laude Platonicorum interpretum* [In Praise of Those who Expound Plato]).[68] The gold of wisdom, Ficino writes, was given to Plato directly by God. Although the Platonic writings are a manifestation of this divine gift, the difficulty of interpreting them, together with shortcomings in the minds of the readers, meant that this gold could not shine and reveal its worth as it should have done. The Neoplatonists took upon themselves a task of the utmost importance: that of making Plato's teaching available and clearer than in their original form, metaphorically polishing Plato's golden treasure:

> Verum in Plotini primum, Porphyrii deinde, ac Iamblici, ac denique Proculi, officinam aurum illud iniectum, exquisitissimo ignis examine excusis arenis enituit, usque adeo ad omnem orbem miro splendore repleverit.

> [But when that gold [of wisdom, given by God to Plato] was put into the worship first of Plotinus then of Porphyry, Iamblichus, and eventually Proclus, the earth was removed by the searching test of fire, and the gold so shone that it filled the whole world again with marvellous splendor.][69]

Porphyry and Iamblichus are placed next to each other, and indeed in subsequent years, too, Ficino's approach will develop towards a harmonization of these two heirs of Plato, even including their stances on the issue of sacrifice.

As Stéphane Toussaint puts it, between 1486 and 1489 Ficino worked on a series of texts that came to form a sort of 'petite encyclopédie', or 'small encyclopaedia', of Neoplatonic writings related to the topics of sacrifice, magic, and theurgy.[70] Taken as a whole, the collection deals with questions such as: what are the meaning and function of sacrifice, and, most importantly, do sacrificial rituals have a direct influence on the divine? What is the nature of daemons, and what role do they play within ritual practices?[71] Published in 1497 for Aldo Manuzio, the volume contains, among others, translations from Iamblichus's *De mysteriis Aegyptiorum* [On the Mysteries of the Egyptians], Proclus's *De sacrificiis et magia* [On Sacrifices and Magic], Psellus's *De demonibus* [On Daemons] and a selection of passages from Porphyry's *On Abstinence*.[72] But what Ficino presents is not simply a group of translations: the texts are abridged, with parts summarized or interposed with the translator's own comments. This approach reveals Ficino's aim: by selecting authors and passages he means to present and revive a discussion which emerges out of the study of Neoplatonic materials, pivoting on ritual practices.[73]

In the case of *On Abstinence*, the selection ranges from the first to the fourth book but with a special focus on the second book, which deals with animal sacrifice. This selection features ample extracts on the nature of daemons and their role in sacrifice which Ficino had already translated in a long letter he had sent to Braccio Martelli (included in Book 8 of Ficino's correspondence). These extracts are reproduced in the 1497 edition with minor alterations to the translations and to the subdivision of the text.[74] It is noteworthy that in the *Index* placed at the beginning of the printed Aldine edition, the extracts from Porphyry bear a title which emphasizes even more the core of Ficino's engagement with *On Abstinence*: the title chosen is *De divinis atque daemonibus* [On the Divine and on Daemons], rather than simply *On Abstinence*. In reading Porphyry, Ficino pursues a line of investigation which unfolds through the translations, seeking answers to the question of the efficacy of rituals, from the assessment of their effect on the divine to the problem of involving daemonic presences as intermediaries between the world and the divine.[75] There is therefore a distinct religious interest in Ficino's undertaking, as he treats theurgy as central to the Platonists' approach to seeking union with God.[76] In this context, Porphyry has a special role to play, as a direct consequence of his discussion of animal sacrifice.

The fact that Ficino's selective interest in *On Abstinence* pivots on the role of sacrifice emerges explicitly in the letter to Giovanni de' Medici, in which Ficino presents his translation of Iamblichus's *On the Mysteries* and which constitutes the introductory summary (*argumentum in librum Iamblichi*) in the 1497 edition.[77] Here he recapitulates the controversy between Porphyry and Iamblichus on the function of animal sacrifice, explaining how it developed into a fictitious exchange of letters thanks to the introduction of the figures of Abamon the priest and of Anebo, Iamblichus's supposed disciple:

> Porphyrius, qui inter Platonicos propter excellentiam Philosophus appellatur, longam in Aegyptum misit epistolam ad Anebonem Sacerdotem variarum et graviarum quaestionum plenam, ad omnes philosophiae partes spectantium, praesertim ad Deum atque angelos, daemonesque et animas, ad providentiam, ad fatum, vaticinia, magicen, miracula, sacrificia, vota. Porphyrii quaestionibus

respondit Iamblichus eius auditor. Introducit vero Porphyrio respondentem Abamonem Aegyptium Sacerdotem, pro Anebone discipulo suo, ad quem Porphyrius misit espistolam. Huius ergo quaestionis totius atque responsionis profecto divinae, tanquam in Plotino adhuc nimium occupatus, singula ferme non verba, sed sensa traduxi, ut non mirum putari debeat, sicubi divulsa videatur oratio, praesertim inter ipsa disputandi principia ubi levior iactura verborum: nam deinceps verborum etiam contextus magis perpetuus apparebit. Coactus vero sum interdum meum aliquod verbum, vel continuationis, vel intelligentiae gratia interserere.

[Porphyry, who among Platonists is called 'philosophus' because of his excellence, sent to the priest Anebo in Egypt a long letter full of diverse and weighty questions regarding all aspects of philosophy, especially God, and the angels, daemons and souls, as well as providence, fate, prophecies, magic, miracles, sacrifices and vows. Iamblichus, Porphyry's disciple, replied to his questions. In fact he introduced the Egyptian priest Abamon to answer Porphyry on behalf of Anebo, his disciple, to whom Porphyry had sent the letter. Since until now I have been very occupied with Plotinus, I have not translated each and every word of this whole enquiry and its divine reply, but have instead conveyed the meaning. So one should not be surprised if the discourse seems disjointed in places, especially at the beginning of the discussion where the loss of words is less serious, for thereafter the sequence of words will appear less broken. I have been obliged occasionally to insert some words either for continuity or for clarity.][78]

As the presentation of his approach in this letter makes clear, Ficino reads Porphyry's and Iamblichus's interpretations of theurgy by stressing their close connections. In a letter to Pierleone da Spoleto, who is mentioned further on in this summary as well, Ficino seems to have in mind a sort of Neoplatonic discourse involving different authors when he writes: 'You are waiting for Proclus from us. Expect Proclus at the same time as Iamblichus, the divine Iamblichus, with his wonderful answers to Porphyry's many serious questions, and his revelation of the divine mysteries of the Egyptians and the Assyrians'.[79] Once again, Ficino talks about questions and answers, emphasizing the fact that his work on the translation will provide the reader with materials about a debate unfolding in Neoplatonism, rather than simply with individual positions.

With regard to Iamblichus and Porphyry in particular, one could even say that Ficino did not set out to translate two works — *On Abstinence* and *On the Mysteries* — but rather a specific controversy between the philosophers; and yet he did so in the spirit of stressing the points of contact between the two, delineating a harmonious development of Platonism after Plato. Furthermore, in the letter to Giovanni de' Medici Ficino openly declares that the method he used to represent this controversy did not involve a word-by-word translation, but rather a mixture of translating and paraphrasing. He thus actively intervened in the texts by selecting and adapting: these are not simply translations. Both in the case of Iamblichus and of Porphyry, Ficino bridges the gap between different topics, adding clarificatory passages and emphasizing the fact that the texts unfold as a dialogue. It is noteworthy that he also introduces several short titles that divide the writings into distinct thematic sections. Ficino thus constructs his own abridged versions, in which certain topics emerge strongly, while others are left completely unmentioned. The translator enters the controversy between Iamblichus and Porphyry, highlighting what he considers to be the most important aspects. Ficino mentions that he had been pressed for time because of the task of translating Plotinus, but far from being simply an efficient method, this approach reveals the translator's specific interests in those Neoplatonic writings, and his own strategy of making them available in Latin while simultaneously providing an interpretation.[80]

The work of Ficino in the transmission of these texts was influential, and the 'small encyclopaedia' was reissued several times (for instance in 1516 and again in 1552).[81] In the case of *On Abstinence*, Ficino's paraphrase is all the more relevant because it was the first attempt to render Porphyry's work in Latin (if we exclude the translation, by George of Trebizond, of some passages of *On Abstinence* incorporated by Eusebius in his *Praeparatio evangelica* [Preparation for the Gospel]).[82] The first complete translation was published only fifty years later, in 1547, while the *editio princeps* of the Greek original, prepared by Piero Vettori, appeared in 1548.[83] Also in the case of Iamblichus, Ficino was the first to attempt a Latin translation, producing a text which in turn enjoyed its own manuscript dissemination.[84] Moreover the impact of Ficino's translation on the reception of the work is visible already in the fortune of the title *De mysteriis* (which was Ficino's personal choice) in place of *Master Abamon's Reply to Porphyry's Letter to Anebo*.[85] Ficino's title was then adopted also by the author of the first complete translation, Niccolò Scutelli.[86]

Ficino was conscious of the difficulties of translating and adapting such works for a Latin readership. Hankins has drawn attention to the fact that Ficino frequently poses the question of whether a particular writing (with special reference to the Platonic dialogues) is at all translatable in another language.[87] Reading and translating several works at the same time can thus have an important explanatory function, and indeed in his preface to the translation of Plotinus Ficino mentions directly the works of Porphyry as an instrument for approaching and interpreting Plotinus.[88] This cross-interpretation of Neoplatonic sources is part of the process of polishing the gold of Plato, creating the sense of a cooperative enterprise within the development of Neoplatonism. In the above-mentioned letter to Braccio Martelli, Ficino uses this conception as a background to narrate his engagement with Plotinus and his followers in terms of a dialogue with the living presences of these philosophers, summoned by means of daemonic magic. Ficino writes that while he was a guest of Filippo and Niccolò Valori, and working on daemons, Plotinus manifested himself, uttering mysterious, divine words. Porphyry was then summoned with the aim of clarifying the words of his master on the nature of daemons. The narrative frame is similar to that used in the letter to Giovanni de' Medici which served as proemium to the translation of *On the Mysteries*, where Ficino addresses Iamblichus as 'great priest', entreating him to offer to Giovanni his divine words and mysteries as present on the occasion of becoming Cardinal. By imagining the summoning of Plotinus and Porphyry, Ficino places himself in their company as a direct interlocutor in charge of translating their statements from Greek into Latin.[89]

The scene reveals the timeframe and motives of Ficino's translations: he interrupted his translation of Plotinus in order to expand the investigation on the problem of daemons by turning to the translation of Porphyry. But it also clearly points to the central issues in Ficino's reading of *On Abstinence*: how to interpret the function of sacrifices, and whether Platonic theology, and daemonology in particular, is combinable with Christianity — issues which, as we saw, Bessarion had addressed. Indeed Porphyry's talk opens with a statement, placed as a highlighted heading to the first section, which is reminiscent of Bessarion's emphasis on the Neoplatonic interior offering to the highest deity: 'The followers of Plato offer nothing but contemplation to God and to the Soul of the world, but to the souls that move the stars they offer flowers and the fruits of the earth and of trees'.[90] This draws on the same paragraph from *On Abstinence* (II.34) quoted by Bessarion, showing that Ficino, too, is eager to pick the passages which are more easily combinable with the Christian idea of offering to the one God. At the basis of this approach lies the belief that it is possible to find in Platonic philosophy the seeds of those truths which will be revealed and expounded in Christianity.[91] As Guido Giglioni puts it, 'a virtuous hermeneutical circle seemed to connect Platonism with Christianity'.[92] Ficino, and Bessarion before him, thus adopt this perspective when they seek to specify a connection between Porphyry's understanding of sacrifice and the Christian ritual.[93]

But further in this letter Ficino discloses a key aspect which Bessarion had not mentioned: the direct link between sacrificing and eating animals. Another section in the letter is titled: 'A wise man will abstain from eating the flesh of animals and from sacrificing them, for through these practices evil daemons are summoned to us'.[94] The source is Porphyry's statement in Book 2 that 'an intelligent, temperate man' should know the danger connected with offering animals, namely that of attracting bad daemons, hungry for the fumes rising from the altars.[95] In Ficino's paraphrase evil daemons are summoned by both practices, eating and sacrificing animals, as the connection between them is strongly emphasized. The roots of this connection are to be found in the interpretation of what a daemon is: this is the main focus of interest for Ficino, who follows the unfolding of this Neoplatonic discussion from Iamblichus and Porphyry, to Proclus and Psellus.

1.4. Carnivorous Daemons?

In his paraphrase of Iamblichus's work, Ficino dedicates a section to discussing in what ways sacrifices are considered to be useful ('Quae ratio sacrificiorum, quae utilitas', deriving from *On the Mysteries* v.6).[96] Here Porphyry's interpretation of sacrifice and that of Iamblichus are sketched in opposition to each other. For Porphyry sacrifice is simply a means to venerate the gods; for Iamblichus it is an active measure to intervene in the world, for instance with the aim of preventing a plague or famine.[97] Of course underlying this distinction is a radically different way of understanding what is appropriate to the gods, and if and how humans can influence them — and this point constitutes the basis for Iamblichus's defence of animal sacrifice against Porphyry's attempt drastically to limit this practice, and ideally even to substitute it with purely vegetable offerings. In another paragraph, which Ficino titles 'On the sacrifices of animals' ('De sacrificiis animalium'), Iamblichus defends, against Porphyry, the legitimacy of manipulating dead animal bodies during sacrifice.[98] Iamblichus admits that touching these bodies, or inhaling the fumes of their burning flesh, might pollute those who are present at the sacrificial rite — and this is the reason why the priests have regulations about dealing with animals to be sacrificed. But in no case can these bodies, or the fumes, have the negative effects that Porphyry had envisaged; and indeed animal sacrifice appears for Iamblichus as a necessary practice, at least as an offering to the material deities, because like demands like and thus material offerings are appropriate for material deities (for the immaterial gods, on the other hand, an immaterial offer would be appropriate).[99] Also, not all humans are in the requisite spiritual condition to make immaterial offers; therefore, both the offerant and the deity to which the offer is due should be taken into account when choosing the appropriate sacrifice, and for Iamblichus the material sacrifice of animals has an important role to play in this context.[100] Animal sacrifice creates a connection between daemons and humans, and this connection is the channel for theurgy.[101] Here Ficino paraphrases the arguments presented in *On the Mysteries* v.14, where Iamblichus states:

> And so, in sacrifices, dead bodies deprived of life, the slaughter of animals and the consumption of their bodies, and every sort of change and destruction, and in general processes of dissolution are suitable to those gods who preside over matter — not to them in themselves, but because of the matter over which they rule.[102]

Noteworthy here is the direct connection between the acts of offering and eating: animals are to be slaughtered *and* eaten as part of a theurgic ritual that will influence the material realm, which is under the influence of the gods.

In Porphyry's view, on the other hand, the main problem with killing is that it has dangerous consequences which are directly connected to eating. In the first instance, the blood and the fumes provide nourishment not for humans, but rather for bad daemons, which are summoned by the violent act of shedding blood and by the smoke from burning meat. Abstinence from eating animals can be seen, in this context, as a way to resist this fall into a daemonic spiral of violence, since Porphyry holds these evil daemons responsible for the suffering and violence in the world.

Indeed, Ficino writes in his paraphrase of *On Abstinence* that 'there is no evil which they [i.e. the evil daemons] would not dare to perform'.[103] He faithfully translates the explanation Porphyry had given for the daemons' behaviour: 'they delight in libation and the fumes from roasted meats', from which their 'spiritale corpus' ('pneumatic body') is literally nourished, fattening up on such food, because 'it lives on the vapours' and it 'draws strength from the smell of blood and the fumes of the burning meat'.[104] In the version presented in the letter to Martelli this point is further emphasized by the fact that it is followed by a short title-summary, which is omitted from the longer version in the 1497 edition. The title reads: 'Those who sacrifice animals draw to themselves evil daemons without realizing it; certainly we should offer in sacrifice only inanimate things to the good daemons, that is to say to the angels, with purity of mind'.[105]

Animal sacrifice is therefore a violent practice that calls up further violence through these daemonic presences, and this is why innocuous fruit and vegetables are not only appropriate but preferable for practicing piety understood as veneration of the gods. 'The first men who made sacrifices' — argues Porphyry in Ficino's wording — 'did not offer animals, but herbs and flowers to begin with, and then plants and burnt spices. Those who were the first to start eating flesh seized animals due to lack of fruits, for previously they used to eat the fruits of the earth'.[106] Once again, Ficino's abridged version emphasizes the strong connection between eating and sacrificing: the ancients started to eat and sacrifice animals as a consequence of lack of vegetable nourishment. Ficino then proceeds to translate Porphyry's list of the reasons for sacrifice: first, to venerate the gods; also to express gratitude; and finally to ask them either to give us what we need, or to ward off evils.[107] Indeed Porphyry does not reject sacrifice *tout court*, but rather insists at once on the avoidable violence of animal sacrifice, and on the consequences to be drawn with regard to eating animals. Sacrifice still plays an important role, even if animals are replaced by inanimate offers on the altar. This substitution even has the effect of bringing to light what constitutes the essence of sacrifice according to Porphyry, because by eliminating the violence of slaughtering, and the expectations and dangers connected with it, the type of religiosity appropriate to the philosopher properly emerges.

Ficino continues his paraphrase with a very direct statement: 'Indeed it is abominable to slaughter animals', sharpening the ultimate aim of Porphyry's argument.[108] It is at this point, still paraphrasing from Book 2 of *On Abstinence*, that Ficino translates an important clarification of Porphyry on daemonology. The section titled 'On the species of the good and the bad daemons' begins with the remark that Plato did not distinguish precisely between various types of those invisible beings called daemons: it is therefore of the utmost importance that the major differentiations should be pointed out, and especially the main subdivision between good and bad daemons.[109] In the letter to Martelli, Ficino intervenes at this point by adding a comment which does not derive from *On Abstinence*: he writes that all daemons emanate from the universal soul, 'that is, from the very idea of souls'.[110] As such, all daemons have a 'tenue corpus' ('subtle body'), and indeed the way in which the daemons control their bodies is the foundation of the main differentiation between the good and bad types.

The importance of the body and shape of the daemons was already apparent in the theory that the evil ones fatten up on the flesh of sacrificed animals. Indeed, one important characteristic of daemons is that their bodies can change: in Book 16 of *Theologia platonica* [Platonic Theology], Ficino had alluded to *On Abstinence* when he stated that according to the Platonists 'not just our souls but the souls too of many daemons change their own bodies at times.'[111] This physical presence of daemons explains why Porphyry (and in this case Ficino, too, paraphrasing *On Abstinence*) insists that good and bad daemons act differently, that is to say that their positive or negative intentions are evident in the way they intervene in the world — in the case of the evil ones, by enjoying meat and causing havoc.

This discussion of the bodies of daemons continues straight into the next translation featured in the 1497 edition, the extracts from Psellus *De operatione daemonum* [On the Workings of Daemons], which Ficino titles simply *De demonibus*. Indeed the selection starts with the statement: 'The nature of daemons is not without body, but it has a body'.[112] As Walter Stephens has noted, it is highly significant that Ficino should open his translation with this statement, which is not the beginning of Psellus's treatise: 'Under Ficino's scissors, Psellus's treatise concerns the corporality of daemons more than their activities'.[113]

But even if possessing a subtle body is a common characteristic of daemons, the distinction between good and evil ones is fundamental for Ficino, and this distinction is based both on the physicality of the daemons themselves and on the effects they have on human and animal bodies.[114] It is on the discussion of these different types of daemonic presences that Ficino constructs his discussion of Neoplatonic daemonology, sliding from Iamblichus, to Porphyry, to Psellus. But it is the section on Porphyry which makes clear why killing animals constitutes a major problem in this context, and highlights the reasons for Ficino's interest.

If we compare the first version of his translations from Book 2 of *On Abstinence* (the extracts featured in the letter to Martelli), and the 1497 version, a notable difference is apparent. This regards the topic of summoning evil daemons by slaughtering animals, and it shows that Ficino continued to reflect on the key role of animal sacrifice. In the 1497 version, the last two sections of Book 2 feature the topic of protection from bad daemons. They are titled: 'De sacrificiis ad daemones malos, et de abstinentia et cautione a malis daemonibus' ('On sacrifices to the evil daemons, and on abstinence and protection from evil daemons'); and 'De vero cultu et sacrificio et cautione a malis daemonibus' ('On the true ritual and sacrifice, and on warding off bad daemons').[115] Here Ficino has changed the titles he had employed in the earlier letter, which had instead emphasized the prohibition for the wise man to sacrifice and consume animals, insisting on the key word 'abstinence'. They read: 'Puritas et abstinentia a malis daemonibus nos tuetur, quibus contemplatores sacrificare non debent' ('Purity and abstinence protect us from evil daemons, to which those dedicated to contemplation should not sacrifice'); and 'Sapiens abstinebit tum cibo, tum sacrificio animalium: per haec enim mali ad nos daemones advocantur' ('The wise man will abstain both from eating and from sacrificing animals because through these activities evil daemons are attracted to us').[116] The new version now contains an extract translated faithfully from *On Abstinence* II.47–48, which deals with the effects of violent death. After stating (in both the letter and in the collection of translations) that 'all theologians' were right in assigning a key role to the practice of abstinence, the 1497 version continues with a reference to a special reason for abstaining from animals provided by 'the Egyptian'. Ficino, following Porphyry, writes that 'a base and irrational soul, which abandons its body violently, having been stripped of it, later draws close to it and everywhere continues to linger, whence the souls of human beings who died violently also remain and linger near the body'.[117] Certainly killing animals on the altar is an instance of a violent death: the daemonic lingering of the soul in the dead body, continues the passage, was used in divinatory practices, during which parts of animals were swallowed, and thus the souls of those animals, too, entered the body of the person performing the ritual, bringing about a connection between human and animal as a result of a violent act.[118] Once again, Ficino maintains a firm link between killing violently and eating the products of such slaughter, rendering Porphyry's images of daemonic infestation in vivid language.

In both the letter and the 1497 translation, Ficino ends the selection from Book 2 of *On Abstinence* with a conclusion that abridges a longer paragraph in which Porphyry claims that the best offering to the gods is a pure mind not affected by the unsettling effect of passions. Interestingly, while in the letter Ficino had adapted the recipient of the offering, changing it from Porphyry's plural, 'gods' ('theói', II.61.2) to a singular, 'Deum', in the printed version Ficino reintegrates the original plural ('apud Deos').[119] From the scenes of burning meat and daemonic possession, Ficino guides the reader of his abridged translation to the same conclusion that Bessarion had already stressed in his use of *On Abstinence*: Porphyry liberates Neoplatonism from a cruel pagan ritual, leading to an interpretation of sacrifice as a purely spiritual offering.[120] The scenes of slaughter on the altar and the summoning of hungry daemons work as a counterpart that lets the non-violent essence of sacrifice emerge — and Porphyry is the emblem of this restitution. The bodily, violent aspects of sacrifice are given a higher meaning, sublimated into a spiritual offering which leaves the animals untouched. Platonism thus appears, through Porphyry, compatible with Christianity. But Ficino achieves something else as well: he integrates Porphyry's understanding of sacrifice within a broader picture, softening the points of conflict with other Neoplatonic strands, and especially with Iamblichus.[121]

1.5. Strangling the Pythagorean Cock: Ficinian Daemons in Porphyry and Iamblichus

The reference to the 'Egyptian' in the 1497 paraphrase discloses further the reasons for Ficino's interest in animal sacrifice: as Gillian Clark has pointed out, the Egyptian is Hermes Trismegistos, and in 1463 Ficino had worked on translating fourteen treatises from the *Corpus Hermeticum*.[122] This was the first of Ficino's most important translations,[123] and he chose the title *Pimander* for his version of the text (once again, a successful Ficinian title that would become synonymous with the entire Hermetic Corpus — *Pimander* being the title of the first treatise in the collection).[124] The topic of the ninth treatise is the origin of beauty and the good, which rests solely in the divine; but the discussion soon proceeds to draw a radical differentiation between good and evil, encouraging the human being to side with the former, and flee the latter.[125] It is in this context that the evil daemons enter into the picture, as Ficino translates as follows: 'there is no part of the world which is devoid of daemons, their light descends entirely from God himself. Thus the daemon, insinuated into the human being, scatters the seed of its own action'.[126]

The fruits which germinate from these 'seeds' are terrible, violent actions, such as homicide, sacrilege, and indeed slaughter (literally throat-slittings, 'iugulationes'), together with 'all other things which are the work of evil daemons ('mali daemones')'.[127] Ficino's translation conveys the sense of the intimate infiltration of daemons, influencing human actions. This, for Ficino, is true for all kinds of daemons, but in the case of the evil ones the infiltration is particularly problematic because it stimulates violence. Although the text does not add further details about the type of slaughter which is inspired by the evil daemons, there is evidently a connection with the topic of sacrifice in Ficino's paraphrase of Porphyry, on which he worked around twenty years after translating *Pimander*. The *trait d'union* is the claim that bloodshed, in all its forms, of animals or humans, tends to be both an expression and a catalyst of violence, deriving from daemonic possession of the evil kind.

In the *summa* which introduces the commentary on Plotinus' *Ennead* III.4, Ficino brings together Iamblichus, Porphyry and the 'Egyptian priest' in order to present an overview of the different types of personal daemons. He labels this section of the commentary simply 'On daemons': here he mentions Socrates's daemon ('daemon Socraticus'),[128] but he also summarizes the theory, already discussed in the *Theologia platonica*, that there is a precise relation between the daemons which inhabit specific parts of the air (from thicker to purer) and the ways in which they affect the different lives of human beings (depending on whether these latter are more or less inclined to imagination or to intellectual activity). The airy bodies of daemons literally surround humans all the time, and have great power over us: 'The theologians suppose, therefore, that the daemons know the best possible way easily to perturb each person, and that, troubled themselves by a sort of perturbation, they trouble us from day to day'.[129] This perturbation can vary from connecting our imagination with theirs, to supporting the aspiration to an intellectual life.[130] Ficino insists on the actual, constant presence of daemons, expressing a certain concern about the extent of their influence. As D. P. Walker observed, Ficino seems rather anxious when he discusses daemons.[131] He is well aware of the fact that *dáimon* is a multifaceted concept, embracing very different kinds of presences, and he tries to impose order by defining their actions, using as a starting point the Neoplatonic works he translates or comments upon.[132]

In *Ennead* III.4, Plotinus had explained that the guiding spirit or *dáimon* stimulates a development of human life out of the lower level of animality towards the higher realm of the sage who is united with the One.[133] Rather than simply living the possibility of choosing between a good and a bad life, Ficino focuses on the nature of the daemons: there are good and bad ones, and both can influence human actions in different ways. In the *Theologia platonica* Ficino writes:

> Non desunt daemones boni nobis, qui genii nominantur, ingenii duces assidui, qui non vi, sed persuadendo ducant. Sunt et mali, non tamquam duces naturaliter ordinati, sed adversarii, ut ita dixerim, peregrini, quod in hac vita per philosophiam sacrificiaque propulsari Platonici putant.

> [We are not without the good daemons: they are called genii [because] they are tireless leaders of our own ingeniousness; and they lead us not by force but by

persuasion. There are bad daemons too who are naturally assigned to us not as leaders but as adversaries or, one might say, as strangers; the Platonists think that they are warded off in this life by philosophy and by sacrifices.][134]

This explains why sacrifice plays a key role not just for the post-Plotinian Platonists, but for Ficino as well: the distinction between good and evil daemons demands that strategies be presented for dealing with both kinds of presences.

Animal sacrifice is one such strategy which leads directly to the core of the controversy: does it ward off evil presences, or does it actually attract them? Which daemonic beings are involved in the practice? It is noteworthy that an animal, a cock, is indirectly involved also in Plotinus's *Ennead* III.4, on which Ficino comments. For the editor of the *Enneads*, Porphyry, the discussion of the guiding spirits presented an immediate point of connection with the episode of the summoning of the 'visible manifestation of Plotinus's presiding spirit'.[135] The spirit is evoked in a ritual performed by an Egyptian priest and his assistant, who is in charge of holding the sacrificial birds. But just when the *dáimon* has been revealed to be a Divinity, and not just a lower spirit, the assistant strangles the birds, either out of fear of the powerful presence, or jealousy of the purity of the manifested spirit.

Ficino reflects precisely on the strangling of the birds (or rather, of the cock, following in the Pythagorean tradition) by explaining what this image of sacrifice means metaphorically.[136] In a *Short Commentary on the Pythagorean Symbols*, Ficino includes discussion of the saying that one should nourish a cock, not sacrifice it.[137] The cock represents a certain power of the soul through which humans are capable of predicting future events, by means of an affinity with celestial bodies and spirits. The reason is that cocks are animals which can so precisely measure the passing of time that a certain part of the night is even called *gallicinium*.[138] Thus it is obvious that they have some kind of power akin to that of foreseeing the feature. Via metaphor, the conclusion is that the cock — representing this power of the soul — should be 'nourished', and this happens when we live in such a way that we can attune to the celestial motions, by cultivating tranquillity of spirit. But under no circumstances should the cock be sacrificed, that is to say strangled like the birds which were used to evoke Plotinus's guiding spirit.[139]

This interpretation of the role of the cock reveals Ficino's tendency to recognize the unfolding of entire traditions below the surface of a single saying.[140] Of course Ficino also has in mind the biblical passages in which cocks are mentioned at key points: notably Job 38: 36, where wisdom (*sapientia*) is attributed to the bird; and the cock's marking of time passing in the Gospel of Matthew 26: 74.[141] But Ficino's interest in the Pythagorean saying can be also considered in the broader context of his examination of sacrifice. Leaving aside the parallel with the soul's power of foreseeing the future, the contrast between nourishing and sacrificing the cock offers an important way into Ficino's discussion of animal sacrifice through his reading of Porphyry and Plotinus. The line to draw is subtle: we could think of the assistant to the Egyptian priest, holding the animal, but without using too much force. Animals are often assigned an important function in Neoplatonic rituals dealing with evil daemons; yet, when the blood flows, the ritual of protecting humans from evil presences can, especially from a Porphyrian perspective, tilt into a summoning of violence itself. Furthermore, it is precisely on that critical point, when violence explodes on the altar, that the combination of Neoplatonism and Christianity becomes problematic. Yet, Ficino aims to show that one should not identify Platonism with the kind of magic that summons evil presences: in opposing evil magic, Platonism is thus on the side of Christianity.

The image of nourishing without sacrificing reflects Ficino's attitude with regard to these key points. Just as a delicate balance must be preserved between using the animal and killing it, so Ficino attempts to reconcile different Neoplatonic traditions rather than opposing one to another. This approach appears in his reading of Porphyry's and Iamblichus's interpretations of daemonology and animal sacrifice: not only does he read Porphyry from an Iamblichan perspective, but he also works in the opposite direction, integrating Iamblichus's vindication of animal sacrifice into the safer territory of Porphyry's sublimated, non-violent sacrifice.[142]

Despite his constant conciliatory attempts, it is clear that Ficino has a predilection for Iamblichus over other Neoplatonists, including Porphyry. In a letter to Pierleone, included in the eleventh book of the correspondence, Ficino even assigns to Iamblichus a fundamental position within Platonism, and especially within his own love of the Platonic tradition: 'I love Plato in Iamblichus, I admire him in Plotinus, but I venerate him in Dionysius'.[143] Iamblichus, the first in this list, is the Neoplatonist in whom Ficino not only recognizes but even loves Plato. With regard to sacrifice, Ficino shows what has been called a 'neo-Iamblichan appreciation of the use and power of ritual'.[144] For instance, in *De vita coelitus comparanda* [On Obtaining Life from the Heavens] Ficino connects the knowledge he gained from sources like Iamblichus with observations derived from personal experience:

> Accepi a Platonicis malos daemonas plurimum septentrionales existere, quod etiam Hebraeorum astronomi confitentur, noxios Martiosque daemonas in septentrionem ponentes. [...] Didici a theologis et Iamblicho imaginum fictores a daemonibus malis occupari saepius atque falli.

> [I learned from the Platonists that evil daemons are mostly Northern, which even the Hebrew Astronomers confess, placing harmful Martial daemons in the North [...]. I learned from the theologians and Iamblichus that makers of images are often possessed by evil daemons and deceived.][145]

In Iamblichus, Ficino finds a wealth of material for studying the entire spectrum of daemonic presences.[146] Porphyry's daemonology in *On Abstinence*, on the other hand, has less to offer to Ficino, not only because of his emphasis on the dangers connected with summoning evil daemons, but also because of the focal point of his entire discourse, which is the connection between sacrificing and abstaining from eating animals. There is, nevertheless, one distinct advantage in associating Porphyry with Iamblichus, within the broader project of combining Christianity and Platonism: this lies in Porphyry's rejection of certain violent rituals. Thus, while Ficino subdivides the Neoplatonists between those he considers to be closer to Christianity, offering an account of spirituality consistent with it (including Iamblichus) and those who are further away (like Porphyry), Porphyry's aversion to violence remains appealing to him.[147]

Ficino brings together Porphyry and Iamblichus by showing that the latter reinforced the theory that the former had already formulated with regard to the prophetic role of daemons:

> Porphyrius ait eos regulis astronomicis oracula reddidisse, atque ideo frequenter ambigua, et merito, quoniam Iamblichus probat prophetiam veram, atque certam, nec malis daemonibus convenire, nec humanis artibus, vel natura, sed spiratione divina purgatis mentibus provenire.

> [Porphyry says they [daemons] have rendered oracles by astronomical rules and therefore frequently ambiguously. Porphyry is right to say 'ambiguously', since Iamblichus demonstrated that true and certain prophecy cannot come from such evil daemons, nor is it produced by human arts or by nature; it is only produced in purified minds by divine inspiration.][148]

Ficino remarks that Iamblichus had preferred the Chaldeans over the Egyptians: the reason is that the Chaldeans 'were not preoccupied with daemons'.[149] Thus on the one hand Ficino acknowledges the important role that magic and ritual play in Iamblichus's *On the Mysteries*, and creates on this point a common basis for bringing Porphyry and Iamblichus into fundamental agreement.[150] But on the other he stretches Iamblichus in the direction of Porphyry in preferring spiritual sacrifice over pagan sacrifices, including the killing of animals.

Ficino intertwines Iamblichus's and Porphyry's views on daemonology repeatedly, not only by translating key passages by both authors on daemonology, but even by constructing a sort of dialogue between the two. In his comment on Plotinus's *Enneads* III.5, Ficino writes that humans who are too prone to satisfy their belly tend to become receptacles for impure daemons, 'as Porphyry says'. Yet, although, 'as Iamblichus says', such daemons can obtain nutriment even without human intervention, nevertheless humans can be contaminated by such daemonic presences, as in the case of particularly arrogant ('superbi') people, who are agitated by similarly inclined daemons, once again 'as Porphyry says'.[151] Ficino does not entirely omit Porphyry's view that it is not general gluttony, but specifically meat-eating, which attracts the evil daemons.[152] Minimizing Porphyry's emphasis on meat, however, is one of the ways in which he narrows the gap between the two Neoplatonists. This enables him to state what 'the Platonists' believed about daemons, as if they shared one coherent opinion on the matter. In the *Theologia platonica* Ficino groups the personae of the exchange between Porphyry and Iamblichus, Anebon and Abamon, together with the Platonists Plotinus, Iamblichus, and Julian, because they all 'claimed that not only God, but all mind as well, whether angelic or animal, extends itself whole through infinity'.[153]

The most obvious sign of Ficino's conciliatory approach appears in his terminology. He uses the term 'Platonici', Platonists, to emphasize the sense of uniformity.[154] Porphyry's and Iamblichus's different stances on the topic of daemonic presences and theurgy derive from major divergences on the level of ontology. As Daniela Taormina has remarked, the importance of theurgy for Iamblichus stems from his view that the summoning of external powers is essential to achieve union with the divine, because the human soul is placed in between the intelligible and the sensible realms. According to Porphyry, on the other hand, the soul never loses its intelligible nature, and thus the theurgic summoning of daemons does not have the same important function.[155] As we saw before, daemons can be very dangerous presences for Porphyry. The theoretical gap between Porphyry and Iamblichus's positions, in any case, cannot be easily overlooked.

Ficino was not the first to appreciate Porphyry's stance on the dangers of theurgy. In Book 10 of *The City of God*, Augustine dedicated a section to Porphyry's arguments in the lost *Letter to Anebo*.[156] According to Augustine, Porphyry is torn between embracing a fully philosophical approach to the divine, and justifying certain theurgic practices, at least as means for purifying the soul. But the letter, Augustine claims, has the merit of expressing more clearly the dangers of such rituals:

> Melius sapuit iste Porphyrius, cum *ad Anebontem scripsit Aegyptium*, ubi consulenti similis et quaerenti et prodit artes sacrilegas et evertit. Et ibi quidem omnes daemones reprobat, quos dicit ob inprudentiam *trahere humidum vaporem* et ideo non in aethere, sed in aëre esse sub luna atque in ipso lunae globo.

> [Porphyry showed a greater degree of wisdom when *he wrote to Anebo the Egyptian*; for here, acting the part of an inquirer seeking guidance, he exposes and overturns the sacrilegious arts. On this occasion, indeed, he condemns all daemons, who, he says, are foolish enough to be *attracted by the turbid fumes of sacrifice*, and who must therefore dwell not in the aether, but in the air below the moon and on the moon's sphere itself.][157]

For Augustine the problem of dealing with the evil daemons is at the centre of Porphyry's daemonology; the same emphasis is apparent in Ficino's selective translation, even if Augustine and Ficino have very different agendas when dealing with Porphyry's legacy. In Augustine's account there is no subtle balance between warding off certain daemonic presences while welcoming the role of others as intermediaries between humans and the Divine: all daemons are malevolent. Augustine detects Porphyry's anxiety in dealing with the matter, and suggests that this might be due both to the clash between the belief in daemonic powers and his philosophical approach, and to the desire to avoid disrespect towards his addressee, Anebo.[158] But the main reason could be one which Augustine does not mention because he himself does not consider it to be of any importance: the influence that the choice of a vegetarian diet would have on participation in veneration and piety.

Despite a certain approbation of Porphyry's approach with regard to pagan sacrifices, Augustine emphatically disagrees with Porphyry about the key tenet of *On Abstinence* — the fact that animals should not be used as food. This becomes clear in a work addressed to the Manichean Adimantus (*Contra Adimantum* [Against Adimantus]), who, according to this text, had argued in favour of a vegetarian diet. Augustine's reply hinges on the meaning of sacrifice: the Manicheans come to the conclusion that meat should be avoided because they believe that 'it is a sacrifice [*immolatio*] when any kind of animal is prepared to become supper for humans'.[159] What matters for Augustine is not simply that this conclusion is wrong but that it is anti-Christian. According to Augustine, the Manicheans misinterpret a passage from Paul's First Letter to the Corinthians (10: 20), which states that 'what the pagans offer [on the altars], is offered to the daemons and not to God'. Augustine comments that 'the Apostle clearly means the victims which are offered in the temple to the daemons, and not the dishes which humans prepare for themselves'.[160] Thus even if Scripture (1 Corinthians 10: 21) does seem to present a parallel between offering and eating animals, linking both actions to the presence of malevolent daemons ('You cannot drink from the cup of God and of the daemons. You cannot sit at the table of God and of the daemons'), Augustine nevertheless insists that eating animals is a distinct action from sacrificing them.[161] Daemons might be attracted by sacrifice, but not by consuming animal flesh, which is not a sacrificial act at all. A proper Christian will thus abstain from the pagan action of sacrificing animals, but will continue to eat them. Augustine underlines that a Christian should beware of indulging in excessive consumption of meat, but that eating animals simply for one's nourishment and health is fully in accordance with the Scriptures.[162] Abstaining from animal flesh is not only unnecessary, but potentially dangerous, as it is founded on a misunderstanding: God does not require vegetarianism.[163]

Augustine's insistence on the necessity of separating sacrificing and eating animals makes clear that from a Christian perspective the legacy of Porphyry is equally useful in arguing against the former aspect (pagan sacrifice), and problematic with regard to the latter (the dietetic consequences). Ficino's aims are profoundly different from Augustine's: Ficino is not arguing against a sect that threatens the cohesion of the Church. Porphyry's stance on pagan sacrifice can be read in harmony with other approaches to theurgy only by neglecting to address the key problem: in view of the interconnection of sacrificing and eating animals, Porphyry maintains that the philosopher should ideally abstain from both. Keeping the balance between different Neoplatonic strands in order to create the sense of a uniform tradition on daemonology proves just as difficult as holding the Pythagorean cock without strangling it.[164] Yet, this is precisely what Ficino sets out to achieve in combining Iamblichus and Porphyry.

Ficino wants to have it both ways. He adopts a selective approach to Porphyry, in order to be able to shorten the distance dividing him from Iamblichus, whom in general he finds more congenial. This means that with regard to animals, too, he tends to make use of Porphyry's critical stance on sacrifice, but without omitting his reasoning about the dietary implications. Striking such a balance means that the contiguity of sacrificing and eating animals on which Porphyry had insisted is at least partly blurred. But the animals, as real presences that tend to pass from the altar to the plate, suspended between life and death like the Pythagorean cock, keep upsetting this harmonious plan.

1.6. Rational Animals: An Exercise in Translating Porphyry

Held dangerously by the neck, the cock of the Pythagorean proverb not only serves as a metaphor for a power of the soul, but also stands as an animal used in a sacrificial context, reminiscent of Ficino's engagement with this topic through his translations. After all, the cock is here a 'Pythagorean symbol', and Pythagoras is one of Porphyry's main authorities for abstaining both from sacrificing and eating animals. In the early 1460s Ficino worked on Iamblichus's *De secta pythagorica* [On the Pythagorean Sect], the first part of which is dedicated to Pythagoras's life and philosophy.[165] There Iamblichus had named cocks among the very few animals which the Pythagoreans sacrificed, though only on exceptional occasions. Pythagoras

> sacrificed to the gods frankincense, millet, cakes, honeycomb, myrrh and the other fragrances. Neither he nor any other of the learned philosophers sacrificed any living thing, and he told the 'hearers' and the 'civic' followers to sacrifice live creatures only rarely: a cock, a lamb, some other young creature, but not oxen.[166]

One of the main reasons given by Iamblichus for Pythagoras's abstinence is that it promotes peace among all creatures, animal and human. By avoiding aggression towards animals, the Pythagoreans came to envision war as an even worse case of violence, and opposed it in all its forms.[167] This argument deploys the link between violence against animals and against humans differently than Porphyry had done: while Porphyry claimed that the Pythagorean vegetarian diet was not a response to an innate tendency of humans to be aggressive towards each other, Iamblichus emphasized how the decision not the kill animals had a positive effect on intra-human relations as well.[168]

Yet, Iamblichus tends to interpret Pythagorean sentences as being allegorical figures, rather than practical dietary prescriptions. Porphyry, by contrast, inter-weaves the same Pythagorean materials in his arguments in favour of a precise dietary choice, the vegetable diet. Once again, Ficino is thus presented with the challenge of dealing with different Neoplatonic interpretations of the same Pythagorean background. For instance, in a series of annotations to Iamblichus's *On the Pythagorean Life*, Ficino includes the following explanation of Pythagoras's prohibition, reported by Iamblichus against eating the heart of animals ('cor ne edas'): 'The brain is the instrument of thinking, the heart of passions. He who entangles the brain in various, harmful and useless thoughts, devours it. He who subjugates the heart to unnecessary passions, eats it'.[169] Ficino, following Iamblichus, emphasizes this allegorical reading, also employing the same interpretation of Pythagoras's prohibition in a letter.[170] For Porphyry, too, eating the heart had symbolical value, but at the same time functioned as a reminder that the heart is a piece of meat, and that the philosopher should anyway abstain from ingesting animal parts.[171] The heart and the brain are special organs, respectively seat of the passions and of ratiocination: therefore the sacrificial image of eating an animal organ is connected to the allegorical meaning endorsed by Ficino, developing the practical implications of the tenet that no part of any animal should be consumed as food. Indeed Iamblichus himself in *On the Pythagorean Life* had introduced the discussion of Pythagoras's prohibition with the general statement that 'animals are akin to us, sharing life and basic constituents and composition, linked in a kind of brotherhood'.[172] Avoiding eating the brain and the heart, in this context, could thus reflect the belief in the kinship of humans and the animals.

In Book 3 of *On Abstinence* Porphyry considers whether the kinship between humans and animals provides a further argument in favour of abstaining from meat-eating. Here he develops one particular facet of the human–animal proximity, implicitly addressed by the image of devouring the brain: the shared capability to think rationally, even if in different ways or different degrees. Porphyry's arguments on animal rationality are based on Stoic terminology: the animals have both an internal and an external *lógos*, that is to say that their silent thought-processes become explicit through their use of voices, which are to be considered languages in their own right.[173]

In *On the Pythagorean Life*, Iamblichus refers to stories about Pythagoras's alleged ability to promote non-violent behaviour and mutual respect among both rational and non-rational creatures. Such behaviour could include a change of dietary habit, as with the bear which was fed fruit and bread by Pythagoras, and convinced never to catch living creatures again.[174] This episode shows that Pythagoras was capable of communicating with and even teaching animals, despite their supposed lack of reason. Rationality as a criterion of distinction between humans and animals is crucial for Porphyry too, and Ficino was well aware of its connection to the topic of eating animals. Book 3 of *On Abstinence* deals with the ethical implications that can be drawn from considering the similarities and differences between the animal and the human soul. The main question is the following: if animals are rational is it justified to kill them or is it rather, in general, a crime, something impious, regardless of whether one kills an animal in order to sacrifice it or to gain nourishment from its flesh?[175]

Ficino summarizes this main issue in the section of his abridged translation of Book 3 of *On Abstinence*.[176] This begins with a paragraph in which he selects key passages from Porphyry's discussion on the rationality of animals. Here, Ficino disentangles two main elements of Porphyry's argumentation, the rationality of animals and their inclusion in the territory of justice. Porphyry's main aim in Book 3 is to show that the acknowledgment of animal rationality requires that justice (*díkē*) is due to animals as well. Proving Pythagoras's belief in the rationality of every soul is instrumental to extending justice to all creatures.[177] In the selection which forms the first paragraph of Ficino's translation, there are no references to justice. This shows that Ficino understands translation as an occasion to reshuffle and restructure the original material, presenting to the reader not simply an abridged version, but rather a new logical sequence, and ultimately his own interpretation of Porphyry's main tenets. What he omitted is thus as important as what he included in his translations. He subdivides his selection from Book 3 into four short paragraphs, each of which distils a particular argument. He leaves out arguments related to Stoicism, even though these were pivotal to Porphyry's reasoning.

Ficino's translation begins with reference to Pythagoras and his correct belief that 'a soul endowed with sensation and memory is rational, and has discursive knowledge [*ratio*], and speech, both interior and exterior, since animals speak to each other'.[178] The ethical conclusions are treated separately from this initial claim: they are addressed in the subsequent paragraph, which Ficino titles 'nefas est animalia caedere' ('it is abominable, or unlawful, to kill animals').[179] When Ficino then turns to the topic of justice, he does not immediately concur with Porphyry's emphatic conclusion that if animals are rational then they should be treated justly. Instead, Ficino opens the second section of his translation from Book 3 with the translation of a passage in which Porphyry deals with 'marginal cases', contexts in which animals are killed not for nourishment, but for fun or simply for the enjoyment of cruelty, as in circuses and hunts.

In Ficino's selection, the emphasis lies on the mere acknowledgement of animal rationality, which has the effect of weakening Porphyry's insistence on its strictly ethical value. Indeed it is significant that Ficino chooses to end his translation from Book 3 with a very short paragraph in which the argument culminates, and which he entitles: 'A certain [degree of] reason is present even in animals'.[180] Ficino includes Porphyry's discussion of ancient philosophers who discussed animal rationality — from Pythagoras to Apollonius of Tyana, Empedocles, Democritus, Plato, and Aristotle.[181] He also translates a sentence in which Porphyry relates a theory about the relationship between the place inhabited by a creature and its rationality: 'those who [are] in water', for instance, and 'those that are in the earth vary among themselves with regard to the degree of reason'.[182] This passage might have resonated with Ficino's own understanding of the cosmos and the rationality of the creatures inhabiting it.[183] Indeed in Book 4 of the *Theologia platonica* (written fifteen to twenty years before the translation project) Ficino had explained that:

> Animam ipsam terrae rationalem esse necessarium est, quandoquidem animalia quaedam terrae ratione non carent, praesertim cum opera terrae pulchriora sint quam hominum opera. Si anima huius infimi globi ratione capta non est, neque etiam superiorum globorum animae sunt rationis expertes. In terra et aqua talis est distinctio partium, quod terrenorum corporum quaedam sunt minus pura, quaedam purissima. Illas animas irrationales habent, ista rationales. Idem in aqua, ubi sunt pisces irrationales in luteis partibus aquae; sunt enim daemones aquaei [...] in quibusdam sublimioribus exhalationibus aquae, quales sint in hoc aere nubiloso.

> [The soul of the earth must be rational since certain of earth's animals do not lack reason, and since especially the works of the earth are more beautiful than men's works. If the soul of this lowest sphere has not been robbed of reason, the souls of the higher spheres are also not without reason. In earth and water the different parts are distinguished such that some of the earthly bodies are less pure, others are very pure. The former have irrational souls, the latter rational. The same occurs in water, where irrational fishes live in the muddy parts, but where water daemons [...] live in certain rarefied water vapors such as those in the cloudy air.][184]

It is noteworthy that Ficino here adopts the same argumentative strategy that occurs

repeatedly in the selection of passages on animal rationality from *On Abstinence*:
the comparison between creatures endowed with different degrees of reason
challenges the strict division between absolutely rational and absolutely irrational.[185]
A few lines later Porphyry's conception of daemons is brought into the discussion
of the relationship between the places the creatures inhabit and their level of
rationality.[186] In Book 2 of *Theologia platonica*, Ficino alludes to both Porphyry and
Iamblichus with regard to the role of rationality within the distinction between matter
and spirit. Even before he began to translate the Neoplatonic daemonology, Ficino's
approach stressed the harmonious development of a Neoplatonic understanding of
rationality: the 'Platonists' view rests,' he wrote, on the philosophical assumption
that 'rational spirits, because in no way do they stem from matter, possess no fixed
dimension in themselves and are not bound to dimension at all'.[187] When Ficino
turned to translating Iamblichus and Porphyry, precisely this approach informed
the exercise of abridging the texts and appropriating them within his own work.

The translation from Book 3 of *On Abstinence* ends, as mentioned, with a
reminder that rationality is present in creatures in varying degrees of perfection,
rather than being simply present or absent. Although Ficino's own understanding of
rationality in *Theologia platonica* rests on a separation of spirit and matter, implying
a radical distinction of humans from all animals, the idea of a gradation among
the creatures is also present.[188] For instance in Book 10, while arguing against the
Epicurean doctrine that nothing divine can be attached to a mortal thing, Ficino
sketches a 'chain of being' ('rerum series'), from the elements, to metals, to plants
and animals, and finally to humans and daemons.[189] With an approach somewhat
similar to that employed by Porphyry in the passages he translates, Ficino describes
the transition from animals to humans as follows:

> In brutis ostrea uno tantum superant plantas, quod sensum habent tactus,
> sed fixa terrae paene nutriuntur ut arbores. [...] Sunt et simiae, canes, equi
> et elephantes et aliae bestiae hominibus in quibusdam figuris, gestibus,
> artificiisque persimiles. Sunt stolidi homines et ignavi, ut apparet, his quoque
> quam proximi. Sunt heroici homines, aliorum duces, supernis numinibus
> cognatissimi.

> [Among animals, the oysters are superior to plants only in that they have a sense
> of touch, but they can stay rooted to the bottom and are nourished more or less
> like trees. [...] There are also monkeys, dogs, horses, elephants, and other beasts
> that resemble men in their various shapes, gestures, and accomplishments.
> There are dullwitted, lazy men too who obviously closely approximate to these
> animals [and] there are heroic men, leaders of others, who are next of kin to
> the divine spirits.][190]

The cases of brutal humans and of (almost) human–like animals blur the line
dividing the two categories, animal and human. The sense of a continuity is
intensified when Ficino introduces daemons into the picture and discusses the
presence or absence of rationality. Once again, Ficino draws a line which runs
from the 'Egyptians' through Neoplatonism, naming Porphyry explicitly.[191] All
Platonists, Ficino argues, share the same view about rationality: 'not only must
rational immortal creatures and at the same time irrational mortal creatures exist for

the world's perfect harmony, but also many rational and mortal creatures in between them, not only in earth, but also in the other elements'.[192] Ficino subordinates Porphyry's constant reference to the ethical impact of attributing rationality to his own interests in the nature of daemons.[193]

Another Porphyrian aspect on which Ficino does not linger is the problem of the link between the ritual sacrifice of animals and the summoning or casting out of evil presences. As we saw, this was one major root of the controversy between Iamblichus and Porphyry, and despite his attempts to harmonize the two Neoplatonists, it is clear that Ficino feels closer to the former than the latter. Yet, in this case, he does not simply omit to discuss the effects of ritual slaughter, but rather refers his readers to the works of someone who dealt with this matter in more detail:

> Explorato quoque dignissimum est Hebraicum illud, in mactandis animalibus rebusque nostris sacrificio dissipandis mala coelitus imminentia, a nobis ad nostra deflecti. Sed haec Pico nostro exploranda relinquimus.

> [It would be very worthwhile to explore that Hebrew notion, namely that in ritual slaughter of animals and in the scattering of our possessions as a sacrifice, the evils menacing us from the heavens are deflected from us to our possessions. But we leave these things for our friend Pico to explore.][194]

Readers interested in the apotropaic effect ascribed to ritual animal slaughter as a means to keep evils at bay should thus turn to the study of the 'Hebrew notion', that is to say to cabalistic sources: Ficino envisages Giovanni Pico della Mirandola's work as a guide in approaching this difficult topic. Indeed, despite focusing on different facets of ritual sacrifice, Pico, too, employs Porphyry's treatment of animal sacrifice as a point of reference. But he, too, transposes Porphyry's discussion into yet another area, different from the destination to which Ficino had brought it. For Pico, animal sacrifice has a metaphorical significance.

1.7. Becoming Human by Sacrificing Animals: Pico's *Conclusiones*

When Pico first published his *Conclusiones*, in 1486, Marsilio Ficino's project of translating Neoplatonic texts on daemonology was just about to begin.[195] Pico's eclectic collection interweaves a whole spectrum of theses taken from Neoplatonic sources, ranging from Plotinus to Porphyry, Iamblichus, and Proclus.[196] He engages directly with Porphyry's daemonology in two *conclusiones*, which deal in particular with the conception of evil daemons. The ninth thesis introduces Porphyry's distinction between two types of evil daemons ('There are two kinds of evil daemons: on the one hand, there are the souls and substantial daemons, on the other material powers and accidental daemons').[197] The thesis that follows presents Pico's explanation of this theory.[198] It is in the section featuring the cabalistic conclusions that the topic of sacrifice, especially animal sacrifice, comes to play the crucial role. Indeed the opening thesis of the *Conclusiones cabalisticae numero XLVII secundum secretam doctrinam sapientum hebreorum cabalistarum* centres upon a parallel between two different types of sacrifice,[199] one of lower and the other of higher value: 'Just as man and the lower priest sacrifices to God the souls of the irrational animals, so Michael, the higher priest, sacrifices the souls of the rational animals'.[200] The parallel hinges on two main points: the contrast between rational and irrational animals, and the distinction between a lower and higher sacrificial practice. It is not easy to identify Pico's sources for this compressed, enigmatic thesis (although there is an echo of Iamblichus's differentiation of sacrificial offering in *De mysteriis*).[201] By considering the broader treatment of both aspects — rationality and sacrifice — it will be possible to understand what connects Pico's interest in the topic of sacrifice with the wider fifteenth-century reception of Porphyry's argumentation on sacrificing animals in *On Abstinence*.[202]

On the first point, rationality, Pico explains in *Heptaplus*, a commentary in seven parts on the six days of the Creation, that there are three kinds of irrational animal. This distinction resonates with the discussion of animal rationality in Ficino's selection from *On Abstinence*.[203] Intertwining Plotinus (Pico acknowledges Ficino's Latin version) and biblical references, Pico writes that the three categories of irrational land animal are cattle (*iumenta*), reptiles (*reptilia*), and wild animals (*bestiae*). Each of the three groups occupies a precise position in the *scala naturae*: the reptiles have an imperfect form of imagination (*phantasia*) and can be placed in between plants and animals; the beasts of prey, on the other hand, are endowed with perfect imagination, and thus occupy a middle position within the realm of animals. Finally, cattle are the animals closest to humans, and enjoy a 'medium condition between brutes and humans'.[204] Unlike the beasts of prey, they can be tamed, and so somehow participate in reason, even if not fully.

Despite this somewhat gradual differentiation, from the point of sacrificial practice — the second main aspect in Pico's thesis — the division between rational and irrational creatures is radical: the lower priest sacrifices irrational souls, and the higher rational ones. The criterion of rationality points to a different understanding of the human-animal distinction, based on the roles played by animals and humans during sacrifice. In *Heptaplus* VI.5 Pico invokes the authorities of Iamblichus, Porphyry, and in general the Platonists and Pythagoreans, in order to argue that religious practices (including *mysteria*, vows, hymns, and supplications) are not only useful but also necessary. Further, both the *Conclusions* and the *Heptaplus* emphasize religious practice as that which is properly human: Pico's focus is on how the practice of sacrifice defines the position of humans in the cosmos.[205] The main point of distinction from the world of animals is not rationality, but rather the fact that humans perform religious acts, while animals in sacrifice play the role of the offering.

This emphasis on the role of sacrifice in defining humanity is noteworthy given that Pico (in his conciliatory fashion) mentions Porphyry alongside other 'Platonists', including Iamblichus: all of them, Pico writes, 'confirm' the crucial role of religious practices unanimously, 'with one voice'.[206] Pico's references to Porphyry thus appear within a broader context consonant with the general fifteenth-century approach to the rediscovery of *On Abstinence*: from Bessarion to Ficino, the identification of a 'Platonic' view of the cosmos, and the synthesis of biblical and Neoplatonic conceptions, are the two main features that account for the rising interest in Porphyry's discussion of (animal) sacrifice.

The first of these cabalistic theses by Pico indicates a view of the practice of sacrifice as an interior offering in prayer.[207] 'Sacrifice' may sound redolent of the offerings of animals on the altar, but the higher interpretation consists in the immolation of a human being to the divine: the latter takes place through 'role changing', by means of which the human takes the position of the animals he sacrificed on the altar, and in turn becomes an offering. It is worth remembering here that Bessarion referred to Porphyry in a similar context, arguing that the rejection of animal sacrifice in *On Abstinence* encouraged us to step away from the materiality of external offerings in order to grasp the deeper nature of religious practice, thus providing a Neoplatonic theory of sacrifice which was perfectly compatible with Christianity. The immolation of Christ as the lamb, instead of the offering of a real animal, marked this evolution from the blood and smoke of pagan sacrifices to the sublimated offering of the host in Christianity. For Bessarion, Porphyry had an important role to play within this trajectory.

Concise and esoteric, Pico's thesis does not go as far as Bessarion in developing the idea of an evolution in the practice of sacrifice, even if Pico's work is driven by a similar conciliatory approach.[208] Pico rather presents a contrast between the sacrifice proper to the lower priest (like Aaron, the first priest of the Israelites) and the higher offering performed by the archangel Michael, who presents human souls to God.[209] It suggests a metaphorical sublimation of sacrifice, and it emphasizes that in both cases, whether animals or humans are immolated, it is their souls, rather than their bodies, that are sacrificed. Even if Pico keeps the precise cabalistic background intentionally veiled, yet it is clear that he has in mind a contrast between the sacrificial practice in the Old Testament, and its overcoming in Michael's sublimated offer.[210] The offer is purely spiritual, and it does not involve slaughter.

The circulation of commentaries on Pico's cabalistic *Conclusiones* testifies to attempts by its readers to expound the esoteric content. In particular, three versions of a commentary are attested, and are attributed respectively to a Brother Christophorus of Forlì, to Arcangelo da Borgonovo, and to Francesco Cusano.[211] Thanks to a manuscript discovered by Chaim Wirszubski, containing an explicatory preface by Cusano,[212] it is now known that these three versions had a common origin: a commentary prepared by the Franciscan Francesco Zorzi (1466–1540), who was profoundly influenced by Pico (even though Pico is never mentioned in his main work, *De harmonia mundi*).[213] Through the filter of the different versions, we can thus glimpse Zorzi's own commentary, the starting point for a whole tradition of commentary upon Pico's *Conclusiones*.[214]

Borgonovo's commentary (*Cabalistarum selectiora dogmata*) was published in 1569, the year of his death. The commentary opens with a discussion of the sacrificial practice of the priests of the Old Testament, explaining the role of the 'lower priest' referred to in Pico's thesis. The animals offered in sacrifice had to be 'clean' ('munda'), without stain ('sine macula'): the reason is that 'sacrifices have a certain symbolic connection ('symbolum') with the one they are offered to and with those which are atoned for, yet [it is] such an obscure connection that not even the human mind can grasp it'.[215] Sacrifice, then, is an action by which humans seek contact with the Divine. It is an action like no other, since it defines what a human being is, as opposed to animals:

> Deo enim sacrificare (inquit Aristoteles ethicorum quinto, et Proclus in de orationibus et obsecrationibus libro, itemque Plato, Plotinus, et Porphyrius) est homini proprium sicut mugire bobus, et latrare canibus. Et his praeterea addunt quod qui hoc peragere contempserit, extra hominis naturam depelli meretur, eique hominis nomen denegari.[216]

> [To sacrifice to God (as Aristotle says in the fifth book of the *Ethics*, and Proclus in the book *On Orations and Supplications*, and also Plato, Plotinus and Porphyry) is peculiar to the human being just as lowing is peculiar to cattle and barking to dogs. And they add that he who does not care to do this, deserves to be cast out of human nature, and to be deprived of the name of human.]

Beginning with a reference to the role attributed to sacrifice especially in the Platonic tradition, the text underlines that praying and making offerings on the altar are the activities that distinguish humans from animals. Understanding the practice of sacrifice is therefore a way to understand humanity itself.[217] Yet, sliding away from this Platonic background into the interpretation of sacrifice founded on biblical sources, the author traces an evolution of sacrificial practice: reconstructing how sacrificial rituals changed through time enables us to recognize the trajectory of human approaches to seeking the connection with God.

The commentary explains that shedding the blood of animals was intended as a method to expiate sin, as everything is cleansed by blood.[218] But even before animals were sacrificed, the Old Testament shows that humans sacrificed crops, following what the commentary calls 'the law of nature', which preceded the written, Mosaic law. According to the commentary, God's design emerges clearly through the changes that occurred in the choice of the sacrificial offer: from the least worthy (crops), to the more worthy (animals), and finally to the worthiest offer of all — Christ.[219] The written law, too, is thus ultimately overcome by the 'law of love', and the most perfect animal (Christ, the lamb) takes the place of the animals slaughtered on the altars of the Old Testament. Having sketched this evolution, the text then comes back to the meaning of the cabalistic thesis, and interprets it as follows: just as the priest (of the Old Testament) offered the soul of animals under the written law, so Michael, who is priest and ruler over souls, offers them to God, and in so doing he redeems them.[220]

The reference to Porphyry, who is placed next to Aristotle, Plato, and Proclus, is general, and the author does not use *On Abstinence* to further exemplify how animal sacrifice overcame non-violent offerings, and was then in turn overcome by Christianity. It is worth remembering that this is precisely the context in which Jacques Boulduc was later to recur to Porphyry in his *De ecclesia ante legem*, integrating Porphyry's apology of vegetable offering within a biblical history of sacrifice which is consonant with the one found in this commentary. Nevertheless, the cornerstone of the commentary's interpretation effectively concurs with Porphyry: this is the idea that sacrifice is a fundamental but not necessarily violent human activity. It is interesting to note that Heinrich Cornelius Agrippa von Nettesheim offers a similar explanation of sacrifice in a section of *De occulta philosophia* [On Occult Philosophy] in which he comments on the function of the archangel Michael as priest who 'sacrifices the souls of human beings and this by separating the soul from the body, rather than the body from the soul'.[221] Agrippa here employs a direct reference to Porphyry in order to invoke the interpretation of the highest sacrifice as a sacrifice of one's own soul, just as Christ offered himself as victim. Agrippa adds that all external offers are simply means by which the soul can be cured, as is the case with exorcisms by which a malignant daemon must be cast away (the reference is here to Proclus).[222] Yet, Christ himself had renounced all animal sacrifice, limiting his offerings to simple bread and water, as the basis of human nutrition. Agrippa, too, integrates Porphyry within his interpretation of how sacrificial practice evolved towards non-violence; the remark on bread and water even goes further, hinting that animals are neither essential on the altar, nor on the plate.[223]

This non-violent core of sacrifice is still more prominent in Brother Christophorus's commentary on Pico. In general terms, the commentary on this thesis appears very similar to the one printed under the name of Borgonovo — further evidence for the hypothesis that they both stemmed from an original corpus of notes by Francesco Zorzi. Yet, this text contains some different formulations which add further details to the interpretation of animal sacrifice already sketched. The most relevant one features in the explanation which follows immediately the quotation of the thesis ('Sicut homo et sacerdos inferior sacrificat animas animalium irrationalium, ita Michael sacerdos superior sacrificat animas animalium rationalium'):

> Nota quod dicit Proclus in libro de orationibus et obsecrationibus, et Aristoteles 5. Ethicorum de mente Platonis, item Plotinus et Porphirius, quod sicut mugire est proprium bobus et latrare canibus ita deum orare est proprium hominibus et sacrificare, quod idem est.[224]

> [Note what Proclus says in the book *On Orations and Supplications*, and Aristotle in the fifth book of the *Ethics*, expounding Plato, and also [what] Plotinus and Porphyry [say], namely that just as lowing is peculiar to cattle and barking to dogs, so praying to God is peculiar to the human being, and sacrificing, which is the same [i.e. as praying].]

The emphasis given to the equivalence of sacrificing and praying contributes to identifying the essence of sacrifice with an internal action, which does not need to be performed on the altar through animal slaughter: it is not by chance that Porphyry is here, once again, a point of reference.

A similar passage is to be found in Zorzi's *De harmonia mundi*, a detail which shows once more the impact of Pico's eclectic discussion of sacrifice, and its further reception in the commentary. Zorzi writes that 'Didymus, Iarchas, Porphyry, Proclus in *On Orations and Supplications*, where he expounds on Plato, Iamblichus and Porphyry' agree that 'prayers are necessary, so that through them we are led back to our homeland, from which we are foreigners as long as we live here on earth'.[225] It is significant to note that a specific form of religious observance —

prayers, rather than sacrifice — plays the crucial role of directing the human being back to his origin.[226] Indeed in another passage which also resonates in the commentary, Zorzi states that what is peculiar to humankind is praying:

> Si Deus necessario agit, ad quid sacrificia? Ad quid orationes? Ad quid divinus cultus? Cur orare nobis proprium est (ut Plato, Porphyrius, Iamblichus, et Proclus docent) si Deus orationibus non flectitur?[227]

> [If God's actions are necessary, what is the function of sacrifice? And that of orations? And what is the scope of divine veneration? Why is praying proper to us (as Plato, Porphyry, Iamblichus and Proclus teach) if God is not moved by orations?]

Sacrificing is here indirectly subsumed within the category of a form of prayer: praying is the specific action of humans, setting them apart from all other animals, and paving the way for the return to God.[228]

Animal sacrifice per se appears to be overcome by non-violent prayer, and the reference to Porphyry is emblematic of this shift; at the same time, the place of animals within religious practice is still the crucial term of comparison for highlighting human specificity. Porphyry plays an important role in Zorzi's explication of the original function of animal sacrifice and its symbolic sublimation in prayer. At the same time Zorzi reflects on an issue which was essential to Porphyry's reasoning on animal sacrifice, but which lost its centrality in the discussion of the two types of sacrifice sparked by Pico's cabalistic readings: the connection between sacrificing and eating animals.

1.8. Symbolic Sacrifice: Francesco Zorzi and the Afterlives of Porphyrian Sacrifice

References to Porphyry are plentiful in *De harmonia mundi*.[229] Indeed, the most important strands of Renaissance engagement with Porphyry's discussion of sacrifice in *On Abstinence* converge in Zorzi's work: the effort to read Porphyry from a Christian perspective, the focus on the strictly daemonological aspects, the inclusion of cabalistic sources in the framework of interpretation (as in Pico), and especially the use of Ficino's translation of *On Abstinence*, which Zorzi quotes verbatim. As noted by Campanini, it would be impossible to understand Zorzi's view on the compatibility of Christianity and pagan authors without considering the contribution of Ficino, especially in the form of his translations of Neoplatonic sources.[230]

An instance of how these aspects come together, reflecting the pervasive presence of Porphyry in Renaissance debates on sacrifice, is a passage in which Zorzi quotes from Book 2 of *On Abstinence*, which he titles 'On the Good and the Bad Daemons', echoing a section of Ficino's translation titled 'On the Species of Good and Bad Daemons'. Describing the activity of the evil daemons, Zorzi quotes Porphyry in Ficino's version: 'There is no evil that they would not dare to perpetrate. They have a completely violent and wicked attitude, clearly deprived of the protection of good daemons'.[231] Ficino's special interest in the role of the evil daemons in

Porphyry thus resurfaces in Zorzi's own explanation of the behaviour of certain daemonic presences which intervene to punish those who act against God's will. Detached from its context — the daemonological consequences of animal sacrifice — Porphyry has here become the authority with regard to the existence of such evil daemonic entities. A further testimony of the reception of Porphyry's daemonology via Ficino, is Agrippa's *De occulta philosophia*, in which the same passage is introduced by the words 'Porphyry says [the following] about this type of daemons' — that is to say, the evil type.[232]

Yet despite the clear and diffuse influence of Porphyry (and Ficino's Porphyry in particular) in *De harmonia mundi*, there are two passages where the lack of direct reference to Porphyry is striking. The first is in the discussion of the evolution of sacrifice from vegetable offerings through the animal sacrifices of the Old Testament, to the immolation of Christ. The second regards the symbology of meat-eating and includes a statement which can be read as an explanation about Zorzi's own choice of a vegetable diet.[233] A main reason for not mentioning Porphyry in these two key passages may be Zorzi's Christian concern. Zorzi is aware that despite previous attempts to integrate Porphyry within Christianity, such as Bessarion's, Porphyry's attacks on Christians remained problematic. This is why Zorzi calls Porphyry a 'rabid dog', and underlines that the pagan cults were overcome by Christianity, and Porphyry's gods defeated by Jesus.[234]

Nevertheless, Porphyry's stance on animal sacrifice presented one obvious advantage over the Christian conception of sacrifice: it did make it unnecessary to explain why God would require the immolation of animals, rejoicing in the violent act of shedding their blood. In the commentary on Pico's *Conclusiones*, the explanation hinged on the need to 'wash away' sin through blood. In *De harmonia mundi*, Zorzi asks directly: 'what is the function of sacrifices, and why is it ordered that goats, randomly chosen, are offered to expiate sin'?[235] He admits that it is difficult to understand why God would 'be delighted by the shedding of animal blood, by the roasting and burning of meat, and of their smells, and the smells of other things, as is said in many passages: "And God smelled a pleasant odour"'.[236] In the first instance, such passages must thus be interpreted as referring to a deep, mysterious meaning of sacrifice, according to which animal sacrifice is a symbol for the offering and death of the animal part of the human soul. Indeed the 'animal part' in humans is the seat of the devil, in which sin has its roots: that 'animal part' is the animal which needs to die on the altar. Symbolically, the killing of animals means subduing and cleaning the bestiality of sin, eradicating it from the depths of humanity. Through sacrifice, the death of this symbolical animal opens the path to a spiritual rebirth, by analogy with the generation of a plant, when the sprout germinates while part of the seed decays.

This symbolical turn allows Zorzi to emphasize the transition from the Old Testament practice of animal sacrifice to the immolation of Christ in the New Testament. He explains this evolution by using the example of the scapegoat: the animal is cast into the desert as a sacrificial symbol that all evils can be collected in an animal body and expiated with the creature's death. But of course this is precisely

Christ's function, and thus Zorzi slides from the symbology of animal sacrifice to the meaning of Christ's sacrifice, through which all sins are washed away. Zorzi underlines that Christ died for 'his sheep', a term that stands symbolically for humans, but which suggests a reversal of the roles: from the sacrifice of animals to save humans, to the sacrifice of Christ the shepherd to save his flock.[237] A passage from Zorzi's *Commento sopra il Poema* [Commentary on the Poem] adds further facets to the meaning attributed to the image of saving the sheep, while at the same time explaining Christ's spiritual offer:

> ['l Propheta] canta nel Salmo 35°, Salverai, o Signore gli huomini, e gli giumenti.[238] Per la vera intelligentia, nel cui luogo, sappi che 'l Propheta vuol dire, che 'l se salverà l'huomo i. la parte rationale; ché, come dice Aristotele, l'huomo si è l'intelletto, e la ragione; e per gli giumenti, se intendono li corpi, o le parti animali, quando però saran transmutate in sorte, e conditioni spirituali. E contenendo l'huomo in sé tutte le cose [...] salvandosi l'huomo, se vengono a salvare tutte le cose, che vertualmente sono contenute in lui .[239]

> [In Psalm 35, the prophet sings: 'Lord, you will save humans and cattle'. You should know that by true intelligence, as is said in the corresponding passage, the prophet means that the human being, that is to say, the rational part, will be saved; indeed, as Aristotle said, the human being is the intellect, reason; by cattle are meant the bodies, or the animal parts, but when they will be transformed into spiritual kind and condition. And since the human being contains everything within himself [...], by saving him everything that is virtually contained in him will also be saved.]

Just as he interprets cattle as a symbolic image of the body (or the 'animal part', an expression used in *De harmonia mundi* as well), in answering the problem of God's delight in animal sacrifice, Zorzi steers away from the real practice of sacrifice, and directs attention to the symbolical meaning. He supports this approach with rather vague references to the doctrines of the 'Jewish masters' ('doctores Hebraei'). But he might also have in mind the Neoplatonic sources on daemonology when he writes that it is not God himself who takes part in sacrifice by eating the offering, but rather there are certain 'virtues', or powers, which can taste 'thick foods' made of earthly matter.[240] These powers are not evil, unlike those daemons that according to Porphyry are summoned by the blood of animals slaughtered on the altar; but just like those daemons, they appear to intervene physically in the ritual by eating the offer.

Zorzi is careful to remark that God, on the contrary, does not eat material food, nor does he enjoy any smell or taste, so that when the Old Testament describes such practices of 'feeding God', these must be interpreted in a higher, symbolical sense. God, then, does not eat the flesh of animals — and apparently neither did Zorzi himself.[241] This is the second passage in which the absence of Porphyry is particularly striking, given that Zorzi draws dietetic conclusions from a broader discussion centred on comparing the original habits of humans with the current, corrupted ones, a comparison which Porphyry had also insisted upon. But unlike that of Porphyry, Zorzi's comparison is based on the biblical account of how human diet changed from prelapsarian vegetable food, to a violent diet including meat after the flood. The question of the legitimacy of animal sacrifice might also be in the background, given the story of Noah's sacrifice to God straight after the flood (a detail to which, as we saw, Boulduc draws attention, too). As Zorzi explains in the following passage, all acts of tearing apart and killing pertain to a violent law which is not the law of the Gospel:

> Nam in horto voluptatis positus fuit homo, ut ederet de fructibus arborum, et excoleret illas [...] a quod loco eiecto homini ante, et post diluvium, et in utraque lege, Mosaica, et Evagelica, etiam semper olera eadem concessa fuere, nisi quae aliquo gravi excessu virosa et nocua effecta sunt in radicibus, stipitibus, foliis, aut fructibus sese vitanda reddidere. Carnes autem ante diluvium non erant in usu, immo (ut aliqui asseverant) interdictae, metalla vero (quibus thesaurizatur in hac peregrinatione) in Evangelio denegantur, quae sub Martis ditione (ut diximus) continentur. Sic animalium sanguis, morticina praedata, dilaniata rostris, vel unguibus, aut dentibus, et huiusmodi, quae Martia sunt, et ex parte sinistra in lege prohibentur his, qui in dextris collocandi sunt, a quibus (ne ultra progrediamur, quam liceat) abstinendum duximus.[242]

> [The human being was placed in the garden of delight to eat the fruits of the trees, and cultivate them [...] and after being expelled from that place before and after the flood and in both laws, the Mosaic and the Gospel one, and indeed always, the same vegetables were permitted, apart from those that, due to something severely excessive in them, are proven poisonous and dangerous in the roots, in the trunks, leaves or fruits and are therefore not edible. But flesh was not used as food before the flood, and it was even (as some say) prohibited, and in fact metals (with which treasures are accumulated in this [earthly] peregrination) are rejected in the Gospel: they are included, as we said, under the dominion of Mars. Thus the blood of animals, the hunted corpses, torn apart by beaks, claws, or teeth, and all things that belong to Mars, being on the left side in the law are prohibited to those who shall be placed on the right hand side; and from these (so as not to go beyond what is permitted) we decided to abstain.]

According to this statement, abstinence from consuming the flesh of animals keeps the human being away from the unlawful, violent aspects which belong to Mars. Abstinence also separates Adam from the history of corruption after the Fall. Eating vegetables is thus almost a journey back to the condition before the Fall: in the Garden of Eden there was no violence, and no animal blood was shed, neither for sacrifice, nor for food. Only a few decades after the publication of Zorzi's *De harmonia mundi* in 1525, Francesco Pucci was to recur to the same biblical image of Adam's condition before the Fall to argue that the diet of the first human being had also been exempt from any kind of violence: Adam had been, indeed, a vegetarian.[243] Zorzi combines elements of astrology (a science whose invention he attributes to the Egyptians and Chaldeans), with dietetic notions about the consumption of plants, and with biblical exegesis, in particular regarding the difference between the Old and the New Testament.[244] It is owing to this context that the conclusion about abstinence from animal flesh, expressed almost in passing, reveals its crucial role, connecting Zorzi's symbolical reinterpretation of animal sacrifice with concern about the human uses of animals. It is at this level that Zorzi's view appears to be remarkably close to Porphyry's, even if he does not mention Porphyry directly as a source. Again, despite a certain sympathy towards Porphyry, who 'feeds the wondering minds with the variety of his doctrines', Zorzi probably means to underline that his own approach, unlike Porphyry's, is rooted in the revelation of Christian truth.[245] His image of an original state in which man was vegetarian and cruelty had not yet shaped the relationship between the creatures derives from the biblical description of the Garden of Eden, rather than from the ideal of a Golden Age in which the ancients preferred vegetable food, as in Porphyry. Nevertheless, Zorzi follows in the footsteps of previous readers and translators of Porphyry, and especially of Ficino in bringing together pagan philosophers with Christianity on key doctrinal points: abstinence from animals, for Zorzi, becomes one such focal point, where the interpretation of the Scripture harmonizes with Porphyry's view.

Notes to Chapter 1

1. About the pervasiveness of animal sacrifice in the Mediterranean basin, within different religious strands, see Daniel C. Ullucci, *The Christian Rejection of Animal Sacrifice* (Oxford & New York: Oxford University Press, 2012), Chapter 1.
2. *OA*, II.1–2; p. 55.
3. Mark J. Edwards, 'Two Images of Pythagoras: Iamblichus and Porphyry', in *The Divine Iamblichus: Philosopher and Man of Gods*, ed. by Henry J. Blumenthal & E. Gillian Clark (Bristol: Bristol Classical Press, 1993), pp. 159–72 (p. 159): 'The man who was to write the *De Abstinentia* neither denies nor upbraids the occasional sacrifices which are attributed to Pythagoras in his sources'.
4. See a very clear sketch of the problem in Ullucci, *The Christian Rejection of Animal Sacrifice*, pp. 58–59.
5. *OA*, 1.26.2–3; p. 40. Cf. Porphyry, *Vie de Pythagore*, in *Vie de Pythagore. Lettre à Marcella*, ed. by Edouard des Places (Paris: Les Belles Lettres, 1982), pp. 52–54 (§ 36). On Porphyry's *Life of Pythagoras*, and on the differences with Iamblichus's *On the Pythagorean Way of Life*, see Gillian Clark, 'Philosophic Lives and the Philosophic Life', in *Greek Biography and Panegyric in Late Antiquity*, ed. by Tomas Hägg and Philip Rousseau (Berkeley: University of California Press, 2000), pp. 29–51.
6. Diogenes Laertius, *Lives of Eminent Philosophers*, VIII.19–22. But it is interesting to note that Diogenes, too, refers to the opinion that Pythagoras actually offered up small animals (cocks, kids, and suckling animals). This is followed by the remark that, according to Aristoxenos, he even ate animals, with the exception of two notable ones: the ox used for ploughing, and the ram. See also *OA*, II.31.1–2; pp. 67–68, about the prohibition to kill the animals working for humans.
7. The reference is to the diet of the athletes: Diogenes Laertius, *Lives of Eminent Philosophers*, VIII.12–13. I will come back to the discussion of meat's nourishing qualities in Chapter 2 below.
8. *OA*, 1.1.1. & 1.3.3; pp. 31–32.
9. *OA*, II.2.1; p. 55.
10. This is Clark's explanation for the statement, contained in *OA*, II.2.2; p. 55, that humans sacrifice creatures they would never dare to eat (*OA*, p. 144).
11. For a clear overview of the main anthropological interpretations of the connection between sacrificing animals and eating their meat see Cristiano Grottanelli, 'Uccidere, donare, mangiare: problematiche attuali nel sacrificio antico', in *Sacrificio e società nel mondo antico*, ed. by Cristiano Grottanelli & Nicola F. Parise (Bari & Rome: Laterza, 1988), pp. 3–53.
12. Jean-Pierre Vernant and Marcel Detienne, *The Cuisine of Sacrifice Among the Greeks*, trans. by Paula Wissing (Chicago: University of Chicago Press, 1989). See also Grottanelli, 'Uccidere, donare, mangiare', p. 17.

13. See Ullucci's definition (*The Christian Rejection of Animal Sacrifice*, p. 15): 'Animal sacrifice is the ritual slaughter of an animal and the distribution of its parts among humans and imagined superhuman beings. It is one of the most pervasive religious rituals in human history'.

14. Walter Burkert, *Homo necans: Interpretationen altgriechischer Opferriten und Mythen* (Berlin: De Gruyter, 1972), p. 29.

15. On hunting and sacrificing see Mack Burton, 'Introduction: Religion and Ritual', in *Violent Origins: Walter Burkert, René Girard, and Jonathan Z. Smith on Ritual Killing and Cultural Formation*, ed. by Robert G. Hamerton-Kelly (Stanford, CA: Stanford University Press, 1987), pp. 1–70 (p. 23).

16. *OA*, II.29.1; p. 66.

17. See Theophrastus of Eresus, *Commentary 6.1: Sources on Ethics*, ed. by William W. Fortenbaugh, with Contributions on the Arabic Material by Dimitri Gutas (Leiden: Brill, 2011), p. 569; and Theophrastus of Eresus, *Commentary 5: Sources on Biology (Human Physiology, Living Creatures, Botany: Texts 328–435)*, ed. by Robert W. Sharples (Leiden: Brill, 1995), pp. 39–40. See also Diogenes Laertius, *Lives of Eminent Philosophers*, v.50.

18. For Porphyry's borrowings from Theophastus see Theophrastus of Eresus, *Commentary 5*, p. 411. Cf. *OA*, II.5.1; p. 56.

19. *OA*, II.7.2 & II.9.1–2; pp. 57 & 58.

20. *OA*, II.12.1; p. 59.

21. Cf. Giulia Gasparro Sfameni, 'Critica del sacrificio cruento e antropologia in Grecia: da Pitagora a Porfirio. II. Il *De abstinentia* porfiriano', in *Sangue e antropologia nella teologia: Atti della VI settimana, Roma, 23–28 nov. 1987*, ed. by Francesco Vattioni (Rome: Edizioni Pia Unione Preziosissimo Sangue, 1989), pp. 461–505.

22. On the relationship between Porphyry and Iamblichus see Richard Sorabji, *The Philosophy of the Commentators, 200–600 AD: Physics* (Ithaca, NY: Cornell University Press, 2005), p. 7.

23. Graziella Federici Vescovini, *'Arti' e filosofia nel secolo XIV: studi sulla tradizione aristotelica e i 'moderni'* (Florence: Vallecchi, 1983), p. 180: 'Tutto si ritualizza e sacralizza.'

24. Clarke, *Iamblichus' 'De Mysteriis'*, p. 6.

25. See the introduction to Porphyry, *Lettre à Anébon l'Égyptien*, ed. by Henri Dominique Saffrey & Alain Segonds (Paris: Les Belles Lettres, 2012), p. xlvii. For a detailed discussion of the content of the *De mysteriis* as a response to Porphyry see Henri Dominique Saffrey, 'Analyse de la réponse de Jamblique à Porphyre, connue sous le titre *De mysteriis*', *Revue des Sciences philosophiques et théologiques*, 84.3 (July 2000), 489–511 (reprinted in Saffrey, *Le Néoplatonisme après Plotin* (Paris: Vrin, 2000), pp. 77–99).

26. Francesco Romano, 'Il vocabolario della "natura" nel *De Mysteriis* di Giamblico', in *The Divine Iamblichus*, ed. by Blumenthal & Clark, p. 87.

27. On the difference between Porphyry's position in *On Abstinence* and in the *Letter* see Sodano's introduction to Iamblichus, *I misteri egiziani*, ed. by Angelo R. Sodano (Milan: Rusconi, 1984), p. 33 (Sodano maintains that Abamon is not Iamblichus's pseudonym). On Porphyry's position(s) on sacrifice in his various writings see Crystal Addey, *Divination and Theurgy in Neoplatonism* (Farnham: Ashgate, 2014), p. 136.

28. On the circulation of Iamblichus's *De mysteriis Aegyptiorum* (forty manuscripts are extant, many incomplete) see Paul Oskar Kristeller, 'Neoplatonismo e Rinascimento', in *Studies in Renaissance Thought and Letters*, 4 vols (Rome: Edizioni di Storia e Letteratura, 1996), IV, 160.

29. Jacques Boulduc, *De ecclesia ante legem libri tres* [...] (Lyon: Landry, 1626). The second edition was published in 1630, together with a new volume entitled *De ecclesia post legem* (Paris: Cottereau, 1630).

30. Boulduc, *De ecclesia ante legem* (1630), p. 4 (1626 ed., p. 3).

31. Boulduc, *De ecclesia ante legem* (1630), p. 5: 'Hoc forsitan naturali lumine ducti Theologi Gentium tribus de causis Diis sacrificandum censuerunt, ut veneremur, ut gratias referamus, ut ab ipsis necessaria petamus, et mala propellamus. Ad haec perficienda votum animi satis esse existimabant, cui et addi posse credebant quaedam ex frugibus munuscola, animalia vero mactare nefas ducebant: inter quos Aegyptios extitisse puto, de quibus Moyses. Porphyrius Philosophus scribit primos qui Diis sacrificare caeperunt, non animalium, sed herbas primum floresque, deinde arbores sacrificasse'.

32. Boulduc, *De ecclesia ante legem* (1630), p. 5 (1626 ed., p. 3). Moshe Halbertal has interpreted sacrifice in terms of a precise dynamic of giving and accepting, and Cain's violence as a reaction to the infringment of this pattern: *On Sacrifice* (Princeton & Oxford: Princeton University Press, 2012), pp. 10, 19–21.

33. Boulduc, *De ecclesia ante legem* (1630), p. 5: 'Inde colligo Cain primogenitum Adae tale sacrificium de terrae frugibus, non nisi exemplo patris, cui in sacrificio succedebat, obtulisse'. In *De oggio Christiano* (Lyon: Boissat and Anisson, 1640) Boulduc shows a specific interest in the sacrifice of wine and cereals.

34. See the index at the end of the 1630 edition of *De ecclesia ante legem*, under 'Idolatria': 'Nulla fuit ante diluvium'.

35. Cf. Genesis 8: 20–21 (all biblical quotations are taken from *The Bible: Authorized King James Version*, ed. by Robert Carroll & Stephen Prickett (Oxford & New York: Oxford University Press, 1998)): 'And Noah builded an altar unto the Lord; and took of every clean beast, and of every clean fowl, and offered burnt offerings on the altar. And the Lord smelled a sweet savour'. Cf. Boulduc, *De ecclesia ante legem* (1630), p. 12.

36. On the Plato-Aristotle controversy see John Monfasani, *George of Trebizond: A Biography and a Study of His Rhetoric and Logic* (Leiden: Brill, 1976), pp. 201–29.

37. George Gemistos Plethon, *De differentiis (Peri on Aristoteles pros Platona diapheretai)* was first published in Greek in 1540 (Venice: Scoto); the first Latin translation, by Niccolò Scutelli, remained unpublished. Plethon wrote this text in Florence in 1439, mainly for an Italian audience. See on this François Masai, *Pléthon et le platonism de Mistra* (Paris: Les Belles Lettres, 1956), pp. 330–31. See also Christopher Montague, *George Gemistos Plethon: The Last of the Hellenes* (Oxford: Clarendon Press, 1986), p. 191. On the differences between Ficino's and Plethon's approaches to the relationship between Platonism and Christianity see Niketas Siniossoglou, *Radical Platonism in Byzantium: Illumination and Utopia in Gemistos Plethon* (Cambridge: Cambridge University Press, 2011), p. 155.

38. On Plethon's 'reputation as a neopagan' see John Monfasani, 'George Gemistos Pletho and the West: Greek Émigrés, Latin Scholasticism and Renaissance Humanism', in *Renaissance Encounters: Greek East and Latin West*, ed. by Marina S. Brownlee & Dimitri H. Gondicas (Leiden: Brill, 2013), pp. 19–34. On Plethon's pagan Platonism see Siniossoglou, *Radical Platonism in Byzantium*, especially part 2. On the *Comparatio* see John Monfasani, 'A Tale of Two Books: Bessarion's *In Calumniatorem Platonis* and George of Trebizond's *Comparatio Philosophorum Platonis et Aristotelis*', *Renaissance Studies*, 22.1 (2008), 1–15.

39. See especially George of Trebizond, *Comparatio philosophorum Platonis et Aristotelis* (Venice: Penzio, 1523; facsimile edn Frankfurt am Main: Minerva, 1975), Book II, section 2 [unnumbered]: 'Sacrificia non illis primis, sed coelo ipsi, et soli, ac lunae, his inferioribus diis [...] offerenda esse censet'. For a useful overview of George of Trebizond's charges against Platonic theology, and Bessarion's answers, see Sears Reynolds Jayne, *Plato in Renaissance England* (Dordrecht: Kluwer, 1995), p. 65.

40. George of Trebizond, *Comparatio*, Book II, section 2: 'Nec quos deos appellat solum colit atque adorat, verum etiam daemones, horum naturam mediam esse putat, inter hominum naturam, et ultimorum deorum'. And ibid.: 'Iccirco per divinationem quoque hominum, daemones transeunt. Sacerdotalis etiam ars, in extis et sacrificiis et invocationibus, et divinationibus generibus universis, maleficisque artibus, per demonas afficitur'.

41. Of course, paganism is a complex concept, especially if applied to fifteenth-century thinkers. On the appropriateness of its use in the case of Plethon and of his contemporaries see: John Monfasani, 'Platonic Paganism in the Fifteenth Century', in *Reconsidering the Renaissance: Papers from the Twenty-first Annual Conference of the Center for Medieval and Early Renaissance Studies*, ed. by Mario A. Di Cesare (Binghamton, NY: Medieval and Renaissance Texts and Studies, 1992), pp. 45–61; and Siniossoglou, *Radical Platonism in Byzantium*, especially pp. 15–23.

42. See John Monfasani, 'The Pre- and Post-History of Cardinal Bessarion's 1469 *In Calumniatorem Platonis*', in *'Inter graecos latinissimus, inter latinos graecissimus': Bessarion zwischen den Kulturen*, ed. by Christian Kaiser, Claudia Märtl, & Thomas Ricklin (Berlin: De Gruyter, 2013), pp. 347–66 (pp. 352–53). On the danger of Bessarion's operation see Daniel P. Walker, 'Orpheus the Theologian

and Renaissance Platonists', *Journal of the Warburg and Courtauld Institutes*, 16.1–2 (1953), 100–20 (p. 118): '[Bessarion] was acutely conscious of the danger of making Christianity fit Platonism, instead of the other way round. He constantly indicated points where Plato is not reconcilable with orthodoxy'.

43. *ICP*, III.4.2; pp. 227–29. I quote from the Latin version of the text.

44. *ICP*, III.4.1; p. 229.

45. On sacrifice and popular festivities in Plato see *Laws*, Book VIII. Bessarion refers to this book directly (*ICP*, III.5.3; p. 237).

46. *ICP*, III.4.2; p. 229.

47. *ICP*, III.4.2; pp. 230–31. It is relevant that the key quotation from *On Abstinence* is included by Eusebius in his *Praeparatio evangelica* translated by George of Trebizond in 1448 and published in 1470: 'Silentio autem sancto et cogitatione integra ab omnique morbo remota eum colimus' (Eusebius of Caesarea, *De evangelica praeparatione*, trans. by George of Trebizond (Venice: Jenson, 1470), Book 4, chapter 5, unnumbered). The same passage is included in Ficino's selected translation from Book 2 of *On Abstinence* (on which see sections 3 & 6 below): *OMF*, I, 1934: 'silentio puro, purisque de ipso intelligentiis ipsum rite colemus'. As Sebastiano Gentile has shown, Ficino used this translation by George of Trebizond: 'Sulle prime traduzioni dal greco di Marsilio Ficino', *Rinascimento*, 2nd s., 40 (1990), 57–104 (63).

48. This conciliatory role also explains Bessarion's sympathy for Porphyry (Monfasani, *George of Trebizond*, p. 220).

49. See for instance Kristeller, *Studies in Renaissance Thought and Letters*, IV, 160.

50. Crystal Addey (*Divination and Theurgy in Neoplatonism*, pp. 127–69) has claimed that the opposition between Porphyry's and Iamblichus's views could nevertheless be interpreted in the tradition of Platonic dialogical opposition, rather than simply as contrasting views.

51. This is Mohler's position, commented upon by Monfasani, *George of Trebizond*, p. 220.

52. *ICP*, III.5.3; p. 237. Cf. *OA*, II.34.2; p. 69.

53. *ICP*, III.5.3; p. 237: 'Nullum enim animal illic immolatur, atque ob eam rem ara pia est nuncupata'. Cf. *OA*, II.28.1; p. 66.

54. Porphyry, *Against the Christians*, ed. by Robert M. Berchman (Leiden: Brill, 2005), p. 186. Cf. *DCD*, XL.2, 411 (Book XIX.22): 'doctissimus philosophorum, quamvis Christianorum acerrimus inimicus'.

55. Porphyry, *Against the Christians*, p. 184 (cf. *DCD*, XL.1, 485 (Book X.24): 'Eum quippe in ipsa carne contempsit, quam propter sacrificium nostrae purgationis adsumpsit, magnum scilicet sacramentum ea superbia non intelligens, quam sua ille humilitate deiecit verus benignusque Mediator').

56. Porphyry, *Against the Christians*, p. 184: 'But Porphyry, being under the dominion of these envious powers, whose influence he was at once ashamed of and afraid to cast off, refused to recognize that Christ is the principle by whose incarnation we are purified'. Ibid., p. 172: '[Porphyry] says "[they] censure the rites of sacrifices, the victims, the incense, and other things exercised in the cults of the temples, whether the same cult began with themselves, or with the God whom they worship." (See respectively *DCD*, XL.1, 485 (Book X.24); and Augustine, *Epistulae*, in *Corpus scriptorum ecclesiasticorum latinorum*, XXXIV.2, ed. by Alois Goldbacher (Prague, Vienna, & Leipzig: Tempsky & Freytag, 1898), nr. 102.16; p. 558).

57. *ICP*, III.15.1; p. 299.

58. Porphyry, *Against the Christians*, p. 189: 'Plato and Porphyry many times made certain statements, and if they could have shared these with one another, perhaps they would have become Christians'. Cf. *DCD*, XL.1, 653 (Book XXII.27). See also Monfasani, *George of Trebizond*, p. 219.

59. But see Ullucci, *The Christian Rejection of Animal Sacrifice*, p. 7, on the interpretation of Christ's death as 'equivalent to animal sacrifice'.

60. *OA*, II.36.1; p. 69.

61. *ICP*, III.5.3; p. 235.

62. *OA*, II.34.2; p. 69. On this aspect of Porphyry's discussion of animal sacrifice see Michael B. Simmons, *Universal Salvation in Late Antiquity: Porphyry of Tyre and the Pagan-Christian Debate*

(Oxford & New York: Oxford University Press, 2015), pp. 40–41. In particular Simmons explains that Porphyry provides detailed instructions about animals and parts of animals suitable to be sacrificed to each deity, pointing to 'an allegorical meaning to various elements related to the practice'. Yet, according to Simmons, this does not happen 'at the exclusion of the practice itself'.

63. See Nicholas Banner, *Philosophic Silence and the 'One' in Plotinus* (Cambridge: Cambridge University Press, 2018).

64. *OA*, II.61.6; p. 79.

65. See John Monfasani, 'Prisca theologia in the Plato-Aristotle controversy before Ficino', in *The Rebirth of Platonic Theology: Proceedings of a Conference Held at The Harvard University Center for Italian Renaissance Studies (Villa I Tatti) and the Istituto Nazionale di Studi sul Rinascimento (Florence, 26–27 April 2007), for Michael J. B. Allen*, ed. by James Hankins & Fabrizio Meroi (Florence: Olschki, 2013), pp. 47–59. On the role of Pythagoras within the Renaissance rediscovery of Platonism see Joost-Gaugier, *Pythagoras and Renaissance Europe*, p. 25: 'Bessarion proposed a new role for Pythagoras, as a conduit from ancient philosophy to Christianity: Not only was Pythagoras a precursor of Christianity, he was one of its inspirators'.

66. Basil Bessarion, *De sacramento Eucharistiae*, in *Kardinal Bessarion als Theologe, Humanist und Staatsmann*, ed. by Mohler, III, 1–69 (esp. p. 53).

67. As Monfasani points out, the text had been withdrawn from the press in 1466 and was published only three years later (cf. Monfasani, 'The Pre- and Post-History History of Cardinal Bessarion's 1469 *In Calumniatorem Platonis*', p. 355).

68. Kristeller noted that the timing of this exchange and of Ficino's translation of Plato suggests mutual acknowledgement of their respective engagement with and approach to Plato (Kristeller, *Studies In Renaissance Thought and Letters*, IV, 268–69).

69. *OMF*, I, 617. *LMF*, I, 53.

70. See Stéphane Toussaint, 'Introduction', in Iamblichus, *De mysteriis* (Enghien-Les-Bains: Éditions du Miraval, 2006), p. vii (facsimile edn of Venice: Aldus Manutius, 1497).

71. On the meaning of theurgy and the link with sacrifice in Ficino's paraphrase of Iamblichus's *De mysteriis*, see Guido Giglioni, 'Theurgy and Philosophy in Marsilio Ficino's Paraphrase of Iamblichus's *De mysteriis Aegyptiorum*', *Rinascimento*, 52 (2012), 3–36 (pp. 7–8). Giglioni remarks on the significant fact that in Niccolò Scutelli's translation of *De mysteriis*, *theurgia* is rendered with *sacrificia* (p. 8).

72. Ficino had already worked on Iamblichus's *De secta pythagorica* in the 1460s. See Christopher S. Celenza, 'Temi neopitagorici nel pensiero di Marsilio Ficino', in *Marsile Ficin ou les mystères platoniciens: Actes du XLIIe Colloque International d'Études Humanistes. Centre d'Études supérieures de la Renaissance. Tours, 7–10 juillet 1999*, ed. by Stéphane Toussaint, Les Cahiers de l'humanisme, 2 (Paris: Les Belles Lettres, 2002), pp. 57–70 (p. 63). See also Cesare Vasoli, 'Pitagora in monastero', *Interpres*, 1 (1978), 256–72 (p. 256). On Ficino's translation of Proclus see Michael J. B. Allen, 'Marsilio Ficino', in *Interpreting Proclus From Antiquity to the Renaissance*, ed. by Stephen Gersh (Cambridge: Cambridge University Press, 2014), pp. 353–79 (esp. pp. 358–61).

73. For a thorough discussion of Ficino's interest in daemonology as it emerges in these translations, see Maude Vanhaelen, 'L'Enterprise de traduction et d'exégèse de Ficin dans les années 1486–1489: démons et prophétie à l'aube de l'ère savonarolienne', *Humanistica*, 1 (2010), 125–36. On Ficino's harmonizing attitude with regard to Platonism and Christianity, and on the role of Porphyry in particular, see ibid., p. 130.

74. Because of the presence of these extracts, Ficino's translations of Porphyry can be dated to 1486–88: *Marsilio Ficino e il ritorno di Platone: mostra di manoscritti, stampe e documenti, 17 maggio-16 giugno 1984*, ed. by Sebastiano Gentile, Sandra Niccoli, & Paolo Viti, exhibition catalogue (Florence: Le Lettere, 1984), pp. 122–23. Ficino used two Greek manuscripts to translate Porphyry.

75. See Cesare Vasoli, *Quod sit Deus: studi su Marsilio Ficino* (Lecce: Conte, 1999), p. 108.

76. As Gillian Clark puts it with regard to Platonic asceticism, 'the philosopher thus becomes a religious leader'. (Clark, 'Introduction', in Iamblichus, *On the Pythagorean Life*, p. xiii). According to Stéphane Toussaint ('L'individuo estatico: tecniche profetiche in Marsilio Ficino e Giovanni Pico della Mirandola', *Bruniana & Campanelliana*, 6.2 (2000), 251–379), there is a mystical element in Ficino's approach to theurgy.

77. Some of the translations were dedicated to Giovanni de' Medici, before their publication for Manuzio (see *Supplementum ficinianum: Marsilii Ficini Florentini philosophi Platonici opuscula inedita et dispersa*, ed. by Paul Oskar Kristeller, 2 vols (Florence: Olschki, 1937), I, cxxxiii–cxxxv; and Toussaint's introduction to Iamblichus, *De mysteriis*, p. v).

78. *OMF*, I, 897–98 (correcting 'vel levior' in 'ubi levior'). *LMF*, VIII (translation of Book 9 of Ficino's *Letters*), 14–15 (modified).

79. *LMF*, VIII, 9; *OMF*, I, 895: 'Expecta Proclum simul, atque Iamblichum, divinum illum Iamblichum, plurimis et gravissimis Porphyrii quaestionibus mirifice respondentem, et interea Aegyptiorum Assyriorumque divina mysteria revelantem'. On Ficino and Pierleone see Maike Rotzoll, *Pierleone da Spoleto: vita e opere di un medico del Rinascimento* (Florence: Olschki, 2000), pp. 26–28. On Pierleone's interest in the Neoplatonic works translated by Ficino, and on their presence in his library, see Vanhaelen, 'L'Enterprise de traduction et d'exégèse de Ficin', p. 134.

80. On Ficino's reading of Plotinus see Stephen Gersh, 'Marsilio Ficino as Commentator on Plotinus: Some Case Studies', in *Plotinus' Legacy: The Transformation of Platonism from the Renaissance to the Modern Era*, ed. by Stephen Gersh (Cambridge: Cambridge University Press, 2019), 19–43.

81. On the afterlife of Ficino's daemonology see Giglioni, 'Theurgy and Philosophy', p. 15.

82. On this translation see Monfasani, *George of Trebizond*, pp. 78–79. On the influence of Eusebius's portrait of Porphyry on Ficino see Conti's introduction to Marsilio Ficino, *Commentarium in Epistolas Pauli*, ed. by Daniele Conti (Turin: Aragno, 2018), pp. li–lii & lxxxvi–lxxxvii.

83. On the history of the editions see Bouffartigue & Patillon, 'Introduction', pp. lxxix–lxxxiii. The first complete Latin translation was prepared by Giovanni Bernardo Feliciano: Porphyry, *De abstinentia ab esu animalium* (Venice: Gryphius, 1547). See on this Cecilia Muratori, 'Medical and Ethical Aspects of Vegetarianism: On the Reception of Porphyry's *De abstinentia* in the Renaissance', in *Medical Ethics: Premodern Negotiations between Medicine and Philosophy*, ed. by Mariacarla Gadebusch Bondio (Stuttgart: Steiner, 2014), pp. 143–60.

84. Martin Sicherl, *Die Handschriften, Ausgaben und Übersetzungen von Iamblichos 'De mysteriis': eine kritisch-historische Studie* (Berlin: Akademie Verlag, 1957), p. 183.

85. This is emphasized by Henri Dominique Saffrey and Alain-Philippe Segonds in their edition of Iamblichus, *Réponse à Porphyre (De mysteriis)* (Paris: Les Belles Lettres, 2013), p. xi; and Giglioni, 'Theurgy and Philosophy', p. 6. Ficino was assisted in translating *De mysteriis* by Pierleone da Spoleto: see Gentile, 'Le prime traduzioni dal greco di Marsilio Ficino', p. 73; and *Marsilio Ficino e il ritorno di Platone*, ed. by Gentile, Niccoli, & Viti, pp. 126–28.

86. Cf. Henri-Dominique Saffrey, 'Les Livres IV à VII du *De mysteriis* de Jamblique relus avec la *Lettre de Porphyre à Anébon*', in *The Divine Iamblichus: Philosopher and Man of Gods*, ed. by Blumenthal & Clark, pp. 144–58 (p. 145). The *editio princeps* of *De mysteriis* was published in 1678 (Sicherl, *Die Handschriften, Ausgaben und Übersetzungen von Iamblichos 'De mysteriis'*, p. 195).

87. James Hankins, *Plato in the Italian Renaissance*, 2 vols (Leiden: Brill, 1990), I, 316: 'He declares in a number of places that the Platonic dialogues were sacred texts, and as such were, strictly speaking, untranslatable'.

88. *OMF*, II, 1548: 'Atque utinam in mysteriis huius interpretandis adminiculum Porphyrii, aut Eustochii, aut Proculi, qui Plotini libros disposuerunt, atque exposuerunt, nobis adesset'. The passage is translated and commented upon by Hankins, *Plato in the Italian Renaissance*, I, 317 ('in interpreting his [i.e. Plato's] mysteries I had the aid of Porphyry, Eustochius, or Proclus who set in order and expounded the book of Plotinus').

89. *OMF*, I, 875: 'Porphyrius quidem Graecis nobiscum locutus est verbis, quorum ego summam verbis tibi Latinis interpretabor'. *LMF*, VII, 33: 'Now Porphyry spoke with us in Greek, but I shall translate for you in Latin the essence of what he said' (translation modified).

90. *LMF*, VII, 33. *OMF*, I, 876: 'Platonici Deo et animae mundi nihil praeter contemplationem sacrificant, animabus autem stellas moventibus flores sacrificant atque terrae arborumque fructus.'

91. See on this Cesare Vasoli's chapter 'Ficino e il *De christiana religione*', in *Filosofia e religione nella cultura del Rinascimento* (Naples: Guida, 1988), pp. 19–73 (p. 61).

92. Giglioni, 'Theurgy and Philosophy', p. 5.

93. For a discussion of the place of ritual in Ficino's philosophy, between paganism and Christianity, see Christopher S. Celenza, 'Late Antiquity and Florentine Platonism: The "Post-Plotinian"

Ficino', in *Marsilio Ficino: His Theology, His Philosophy, His Legacy*, ed. by Michael J. B. Allen & Valery Rees with Martin Davies (Leiden: Brill, 2002), pp. 71–97.

94. *LMF*, VII, 39; *OMF*, I, 879: 'Sapiens abstinebit tum cibo, tum sacrificio animalium, per haec enim mali ad nos daemones advocantur.'

95. *OA*, II.42.3; p. 73.

96. On this paraphrase see the seminal work by Guido Giglioni, 'Theurgy and Philosophy' (especially p. 9 regarding Ficino's technique of combining passages of word-by-word translation with summaries and original insertions).

97. *OMF*, II, 1895: 'Porphyrius offerri sacrificia diis hac ratione putat, ut eos veneremur eiusmodi donis, ut maiores saepe solemus, atque etiam, ut pro bonis acceptis divinitus ita gratiam referamus, pro bonis bona reddentes. Iamblichus causam eiusmodi ductam inquit ex communi hominum ad homines consuetudine, neque convenire naturae deorum mores humanos supra modum exuperanti. Maximam vero sacrificiorum efficaciam tales modi declarationesque sacrificiorum non omnino demonstrant, efficaciam, inquam, sine qua non liberamur a peste, fame, penuria, nec impetramus opportunos imbres, imo et per quam purificationem quoque perfectionemque consequimur animorum'.

98. *OMF*, II, 1900.

99. Iamblichus, *On the Mysteries*, ed. by Emma C. Clarke and others (Atlanta: Society of Biblical Literature, 2003), p. 249 (v.14).

100. See Beate Nasemann, *Theurgie und Philosophie in Jamblichs 'De mysteriis'* (Stuttgart: Teubner, 1991), pp. 165–92.

101. Saffrey, *Le Néoplatonisme après Plotin*, p. 95.

102. Iamblichus, *On the Mysteries*, pp. 249–51 (v.14). On Iamblichus's understanding of the efficacy of sacrifices see Emma C. Clarke, *Iamblichus' 'De Mysteriis'*, p. 40.

103. *OMF*, I, 877 (cf. also II, 1935): 'Nullum ergo malum est, quod non audeant perpetrare'.

104. My translation, but cf. *LMF*, VII, 37. *OMF*, I, 878 (cf. also p. 1936): 'hi sane sunt duntaxat qui libamine, nidoreque carnium oblectantur, his enim spiritale corpus eorum pinguescere solet. Vivit namque hoc vaporibus fumigationibusque atque varias admodum (ut par est) per varia nidoreque sanguinis et carnium vires assumit'. Cf. *OA*, II.42.3; p. 73.

105. My translation, but cf. *LMF*, VII, 37. *OMF*, I, 878: 'Qui sacrificant animalia clam daemones ad se malos alliciunt, daemonibus vero bonis, id est angelis, res duntaxat inanimata puritate mentis consecrare debemus'.

106. *OMF*, II, 1934: 'Primi sacrificatores non animalia, sed herbas primum, floresque, deinde arbores sacrificarunt, atque aromata subfumigarunt. Primi qui animalibus vesci caeperunt, penuria frugum animalia invaserunt, prius enim terrae fructus vescebantur'. Cf. *OA*, II.12.1; p. 59; II.27.1; p. 65; and II.29.1; p. 66.

107. *OMF*, II, 1934: 'Tribus de causis diis sacrificandum est, ut veneremur, ut gratiam referamus, ut necessaria ab ipsis petamus, malaque propellamus'. Cf. *OA*, II.24.1; p. 64.

108. *OMF*, II, 1934: 'Animalia vero mactare nefas est'.

109. See *OMF*, II, 1935. Cf. *OA*, II.37–38; p. 70.

110. See the comment by the editors of *LMF*, VII, 119. Porphyry (*OA*, II.38.2; p. 70) does refer to the universal soul but without using the word 'idea' (see also the note by Bouffartigue and Patillon in Porphyry, *De l'abstinence*, II, 216).

111. Marsilio Ficino, *Platonic Theology*, Latin text ed. by James Hankins & William Bowen and trans. by Michael J. B. Allen & John Warden, 6 vols (Cambridge, MA: Harvard University Press, 2001–06), V, 267–68 (Book XVI.5.4): 'Mitto quod Platonici non nostras solum, sed multorum quoque daemonum animas propria quandoque mutare corpora putant'. Cf. *OA*, II.39.1; p. 71, as noted by Allen and Hankins.

112. *OMF*, II, 1939: 'Natura daemonum non est absque corpore, sed habet corpus'. On the nature of the daemons' bodies see Armando Maggi, *In the Company of Demons: Unnatural Beings, Love, and Identity in the Italian Renaissance* (Chicago: University of Chicago Press, 2006), p. ix.

113. Walter Stephens, 'Habeas Corpus: Demonic Bodies in Ficino, Psellus and *Malleus maleficarum*', in *The Body in Early Modern Italy*, ed. by Julia L. Hairston & Walter Stephens (Baltimore: The John Hopkins University Press, 2010), pp. 74–91 (p. 85).

114. See Maude Vanhaelen, 'Ficino's Commentary on St Paul's First Epistle to the Romans (1497): An Anti-savonarolan Reading of Vision and Prophecy', in *The Rebirth of Platonic Theology*, ed. by Hankins & Meroi, pp. 205–33 (p. 215).

115. *OMF*, II, 1936.

116. *OMF*, I, 878–79 (cf. *LMF*, VII, 39).

117. *OMF*, II, 1937: 'Quoniam videlicet prava, irrationalisque anima, quae corpus violentia suum reliquit, expoliata ad hoc ipsum, deinde se admovet, ubique moras protrahit, unde hominum quoque animae violentia mortuorum immorantur, et circa corpus'.

118. Ibid.: 'Qui enim vaticinantium animalium insinuare sibi animas optabant, praecipua illorum membra deglutientes, velut corda cervorum, vel talparum, vel asturum accipiebant subinde praesentem animam Dei ritu vaticinantem, quae sane una cum sui corporis intus assumptione in corpus humanum se penitus ingerebat. Iure igitur philosophus, Deique sacerdos omnibus dominatus animalibus omnibus abstinet'.

119. Ibid. (cf. also I, 879): 'Nam apud Deos optima est oblatio, pura mens et perturbationum vacuus animus. Hinc Plato bono quidem viro convenire ait sacrificia operare divinisque interesse, malum vero frustra in sacrificiis laborare'. Cf. *OA*, II.61.4; p. 79. On this variation (*deum/deos*) see also Denis J.-J. Robichaud, 'Ficino on Force, Magic, and Prayers: Neoplatonic and Hermetic Influences in Ficino's *Three Books on Life*', *Renaissance Quarterly*, 70 (2017), 44–87 (p. 59).

120. On the influence on Ficino of Bessarion's interpetation of Porphyry, see Conti's introduction to Ficino, *Commentarium in Epistolas Pauli*, p. xciv.

121. As noted by Conti, Ficino would have encountered the idea of a general agreement of Porphyry and Iamblichus with regard to the superiority of spiritual to material offerings in Eusebius's *Praeparatio evangelica*: Ficino, *Commentarium in Epistolas Pauli*, pp. xcvi & 29. On Ficino and Eusebius see John Monfasani, 'Marsilio Ficino and Eusebius of Caesarea's *Praeparatio Evangelica*', *Rinascimento*, 49 (2009), 3–13. Monfasani points out that Ficino reads Eusebius to substantiate the idea that Platonism and Christianity can be harmonized. In this respect, there is a clear parallel between Ficino's readings of Eusebius and of Porphyry. See also Guido Bartolucci, 'Marsilio Ficino, Eusebio di Cesarea e un trattato sulle religioni degli Antichi', *Accademia*, 9 (2007), 37–55.

122. *OA*, p. 158. On the *Corpus Hermeticum*, its content and legacy, see André-Jean Festugière, *La Révélation d'Hermès Trismégiste*, 4 vols in 3 (Paris: Les Belles Lettres, 1981), II, 1–27 ('Le Dossier des Hermetica').

123. On Ficino's view regarding Hermes's position in the development of 'prisca theologia', see Gentile, 'Sulle prime traduzioni dal greco di Marsilio Ficino'. See also Frederick Purnell, Jr, 'Hermes and the Sibyl: A Note on Ficino's *Pimander*', *Renaissance Quarterly*, 30.3 (1977), 305–10 (p. 307).

124. On Ficino's translation of Pimander and its fortune see *Marsilio Ficino e il ritorno di Platone*, ed. by Gentile, Niccoli, & Viti, pp. 37–45. See Hermes Trismegistos, *Hermetica: The Greek Corpus Hermeticum and the Latin Asclepius in a New English Translation, with Notes and Introduction*, ed. by Brian P. Copenhaver (Cambridge: Cambridge University Press, 1992), p. xli. Copenhaver highlights that Ficino 'worked from a Greek manuscript that ends at C. H. XIV, and the new print technology amplified the influence of this truncated version after 1471, when his new translation first appeared in print'. On Ficino's portrait of Hermes see Hermes Trismegistus, *Pimander sive de potestate et sapientia Dei*, ed. by Maurizio Campanelli (Turin: Aragno, 2011), pp. xxiii–lx; on the 'quality of Ficino's translation', pp. ccxvii–ccl: Campanelli demonstrates that Ficino aimed at providing an elegant translation, sometimes expanding the Greek text. See also Maurizio Campanelli, 'Marsilio Ficino's Portrait of Hermes Trismegistus and its Afterlife', *Intellectual History Review*, 29.1 (2019), 53–71. On Ficino's translation of Pimander see also Ilana Klutstein, 'Marsile Ficin et Hermès Trismégiste: quelques notes sur la traduction du Pimandre dans la Vulgata de Ficin', *Renaissance and Reformation / Renaissance et Réforme*, n.s. 14.3 (1990), 213–22.

125. On this see also *OMF*, II, 1847 (*Commentaria*): 'Vos ergo seligite divina semina spiritales facti, et malorum semina daemonum, qui nos materiali affectione dormientes occupare vigilant, cauti nunc effugite'.

126. *OMF*, II, 1846: 'Nulla profecto mundi pars daemonum praesentia destituta, horum lumen ab ipso Deo totum descendit. Demon denique transfusus in hominem, semina proprie notionis

inspergit'. Cf. [Hermes Trismegistus], *Pimander*, ed. by Campanelli, p. 54: 'Nulla profecto mundi pars demonum presentia destituta. Horum lumen ab ipso Deo totum descendit. Demon denique transfusus in hominem semina proprie operationis inspargit'. In translating, I correct 'notionis' to 'operationis'. Cf. *Hermetica*, ed. by Brian Copenhaver, pp. 27–28.

127. *OMF*, II, 1846: 'Mens autem conspersa seminibus pregnans, inde parit adulteria, stupra, homicidia, paricidia, sacrilega, divinorum contemptum, iugulationes, eversiones urbium, pestes hominum, et reliqua omnia quaecunquae malorum sunt opera daemonum'. [Hermes Trismegistos], *Pimander*, ed. by Campanelli, p. 54: 'mens autem conspersa seminibus pregnans inde parit adulteria, stupra, homicidia, parricidia, sacrilegia, divinorum contempum, iugulationes, eversiones urbium, pestes hominum ac reliqua omnia, quotcumque malorum sunt opera demonum'. *Hermetica*, ed. by Brian Copenhaver, pp. 27–28: 'no part of the cosmos is without a demon that steals into the mind to sow the seed of its own energy, and what has been sown the mind conceives — adulteries, murders, assaults on one's father, acts of sacrilege and irreverence, suicides by hanging or falling from a cliff, and all other such works of demons. Few seeds come from god, but they are potent and beautiful and good — virtue, moderation and reverence'. The Italian translation of Ficino's *Pimander*, by Ficino's friend Tommaso Benci, renders *iugulationes* with *scannamenti* (*Il Pimandro di Mercurio Trismegisto, tradotto da Tommaso e in linga Fiorentina* (Florence: [Torrentino], 1549), p. 53).

128. *OMF*, II, 1708.

129. Ficino, *Platonic Theology*, V, 308–09 (Book XVI.7.17): 'Hinc ergo fieri, ut qua via quemque perturbare facilius valeant, rectissime calleant atque ipsi perturbatione quadam affecti nos quotidie turbent.'

130. *OMF*, II, 1708: 'Ubi vero secundum imaginationem vita disponitur, externus daemon noster est aerius in aere videlicet infimo, ac per imaginationem nostram imaginatione sua nos agitans; ubi vero secundum rationem vivitur, daemon foris ex aere medio ratione sua rationem versat humanam; ubi denique intellectualis vita est, daemon ex aere summo per intelligentiam aspirat intelligentiae'. See Michael J. B. Allen's explanation of this relationship in 'Summoning Plotinus: Ficino, Smoke and the Strangled Chickens,' in *Reconsidering the Renaissance*, ed. by Di Cesare, pp. 63–88 (p. 67).

131. Daniel P. Walker, *Spiritual and Demonic Magic from Ficino to Campanella*, 2nd edn (University Park: Pennsylvania State University Press, 2000), p. 45.

132. Ficino exploits the polisemantic character of the word *dáimon*. See the detailed presentation of Neoplatonic daemonology in Andréi Timotin, *La Démonologie platonicienne* (Leiden: Brill, 2012).

133. Plotinus, *Enneads*, trans. by Stephen MacKenna, abridged with an Introduction and Notes by John Dillon (New York: Penguin, 1991), pp. 166–73.

134. Ficino, *Platonic Theology*, VI, 182–83 (Book XVIII.10.3).

135. See *OMF*, II, 1708: 'Videtur itaque sacerdos Aegyptius daemonis Plotinici radios congregasse, atque (ut Porphyrius testis est) praesentium oculis ostendisse'. Cf. also Plotinus, *Enneads*, p. 166.

136. On the sacrifice of birds see Alexandra Villing, 'Don't Kill the Goose that Lays the Golden Egg? Some Thoughts on Bird Sacrifices in Ancient Greece', in *Animal Sacrifice in the Ancient Greek World*, ed. by Sarah Hitch & Ian Rutherford (Cambridge: Cambridge University Press, 2017), pp. 63–101.

137. *Supplementum ficinianum*, II, 100–01 (and cf. Celenza, 'Late Antiquity and Florentine Platonism', p. 90).

138. *Supplementum ficinianum*, II, 101: 'Gallum nutrias quidem etc. Est vis quedam anime que cognatione quadam celestium corporum et spirituum / sepe ita cietur ut futura presagiat. [...] Hanc anime vim per gallum significari ideo arbitror, quia galli ea natura est, qua et tempora metiatur et ipsorum temporum mutationes ita sentiat, ut nunquam fallatur. Inde pars quedam noctis gallicinium appellata'. See also Christopher S. Celenza's translation and comment on this passage in *Piety and Pythagoras in Renaissance Florence: The 'Symbolum Nesianum'* (Leiden: Brill, 2001), p. 24.

139. *Supplementum ficinianum*, II, 102: 'Hanc igitur vim nutrire bonum est. Nutritur autem si ita vivamus ut sit tranquillus et a turbulentis curis solutus animus, adeo ut motus sentire celestes denique valeat. Non tamen sacrificandus est, quia naturalis est hec vis, quapropter nullum

meritum habitura est sacrificium'. Cf. Celenza's clear interpretation of this passage in *Piety and Pythagoras in Renaissance Florence*, p. 25. Cf. also Celenza, 'Late Antiquity and Florentine Platonism', p. 90: 'Commenting on the Pythagorean saying "nourish the cock, but do no sacrifice him, since he is sacred to the sun and the moon", Ficino expounds the prophetic powers which he believes the soul possesses'.

140. Celenza (*Piety and Pythagoras in Renaissance Florence*, p. 22) states that 'He [i.e. Ficino] took them [i.e. the symbols] seriously as *monumenta* of the *prisca theologia* tradition'.

141. *Supplementum ficinianum*, II, 102.

142. Celenza, 'Late Antiquity and Florentine Platonism', p. 93: 'Ficino reads Porphyry and Plotinus through Iamblichan eyes'.

143. *OMF*, I, 925: 'Amo equidem Platonem in Iamblicho, admiror in Plotino, in Dionysio veneror'. The passage is translated and commented upon in Celenza, 'Late Antiquity and Florentine Platonism', p. 84. See also Michael J. B. Allen, *Plato's Third Eye: Studies in Marsilio Ficino's Metaphysics and its Sources* (Farnham: Ashgate, 1995), p. 353.

144. Celenza, 'Late Antiquity and Florentine Platonism', p. 91.

145. *OMF*, I, 551; Marsilio Ficino, *Three Books on Life*, ed. by Carol V. Kaske and John R. Clark (Tempe: Arizona Center for Medieval and Renaissance Studies, 2002), p. 317 (III.15.49–54).

146. See also Marsilio Ficino, *Comment on and Chapter Summaries of the Phaedrus*, in *Commentaries on Plato*, ed. and trans. by Michael J. B. Allen, 2 vols (Cambridge, MA: Harvard University Press, 2008), I (*Phaedrus and Ion*), 115–16.

147. Celenza, 'Temi neopitagorici nel pensiero di Marsilio Ficino', pp. 69–70.

148. *OMF*, I, 571; Ficino, *Three Books on Life*, p. 391 (III.26.116–21). On this passage see also Conti's introduction in Ficino, *Commentarium in Epistolas Pauli*, p. lxxxvii. On Ficino's use of Iamblichus with reference to *De vita* see Robichaud, 'Ficino on Force, Magic, and Prayers'.

149. Ficino, *Three Books on Life*, pp. 389–90 (III.26.93–96); *OMF*, I, 571: 'Chaldaeos vero daemonibus non occupatos'.

150. Celenza ('Late Antiquity and Florentine Platonism', p. 93) rightly states that the emphasis on magic and ritual, which derives from the reading of Iamblichus, even leads Ficino to drawing 'Plotinus and Porphyry into the orbit of the affirmation of magic, though they would have denigrated it, at least in the philosophical life'.

151. *OMF*, II, 1716: 'ut ait Porphyrius, homines ventri dediti vasa fiunt daemonum immundorum. Quamvis enim daemones si quo indigent nutrimento, ut ait Iamblichus, id absque nostra opera sibi passim suppeditare possint: tamen probabile est, posse quasdam illecebras ab homine illis offerri, et incontinentes daemones incontinentibus hominibus commisceri. Superbi vero superbioribus daemonibus agitantur. Nam primum esse in eis superbiam Porphyrius ait'.

152. Ibid.: 'Postremi daemones odoribus et vaporibus indigent crassioribus, qui ex sanguine carni-busque mittuntur, maxime coctis et a nobis assumptis. Quare si Porphyrio credis, dices hoc induxisse nos ad animalia devoranda'.

153. Ficino, *Platonic Theology*, I, 126–27 (Book II.6.7): 'Plotinus Iamblichusque et Iulianus Platonici non deum tantum, sed omnem quoque mentem, sive angelicam sive animalem per immensum se integram fundere voluerunt'. See also Ficino, *Commentarium in Convivium Platonis De Amore*, ed. by Pierre Laurens (Paris: Les Belles Lettres, 2002), p. 133 (VI.3): 'Esse vero alios quodsam malos demones Platonici nonnulli et Christiani theologi voluerunt. Sed de malis demonibus nulla ad presens nobis est disputatio'.

154. See for instance Ficino, *Platonic Theology*, Book XVIII.10.3.

155. Daniela Patrizia Taormina, *Jamblique: critique de Plotin et de Porphyre. Quatre études* (Paris: Vrin, 1999), p. 10.

156. On Augustine's interpretation of Porphyry see Gillian Clark, 'Augustine's Porphyry and the Universal Way of Salvation', in *Studies on Porphyry*, ed. by George Karamanolis & Anne Sheppard (London: Institute of Classical Studies, University of London, 2007), pp. 127–40.

157. Porphyry, *Lettre à Anébon*, p. 44; *The City of God Against the Pagans*, ed. by Robert W. Dyson (Cambridge: Cambridge University Press, 1997), p. 407. Cf. also *DCD*, XL.I, 464 (Book X.11).

158. Porphyry, *Lettre à Anébon*, pp. 45–47 (see also *DCD*, XL.I, 465 (Book X.11)); Augustine, *City of God*, p. 408.

159. Augustine, *Contra Adimantum*, in *Corpus scriptorum ecclesiasticorum latinorum*, XXV.I, ed. by Joseph Zycha (Prague, Vienna, & Leipzig: Tempsky & Freytag, 1891), 113–90; p. 152 (§ 14): 'Sed quoniam Manichaei etiam cum ad hominis cenam quaeque animalia praeparantur, immolationem esse dicunt'.

160. Ibid., p. 152: 'Propterea et illum commemoraverunt locum, ubi apostolus ait: "Quae immolant Gentes, daemoniis immolant, et non deo", cum apostolus apertissime de victimis loqueretur, quae in templo offeruntur daemonibus, non de his escis, quas sibi homines praeparant'.

161. Ibid.: ' "Non potestis calicem domini bibere et calicem daemoniorum. Non potestis mensae domini participare, et mensae daemoniorum" '.

162. Ibid., p. 148: 'De eo, quod scriptum est in Deuteronomio: "secundum desiderium animae tuae occide et manduca omnem carnem iuxta voluptate, quam dedit tibi dominus. Cave autem, ne sanguine manduce, sed effunde tamquam aquam super terram". His verbis legis Adimantus contrarium esse arbitratur, quod in Evangelio dominus ait: "non graventur corda vestra cruditate et vinolentia et curis saecularibus et quod ait apostolus: bonum est non manducare carnem neque bibere vinum et iterum: non potestis mensae domini partecipare et mensae daemonorum". Nos autem omnia haec, sive quae in vetere sive quae in novo testamento scripta sunt, et suis causis exigentibus posita dicimus et sibi adversa non esse monstramus'.

163. On the notion that humans should use animals according to God's design of the Creation see Gillian Clark, 'The Fathers and the Animals: The Rule of Reason?', in *Animals on the Agenda*, ed. by Andrew Linzey & Dorothy Yamamoto (London: SCM Press, 1998), pp. 67–79.

164. On Ficino's attempt at harmonizing different Neoplatonic approaches see Vanhaelen, 'L'Enterprise de traduction et d'exégèse de Ficin dans les années 1486–1489', p. 130.

165. The first book of *De secta pythagorica* is entitled 'De vita pythagorica' and is often erroneously rendered as 'Life of Pythagoras': see Iamblichus, *On the Pythagorean Life*, p. ix. On Ficino's engagement with *De secta pythagorica* see Denis J.-J. Robichaud, *Plato's Persona: Marsilio Ficino, Renaissance Humanism, and Platonic Traditions* (Philadelphia: University of Pennsylvania Press, 2018), pp. 91–94, 127–28. See also Gentile, 'Le prime traduzioni dal greco di Marsilio Ficino', pp. 73–79 (for a discussion of the dating of Ficino's translation see esp. p. 80).

166. Iamblichus, *On the Pythagorean Life*, p. 66. See also p. 7 on a fruit offering given to Pythagoras on an altar.

167. Ibid., pp. 81–82: 'He required abstinence from living creatures for many reasons, and especially because the practice makes for peace: people who were accustomed to be disgusted by the killing of animals, thinking it contrary to law and nature, found the killing of a human being even more contrary to divine law, and ceased to make war'.

168. On the connection between vegetarianism and cannibalism see Chapter 3 below.

169. *Supplementum ficinianum*, II, 100: '(ibd. ad verba: cor ne edas). Cerebrum est instrumentum cognitionum, cor passionum. Vorat cerebrum, qui multigenis et noxiis et inutilibus cogitationibus ipsum involvit. Edit cor qui superfluis passionibus ipsum subicit et in illis diu sistit'. See also the same Pythagorean image in *Angelo Poliziano's 'Lamia': Text, Translation, and Introductory Studies*, ed. by Christopher S. Celenza (Leiden: Brill, 2010), pp. 23, 87, 201.

170. Cf. Angelo Poliziano, *Lamia*, ed. by Ari Wesseling (Leiden: Brill, 1986), pp. 33–34. Wesseling points out that Ficino recurs to the same Pythagorean metaphor in the first letter of the fourth volume of the correspondence: 'Mandavit discipulis suis Pythagoras, nec cerebrum corve commederent. Id est, neque cerebrum cogitationibus consumerent supervacuis, neque immoderatis curis urerent'. (See *OMF*, I, 751.)

171. On the different interpretations of this prohibition in Platonism, and within a broader frame of dietary restrictions, see Robert M. Grant, 'Dietary Laws among Pythagoreans, Jews, and Christians', *The Harvard Theological Review*, 73.1–2 (1980), 299–310 (p. 301): 'Porphyry tells us that not eating the heart means not grieving oneself with troubles, but when he comes to various pieces of meat and to beans he gives an allegorical explanation but at the same time insists on abstinence. [...] The later Neoplatonist Iamblichus gives thorough-going allegorical explanations in both his *Pythagorean Life* and his *Protrepticus*'.

172. Iamblichus, *On the Pythagorean Life*, p. 48: 'He also forbade them to eat the heart or the brain, and told all Pythagoreans to abstain from these, for these are the governing organs and, as it

were, the seats and abodes of thought and life: their nature is that of the divine reason and he declared them sacred'.

173. On Porphyry's rhetorical strategy, which often involves appropriating the language of his opponents, see G. Fay Edwards, 'The Puzzle of Porphyry's Rational Animals' (unpublished PhD thesis, King's College London, 2013). On Porphyry and animal rationality see below Chapter 4, sections 4 & 5.

174. Iamblichus, *On the Pythagorean Life*, p. 24.

175. *OMF*, II, 1938. On Porphyry's argument on animals see G. Fay Edwards, 'Reincarnation, Rationality, and Temperance: Platonists on Not Eating Animals', in *Animals: A History*, ed. by Peter Adamson & G. Fay Edwards (Oxford & New York: Oxford University Press, 2018), pp. 27–55. See also Kevin Corrigan, 'Humans, Other Animals, Plants and the Question of the Good: The Platonic and Neoplatonic Traditions', in *The Routledge Handbook of Neoplatonism*, ed. by Pauliina Remes & Svetla Slaveva-Griffin (Abingdon: Routledge, 2014), pp. 372–90.

176. *OMF*, II, 1932–39.

177. *OA*, III.1.4; p. 80.

178. *OMF*, II, 1937: 'In libro tertio dicit se afferre opinionem veram et Pythagoricam: omnem scilicet animam sensibus et memoria praeditam, esse rationalem, haberetque rationem, orationemque, tum interiorem, tum exteriorem, qua inter se loquantur animalia'.

179. Ibid., p. 1938.

180. Ibid. ('Ratio quaedam inest etiam animalibus').

181. The following passages offer an overview of Ficino's selective translation on the topic of animal rationality: *OMF*, II, 1937: 'Melampus et Tiresias atque Tales, nuper vero Apollonius Theaneus, quem dicunt in amicorum coetu, cum audiret hirundinem alii nuntiare, asinum prope urbem onustum tritico cecidisse, triticumque humi diffusum' (cf. *OA*, III.3.6; p. 81). *OMF*, II, 1937: 'Subiungit Aristotelem, Platonem, Empedoclem, Democritum, aliosque quicumque veritatem de animalibus perscrutari sunt, participationem rationis, orationisque in animalibus comperisse' (cf. *OA*, III.6.7; p. 84). *OMF*, II, 1937: 'Differentiae vero corporum facile quidem, et difficile passivam reddunt animam, atque magis minusque promptam habere rationem praestant, verum secundum essentiam variare animam nequeunt, quando neque sensus, neque passiones reddunt inter se differentes, neque faciunt ut perfectum transgrediantur. Concedatur itaque secundum magis et minus esse in his differentiam rationis' (cf. *OA*, III.8.6–7; p. 85).

182. *OMF*, II, 1938: 'Non absurde quidnam conati sunt ostendere multa etiam ex locis quae sortita sunt, prudentiora esse quam nos. [...] Deinde quae in aqua, deinde quae in terra inter se rationis gradu differre, si enim deorum dignitatem quodammodo metimur etiam in locis, sic et animalium perpendimus dignitatem'.

183. For a detailed discussion of Ficino's understanding of rationality, and of animal rationality in particular, see Maria-Christine Leitgeb, 'Marsilio Ficino — der Philosoph der Tierseelen?', in *The Animal Soul and the Human Mind: Renaissance Debates*, ed. by Cecilia Muratori (Pisa & Rome: Serra, 2013), pp. 45–60.

184. Ficino, *Platonic Theology*, II, 266–67 (Book IV.1.14).

185. For instance, see *OMF*, II, 1937–38: 'neque ex eo quod nos magis quam animalia intelligamus, propterea illa intellectione omnino privemus, sicut neque volare perdices negamus quoniam astures velocius volent' (cf. *OA*, III.8.8; p. 85). For further on this issue see Ficino, *Platonic Theology*, II, 98–99 (Book v.14.6–7).

186. Ficino, *Platonic Theology*, I, 267 (Book IV.1.14): 'Porphyry adds both that those daemons in whose bodies fire abounds besides the water's vapor are only seen, and that this happens in the East and South; but the daemons in bodies where there is a great deal of earth besides can also be touched'.

187. Ibid., I, 127 (Book II.4.7).

188. On Ficino's argumentation about the human distinction from and superiority over animals, see Paul Oskar Kristeller, *Die Philosophie des Marsilio Ficino* (Frankfurt am Main: Klostermann, 1972), p. 368.

189. Ficino, *Platonic Theology*, III, 116–17 (Book x.2.1).

190. Ibid., III, 116–17 (Book x.2.2).

191. Ibid. (Book x.2.3): 'the Egyptians maintain — and they are followed by Origen, Numenius, and Porphyry — that there are many demons who lift their rational souls towards higher things and many others who deflect them towards lower things'.

192. Ibid. (Book x.2.7): 'ad consonantiam mundi perfectam esse oportere non solum animalia quaedam rationalia immortaliaque atque contra animalia irrationalia et mortalia simul, verumetiam multa haec media rationalia quidem, sed mortalia non in terra solum, sed etiam in caeteris elementis.'

193. Ibid., 123 (Book x.2.7): 'The Egyptians' theory, supported by all the Platonists, especially Proclus, leads to the same conclusion. They say that not only do men have eternal souls in a mortal body, but many daemons as well, some of them close to us, others far superior to us, whose bodies come into being and gradually pass away although they live longer than our bodies and more splendidly'.

194. *OMF*, I, 566. Ficino, *Three Books on Life*, p. 369 (III.22.104–07).

195. According to Biondi, this explains why Pico insisted that he had been the first to provide an overview of Platonic philosophy (cf. Giovanni Pico della Mirandola, *Conclusiones nongentae: le novecento tesi dell'anno 1486*, ed. by Albano Biondi (Florence: Olschki, 1995), pp. xxiv–xxv).

196. The section dedicated to the theses 'secundum doctrinam Platonicorum' includes a list of sentences attributed to Adelandus Arabus. See on this Eugenio Garin, *Giovanni Pico della Mirandola: vita e dottrina* (Florence: Le Monnier, 1937), p. 110.

197. Pico della Mirandola, *Conclusiones nongentae*, p. 38: '9. Duplex malorum daemonum genus: alterum animae sunt et substantiales daemones, alterum materiales potentiae et accidentales daemones'.

198. Ibid., p. 40: '10. Duplex genus daemonum, de quibus dixit secundum Porphyrium praecedens conclusio, nihil credimus esse aliud, quam membrorum legem, et potestates harum tenebrarum, de quibus apud Paulum, quamvis de quiditate et substantia harum potestatum eos non credo convenire'. See Toussaint, 'L'individuo estatico', pp. 350–60.

199. Next to this set of forty-seven Cabalistic theses ('secundum doctrinam sapientum hebreorum Cabalistarum'), Pico's *Conclusiones* contain a second one (*Conclusiones cabalisticae numero LXXI[I] secundum opinionem propriam, ex ipsis hebreorum sapientum fundamentis christianam religionem maxime confirmantes*). I always refer to the first set here.

200. Pico della Mirandola, *Conclusiones nongentae*, p. 56: 'Sicut homo et sacerdos inferior sacrificat Deo animas animalium irrationalium, ita Michaël sacerdos superior sacrificat animas animalium rationalium'.

201. Ficino and Pico read *De mysteriis* in the same codex: see Toussaint, 'L'individuo estatico', p. 367.

202. On this *conclusio* see Chaim Wirszubski, *Pico della Mirandola's Encounter with Jewish Mysticism* (Cambridge, MA: Harvard University Press, 1989), pp. 21–22.

203. On Pico's human-animal distinction, with special focus on *Heptaplus*, see Crofton Black, *Pico's 'Heptaplus' and Biblical Hermeneutics* (Leiden: Brill, 2006), pp. 40 & 204.

204. *Heptaplus* V.5, in Giovanni Pico della Mirandola, *De hominis dignitate, Heptaplus, De ente et uno, e scritti vari*, ed. by Eugenio Garin (Florence: Vallecchi, 1942), p. 300: 'Inter animalia terrae tria memorat Moses: iumenta, reptilia et bestias, in quibus tres differentias brutorum irrationalium [...]. Sunt iumenta, quae, et si carent ratione, displinae tamen humanae quoquo modo capaces cum sint, rationis aliquid participare videntur, mediam quasi sortita conditionem inter bruta et homines'.

205. As Brian Copenhaver fittingly puts it, 'In the *Heptaplus* of 1489 we can still hear the Kabbalist voice of the *Conclusions*, but mainly because Pico's earlier works since the *Commento* of 1485–86 have prepared us to listen for it' ('Giovanni Pico della Mirandola', in *The Stanford Encyclopedia of Philosophy*, ed. by Edward N. Zalta, <https://plato.stanford.edu/archives/fall2016/entries/pico-della-mirandola/> [accessed 22 July 2019]).

206. Pico della Mirandola, *Heptaplus*, VI.5, p. 320: 'Hinc platonicae et pythagoricae disputationes a sacris precibus exorsae desinunt in easdem quibus et Porphyrius et Theodorus et omnes Academici nihil utile magis immo necessarium homini esse uno ore confirmant'.

207. See Wirszubski, *Pico's Encounter with Jewish Mysticism*, p. 159: 'Pico's interpretation of the sacrificial offering of the soul to God as the ecstatic separation of the soul from the body affords

a glimpse of an identifiable variation of the mystic way: mysticism of prayer'.

208. According to Mariateresa Fumagalli Beonio Brocchieri (*Pico della Mirandola* (Casale Monferrato, Alessandria: Piemme, 1999), p. 130), in *Heptaplus* Giovanni Pico understands the Cabala as anticipation of Christian mysteries. Eugenio Garin has pointed out that while Pico aims to show that different philosophical strands converge on certain crucial topics, Bessarion instead 'platonizes' Aristotle and 'plotinizes' Plato (Garin, *Giovanni Pico Della Mirandola*, pp. 58, 76, 79).

209. On this interpretation see Giovanni Pico della Mirandola, *Conclusioni cabalistiche*, ed. by Paolo Edoardo Fornaciari (Milan: Mimesis, 1994), p. 73.

210. Saverio Campanini, 'Francesco Giorgio's Criticism of the *Vulgata*: Hebraica Veritas or Mendosa Traductio?', in *Hebrew to Latin, Latin to Hebrew: The Mirroring of Two Cultures in the Age of Humanism*, ed. by Giulio Busi (Turin: Aragno, 2006), pp. 206–31 (p. 205): 'Pico's theses, very brief and intentionally obscure in some points, relied heavily on Flavius Mithridates' translations of kabbalistic literature'. Flavio Mithridates, as is well known, provided Pico with translations of cabalistic literature. Giulio Busi has worked extensively on Mithridates's translations and their influence on Pico (see for details of this project: <www.pico-kabbalah.eu> [accessed 21 July 2019]). Pico did not have direct access to the original cabbalistic literature: Mithridates's translations worked as a filter (see Saverio Campanini, 'Pici Mirandulensis bibliotheca cabbalistica latina: sulle traduzioni latine di opere cabbalistiche eseguiteda Flavio Mitridate per Pico della Mirandola', *Materia Giudaica*, 7.1 (2002), 90–96). On Pico's study of Hebrew and Mithridates's translations see also Black, *Pico's 'Heptaplus' and Biblical Hermeneutics*, pp. 20–25.

211. Paola Zambelli identified 'frater Christophorus' with the cardinal Cristoro Numai (*L'apprendista stregone: astrologia, cabala e arte lulliana in Pico della Mirandola e seguaci* (Venice: Marsilio, 1995), pp. 180–81). More recently this identification has been questioned by Campanini: 'Francesco Giorgio's Criticism of the *Vulgata*', p. 205 (see also his 'Ein unbekannter Kommentar zum "Hohelied" aus der kabbalistischen Schule von Francesco Zorzi: Edition und Kommentar', in *Erzählende Vernunft*, ed. by Günter Frank, Anja Hallacker, & Sebastian Lalla (Berlin: Akademie Verlag, 2006), pp. 265–81.

212. Cf. Chaim Wirszubski, 'Francesco Giorgio's Commentary on Giovanni Pico's Kabbalistic Theses', *Journal of the Warburg and Courtauld Institutes*, 37 (1974), 145–56. See also François Secret, 'Notes sur quelques kabbalistes chrétiens', *Bibliothèque d'Humanism et Renaissance*, 36.1 (1974), 67–82 (pp. 71–74).

213. Francesco Zorzi, *L'armonia del mondo / De harmonia mundi*, ed. by Saverio Campanini (Milan: Bompiani, 2010), see pp. xxiii & lxxi, where Campanini also remarks that Zorzi never mentions Ficino, who is one of the main sources of inspiration for *De harmonia mundi*. Guy Le Fèvre de la Boderie translated into French *De harmonia mundi* (1576) and Pico's *Heptaplus*: see Cesare Vasoli, 'Da Marsilio Ficino a Francesco Giorgio Veneto', in *Filosofia e religione nella cultura del Rinascimento*, pp. 233–56 (p. 235).

214. Wirszubski, 'Francesco Giorgio's Commentary and Pico's Kabbalistic Theses', p. 148: 'Francesco Giorgio's commentary may well have been a book or books written by his disciples from lecture notes after his death, rather than a book written by himself.' See Campanini in *L'armonia del mondo*, p. xxiii. Cf. also Wirszubski, 'Francesco Giorgio's Commentary on Pico's Kabbalistic Theses', p. 152.

215. Giovanni Pico della Mirandola and Arcangelo da Borgonovo, *Cabalistarum selectiora obscurioraque dogmata* [...] (Venice: Franceschi, 1569), f. 2v: 'habent enim sacrificia cum eo cui offeruntur, et cum his qui expiantur, symbolum quoddam: adeo tamen occultum, ut ipsum capere nequeat humanum ingenium'.

216. Ibid.

217. On this key role of sacrifice see Douglas Hedley, *Sacrifice Imagined: Violence, Atonement, and the Sacred* (London: Bloomsbury, 2011), pp. 4–6; on the specific role of animal sacrifices and the disappearence of that particular ritual from Judaism after the destruction of the Temple in AD 70, see p. 3.

218. Pico della Mirandola and Arcangelo da Borgonovo, *Cabalistarum selectiora obscurioraque dogmata*, f. 3r: 'Sanguis enim animalium expurgare videtur peccatum in carne contractum ex sanguine animalis nostri iuxta illud Apostoli omnia pene mundantur in sanguine'. On the concept of

regeneration through blood see Hedley, *Sacrifice Imagined*, p. 155 (with particular reference to Joseph de Maistre).

219. Pico della Mirandola and Arcangelo da Borgonovo, *Cabalistarum selectiora obscurioraque dogmata*, f. 3r–v: 'et sicut lex scripta perfectior lege naturae extitit, ita Deus in illa perfectiora animalium sacrificia videlicet instituit; sunt enim animalia frugum primitiis perfectiora, et quoniam evangelica lex caeteris perfectior existit; hinc Deus nobilius sacrificium instituit, est enim lex amoris, et filialis timoris, sacrificium scilicet agni immaculati Christi, vices omnium, quae offerebantur supplentis'.

220. Ibid., ff. 3v and 6r.

221. Heinrich Cornelius Agrippa von Nettesheim, *De occulta philosophia libri tres*, ed. by Vittoria Perrone Compagni (Leiden: Brill, 1992), section entitled 'De sacrificiis et oblationibus eorumque generibus et modis', p. 577: '<Tum sicut mortalis hic sacerdos in hoc inferiore mundo sacrificat Deo anima animalium irrationabilium per interitum corporis ab anima, ita Michaël archangelus, sublimioris mundi sacerdos, sacrificat animas hominum idque per separationem animae a corpore, non corporis ab anima, nisi per accidens sicut contingit in furore, raptu et extasi et somnio similibusque animae vacationibus, quem Hebraei vocant mortem osculi>' (< > indicate that the passage was subsequently added to the initial version of the text). It is noteworthy that several references to Porphyry belong to the additions inserted after 1510 (i.e. the date of the first draft).

222. Agrippa von Nettesheim, *De occulta philosophia libri tres*, p. 578: 'Externa autem sacrificia, ut ait Heraclitus, medelae quaedam sunt animarum, a summo medico institutae; possidet enim malus daemon hominem, quod ait Proclus, quousque per sacrificia expietur: exquiruntur igitur sacrificia ad Deum et virtutes coelestes placandas et ad expiandum hominem, qui et ipse Dei et mundi gerit imaginem'.

223. Ibid., p. 577, for the definition of sacrifice: 'Sacrificium autem est oblatio, quae et sacra fit offerendo et sacrat seu sanctificat offerentem, nisi illum aut irreverentia aut aliud quoddam impediat peccatum'.

224. Forlì, Biblioteca Comunale 'Saffi', Ms. O.VII.57 (fondo Piancastelli), f. 1r. The table of contents of the miscellany (f. 136r) presents the text of the first set of cabalistic conclusions as: 'Expositio 47. conclusionum cabalistarum Pici Mirandulae de mente [...] Georgii Veneti'. The name of the copiyst Brother Christophorus from Forlì is indicated on f. 140v. A transcription of this passage with Italian translation, is included in Zambelli, *L'apprendista stregone*, pp. 188–89. I have amended the transcription at a few points. The miscellany contains also the *Conclusiones Pici Mirandulae Cabalisticae numero 72* (ff. 25r–66r), and other texts, such as: an *Exameron mysticum* (ff. 67r–110v); an *Expositio* on the Canticle (ff. 113r–135v); and the representation of a sefirotic tree (inserted after f. 111; on this see Saverio Campanini, 'A Sefirotic Tree from a Miscellany of Christian Kabbalistic Texts', *Manuscrits hébreux et arabes*, 38 (2014), 387–401). Cf. Pico della Mirandola and Arcangelo da Borgonovo, *Cabalistarum selectiora obscurioraque dogmata*, f. 4v.

225. Zorzi, *L'armonia del mondo*, p. 950: 'Ibi namque solus Deus est summus princeps, qui cives suos replet suavitate mirifica [...]. In hanc sententiam veniunt Didymus, Hiarchas, Porphyrius, Proculus, in de orationibus, et precibus, ubi docet de mente Platonis, Iamblici, et Porphyrii orationes esse necessarias, ut per eas reducamur ad patriam, a qua quamdiu hic sumus peregrinamur, inquit Paulus'.

226. Yet it is noteworthy that Iamblichus understands prayer as integral to the theurgic ritual: Iamblichus, *On the Mysteries*, p. 275 (Book v.26).

227. Zorzi, *L'armonia del mondo*, p. 132.

228. On Zorzi's understanding of sacrifice, in the context of his conception of the human see Vasoli, 'Da Marsilio Ficino a Francesco Giorgio Veneto', p. 247.

229. Zorzi shows that he is familiar with several works by Porphyry besides *On Abstinence*, including *De antro nympharum*, Porphyry's lives of Plotinus and Pythagoras, and the *Isagoge*.

230. See on this Campanini's introduction to Zorzi, *L'armonia del mondo*, p. lxxi.

231. Zorzi, *L'armonia del mondo*, pp. 2076–78: 'Nullum est malum, quod perpetrare non audeant. Habent omnino violentum, et male sanum morem, desertum videlicet custodiam daemonum meliorum'. Cf. *OMF*, ii, 1935: 'Consentaneum est aliquid ab eo semper effluere, atque nutriri.

In commensuratione quidem corpus bonorum consistit, quemadmodum et corpora nobis manifestorum, sed maleficorum daemonum inconcinna sunt, ac affectione passiva locum incolunt terrae vicinum. Nullum ergo malum est quod non audeant perpetrare, haben enim omnino violentum et malesanum morem, desertum videlicet custodia daemonum meliorum, ideoque vehementes, repentinasque insidias plurimum machinantur, et proruunt, ac dum agunt incursiones, partim latere conantur, partim inferunt violentiam'. The reference is to *OA*, II.39.2–40.3; pp. 71–72.

232. Agrippa von Nettesheim, *De occulta philosophia*, p. 449 (III.16): '<De hoc daemonum genere inquit Porphyrius: "Locum incolunt terrae vicinum, imo intra ipsam terram. Nullum est malum, quod perpetrare non audeant; habent omnino violentum et male sanum morem ideoque vehementes repentinasque insidias plurimum machinantur moliunturque: ac, dum agunt incursiones, partim latere solent, partim vero inferre violentiam omnibusque rebus inique discoriterque factis admodum delectantur".>'.

233. I agree with Campanini that despite a certain ambivalence in the passage, this is ultimatately the meaning of it (Campanini's introduction to Zorzi, *L'armonia del mondo*, p. xii).

234. Zorzi, *L'armonia del mondo*, pp. 1196, 1198.

235. Ibid., p. 1336 (I translate slightly differently from Campanini): 'Ad quid sacrificia, et cur hirci sorte delecti pro peccato offerri iussi sint'.

236. Ibid., p. 1336: 'quod quidem prima fronte durum videtur et extraneum, Deum videlicet delectari sanguine animalium fuso, carnibus assatis, aut combusti, et horum atque aliarum rerum odoramentis, ut plerisque in locis dicitur: Et odoratus est Dominus odorem suavitatis'.

237. Ibid., p. 1340.

238. I have discussed Anton Francesco Doni's use of this same verse from Psalm 35 ('Homines et iumenta salvabis, Domine') in 'Real Animals in Ideal Cities: The Place and Use of Animals in Renaissance Utopian Literature', special issue of *Renaissance Studies* dedicated to *The Animal in Renaissance Italy*, edited by Stephen Bowd & Sarah Cockram, 31.2 (2017), 223–39.

239. Francesco Zorzi, *L'elegante poema e commento sopra il poema*, ed. by Jean-François Maillard (Milan: Archè, 1991), p. 126 (*Canto XI con Noè*, Commento). Note that in this *Commento* Zorzi appears to draw dietetic conclusions from the theory that the human being contains everything within himself, implying that humans are omnivores: 'L'huomo veramente che contiene ogni cosa mangia de tutti li cibi, carne, pesce, grano et herba' (p. 116). The *elegante poema* echoes 'the language, the metrics and the style of the *Divina Commedia*': see 'Campanini, 'Francesco Giorgio's Criticism of the *Vulgata*', p. 204.

240. Zorzi, *L'armonia del mondo*, p. 1336: 'crassior[es] cib[i] ex terrea materia'.

241. The problem of God's nourishment is addressed in a television interview by Matteo Bellinelli with Isaac B. Singer: 'Why is God not a vegetarian? [...] He should have been the first of the vegetarians' (*Come mai Dio non è vegetariano? Intervista di Matteo Bellinelli* (Bellinzona: Edizioni Casagrande, 2005), p. 42).

242. Zorzi, *L'armonia del mondo*, p. 460 (correcting 'vitandam' to 'vitanda').

243. See on this below Chapter 4, section 5.

244. Zorzi, *L'armonia del mondo*, p. 122.

245. Ibid., p. 168: 'Porphyrius dogmatum varietate multivagos animos depascit'.

CHAPTER 2

❖

Health

2.1. Introduction: Can a Vegetarian Philosopher Be Healthy?

According to Galen 'the best physician is also a philosopher'.[1] In his appeal to Firmus Castricius, Porphyry highlights the effects of this diet on the body, suggesting that vegetarianism is an excellent way to take good care of the body and of the soul at one and the same time. Porphyry thus accuses Firmus of unreasonableness in changing his mind, because the vegetarian diet had once had undeniable benefits for Firmus's own body and soul:

> For as I reflect by myself on the cause of your change, I cannot say that you would do so for health and strength, as the uninstructed multitude would say. On the contrary, you yourself used to acknowledge, when you were with us, that the fleshless diet contributes to health and to a suitable endurance of hard work in philosophy; and experience shows that in saying that, you spoke the truth.[2]

Porphyry's thesis is thus that the strength provided by vegetable food makes one a better philosopher, and a healthy one too — and further, enjoying the health of a strong body is a prerequisite for performing 'strong' thinking as well. Thus Firmus's dietetic change is for Porphyry the proof that his friend had not understood the basic principle that an appropriate diet makes the body healthy and the mind sharp. Diet, in other words, is the foundation of any philosophical endeavour, and according to Porphyry experience shows that the vegetable diet is superior to the carnivorous one in this respect. It is therefore out of the question that Firmus could have reverted to the carnivorous diet to improve his health. Was it then just gluttony that prompted him to eat meat again?

If enjoying meat did play a role in the decision, Firmus would be in the company of a philosopher who, like him, had also gone back to meat-eating after a period of abstinence: Seneca (4 BC–AD 65). In letter 108 to Lucilius, Seneca writes that he gave up meat convinced by the arguments of Sotion and Sextius, who believed that humans can derive enough nourishment from plants, without the need to shed blood and indulge in the 'diet of lions and vultures'. Seneca admits that the vegetable diet had had a clearly beneficial effect on him, too: 'Inspired by this argument I began to abstain from living creatures, and after a year the habit was not only easy for me but welcome. I believed that my spirit was more lively, and I would not declare today that it was not so'.[3] Inevitably, Seneca himself therefore poses the question that Porphyry implies as well: 'You wonder why I stopped?' In the case of Seneca the reason had to do with circumstantial events, and not with doubts about the benefits of vegetarianism for body and soul:

> In primum Tiberii Caesaris principatum iuventae tempus inciderat: alienigena tum sacra movebantur et inter argumenta superstitionis ponebatur quorundam animalium abstinentia. Patre itaque meo rogante, qui non calumniam timebat sed philosophiam oderat, ad pristinam consuetudinem redii; nec difficulter mihi ut inciperem melius cenare persuasit.

> [The time of my youth coincided with the beginning of Tiberius Caesar's principate: foreign rites were stirring and abstinence from some living creatures was counted as evidence of superstition. So at my father's request, not because he feared false accusations but he loathed philosophy, I returned to my earlier habit, and he had no difficulty in persuading me to enjoy better dinners.][4]

Even if he abandoned the vegetarian diet for personal and political, rather than philosophical or medical, reasons, Seneca still implies that a 'good dinner' is one that includes meat, and that a fleshless diet is a restriction, almost a punishment for the body. He acknowledges that he experienced an enjoyment and delight in eating meat, and that this made it easy to give up vegetarianism despite evident general benefits.

Porphyry is conscious that even if taste and enjoyment might not be considered proper philosophical arguments, they stand in the way of convincing Firmus. Good dinners including meat appear to be the opposite of vegetarianism, the abstinent, frugal diet appropriate to a Platonic philosopher. Therefore the claim that vegetarianism is a kind of abstinence that does not damage the body, but rather improves overall health, and as a result even promotes better philosophical speculation, is key to Porphyry's argument. He does not simply argue that the fleshless diet provides sufficient nourishment for the body despite the restrictions involved, and that it can be as balanced for the body as a traditional one including meat: rather, he claims that the vegetable diet is superior to meat-eating, because 'meat does not conduce to health', but actually 'impedes it'.[5] Porphyry's statement about the health risks of meat is a bold one: it is not merely possible but even essential to abstain from meat entirely in order to achieve health. Furthermore, becoming healthy and remaining healthy, for Porphyry, are both ensured by a diet that is 'abstinent' in the full sense of that word: it must be simple rather than extravagant, based on light foods rather than those that require longer digestion, and thus is naturally fleshless.

Whether a fleshless diet would provide enough nourishment is a question that until recent times has accompanied any discussion of vegetarianism. Thomas Taylor (1758–1835), who in 1823 published an English translation of Porphyry's *On Abstinence*, explains in his introduction that he himself 'found it expedient to make use of a fleshy diet' in order to engage actively in his philosophical activities. He carefully stresses the fact that this was due to the circumstances of his life, as he was 'obliged to mingle the active with the contemplative life', rather than, for instance, unwillingness, or the enjoyment of eating meat. Speaking of himself in the third person, he explains that 'nothing but an imperious necessity, from causes which it would be superfluous to detail at present, could have induced him to adopt animal, instead of vegetable nutriment'.[6] Ironically, in order to translate Porphyry's *On Abstinence* it seems that one requires the energy that only animal food can provide.

A nineteenth-century reader of Porphyry such as Taylor still doubted whether the ethical reasoning in favour of vegetarianism was combinable with the bodily strength required for an active life. Indeed, the objection that vegetarianism might not provide good nutrition for active people is discussed by Porphyry himself. Using the same rhetorical strategy as with the topic of sacrifice, when it comes to health, too, Porphyry refers to the opinions of those philosophical schools that did not adopt a vegetarian diet, mainly Stoics, Peripatetics, and Epicureans.[7]

On the subject of abstinence from meat for health purposes, the main objection is that athletes eat meat to become particularly strong; similarly, meat is used to aid recovery from illness. These cases might seem to suggest that meat-eating is connected to possessing a strong, rather than a weak body. Porphyry's answer is, as on the topic of sacrifices, complex and nuanced: he maintains that a vegetable diet is healthy, but specifies that it might well be unsuitable for people whose professions require sheer bodily strength (sailors, soldiers), or professional athletes, or those in public life.[8] Vegetarianism is the diet appropriate to a philosopher, such as Firmus, and to a philosopher it promises a healthy body which will be best suited for philosophical activities. As Catherine Osborne succinctly puts it: 'Porphyry is not engaged in converting society as a whole to a vegetarian diet'.[9]

The fact that most ancient philosophers had arguably not been vegetarians is a stumbling block for Porphyry: did they not realize the benefits of vegetarianism for health? Porphyry stretches his evidence as much as possible on the subject, claiming that Pythagoras had been in fact the first to propose a vegetarian diet for athletes (1.26).[10] As already mentioned in Chapter 1, it is striking that Plotinus is never mentioned in *On Abstinence*: one wonders whether this absence is due to the fact that although Plotinus had adopted a generally abstinent mode of life, it was one that did not involve abstinence from animal flesh.[11] In the *Life of Plotinus*, Porphyry claims that his master refused to take any medication that contained animal products. This information is intended to suggest that Plotinus had been a vegetarian, since he avoided even small parts of animals in the form of medicine.[12]

Porphyry tries to create a tradition of philosophical vegetarianism, from Empedocles to Pythagoras, and via Plotinus (even if he remains in the background) to Porphyry himself. He aims at persuading Firmus to revert to this tradition, rather than allying himself with the non-vegetarian philosophical currents.[13] Vegetarianism is therefore presented in the first instance as the appropriate diet to bring the philosopher's life into accord with his view of nature; indeed, in all likelihood the philosopher would not need to be involved in bodily activities requiring exceptional strength. Porphyry thus distinguishes between the energy needed for physical activities and the intensity of philosophical speculation, which does not count as physically strenuous in the same way. Thomas Taylor, therefore, would have had no excuse.

Porphyry thus narrows down the generic claim about meat's dangers for health, insisting that philosophers do not require the potential benefits ascribed to meat in any case. In so doing, Porphyry avoids giving direct answers to the more compelling questions involved in assessing the effect of meat on the body: is it possible to stick to a fleshless diet in the long run and also in case of illness? Does meat really promote health or is vegetarianism rather a spiritual exercise in practicing abstinence by depriving the body of pleasure?[14] More specifically, is meat really difficult to digest, as Porphyry implies by contrasting it with the light vegetable diet? Finally, and most importantly, does consuming meat really endanger clear thinking, and what can be observed in the animal world with regard to the relationship between animals' eating habits and their level of intelligence? These questions are directed not only to philosophers, but also to physicians, and it is not by chance that Renaissance readers of Porphyry, who were often philosophers with a medical training as well, would engage with them.

This chapter now presents an overview of the contexts in which the 'health question' regarding vegetarianism was debated between the thirteenth and sixteenth centuries.[15] Religious and medical aspects intertwine especially in the debates on the vegetarian diet of the Carthusian monks. Philosophical asceticism — as in the case of Porphyry — 'aimed to regulate diet, sleep and lifestyle generally so as to free the mind for the hard intellectual work'; it would therefore only support, not endanger, health. Christian asceticism, on the other hand, 'increased preoccupation with the body'.[16] From Arnau de Villanova to Erasmus, writings dedicated to *De esu carnium* [On Meat-eating] among Carthusians reflect the reception of medical theories on meat consumption while also showing the difficulty of deciding whether meat is necessary only for athletes, as Porphyry had suggested, or whether monks, and even scholars, might struggle to thrive without it. This is a problem with which Ficino, too, was concerned, as in *De vita* [On Life] he posed questions which had a rich afterlife, and which Girolamo Cardano in particular developed in their full spectrum of implications.[17] Cardano asks whether a philosopher should opt for a specific vegetable diet, avoiding all types of meat, or whether he should rather endorse an approach of generic moderation, but without excluding any food from the menu. Are there medical, as well as philosophical reasons for preferring the former, rather than the latter? Is the vegetable diet ultimately the best option for a philosopher who wishes to achieve and maintain physical health, while bringing the care of his body into harmony with his view of nature, and of the human's position in the food chain?

2.2. Dangerous Discipline: The Debate on Religious Vegetarianism

The material for answering the questions regarding the impact of meat on the body had been substantially expanded by the time Porphyry's *On Abstinence* had started to circulate around the end of the fifteenth century. The dissemination of Galen's writings, especially those dealing with the properties of foods, had been propelled by the publication of the Latin *Opera omnia* in 1490, and by the Aldine *editio princeps* in Greek in 1525, which 'marked a new era'.[18] *De alimentorum facultatibus* [On the Properties of Foods], which featured sections on the impact of animal products on health, had been included in the first editions of Galen's works, in a Latin translation by William of Moerbeke.[19] In Book 3 of this work, which is Galen's key writing on dietetics, the focus is on 'food from animals, since it has many different properties both in respect of the parts of the animals, and what is contained within them or is produced by them, amongst which are eggs, milk, blood, cheese and butter'.[20] Galen specifies that 'not all the parts of animals possess the same property', but in general terms he believes that meat can be beneficial for health, and in some cases it appears even to be an essential aliment: 'flesh, when well concocted, produces the best blood, especially in the case of animals such as the pig family, which produce healthy humour'.[21] The nutritional value of pork is confirmed, according to Galen, by the fact that if athletes substitute this type of meat with a different food, they become weaker, and can even show signs of malnutrition if they abstain from this meat for long periods.[22] Porphyry's caution with regard to the possibility that certain people might need to consume (large quantities of) meat was thus supported by Galenic medicine, prompting the question whether vegetarianism, from a strictly medical point of view, must be considered harmful. Philosophers might not be athletes — even if it is in terms of *vita activa* that Thomas Taylor was to describe his efforts as a scholar and translator — but would they be in danger of becoming weak and even shortening their lives by choosing a vegetarian diet?

The medieval physician Arnau de Villanova wrote on the question whether a completely vegetarian diet can be considered healthy or not. His *De esu carnium*[23] refers to a specific case at the crossroads of medicine and theology: that of the Carthusian monks, who refrained from eating meat not just over Lent but permanently, eating mostly raw fruits and vegetables, with small quantities of animal products such as cheese and eggs, and including fish on certain occasions.[24] Abstinence from meat had started within the order possibly as early as 1084, and had been officially confirmed by the Carthusian General Chapter in 1254 (around thirty years before Arnau wrote *De esu carnium*).[25] This position attracted accusations of heresy against the Carthusians, as indeed happened in the case of another famous religious group that practiced abstinence from meat, the Cathars.[26] This shows the religious significance of meat, considered part of the 'standard diet' for clerics, and the subversive significance attributed to vegetarianism.

As seen in Chapter 1 above, Augustine had already pointed out the key role of meat-eating in identifying dangerous religious doctrines such as Manicheism, whose adepts practised a vegetarian diet. But the medieval debate on the diet of the Carthusians focuses strongly on the health consequences of this dietary choice: Arnau's *De esu carnium* applies a strategy which involves separating the problem of the potential heresy of vegetarianism within the Church from the medical aspect.[27] In so doing Arnau aims to judge on purely medical grounds whether or not the vegetarian monks were endangering their health with their dietary restriction.[28] In case of illness, he claims, the best foods are wine and egg yolks, because they are easily digested and turn immediately into blood, thus restoring the vital power of the patient.[29] His answer was that he could see no medical objections to vegetarianism, leaving aside any theological issues (for instance regarding the notion that the animals might have been made by God for the purpose of feeding humans, as Augustine had claimed).[30]

The controversy over the Carthusians' dietary choice continued well into the sixteenth century: several writings entitled *De esu carnium* are dedicated to it, thus turning a relatively obscure debate on the dietary choices of a minor religious order into a main focus of discussion on Renaissance vegetarianism. The theologian and Chancellor of the University of Paris, Jean de Gerson (1363–1429), wrote another defence of the Carthusians' diet, *De non esu carnium apud Carthusienses* [On Abstention from Meat Among the Carthusians] in 1401.[31] Though he states that he does not follow an abstinent, meat-free diet, Gerson admits that he nevertheless has deep admiration for this choice.[32] Abstinence from meat-eating was practiced already by the ancient prophets and hermits, as well as by John the Baptist, and Gerson points out that it was not an impediment to preserving body and soul intact, and that it even seems to have played an important role in extending lifespan.[33] In the central part of the short treatise, Gerson considers especially the eventuality that monks might need to eat meat in particular circumstances, such as serious illnesses. Here he refers to Arnau and the theory that in case of illness the 'radical humidity' might be restored just by eating egg yolks, and without meat. Yet if meat should really be necessary to regain health (for instance if the patient feels nauseous at egg yolks), then according to Gerson it would be legitimate for the Carthusians to eat this food: in such cases it would be mandatory to follow the higher, divine commandment 'do not kill', which would be infringed if the patient were allowed to die. The diet of the Carthusians is thus interpreted as part the monks' discipline, and Gerson looks at it favourably, too, as a hygienic practice to promote the health of the body; but it is not a God-given instruction.[34]

This same view is shared by Erasmus in his *De esu carnium*, where the topic of the influence on health returns to the foreground. This work was first published in 1525, and attracted criticism on a number of points, expressed in the *Libellus quo taxatur Delectus ciborum sive liber de carnium esu* [Booklet Which Censors the Enjoyment of Foods, or Book on Meat-eating], published by a group of Leuven Dominicans under the pseudonym of 'Taxander' [The Punisher] and by Erasmus's longstanding critic Jacobus Latomus (Jacques Masson).[35] For Erasmus, too, consuming meat could be considered only a sin against human law, and not a divine precept.[36] Yet, Erasmus presents meat as a necessary food to restore the body to health in case of illness, and he explains in detail why he himself found meat consumption to be key to overcoming phases of deep physical exhaustion:

> Ipse sic affectus sum erga carnes ut, si liceat vitam ac salutem tueri cicere ac lupino, nec pisces nec carnes sim desideraturus. Porro quum ob imbecillem corporis valetudinem et naturale quoddam odium piscium pene singulis quadragesimis soleam periclitari, tamen frequenter ad carnium praesidia vocantibus medicis nunquam obtemperavi, nisi semel in Italia medico iam dies aliquot mortem minitante ni parerem — cui tamen hactenus parvi diebis paucis, ut ius carnium ovorum vitellis temperatum sumerem, ab ipsis carnibus

abstinerem, quas etiam si animus appetisset, non recipiebat stomachus: tanta erat imbecillitas — et nunc dies aliquot in quadragesima idque iussu medici nec sine venia pontificis.

[My own attitude to meat is that if one might preserve life and health with chickpeas and lupin, I would not want fish or meat. Moreover, although because of my poor physical health and a certain inborn dislike of fish I am usually in danger almost every Lent, I have still never complied with doctors who frequently recommend the safeguard of meat. There was one exception, in Italy, when a doctor threatened that I would die in a few days if I did not yield. But I yielded for a few days to the extent that I ate gravy mixed with egg yolks, but still abstaining from meat, which my stomach would not accept even if the appetite were there — such was my weakness. At present I make an exception for a few days in Lent, and that on doctor's orders and not without papal dispensation.][37]

The dramatic tone serves to underline that meat is an exceptional aliment, which Erasmus claims to have included on his menu only in situations of great emergency and following the instructions of physicians. Meat-eating has to be resisted, unless one's health (or rather, life) is in serious danger. Indeed he underlines that if it had been possible to regain health by vegetable nourishment only, he would have gladly avoided meat altogether, but this often goes against the opinion of physicians.

Erasmus's argument makes it possible to appreciate the interaction of religious precepts with the guidelines of medical intervention. Fish was of course the aliment of choice for religious orders that prescribed abstinence from meat only during certain periods, such as Lent. But is it a safe substitute for short periods of abstinence from meat, as well as for practicing permanent abstinence? How much fish would one need to consume as a valuable alternative to meat? And is the consumption of fish instead of meat only possible for people who dedicate themselves to a life in the cloister, rather than for more active types of life?

In the dialogue 'A Fish Diet', which is notably the longest in the collection of *Colloquia*, Erasmus stages a discussion between a fishmonger and a butcher in which all these questions are addressed, showing how religious and medical arguments intertwine in the assessment of the role of meat in human life. The opinions of Gerson, Latomus, and other theologians are mentioned, as well as the controversial diet of the Carthusians: such precise references are explained by the fact that the fishmonger is said to be conversant in theology because he often ate lunch with Dominican monks whom he used to supply with fish.[38] The dialogue begins with a confrontation regarding the two types of products the discussants sell — fish and meat — but then develops into a complex analysis of the friction between the acceptance of religious rules and the preservation of one's own health following the instructions of the physicians.

The discussion reaches a crucial point when the butcher recalls the dietetic difficulties of a friend of his, a sixty-year old scholar named Eros, whose health had always been very poor and who could also tolerate neither fish nor fasting. Erasmus is clearly relating his own experience, stressing the struggle of finding a balance between the requirements of a fragile body, the choice of foods at one's disposal (especially during journeys), and religious and moral convictions. The *Doppelgänger* Eros, the butcher narrates, had been in life danger during a visit to Freiburg during Lent because he had refused to eat meat, surviving on eggs and the food he hated most: fish. Invited for breakfast by a city councillor called Glaucoplutus, Eros was presented with a roast chicken, as indeed had happened to Erasmus during his stay in Freiburg in 1523.[39] Even if Eros hadn't touched the chicken, and had only eaten eggs, rumours had spread in the city, together with the pleasant smell of the roast meat.[40] In this case Eros/Erasmus had persisted in his vegetarianism, or rather in a 'pescatorian' diet, since during his stay in Freiburg he had consumed fish, despite his disgust for it. The butcher narrates that Eros had then managed to recover his health thanks to a diet of eggs and sugary water, adding almond milk and raisins when he travelled.

The dialogue makes clear that abstinence from eating meat must be considered within a complex constellation of factors, especially including a person's physical state. Religious discipline cannot be simply a dietetic matter, as if the moral conduct of a monk were reduced to eating or not eating meat.[41] A Carthusian monk eating meat, claims the butcher in the dialogue, is not so much an aberration as the same monk drunk, for instance, and yet people are particularly quick to judge the morality of monks merely on the basis of their dietetic choices.[42] But sticking to a prescribed religious diet can be a rather dangerous form of discipline. If a general principle can be developed, this must be that under no circumstances should anyone risk one's own life by refusing meat. Ultimately, Erasmus claims that in his case stubbornly sticking to vegetarianism would have been nothing short of committing suicide:

> Primum expende senectutem, perpetuam pene corpusculi huius valetudinem, expende laborem itineris, labores studiorum in quibus supra vires et corporis et animi versor assidue. [...] Hic quis sanus non diceret me esse meiipsius homicidam, si carnibus abstinuissem?

> [Consider first my old age, the almost continuous ill health of this poor body, consider the exertion of travel, the labours of study in which I am constantly engaged beyond both my physical and my mental resources. [...] In these circumstances what reasonable man would not say that I was killing myself if I abstained from meat?][43]

Listing the labours of scholarship next to more vigorous activities has the effect of presenting vegetarianism as a diet which might be appropriate only to people who exercise neither their bodies nor their brains greatly. Indirectly, Porphyry's claim that vegetarianism is suitable for the philosopher is countered by the statement that mental activities, too, require strength that only meat can provide. But at the same time, the emphasis on resisting meat-eating suggests that this kind of dietary abstinence is simply considered by Erasmus to be primarily an exercise in self-discipline, similar to abstaining from drinking wine or from sexual intercourse.[44] Galen, too, had underlined that the best physician and philosopher should not be enslaved to his belly or his genitals, since excessive indulgence would interfere with his capability to work hard.[45] This position is in line with Arnau's approach to the dietary choice of the Carthusians.[46] To recall Seneca, it might be said that meat does indeed provide better dinners — and that is precisely why it has to be avoided when possible without damaging the body.

Fish occupies a notably liminal position in this debate: Erasmus states that he could eat only small quantities of fish, in place of meat, because since early childhood he had had a strong disgust for this food, and in 'A Fish Diet' fish is definitely not presented as a valuable alternative to meat. Furthermore, the fact that fish is considered mainly as a substitute for meat seems to reinforce the idea that the latter was viewed as an essential food, to be replaced only occasionally and with effort.[47] The fishmonger in the dialogue even argues that the prohibition against meat-eating on certain occasions only fuels the desire to consume more of that aliment, and thus he wishes for his sales that fish were prohibited as well: this would, he claims, make them rise rather than endanger his business.[48]

From a medical point of view, substituting meat occasionally with fish could raise the objection that changing diet might cause imbalances.[49] In general terms, Galen had clearly stated that fish is also a dangerous aliment because its environment is often polluted. Stressing the link between fish and pollution, the butcher of Erasmus's dialogue accuses fishmongers of spreading filth, bad smells, and diseases in cities, as well as rivers, the air itself, and ultimately the bodies of humans. A major topic of discussion in this dialogue is the physicians' opinion about the dangers of consuming this food, which is deemed to generate bad humours in the body, and thus cause fever and infections, among other diseases. The fishmonger advances the counterargument that various medicines contain fish, and that meat is far more dangerous. The pestilent blood and corrupted humours coming from butchered animals are such a hazard for public health that city councils commonly ruled that slaughterhouses must be placed outside the city centre.[50] Yet the butcher replies to these accusations against meat by claiming that physicians themselves notoriously abstain from eating fish. The only reason why fish is not officially banned as food is indeed that it is a major source of income for doctors: the more people eat it, the more patients the doctors will have to treat, since fish makes people sick and weak.[51] In any case, the butcher underlines that doctors obviously do not have the benefit of their patients in mind, but simply restrict themselves to treating the diseases rather than banning an unwholesome food altogether.

Furthermore, Galen regarded fish as a light food more appropriate for the frail and the sick than for active people, an idea which again is picked up by Erasmus.[52] In a short dialogue, first published in the 1523 edition of his *Colloquies*, a soldier and a Carthusian monk discuss the differences between their life styles, focusing especially on the question of diet. While the Carthusians allowed themselves small quantities of fish, especially to help the sick recover, Erasmus makes fun of this habit by staging a dialogue in which the monks' consumption of fish plays a crucial role.[53] The soldier argues that a married man, for instance, would not be able to survive on fish.[54] This is a reference to the assumption that meat is the proper, manly food, as well as an elaboration of Galen's principle according to which fish is not a valid meat substitution for people who exercise their body.

But the monk and the soldier also discuss the possibility that food could have a deep effect on the nature of the eater. Rather than simply debating what food is appropriate for each type of human being, assuming that there is an accordance between food and eater (for instance meat for athletes and fish for the elderly), the monk and the soldier also consider the possibility that food could intervene directly in the constitution of a person, altering it. If the monks always choose fish over meat, will they not eventually turn into fish? The ironic reply of the monk refers to the idea that meat, and especially pork, as Galen had said, is supposed to be the best food for humans: if people turned into the food they ate, then the pork-eating soldier should have turned into a pig.

The belief that the eater might turn into the food has its roots in Hippocratic medicine, and especially in the general rule according to which 'like nourishes like', that is to say that a creature is best nourished by the food that resembles it most.[55] Erasmus overturns this ironically by imagining that the opposite would happen in the case of the Carthusian monk and the soldier: they accuse each other of being in danger of turning into the foods they eat.[56] In neither case is the transformation flattering. Pork is the food of brutish, violent human beings, like soldiers, while fish is a weak aliment, and thus in 'A Fish Diet' the butcher describes fish-eaters as pale, malodorous, stupid, and mute: they eat food which tends to rot quickly, and this affects their souls ('animi').[57] Starting at the level of physiology, food reaches the deepest level of a human being's nature, altering not only appearance but character and disposition as well — in short, it affects the body as well as the soul. This is why the most powerful aliment, meat, is also the most unsafe one.

Abstinence from all meat, of the sort that Porphyry had recommended to Firmus, could indirectly provide a solution to the dangers of meat-eating (even if the fishmonger of Erasmus's dialogue ironically asks what will happen to those eating chard, if one turns into the food consumed). But the vegetarian option had been already discussed by Ficino in De vita, where he had pointed to the difficulty of balancing medical and philosophical approaches to vegetarianism, especially when the health of scholars (rather than athletes, soldiers, or monks) is at stake.

2.3. Pork-eaters and Plant-eaters: Ficino

According to Ficino, scholars tend to be melancholic: this is due to the fact that assiduous studying, combined with lack of movement, tends to dry out the brain, which assumes the characteristics of *melancholia* (literally: black bile), namely dryness and coldness.[58] Their activity might not seem to require too much strength, at first sight, but they have to take special care that their organs function well: not just the brain, but also the heart, the liver, and the stomach. In fact, they make use of their bodies for higher activities than, for instance, athletes, so it is particularly important that they should counter their melancholic tendency by carefully choosing the foods they eat.[59] In the first book of De vita, entitled De vita sana [On Healthy Life] and finished around 1480, Ficino thus recommends specific dietary adjustments for the benefit of scholars: they should avoid cloudy wine and certain types of meat (hare and cow), as well as mature cheese and certain plants and pulses (such as fava beans, lentils, or garlic).[60] But other types of meat are recommended: for instance chicken, or the meat of birds, or young quadrupeds. This advice is meant specifically for scholars, and it seems that in order for them to be healthy they will need to eat a certain amount of meat. At the same time, it is clear that meat must be consumed with extreme care especially in cases of melancholia.[61]

In the second book of *De vita*, devoted to the attainment of a long life (*De vita longa*), Ficino turns instead to formulating more general advice for people who do not fall into a particular category or profession, but who just aspire to live healthily and for a long time. Michele Tramezzino, the publisher of the 1548 Italian translation of Ficino's *De vita*,[62] presents the work to the dedicatee, Domenico Veniero, with this catchy summary of its aim:

> Il libro è di tale qualità che ogni spirito gentile dovrebbe desiderare di haverlo tra le mani sempre, perché chi è colui che non desideri vivere sano, e di vivere molto? Che se questo desiderio è così naturale che non è animale che non desideri l'uno e l'altro, quanto si dee maggiormente dire che l'huomo, che è da tanti e così ragionamenti mosso, il debba assai più desiderare?[63]

> [The book is of such good quality that any refined soul should want to have it always to hand. Indeed who does not desire to live a healthy and long life? This desire is so natural that there is no animal that does not want both. Thus, how much more should humans desire it, given their intense and high reasonings?]

For Ficino, whose practical engagement with medicine intertwined with his efforts in diffusing Platonic philosophy, the discussion of how to achieve a long and healthy life thus represented not a tangential interest, but rather a profound concern.[64] In the dedicatory epistle to *De vita* he credits his father for having put him in the care of Galen, physician and Platonist, who taught him how to keep bodies healthy; Plato, on the other hand, taught him how to care for the needs of souls.[65] Ficino's dual approach to the health of human beings is thus a complex medical and philosophical enterprise and is rooted, as Tramezzino fittingly puts it, in the understanding of what it means to be human. In *De vita*, Ficino states that humans must make use of the strategies of medicine, while also being concerned with morals and religion. With the combined help of all three, we may cure our bodies while also taking care of the incorporeal part of our being, and directing our efforts to attaining the truth.[66] A strong, healthy body is thus the foundation for achieving higher aims, and dietetics is the starting point, since perfect digestion is nothing less than the root of life.[67]

De vita longa was written in the 1480s, the years during which Ficino was also engaged in translating Porphyry's *On Abstinence*, and it is therefore noteworthy that Porphyry should be mentioned directly in the text. In Chapter 6 Ficino presents general rules regarding food and drink, and recalls the medical theory that the most appropriate food is that which is closest to a living being's own nature — 'like nourishes like'.[68] Ficino reports that Galen's recommendation of pork for human consumption was based on this principle: 'the ancient physicians, especially Galen, strongly recommend the meat and blood of a pig because of a certain similarity with our body'.[69] Indeed, in a passage already quoted from *De alimentorum facultatibus* Galen, who is a main source for Ficino's dietetics, had stated that eating pork stimulates the production of excellent blood. Furthermore, the similarity between pork and human flesh is testified by the fact that they have a similar taste: people who ate human flesh have mistaken it for pork.[70] Eating meat, and pork in particular, might thus be essential for the perfect nutrition of humans, since the closer an aliment is to a creature the more deeply it nourishes and there can be no doubt that meat is more similar to the human being than vegetables.

Yet, the proximity of humans to pigs poses a crucial problem: if the most nourishing meat is the one which is closest to a creature, then a human would be the best food for a human, and pork would be simply the next best option. The embarrassingly anthropophagic implication of the principle 'like nourishes like' keeps resurfacing in the reception of ancient medical literature. Erasmus, too, hints sardonically at this principle when in 'A Fish Diet' the fishmonger accuses the butcher of regularly selling pies made with human meat, instead of pork, to unsuspecting customers who would not be able to distinguish the difference in flavour.[71]

But it is in the Renaissance best-seller *Liber de homine* [The Book of the Human Being], also known as *Il Perché*, published in 1474, only a few years before Ficino finished *De vita sana*, that the anthropophagic result of this principle is fully displayed and serenely acknowledged. The author, Girolamo Manfredi (*c.* 1430–93), divided the book, which was written in the vernacular, into two main parts: a health regimen divided into chapters according to the six so-called 'non-naturals', factors considered to be key to preserving health (air, food and drink, sleep and waking, exercise and rest, evacuation and repletion, and finally the passions of the soul); and a section devoted to physiognomics (the theory according to which the internal, invisible nature of a creature manifests itself in specific bodily signs).[72] Among the various questions that the book promises to answer in the dietetic part of the health regimen, ample space is dedicated to the issue regarding the medical implications of the physiological similarity between the human being and pork. Following the Galenic tradition, Manfredi states that the flesh of pigs, especially of domestic ones, tends to be viscous and humid: it is thus difficult to digest and generates too much residue. Yet, 'it is true that it is very appropriate for and bears considerable resemblance with the substance of our body, and this to a greater extent than occurs with any other animal, with the exception of the human being'. Therefore, 'when it is digested, it generates excellent blood and good nutriment'.[73] In line with the tradition to which Porphyry, too, referred in his discussion of the athletes' diet, Manfredi explains that meat which is easily digested, like chicken, is appropriate for people who are not excessively active. On the contrary, those who perform intense physical activities should consume food that is not as easily digested and that is very nutritious, such as pork.[74]

These assertions explain Manfredi's daring formulation that 'there is nothing and no food which would be more appropriate to human nutrition than human meat, were it not for the aversion that nature has against it'.[75] As astonishing as this statement might sound, it has deep roots in the ancient medical tradition, from

Hippocrates's 'like nourishes like' principle to Galen's praise of pork. If considered within the discussion of Renaissance vegetarianism, this statement appears to support the consumption of meat, and of pork in particular, as the best possible food for humans.

In *De vita* Ficino limits himself to expounding the theory that 'like nourishes like' by claiming that the best food for nourishing each individual organ is the meat of the same organ in those animals that most closely resemble humans: 'If you want food to take the form of your brain above all, or of your liver, or of your stomach, eat as much as you can of like food, that is, of the brain, liver, and stomach of animals which are not far removed from human nature'.[76] Once again, this seems to imply indirectly that the flesh of certain animals would provide much needed nutrition for the human body — without it, the organs might become weaker — and Ficino had recommended that scholars, especially, should take good care of their brains, hearts, livers, and stomachs.

But when extolling the effects of pork on human health, Ficino adds a sentence which sounds like a warning against the dangers of meat consumption: 'Pork is best, therefore, for bodies which are pig-like, as are those of rustics and hardy men and those which get a lot of physical exercise'.[77] This is yet another variation on the theme that food and eater must resemble each other for optimal nutritional benefit: therefore what is appropriate for a hardy man might not be so for the philosopher. In other words, there is no simple answer to the question 'what is the best food for humans', and even if, following Galen, pork were considered closest to human flesh, still it would be necessary to make distinctions between humans, as not all will benefit from that food.

Indeed, Galen had given further examples of the apparent resemblance between the human eater and the animals that provide the meat. In the short treatise *De subtiliante diaeta* [On the Thinning Diet], which is devoted to providing advice for 'thinning' the humours in the body, Galen stated that 'the horse and the ass would only be consumed by someone who was himself an ass; and to eat leopards, bears and lions you would have to be a wild beast'.[78] The character of each animal species is clearly defined: wild animals are fierce and violent, just as Ficino's pig appeared to be sturdy, like certain humans who delight more in heavy physical activity than in intellectual speculation.

Ficino's scholars would presumably tend not to eat these animals: rather than being inclined towards physical labour (as in the case of pig-like humans) or brute violence (like the eaters of wild beasts) they need to manage the melancholia which comes with their sedentary intellectual lives.[79] The combination of a motionless body and an active mind makes phlegm and black bile (*atra bilis*) rise in the body.[80] One could thus envisage that scholars might benefit from Galen's advice on thinning humours, and indeed there is some overlap between Ficino's and Galen's practical advice (both, for instance, discourage the consumption of hare). Galen does not recommend eating domestic pigs, even if their flesh is the most nutritious food: it is too nutritious for people who are physically not very active. Instead, 'people who exercise little are recommended to eat fish', and plants play a crucial role, since most of them have thinning properties.[81]

The 'nutritional value' of meat, and of pork in particular, could thus be counterproductive for the health of the studious. This is a theory that had a long afterlife beyond Ficino, and it is not surprising to find it clearly presented by Robert Burton in *Anatomy of Melancholy*, where he states that '*porke*, of all meats, is most nutritive in his owne nature, but altogether unfit for such as live at ease, are any wayes unsound of Body and minde'.[82] Those with a delicate stomach should thus be wary of meat, because 'generally, all such meats as are hard of digestion breed melancholy', and pork is certainly one of them. Meat can thus be potentially dangerous, and it is significant that Ficino invokes Porphyry to point out possible consequences of a frequent ingestion of this food:

> Carnes quoque, si quotidie comedantur, ac etiam si pondere pani propinquent, citam putrefactionem inferunt. Unde Porphyrius Pythagoreorum antiquorumque auctoritate fretus, esum animalium detestatur. Nonne homines accepimus ante diluvium longaevos, animalibus perpecisse? Quamquam medici non tam carnium usum vetant, quam abusum.

> [Meat also, if it is eaten daily, even if it is about the same as the bread in weight, quickly causes putrefaction. Whence Porphyry, relying on the authority of the Pythagoreans and the ancients, denounces the eating of animals. Haven't we heard that before the flood humans, who used to live a long time, spared the animals? Yet physicians do not forbid the use of flesh so much as its abuse.][83]

To begin with, Ficino makes a strictly medical connection between Porphyry's appeal in favour of vegetarianism and the consideration that meat tends quickly to become putrid if this is not mitigated by a simultaneous ingestion of bread. He thus chooses to emphasize Porphyry's claim that eating meat can endanger health. Ficino, who of course was aware that the advantages of vegetarianism for health were not Porphyry's only argument, here nevertheless conveys the impression that Porphyry and the Pythagoreans had been concerned purely with this problem when they advocated vegetarianism. It is by laying emphasis on the medical issue that Ficino links Porphyry, Pythagoras, and the Bible. In his translations from *On Abstinence* (as was discussed in Chapter 1) Ficino showed a particular interest in the topic of sacrifice, which is here touched upon indirectly: in Genesis meat consumption begins after the flood, and is inaugurated by a sacrificial offer. In the context of *De vita* Ficino highlights the fact that according to the Bible, the lifespan of those who lived before the flood was incomparably longer than that of those who lived after. Was this due to the vegetarianism of the former? The question is left open by Ficino, who only mentions that physicians encourage reducing rather than eliminating the consumption of meat. By creating a dialogue between Porphyry and the physicians, Ficino softens Porphyry's opinion about diet, suggesting that moderation rather than absolute vegetarianism is sufficient from the medical perspective, despite the fact that even biblical sources refer to the diet before the flood as a vegetarian one that promoted an extraordinary lifespan. Porphyry's *apoché* — which implied refraining from all animal food — is thus reinterpreted in the sense of abstinent moderation, avoiding excess but without necessarily sparing animals.

Even if the extension of lifespan is the nodal point of the whole second book of *De vita* ('To achieve the perfection of knowledge a long life is necessary' is the title of Chapter 1), Ficino makes no explicit claim in favour of radical abstinence from flesh, and meat that is not too moist is in fact recommended.[84] But there are also cases when in Ficino's view humid foods are appropriate, for instance for patients who have a fever and should eat frequent, light suppers, including chicken or pheasant.[85] In the concluding chapters of *De vita longa* Ficino recommends a general approach of moderation with regard to both food and sex, especially in the case of elderly people, and here he recurs to the authority of Pythagoras and Plato in support of the principle that human life should be kept in a condition of 'somewhat equal proportion of the soul with the body', nourishing and exercising both.[86]

But moderation in eating animals, for Porphyry, was not a viable option with regard to the diet of the philosopher: the way of the physicians and the way of the philosopher appear to be incompatible on this point. Ficino concurs with the physicians about the health benefits of including certain types of meat in the diet, while also retaining a certain fascination for the vegetarian ideal presented by Porphyry. This, as shown in Chapter 1, was also due to the fact that Porphyry's 'bloodless' Platonism could be readily harmonized with Christianity. It is significant that in a sermon Ficino draws a parallel between abstaining from meat-eating (as proposed by Porphyry), and the practices of the early Christians. But in this context Porphyry's dietary abstinence is simply one possible expression of a general abstinent attitude. It represents the mind's rule over the body, rather than a specific endorsement of vegetarianism.[87] Therefore, negotiating moderation and absolute abstinence, and tempering the medical tradition with philosophical and religious ideals, Ficino's judgement with regard to the health benefits of vegetarianism remains suspended.

In the works of another philosopher-physician with an interest in Porphyry's dietetic advice — Girolamo Cardano — the issue of assessing the role of meat in human diet is again discussed with attention both to the philosophical and the medical sides of the debate. The eclectic nature of Cardano's investigations in the fields of natural philosophy, medicine, and metaphysics (as well as astrology and mathematics) makes his work a particularly good example of the interdisciplinary nature of Renaissance discussions on diet, and on vegetarianism in particular.[88] Having studied medicine in Pavia, Cardano was familiar with Hippocratic and Galenic theories of the properties of foodstuffs, a topic which he very often addresses in his medical works (from *Contradicentium medicorum libri duo*, to *De sanitate tuenda*, and including the commentary on Hippocrates's *De alimento*, and several *consilia* on specific diseases), as well as in his more metaphysical ones (especially *Theonoston*, but also in the encyclopaedic work *De rerum varietate*, and in *De subtilitate*).[89]

The issue of choosing the most appropriate food(s), and of consuming meat in particular, is central to Cardano's view not only of human health but of the entire construction of the world. It is at this intersection that Porphyry's legacy emerges in Cardano's writings. His discussion of vegetarianism develops core issues addressed already by Ficino: as a physician, Cardano considers it essential to collect evidence about the influence of different types of food on different types of humans (scholars, athletes, or anyone suffering from specific pathologies); as a philosopher, he engages with the role of diet within philosophical traditions, asking the question that Porphyry had asked of Firmus Castricius: which is the diet appropriate to the philosopher? The result of this dual approach is one of the most complex Renaissance reflections on vegetarianism, in which Porphyry's legacy surfaces at key points in the argumentation.

2.4. Cardano on the Power of Food and the Dangers of Meat

Galen had envisaged the possibility that eating the flesh of an animal could actually turn the nature of the eater into that of the animal. This would not simply be an instance of the accord between food and eater on the basis of their similarities, as in the case of pig-like people eating pork; rather, Galen points to the fact that the choice of meat can deeply affect the character of the person eating this food. This issue greatly fascinated Cardano, who, like Ficino, understood the role and impact of food at the intersection of the care of body and soul. In Book 40 of *De rerum varietate* [On the Variety of Things] (1557), dedicated to the investigation of human nature, Cardano states that 'food can change humans in every nature [...]. Therefore it is to be studied diligently who makes use of which food'.[90] Diet is for Cardano an essential tool for investigating human nature, and for understanding just how it can change under the effect of food.

Cardano carefully monitored such changes in himself: as Nancy Siraisi has insightfully reconstructed, Cardano's autobiography, *De vita propria* [On His Own Life], records in some detail how Cardano meticulously controlled his food intake, constantly adapting his diet over the course of his life, according to his age, diseases, and chronic conditions, and in the light of his continual study of medicine. He complains that the extreme sensitivity of his stomach contributed throughout the course of his life to a state of general bodily infirmity: 'Indigestion [...] and a stomach not any too strong were my lot'.[91] He recalls precisely how this condition had worsened with old age: 'From my seventy-second year, whenever I had eaten something more than usual, or had drunk too much, or eaten between meals, or eaten anything not especially wholesome, I began to feel ill'.[92]

Cardano views food both as a source of powerful change and of stress and anxiety, as both the gateway to health and as a main cause of illness. It is thus not by chance that understanding the properties of food and the effects on his body were an essential part of Cardano's medical interest.[93] But in the case of Cardano, personal experience is placed within a broader interpretative frame, which is philosophical and medical at the same time. This is the background of his statement, again in the autobiography, that from his youth he 'persistently held' to the purpose of making it his own 'duty to care for human life'.[94] Cardano's attention to diet and food should thus be seen in the context of his desire to understand human life starting from its very basis, that is to say the nutriment of the body. Food is the root of life itself, as Cardano writes in the *Praefatio* to his commentary on Hippocrates's *De alimento*

[On Nutriment], a simple assertion that explains why the topic of food emerges and is discussed at critical theoretical points throughout his work.[95] Yet the sense of anxiety regarding food remains ubiquitous, too. Food is, for Cardano, a point of conflict between metaphysical and medical arguments and traditions: the assessment of the role of meat for human nutrition, and the fascination with the ideal of a vegetarian diet, reflected in his direct references to Porphyry's *On Abstinence*, play a significant role in Cardano's far-reaching discussion of food as the cornerstone not only of human life, but of his own philosophical endeavour, too.

Some issues addressed by Cardano with regard to meat-eating and vegetarianism appear to be a direct echo of Ficino's treatment of the topic: is there a 'best diet' for humans or does the choice of food always depend on an individual's 'constitution' and especially on the presence of certain diseases? Would such a diet include meat and if so of which animals and in what quantities? Which diet is more likely to extend human life? These questions crystallize around the same dichotomy sketched by Ficino: is a general moderation with regard to food ultimately advisable, or should complete abstinence from certain foods, and especially meat, be recommended?

Cardano's autobiography demonstrates that these questions were not simply theoretical but had very practical effects on his own life. He was accustomed to noting exactly the years when he applied dietary changes, experimenting with medical theories and with dietary practice, and presented his own conclusions to his readers. For instance this is the diet he decided to follow after his fiftieth year:

> Matutina vigilia distorquebar nimis, et prandium semper coena minus fuit: cum post L. annum, mane contentus fuerim pane ex iure, et ab initio etiam ex aqua, et uvis Creticis magnis zibibis appellatis. Post varie egi: nil minus tamen quam ut vitello ovi cum panis unciis 2. aut parum plus, modicoque vini meri, aut sine, prandium exigerem. Vel si dies sit Veneris aut Sabbati pane ex iure chamarum, vel astacorum tentavi carnis modicum [...].

> [Breakfast was always a lighter meal than dinner. I was satisfied in the morning with bread steeped in broth, or even, at first, with bread and water, and with those large Cretan grapes called Zibbibos or red raisins. Later in the day I followed a more varied menu, desiring for the midday meal simply an egg-yolk with two ounces of bread or a little more, and a mild draught of pure wine, or none at all. Or if the day happened to be a Friday, or Saturday, I tried a small piece of meat with bread and cockle broth or crab soup.][96]

This menu reflects a principle of general moderation with regard to a variety of foods. Animal flesh is included, although in small, strictly controlled quantities, and indeed Cardano does not seem to have ever perfectly conformed to a vegetable diet. Personal preferences, as in the case of Erasmus, shape Cardano's menu, interacting with the medical analysis of the properties of food. But unlike Erasmus, Cardano declares that he prefers fish over meat, finding it more easily digestible but also, quite simply, more pleasant: 'I am especially fond of river crabs, because, while my mother carried me, she ate so many of them. Likewise I delight in cockles and oysters. I prefer fish to meat, and eat the former with much more benefit than the latter'.[97] Yet, Cardano underlines the fact that fish should be fresh: the fear of putrefaction, vividly discussed in Erasmus's 'A Fish Diet', still remains.[98]

As the tradition of religious fasting shows, eating fish can be viewed as an instance of abstinence and moderation, in comparison with eating meat, a supposedly more nutritious aliment. But moderation can be interpreted also as the result of a medical approach according to which foods — all foods — can be dangerous. From this perspective, it is not merely the quantity that can be dangerous, but also the type of food. Cardano often applies a system of progressive refinement, pointing out all the foods that are not recommended, and coming to the relatively 'good' ones through this process of elimination. In so doing he follows in the footsteps of a long tradition of discussing the properties of a list of foods, while at the same time giving tailored advice for specific illnesses.[99]

This is a method he applies in some medical *consilia* on the treatment of specific illnesses.[100] One of these is devoted to the respiratory problems ('difficultas spirandi') of the marquess Girolamo Pallavicino of Cortemaggiore, who also suffered from bad digestion ('concoctio'). Identifying foods that support recovery and those that impede it is essential, especially in the case of Pallavicino, who, having digestive problems as well, was not able to eat much. Therefore Cardano identifies those foods that nourish the body well even in very small quantities: his principle is that the quality of a food must make up for the radical restriction in terms of quantity.[101] Thus Cardano begins by stating that the main distinction with regard to foods is whether they nourish well or badly: good foods have a certain nutritional density which ensures that they will neither burden digestion, nor leave the body weak for lack of nutrition. This distinction is therefore crucial for Cardano's understanding of dietetic moderation, both in cases of illness such as Pallavicino's, and as a foundation for Cardano's own everyday practice. Furthermore, Cardano's dietetic recommendations regarding meat and vegetables also stem from this background: for him, the key question is whether a vegetable diet can sufficiently nourish the body and sustain it during periods of illness. Is meat, from the medical and dietetic points of view, a necessary food to preserve or restore good health?

Drawing on Galen's *De alimentorum facultatibus,* Cardano employs the basic differentiation between foods that produce thick ('crassus') and those that provide thin ('serosus') nourishment.[102] Describing the nourishing quality of fish, especially of pike, Galen had explained that this food produces blood that is more fluid and less abundant in comparison with the blood which is produced upon ingesting the flesh of quadrupeds, and which also dissipates quicker.[103] Ideally, the blood produced should be neither too thick nor too thin, but exactly half-way between the two.[104] Cardano refers directly to this Galenic theory: 'the foods that produce bad nutrition are those that provide either too a feeble or too a thick nourishment'.[105] Again, following Galen, Cardano claims that small fish nourish too little, while big ones threaten to nourish too 'thickly'. The nutritional value of plant food is also critically assessed in this *consilium.* In Cardano's view neither roots nor vegetables can be recommended to the sick patient: roots nourish thickly, while fruit and vegetables tend to generate a thin food. Milk should be consumed with extreme caution, and pulses are difficult to digest.[106]

It could be asked what foods might be suitably eaten, in the end. In this *consilium* Cardano recommends only a select few: a special bread preparation (of which he gives the recipe), egg yolks, and certain types of meat. The best type of meat is that of birds and especially of partridges. Among quadrupeds, he recommends the flesh of goats and pigs, although the latter should be consumed cooked. Apart from a few other animals, such as calf, he claims that 'the other [meats] are not useful'.[107] He warmly recommends cockle or tortoise broth: Cardano himself used to consume such broths, and there is considerable overlap between the recommendations in this *consilium* and Cardano's personal dietary choices.

In another *consilium*, devoted to the treatment of melancholy, Cardano states that actually 'no meat of quadrupeds is good', thus further refining the safe choices with regard to animal flesh, at least in pathological cases like the one discussed in this text.[108] He considers river fish better than sea fish, because they produce less melancholic humour; but the best foods of all are only two: egg yolks and milk (even if the latter should be consumed with care by some).[109] Like Ficino, Cardano recommends caution in meat consumption for those prone to being plagued by an excess of black bile, causing the typical symptoms of melancholy.

Poor digestion is traditionally connected to melancholy, and the danger of meat in this respect, a nutritious food but difficult to digest, is a commonplace.[110] Cardano thus presses to its extreme ('no meat of quadrupeds is good') a generally prevalent theory. For instance, the German doctor Georg Pictorius (1500–1569/73),[111] whom Cardano mentions in his works, warned that the meat of certain animals, especially if dried, causes melancholy.[112] Pictorius was very familiar with Ficino's treatment of melancholy in the first book of *De vita*, of which he published an edition with commentary.[113] In 1550, the year of the publication of Cardano's *De subtilitate*, Pictorius's *De bona tuenda valetudine dialogi septem* was translated into Italian and published in Venice with the title *Dialogi del modo di conservare la sanità* [Dialogues on How to Preserve Health].[114] This edition also included a translation of a writing, attributed to Arnau de Villanova but in fact spurious, dedicated to the topic of prolonging youth and delaying old age, and entitled: *Libro di Arnaldo di Villa Nuova Medico et Filosofo acutissimo del modo di conservare la Gioventù e ritardare la Vecchiezza* [The Book by Arnaldus of Villa Nuova, most Insightful Physician and Philosopher, about the Way to Preserve Youth and Delay Senility].

Pictorius's dialogues focus on the discussion of the six non-naturals. The third dialogue in particular is dedicated to food and drink, and it is here that the characters Polilogus and Theophrastus discuss the advantages and disadvantages of different types of meat.[115] To Polilogus's question about the best kind of meat, Theophrastus answers that pork is hot and humid, and thus can be recommended, even if it is not a suitable food for sick people because it is difficult to digest. Other types of meat, such as beef, stimulate the melancholic humour and must thus be considered harmful for health.[116] Accordingly, Theophrastus adds that he particularly enjoys eating fish.[117]

The *Libro di Arnaldo* included at the end of this Italian edition of Pictorius's dialogues, on the other hand, recommends the 'meats of wholesome animals' ('carni di buoni animali'), which together with good bread and wine are considered the foundation of health.[118] This text was a source for Ficino's *De vita longa*, and, as we have seen, Ficino does agree at least to a certain extent with this medical tradition according to which meat plays a key role in human nutrition. But Cardano, more than Ficino, is aware that meat is indeed a special kind of food, nutrious and dangerous at the same time.

2.5. Meat, Violence, and Intelligence: Cardano

Expanding on the principle that food has a direct impact on the living being who is nourished by it, and that therefore dietary choices are of utmost importance, Cardano uses diet as a criterion for operating anthropological distinctions between different human groups. In *De subtilitate* [On Subtlety] he explains that certain people have assumed the characteristics of the foods, and especially of the animals, they eat:

> Mutantur enim (ut dixi) corpora ex alimentis, atque primum sanguis et mores, inde lac et semen, ac foetus, ultimo carnes et vires proprie similes praecantationibus. Itaque Germani cum magna ex parte lacte belluarum maxime vaccarum alantur, iracundi sunt, intrepidique, atque agrestes. Tauri enim tales sunt, qui eodem alimento utuntur. Et Corsicae insulae accolae cum catulis parvis non solum cicuribus, sed etiam agrestibus vescantur, iracundi sunt, crudeles, infidi, audaces, prompti, agiles, robusti: talis enim est natura canum.

> [As I said, bodies are changed by food, and in the first instance blood and the habits, then milk and sperm and the foetus, finally the flesh and the physical strength change in a way that truly resembles an enchantment. And thus the Germans, who eat mainly the milk of beasts and especially of cows, are irascible, fearless, and also rustic. For bulls are like that, and they take the same food. And the inhabitants of the island Corsica, who eat the puppies not only of tame but even of wild animals, are irascible, fierce, treacherous, bold, quick, agile, strong: for this is the nature of dogs.][119]

Cardano sketches a precise sequence: food penetrates into the deepest texture of a body, affecting its vital fluids (blood, milk, and sperm), and changing the consumer's behaviour. The way in which food transforms flesh is so powerful that it truly resembles magic.[120] Just like Ficino, Cardano establishes a very close connection between the flesh of animals and the character that meat imprints on humans; but he expands the theory with more examples, going beyond Ficino's warning about pork. Further, he focuses on one particular 'side effect' that he attributes to meat-eating: meat makes humans violent and aggressive, bringing them closer to the nature of carnivorous beasts.[121]

A passage already quoted from *De rerum varietate*, in which Cardano declares that food has the power to alter any given nature, warns against the brutalizing effects of consuming the meat of wild animals: 'Those who eat the meat of wild animals and the fumes [derived from burning the meat] all become savage and ferocious, the opposite of those who eat plants'.[122] Cardano does not apply this only to certain brutal, human populations, but expounds it in the form of the general principle that anyone who eats the meat of wild animals becomes just as savage as them, as if he had absorbed the character of the animal he ingested. He thus posits a fundamental alternative within the world of animals, which also affects human life: the difference between eating meat or eating plants, that is to say between carnivores and herbivores. He recurs to this dietary alternative between a carnivorous and a vegetarian diet throughout his work, weighing up advantages and disadvantages for human nutrition. In so doing, he uses the description of animals as a constant point of comparison, on the basis that food and the nature of a creature are in accord with each other.

In *De subtilitate* Cardano explains that in the economy of the world, carnivores and herbivores are both essential: the world could not be populated by only one or other of these two groups. Animals are necessarily divided into three groups: herbivores, carnivores, and omnivores. The reason is that only in this way can animals continue to procreate and populate the earth: if all animals ate each other, Cardano argues, they would soon become extinct. Therefore, this differentiation with regard to diet appears to be necessary to ensure the survival of animals as a whole. Nature's wisdom expresses itself in this dietetic diversity: the fact that herbivores and carnivores coexist ensures that the latter cannot, so to speak, eat each other into oblivion.

But while it is clear, within Cardano's reasoning, that not all animals could be carnivores, what would happen if all animals were herbivores? And would it be advantageous for all animals to eat a vegetable diet? Since herbivores, unlike carnivores, are not violent, a world in which all animals ate plants, rather than other animals, would certainly constitute a less ferocious environment. Yet Cardano answers the latter question in the negative, and the reason lies in the effects of vegetable food as compared to meat: 'If all animals were to eat plants, nature would not have attained perfection, because that blood and meat would not derive from the elements broken down and perfectly tempered'.[123] Something intrinsic to the food is responsible for the difference between carnivores and herbivores, and therefore for their behaviour: meat does not nourish in the same way as plants, because the former is made of what Cardano calls 'the elements broken down and perfectly tempered', allowing it to penetrate subtly into the body of the eater. Meat affects the complexion in such a way that it makes the eater even-tempered, balancing out the dangerous prevalence of certain humours over others. Cardano states this in general terms, and by way of opposing plant and animal food: there are notable differences between the types of flesh provided by a variety of animals, as they can be more or less suitable, or stimulate a particular effect, as for instance in the case of pork. Moreover, as Galen had pointed out, all creatures can be said to have a specific complexion — such as hot or cold — only by comparison with others, and individual characteristics should not be forgotten either.[124]

These specifications notwithstanding, there remains a fundamental dissimilarity between the nourishment that plants can offer (light and less able to penetrate), and that provided by meat (extremely nourishing and deeply affecting the body of the eater). Meat is for Cardano a medical puzzle: it is a nutritiously dense food and thus small quantities are often sufficient; eating large quantities, as athletes do, certainly makes the body very strong, but it can both cause illness and, as we have seen, endow the eater with the nature of the animal eaten.[125] For instance, by eating a wolf, and especially its heart, the eater would become cruel, bold, and savage.[126] Nevertheless Cardano underlines that transformations induced by food are more evident in simpler creatures than in more complex ones. Such changes are thus less manifest in animals than in plants, and even less remarkable in humans than in animals, due to the complexity of the changes that affect humans. Plants are the life-form most exposed to the changes triggered by nutrition because according to Cardano they are not modified by other external factors, whereas animals and humans in particular are exposed to a plurality of influences. In other words, nutrition is powerful in the case of plants, and the changes obvious and visible, because of the simplicity of vegetable life, while human life is so complex that the modifications brought about by food are to be considered within a broader context.

But the explanation of how meat nourishes is not simply a medical and physiological one, regarding merely the different nutritional value and effect of meat compared to other foods. Cardano states that it is owing to meat-eating that nature attained perfection, implying that there is a hierarchy of value among living beings, and that carnivores are at the top. At stake in the question of meat-eating, and in the fundamental difference between carnivores and herbivores, is the understanding of the very order of the world. For Cardano, discussing the properties of food and the criteria for choosing a specific diet leads directly to metaphysical speculation about the place of each creature in the universe.

The sense of directionality in nature is conveyed by the conception of 'perfection'. Cardano's *De subtilitate* features the traditional division of the animal kingdom into two main groups: perfect animals (generated in a womb) and imperfect ones (smaller, and often generated spontaneously in putrid areas, without sexual reproduction). But Cardano adds further facets to the idea of a hierarchy of perfection among animals: he claims that even among the group of perfect animals some are more perfect than others, because they not only generate their offspring in the womb, but also take care of them and accompany them through the course of their entire life. There are only two examples of animals of the highest degree of perfection: the human and the elephant. Moreover, in *De uno* [On the One] Cardano introduces another criterion for distinguishing qualitatively between animals: that is to say the number of offspring. This represents another instance of the combination of natural philosophical with metaphysical considerations: Cardano uses a detail regarding the process of reproduction to order the animals according to a principle of increasing perfection. Beginning with the clear statement that 'the one is good: in truth plurality is bad',[127] Cardano here argues that the more imperfect an animal, the more numerous will be its litter, and as a result of applying this criterion the elephant's single pregnancies place this animal at least as high as the human being in the hierarchy.[128] The lack of twin births in elephants and donkeys even appears to place them higher then human beings, who can give birth to twins relatively frequently: it is therefore relevant that Cardano should insert a comment at this point, explaining that the possession of reason still justifies placing humans higher than these animals, regardless of their lower position according to the criterion of generation.[129]

The hierarchical direction is given by investing biological characteristics with metaphysical meaning.[130] Within the discussion on 'perfection', the fundamental distinction between herbivores and carnivores is crucial: among the various criteria that Cardano uses to pinpoint the meaning of 'perfection' in nature, the nutritional power of meat is an important one because it expresses itself in the higher level of intelligence of carnivores in comparison to herbivores. Again in *De subtilitate*, Cardano explains that 'no animal which does not eat meat has acute senses and is sagacious, apart from the elephant'.[131] It is because of the nature of this particular food — meat — that carnivores are, in a word, smarter than herbivores, and are thus closer to 'perfection'. The role of meat in promoting the intelligence of the eater is twofold: Cardano explains that carnivores are the most acute of all living beings not only because of the properties of meat, but also because they have to hunt for their food, which is not always readily available, and these circumstances sharpen their senses and acuteness:

> Ob id igitur carnivora omnia non vescentibus carne, inter pisces, quadrupedia, et aves, sunt sagaciora duabus causis: prima quod cibum habeant fugacem, nam invenire oportet, inde assequi, cum reliquis invenisse sufficiat. Altera, quod iam cibus ipse ex elementis retusis sit, scilicet caro. Ob id etiam neque ulla caro est calidissima, ut in seminibus plantarum, ac partibus earum frequenter licet conspicere. Itaque homo, qui etiam carnibus vescitur, tum maxime volatilium, potuit esse simul tenuissimae, ac densissimae, calidissimae atque temperatissimae naturae.

> [Therefore all carnivores are smarter than animals which do not eat meat, among fish, quadrupeds and birds, for two reasons: first, because their food is fleeting, since they need to find it and pursue it, while the others only need to find it. The second reason is that the food itself is made of the elements loosened, that is meat. This is why no type of meat is very hot, as is often apparent instead in the case of the seeds of plants, and other parts. Therefore the human being, who indeed eats meat, especially of birds, could have at the same time the thinnest and densest, the hottest and most temperate nature.][132]

Cardano labels as 'smart meat-eaters' carnivores (like lions) and omnivores (like humans); he thus treats the herbivores as less smart than those animals which in one form or another do include meat in their diet. But this implies that if humans are to be considered clever creatures, and in fact the cleverest of all, they must belong by nature to the group of those animals which consume meat, which surpass (almost) all herbivores in shrewdness. Even if the human being, unlike carnivores among animals, does not eat exclusively meat but is rather an omnivore like hens, pigs, and monkeys, meat-eating appears to be essential for medical reasons (obtaining a perfectly tempered nature), as well as for metaphysical ones (the connection between intelligence and perfection). From this perspective the human being must have a stronger connection with carnivores than with herbivores: 'Indeed those which eat meat are closer to the human being with regard to sensation than those which eat plants, like dogs, foxes, monkeys, cats, lions, dolphins, bears, eagles'.[133]

The implication of interpreting dietary differences in terms of a scale of intelligence and perfection is that the world appears as hierarchically ordered, with carnivores at the very top. Nevertheless, Cardano's statement regarding the necessary co-presence of herbivores and carnivores on the earth also reflects his view that nature is a complex plurality which cannot be reduced to a simple teleology. It is for the benefit of the preservation of the whole, rather than a single part, that nature has implanted in herbivores and carnivores a taste for a specific type of food — plants and meat respectively. Cardano even goes on to state that the foods to which an animal is attracted are those that are suitable for the preservation of the animal's health. It is therefore perfectly natural that a carnivore should turn to meat and herbivores to plants, but this natural tendency also reinforces the theory that carnivores are by nature smart and alert, unlike herbivores.[134] The human being, who is an omnivore for Cardano, is of course a more complicated case: as Cardano's own autobiography shows, humans need to control carefully their food intake both in terms of quantity and of quality, choosing between a broad variety of options. The question of whether the human being resembles, or should aim to resemble, more herbivores or carnivores, is thus a relevant one in this context. Unlike both groups of animals, humans feel no innate inclination towards eating one type of food only, and can thus choose what to eat, aware that 'food can change humans in every nature': through diet, human beings establish their relation to the other animals and affirm their metaphysical status within the creation.[135]

In *Hyperchen* [Being] Cardano sketches a simple scheme: plants are nourished by elements, animals either by plants or by other animals. When it comes to humans, Cardano does not declare directly which is their appropriate food, but rather establishes a parallel between daemonic possessions of humans and meat-eating. Just as a human can become the prey of daemons, so the animals fall prey to humans, who eat them.[136] At this point, Cardano mentions Porphyry's rejection of meat-eating with very colourful language: Porphyry is said to 'deprecate' the eating of flesh, 'which is a certain corruption'; yet, like the daemons, 'we eat the bloody wounds of animals'. Consuming meat and blood is thus acknowledged as disturbing and violent: an act of hunting that results in haunting.[137] Is it necessary to be an aggressive hunter in order to be considered smart, *sagax*? Is the alternative the one between being associated with violent beasts or with slow, and less 'perfect', herbivores?

The theory that carnivores are intelligent is critically discussed also in Book I of *On Abstinence*, where Porphyry recapitulates the arguments of those opposed to vegetarianism, from philosophical schools to the opinions of the 'ordinary man of the people'.[138] Here Porphyry mentions the 'commonplace' that 'flesh-eating animals are more intelligent than the others: they are hunters, and have this skill with which they get a living and acquire strength and fighting spirit, like lions and wolves'. This would suggest that 'meat-eating does not damage either the soul or the body', highlighting once again the crucial link between the two as they are influenced by diet.[139]

But Porphyry had the theoretical tools to dismiss this theory in the form of two main tenets in *On Abstinence*: that vegetarianism is the diet appropriate specifically to the philosopher, not to any human being in general; and that a vegetable diet might be less nutritious, but it nevertheless provides all the nutrients necessary for preserving good health, unless for the purpose of intense physical work. For Cardano, the picture is more complex, because he considers meat-eating a crucial factor in shaping the scale of intelligence among living beings, and thus it plays a role in nature's striving towards perfection. In Cardano's work, meat becomes a point at which conflicting theories converge: it nourishes thoroughly, yet it can also trigger highly undesirable effects; it expresses a hierarchy in nature in which humans are among the cleverest, yet also the cruellest of animals.

These conflicts did not escape the scrutiny of Cardano's sharpest critic: Julius Caesar Scaliger (1484–1558).[140] In his extensive critical analysis of Cardano's *De subtilitate*, the *Exotericae exercitationes* [Exoteric Exercises] (1557), Scaliger addresses Cardano's interwining of natural philosophical and metaphysical aspects in his treatment of the role and significance of diet, pointing out the problems Cardano left unsolved, especially with regard to the difference between the nature of carnivores and of vegetarians.[141] Cardano's understanding of meat-eating has dietetic and metaphysical implications that, according to Scaliger, were not fully developed in *De subtilitate*. This is thus what Scaliger pursues in his *Exercitationes*, with the intent of showing incongruences and absurdities that derive directly from Cardano's praise of the power of meat in terms of nutrition, and of the smartness of carnivores.[142]

2.6. Meat-eating, Health and Life Extension: Cardano versus Scaliger

In *Exotericae exercitationes* Scaliger points out that the Galenic theory of temperament should have direct repercussions on the lifespan of a creature. According to Galen the reason why pork is supposed to be the best food is that pigs have the best temperament; in turn, the reason for ascribing the best temperament is the similarity of pork to human meat.[143] Apart from the fact that the argument is circular (and that it could also lead to anthropophagy, following in the steps of Girolamo Manfredi), Scaliger notices another problem: having the best temperament should imply that a creature enjoys a long life. Not only is human life shorter than many other animals' lives, but there are plants, such as the palm tree, whose lives are very long compared to ours. Should the best temperament therefore be ascribed to plants? Again, if meat-eating ensures the best temperament, why is it that carnivores, and humans especially, do not live longer than they do? This critique is exemplary of Scaliger's reply to Cardano's treatment of the role and choice of food in human life, and of meat-eating particularly: Scaliger's strategy consists in exposing the contradictions in Cardano's statement. He probes and ridicules in particular his opponent's 'optimism' with regard to the nutritional value of meat.

With his comment on the influence of food on the lifespan, Scaliger deliberately touches a nerve in Cardano's argument. Of course life-extension had been a primary goal of much medical literature before Cardano, as demonstrated not least by Ficino's *De vita longa* and its sources. But for Cardano the length of the lifespan plays an even more crucial role, because he integrates discussion of this aspect of the animals' lives in his treatment of 'perfection'.[144] A long life, for Cardano, is desirable because it is an expression of the order of nature, which is an order of increasing perfection. This is why diet is not only the foundation of health, but it also plays a crucial role in Cardano's discussion of the relationship between a creature's lifespan and its position in the structure of the universe.

In *De subtilitate* Cardano adds the following details about the link between lifespan and a creature's perfection: 'Indeed if we consider the length of life, the camel is closer to humans than the dog, for camels sometimes live a hundred years, while the life of the dog ends at the twentieth year. [...] Sometimes camels enjoy music, dogs not at all'.[145] A long life is here coupled with a high refinement of the senses, providing an alternative hierarchy to the one Cardano had sketched using the criterion of sense alertness, according to which meat eaters like dogs, bears or eagles should be considered more perfect than plant-eaters. The other long-lived animal often mentioned by Cardano, the elephant, is also endowed with notable virtues: Cardano names it as example of *prudentia* and even *humanitas*,[146] and groups it with the monkey with regard to its *ingenium*.[147] The criterion of the extension of the lifespan places vegetarian animals — the camel and the elephant — above the carnivorous dog, despite the latter's proverbial *sagacitas* in hunting for prey. In *De uno*, as already mentioned, Cardano had used yet another criterion, pointing out the connection between the number of offspring and an animal's position in the scale of perfection, with the result that two vegetarian animals, the elephant and the donkey, had to be placed above carnivores, competing with the human being for the highest position. Cardano explained this problematic result by claiming that nature generates more humans than donkeys or elephants not only because these animals have a stronger 'life principle' ('vitae principium'), but also because the existence of humans, unlike that of elephants and donkeys, is necessary to the world. Conversely, nature generates few snakes because they endanger the existence of other 'better animals'.[148] Once again, Cardano intersects different kinds of criteria, stemming from a variety of disciplines — the type of food, the length of life, the metaphysical ideas of the perfection and 'necessity' of the creatures — but always following the idea that nature adapts the needs of all creatures in order to obtain the best possible balance of the whole.

This shows that for Cardano the medical question of how to extend the lifespan cannot be separated from the metaphysical one as to why it should be desirable to do so. But Scaliger notices a conflict in Cardano's answers to these two questions: the medical reflection leads Cardano to praise meat, and yet the metaphysical analysis reveals that vegetarian animals are the longest lived. The latter fact is crucial because the length of the lifespan is directly connected to the position assigned to a creature in the order of the universe. Scaliger thus emphasizes that, despite the human-pig proximity, it is vegetarian animals (the donkey and the elephant), which threaten to destroy completely Cardano's theory of nutrition as an explanation for the ontological order of nature. The elephant lives longer than the pig, and longer than humans, so it should have an excellent temperament, because having an excellent temperament is the foundation for a long lifespan.[149] If food is instrumental in obtaining this, then the elephant must have derived its temperate nature from plants, rather than meat. While Cardano had underlined the proximity of humans to the meat-eaters, and had placed them in the group of omnivores together with the pig, the hen, and the monkey, Scaliger ironically overturns it by claiming that the elephant and the monkey are the animals closest to humans in terms of intelligence, and that neither of them is by nature carnivorous. On the other hand, animals such as midges and fleas should be considered as those most richly endowed with intelligence and thus closest to the human being, since they feed on the purest substance, blood.[150]

As is often the case with Scaliger's critiques, they display and elaborate problems and contradictions which Cardano himself had noticed. In the commentary on Hippocrates's *De aere, aquis, et locis* [On Air, Waters, and Places], Cardano had recognized that elephants, which only consume water and vegetables and do not eat meat, live considerably longer than humans, attaining an age as advanced as two hundred years. Food and drink are necessary to sustain life, but to achieve a long life 'bread and water' are the only requisites: here, Cardano does not mention meat.[151] In *De sanitate tuenda* [On Preserving One's Health], he points out that meat-eating can make an animal's life short, with all the metaphysical consequences this implies. Yet, he presents this as a puzzle: if it is true that meat shortens the life-span, but also that weaker foods such as vegetables, as Hippocrates had stated, are not conducive to a long life either, then it seems that what is left is the use of fruits, seeds, and twigs only, 'and indeed elephants, camels, and deer live on such foods and their lives are longer and healthier and their habits are also pleasing'.[152] On the theory that consuming meat might shorten a creature's life, Cardano mentions here two sources: Porphyry and Plutarch, 'two most skilful philosophers', who wrote 'works on not eating animals', since 'no animal which eats meat has a long life'.[153] The reference to Porphyry echoes Ficino's similar recourse to the same philosopher in *De vita*.

Cardano was thus aware of conflicting evidence with regard to the link between meat-eating and life expectation. Yet Scaliger, in the *exercitatio* dedicated to the problem 'whether the human being be warm in the highest degree', opens the discussion with the passage from *De subtilitate* in which Cardano had claimed that 'the human being, who indeed eats meat, especially of birds, could have at the same time the thinnest and densest, the hottest and most temperate nature'.[154] Scaliger strongly emphasizes the theory that humans are dependent on the consumption of meat, bringing all the consequences of this view to their extremes. He proceeds to show that meat can be held responsible for the beastly behaviour of humans, rather than for their cleverness. He thus attacks the main tenet of Cardano's claim about the benefits of meat, namely the link between meat-eating and the intelligence ('sagacitas') of a creature. First of all, Scaliger asks whether Cardano is justified in claiming that meat is responsible for the uniqueness of human nature: all of the characteristics that Cardano attributes to humans are supposedly derived from meat-eating, and thus meat has to be considered at once the thinnest and densest, the hottest and most temperate food. Yet, meat is not the thinnest aliment, and 'the human who eats meat is not more subtle [*tenuior*] than the one who eats milk and bread with honey'.[155] Scaliger makes full display of his rhetorical skills by overturning Cardano's claim that carnivores are cleverer because they have to hunt for their food: according to Scaliger those who eat roots should be regarded as the smartest of all animals, since their sense of smell is so strong that they can sniff the presence of food through a thick substance, namely soil, rather than a thin one, such as air, as is the case with carnivores following the traces of their prey in water or on the wind. Applying Cardano's own principles, Scaliger comes to the conclusion that moles and worms should be considered to be the animals most endowed with *sagacitas*, not carnivores such as the dog, traditionally the main example of sagacious behaviour.[156]

Following Cardano's approach, Scaliger then presents his own interpretation of how meat nourishes in contrast to plants, and how this affects the intelligence of creatures, and of humans in particular: 'Meat is indeed thick, and nourishes thickly. Even if herbs are thicker, nevertheless the aliment is constituted by their most subtle parts'.[157] Scaliger thus argues that plant food nourishes better than meat, and he stresses that it is in all respects better to be grouped with herbivores rather than with carnivores. The animals which are closest to humans, such as the elephant or the horse, actually feed on plants.[158]

By demolishing step-by-step all the positive effects that Cardano had attributed to meat-eating, Scaliger intends to show that there is a gap between theory (meat is good, and the more similar it is to body of the eater, the better) and practice (meat is difficult to digest, and does not necessarily promote intelligence, either in humans or in animals). Therefore Cardano's theory is not sound, and it is a subtle move on Scaliger's part to show that the crux of the problem does not really consist in justifying the behaviour of the meat-eaters, so much as explaining why plants nourish so well, if they are distant from us, and why vegetarian creatures do not conform to the pattern of a certain slowness and dullness.

Once again, Cardano had himself posed the same question. In the commentary to Hippocrates's *De alimento* Cardano had this objection in mind when he asked: 'how are the human being and the ox nourished by plants?' The fact that the principle of similarity creates difficulty in assessing the nutritional role of plants is shown by the following comment: 'the ox is better nourished by plants than by flesh, and yet flesh is more similar [to it]'. The same is true of the human being, who is better nourished by the flesh of a chicken than by that of the dog, and yet the latter is closer to him than the former. These examples prove that things that are very different from one's body, such as lettuce for an animal, can provide better nutriment that what is very similar.[159]

A possible key to this dilemma is offered to Cardano by Antonio Fracanziano, a colleague at Bologna and author of a commentary on Hippocrates's *De alimento*. Fracanziano states that the aim of nutrition is the conversion of the food into the substance of the eater.[160] Cardano remarks that according to Fracanziano food and eater can thus be similar in quality, and yet contrary in substance.[161] Cardano's own view, however, is much more complex. Cardano acknowledges the transient and mysterious nature of food, which makes it possible for an apple to turn into the flesh of the human who eats it, thus problematizing the Hippocratic guiding principle of similarity. But he also clearly recognizes the problem caused by the intelligence of certain vegetarian animals, and their proximity to humans. But despite having thus elaborated Hippocrates's apparently simple principle of likeness, Cardano inclines to the idea that the similar (even if not exactly identical) nourishes better than the dissimilar. To put it in simple terms, flesh nourishes flesh, as Cardano himself stresses in a page of *Contradicentia medicorum* [On the Contradictions of Physicians] in which he discusses the highly nourishing diet of athletes, heavily reliant on meat.[162] Yet it is important to remember that athletes, as Porphyry had already pointed out, have peculiar dietary requirements, and Cardano himself underlines elsewhere that the condition of the athlete is far from natural.[163]

Scaliger had a particular interest in the study of the properties of plants, and therefore it is not surprising that he should emphasize the problematic status of plants as a form of nourishment in Cardano's argumentation, in contrast to the supposed nutritional primacy of meat.[164] Scaliger dedicated an ample commentary to Theophrastus's *De plantis* [On Plants], in which he puts forward the doctrine that nutrition is different for different types of living beings: what is very good for one species of animal might be intolerable for another, or even cause death.[165] All in all, food occupies a liminal place, because the original substance is transformed into a different one, when food is absorbed into a different body. Given this view, is it still possible to compare different classes of beings (animals, plants, human animals), as Cardano had done, using details about their respective diets to draw conclusions about characteristics such as intelligence? Scaliger uses the example of specific plants, such as the palm tree, to undermine the hierarchy constructed by Cardano on the basis of food: if nobility depends on the lifespan, then the palm tree must be considered one of the noblest life-forms of all.[166]

Ultimately, Scaliger means to show that plants unsettle Cardano's hierarchy both as long-lived creatures and as suitable food. Scaliger highlights how nutritious plants are, arguing that they promote all the qualities that Cardano instead believes to be provided by meat. He ironizes Cardano's view that the best food is not meat, pointing out that in *De subtilitate* Cardano had actually encouraged the consumption of this aliment. In Book 2 of *De subtilitate*, which deals with the basis of nature — the elements — Cardano had stated that cooking meat diminishes its nutritional properties, to the extent that eating raw flesh would be advantageous in extending the lifespan:

> Miscet autem ignis corpora, sed tamen substantias ipsas dividit, ac separat. Propterea panis igne conficitur, caro vero corrumpitur: verum quia usus non admittit, ut carnes crudas edamus, igne eas coquimus. Quod si carnes et ova cruda comedere consuetum esset, ad vitae diuturnitatem non parum conduceret. Verum quia haec edere haud licet, quae cruda possunt, lac, mel, oleum, butyrum, saccarum, olera plaeraque tenuioris substantiae, si edantur, utiliora erunt tam vitae quam valetudini.

> [Fire mixes bodies, but nevertheless it divides the same substances. Therefore bread is baked by fire, meat is certainly corrupted by it. In truth, we cook meat with fire because custom does not allow us to eat it raw. If it were common to

eat meat and eggs raw, this would be a remarkable contribution to a long life. But since it is not permissible to eat it [raw], those things which can be eaten raw, i.e. milk, honey, oil, butter, sugar, and many vegetables of finer substance, will be more useful to life as well as to health, if eaten.][167]

Cardano points out a clash: the most nutritious aliment is also that towards which humans have a natural disgust — raw meat. Dietary theory and practice thus diverge, and Scaliger is quick to point out this incongruence.

To be sure, in praising the benefits of raw meat, Cardano was following a long-standing tradition, which maintained the principle of similarity between food and eater. Girolamo Manfredi — who, as we saw, went so far as to state that human meat should be the ideal food for humans — had explained that raw or undercooked meat is more nutritious than properly cooked meat: the reason is that the process of cooking dissipates what Manfredi calls 'humido substantiale' or 'humido radicale substantifico', or what had traditionally been called 'radical humidity', the original moisture of a creature, responsible for the continuation of its life.[168] As Chiara Crisciani has explained, the medical notion of essential, or radical, humidity implies that the preservation of a creature's humidity is key to extending the lifespan.[169] In order to live a long life, humans would need to integrate their own original moisture with that of the foods ingested. Thus, the advantage of eating raw meat would consist in the fact that this food is supposed to be very humid, and thus best suited for replenishing the eater's own humidity. The more the meat is cooked, the more the humidity is lost, yet the more digestible it becomes, as Manfredi had pointed out.[170]

Cardano was strongly aware that his stomach would not tolerate foods that are difficult to digest. He thus faced an impasse regarding the advantages and disadvantages of eating meat, and raw meat in particular. This unresolved conflict does not escape the attentive analysis of Scaliger, who views the cooking process as a kind of necessary maturation of the food itself, similarly to what happens with fruit. Not only should cooking meat not be considered detrimental, but for Scaliger it can even be beneficial: 'cooking is advantageous. It is almost a process of ripening'.[171]

The main issues at stake, however, are the link between meat-eating, gaining health and a long life, and the hierarchy of creatures according to their diets. Scaliger pinpoints Cardano's indecision with regard to the full spectrum of implications involved in the choice between a vegetable diet and one that includes meat: if we look at examples in the animal world, we notice that vegetarian animals are less violent and live longer, but are less alert and active; furthermore, meat should be the best source of nourishment for the human body, because it penetrates deeply, yet this theory fails to explain why plants can nourish as well as they do, given that this contradicts the theory that like nourishes like. Scaliger is alert to the fact that Cardano's comparisons between carnivores and vegetarians imply deciding which animals should be treated as role models for human behaviour: do humans prefer to associate themselves with the meat-eaters or with the vegetarians? Thus Scaliger reveals what he believes to be the consequences of Cardano's (theoretical) fascination with raw meat: 'troglodytes eat raw meat [...]. You are welcome to imitate them'.[172]

But Cardano was at least equally fascinated by the vegetable diet and by the examples of vegetarian creatures he describes almost as virtuous examples: animals such as the camel and the elephant, meek, long-lived, and of refined disposition. It is therefore not surprising to find a firm statement about the undeniable benefits of the vegetarian diet in the proem to Cardano's *De sanitate tuenda*: 'In the following we will teach that a long-lasting life does not fit [with the consumption of] meat, nor eggs, nor wine [...] but rather with the fruits of the earth, such as bread, almonds, pine-nuts, chestnuts, sugary water'.[173] This appears to be a simple, frugal diet that we would now call 'vegan', as it does not include any animal products, but rather consists of vegetables, nuts, and grains.

Referring to this passage, Siraisi pointed out that it reveals unresolved contradictions in Cardano's work with regard to diet. He seems to remain undecided whether there even exists such a thing as the 'best diet' for humans, or if the choice of diet always depends on an individual's constitution, for instance a certain fragility of the stomach, and especially on the presence of certain diseases (as he argues in the above-mentioned *consilia*).[174] The question arises whether, in spite of divergent recommendations for the treatment of various diseases, one can still recognize some common traits of what makes a good diet for a long life. The opposition between vegetarianism and carnivorousness also appears to be such an unresolved contradiction for Cardano: he contrasts reflections on the advantages of vegetarianism for a long life with medical advice on the best foods to be prescribed in each individual case.[175] Scaliger's critique exploits precisely these frictions, as he aims to show that Cardano's position is untenable and intrinsically contradictory. Yet, reasoning through oppositions and avoiding a clear-cut solution is part of Cardano's own strategy for approaching the issue of choosing between a vegetarian and a carnivorous diet. This is evident also in the stylistic variety of the texts in which he addresses the problem: from medical *consilia* and treatises, to a major work on the structure of the universe (*De subtilitate*), from his autobiography (*De vita propria*) to fictional dialogues (*Theonoston*, especially Book 2). The latter in particular can be read as an attempt to employ the plurality of voices and ironic detachment of the dialogue in order to show that choosing between vegetarianism and carnivorism implies much more than selecting the best food for the body. It is not a matter of imitating troglodytes, or of associating oneself with dull vegetarian animals: rather, this is a choice that goes to the heart of how to understand the human position in the order of being. Porphyry's *On Abstinence* resurfaces in *Theonoston* once more as a main source of inspiration.

2.7. The Meat of Fish: The Role Model of the Hermit in Cardano's *Theonoston*

The second book of *Theonoston*, entitled *De vita producenda* [On Promoting Life], stages a discussion between the hermit ('eremita'), the citizen ('civis'), and the philosopher ('philosophus') on the question of how to extend the lifespan. The prevailing voice is that of the hermit, who functions at least partially as Cardano's alter ego; but the device of the dialogue allows Cardano to create a space of genuine interaction between different approaches, in which irony also has a key role to play. Unlike Cardano himself, the main character in *Theonoston* repeatedly confesses that he is not a physician ('Medicus non sum'): he is only an hermit with some medical knowledge, who before entering the hermitage had specialized in the treatment of gout.[176] Upon receiving the visit of the citizen and the philosopher, the hermit engages in a discussion with them about the best ways to promote one's health and chances of longevity. The diet followed by the hermit seems to be very successful, since he enjoys a long life, as did his previous *socius* at the hermitage. In seeking the reasons for this success, the emphasis is on the connection of care for the body with care for the soul. The hermit serves as an exemplar, as long life and good health are key to his 'beate vivere'.[177]

Written around the end of the 1550s and the beginning of the 1560s, *Theonoston* return to matters that Cardano had already explored in *De subtilitate*, and especially the link between the position of creatures in the universe and their diet. *Theonoston* is important in bringing to the fore the fundamental intertwining of medicine and metaphysics in Cardano's discussion of vegetarianism: the dialogue makes clear that this diet is crucial as a human choice to support long-lasting health. Unlike other characteristics discussed earlier, such as the number of offspring in *De uno*, diet can be subjected to scrutiny and modification, as Cardano's own attempts, recorded in the autobiography, testify.[178]

Furthermore, *Theonoston* uses the form of the dialogue in order to show how to deal with the varied philosophical and medical sources on diet, including Porphyry, and especially how to choose in case of conflicting evidence. Ancient medical sources are mentioned (especially Galen and Hippocrates), but the hermit and his interlocutors are also familiar with more recent literature on diet. They discuss Cardano's own *De sanitate tuenda*, but the main publication under examination is the then new and controversial book by Alvise Cornaro (*c.* 1484–1567), *Della vita sobria* [On the Sober Life], first published in 1558,[179] which according to Cardano was in everyone's hands.[180] Cornaro had recommended an approach based on the strict monitoring of the quantity of food intake, rather than on the choice of different kinds of food. Contrary to Cardano's suggestion in the proem to *De sanitate tuenda* that the quality of food, and especially a vegetable diet, would be the best choice to prolong life, Cornaro had instead proposed that a variety of foods should be consumed, but in very small quantities. In other words, Cornaro had chosen the path of moderation, which had appealed to Cardano as well, at least during some phases of his life.[181]

The hermit in *Theonoston*, on the other hand, attributes his success in maintaining health and promoting long life to specific, qualitative dietetic choices. The first question which is asked in the dialogue regards the various elements that influence longevity: climate, for instance, but also detachment from human society (which was presented favourably in the first book of *Theonoston*), and diet. Cardano lets the hermit cautiously remark that, as Galen had already said, it is easy to make life shorter but not longer.[182] It is possible that all medical strategies might prove ineffective, while there are people who enjoy a long life without even striving for it. The question of 'how to prolong life' is thus immediately presented as a difficult one to answer. But of all the aspects that potentially influence longevity, the hermit shows a relative optimism with regard to one only: food. Accordingly, he provides great detail about his own diet, and that of the *socius* with whom he initially shared life in the hermitage. It emerges that if it is possible to do anything to achieve the prolongation of life, this must in the first instance involve controlling the intake of food.

The approach to the discussion of diet in this text is remarkably holistic: it involves strictly medical considerations, but also broader elements regarding the role of food in human society. At the end of the first book of *Theonoston*, dedicated to the topic of *tranquillitas*, the hermit explains that he found this peaceful state of mind in the solitude of the hermitage, away from society, surrounded only by animals. He asserts that the 'homo tranquillus', the calm man, 'does not mistreat docile animals' such as deer, rabbits, or the birds that fly over the hermit's table.[183] The hermit explains that:

> Hominem enim tranquillum etiam animalia mansueta amant et agnoscunt. Quo circa ex ea die qua hunc eremum ingressus sum, carnem nullam spirantis animalis edi. Nam? Pisces minus nobis natura coniuncti sunt, neque illos miseret nostri, laudoque Plutarchum, Porphyriumque qui de hac materia libros luculentos scripserint.[184]

> [Docile animals love and recognize the quiet man. For this reason, from the day I entered the hermitage I have not eaten any meat of breathing animals. For fish is less connected to us with regard to nature, nor do we have compassion for it. And I praise Plutarch and Porphyry, who wrote splendid books on this topic.]

The discussion of how to live a quiet, happy life, informed by Porphyry's theory, leads to the very practical consideration of diet. The choice of food, it seems, is not of secondary importance for anyone who wants to achieve this blissful condition, and the hermit discloses the details of his own choice. In the first instance, the reason he gives for this narrowing of his diet is ethical rather than medical: he has come to the conclusion that the meek animals are his daily companions. He thus feels a bond with them, and that is why he refuses to hurt them.

This explanation reflects an underlying understanding of nature as a system of relationships among creatures, measured in terms of distance between classes of beings. The specification 'breathing animals' is very important, since it is explained that the hermit eats fish, thus drawing a line between the animals who live on earth or in the air and those who live under water. The fact that they live in a different element, and therefore do not breathe in the same way as animals living on earth, explains why they are treated differently from other animals, which are spared, while fish is hunted and eaten by the hermit: 'Indeed fish is less connected to us with regard to nature, nor do we have compassion for it'. This could be an echo of Plato's statement in *Timaeus* that there is no animal more physically impaired than the fish, because of its unfortunately-shaped body, lacking any limbs: thus the human souls who are guilty of the greatest stupidity and ignorance will face the fate of transmigrating into the body of a fish.[185]

Despite the fact that the hermit cites inspiration from Plutarch and Porphyry, it is noteworthy that his decision to include fish on the menu (thus following not a 'vegetarian' but rather a 'pescatorian' diet) is not supported by arguments in *On Abstinence*.[186] Porphyry had recommended abstinence from all animals, including fish.[187] Instead the hermit justifies eating fish by referring solely to the ontological distance dividing humans from fish; this distance then 'translates' to the ethical level as well, when Cardano lets the hermit state that humans do not feel pity in killing fish. As the development of the dialogue reveals, however, it is fortunate that humans do not feel an affinity with fish, since medically it is an essential food for elderly people.

At first the dialogue focuses more on the quantity of food, rather than on abstention from eating certain creatures on the basis of their closeness to the human being. It is in the former context that the interlocutors discuss Cornaro's suggestion that food intake must be very strictly regulated, and that in general it is advisable to eat very little, and to avoid excesses (fried foods are explicitly condemned).[188] But just how far this *sobrietas* should extend is not an exclusively medical issue: the hermit, for instance, points out that while the abundant food eaten at a *convivium* is to be avoided, eating together (*con-victum*) can still be beneficial and useful, as it encourages wisdom through discussion. Furthermore, food, for the hermit, is connected to enjoyment: good health and long life, to be achieved through careful diet, are ultimately instrumental to making use of the good in life, or in remembering past pleasures and happiness.[189]

But apart from complying with sobriety or moderation, if a general rule must be followed then this is the Hippocratic principle that like nourishes like: in the case of the ageing hermit this means that a dry body requires dry foods, and it is in this context that the importance of fish as a food for the elderly is fully revealed. The *socius* of the hermit lived well beyond one hundred years: 'He used to eat eggs and honey, he soaked bread in a broth of tortoise, and sometimes in fish broth. He also ate fish, but rarely, roasted with honey, which he had in great quantity and produced with great care, and cooked vegetables and sometimes lentils, but well cooked'.[190] The hermit ate similar foods, and also avoided meat.[191]

Drawing directly from Galen's *On the Properties of Foodstuffs*, the hermit claims that rockfish is particularly beneficial, because it is easily concocted and thus produces good humours. A possible point of conflict is to be found in the hermit's explanation of the advantages of fish which breathe, such as dolphins. Fish of this type have much blood in their flesh, and this is what makes them so nourishing: 'thus no fish which does not breathe nourishes well'.[192] It seems that it is the resemblance to meat — an aliment excluded from the hermit's diet — which shows the nutritional value of certain types of fish.

But the real stumbling block is that of explaining why fish is a suitable type of food at all, and even one that could have a beneficial effect on longevity. The ontological distance between the creatures, which is at the basis of the justification for eating meat, works at the same time as a possible impediment from a medical point of view. But why, then, do fish nourish effectively, if they are so different from us? Cardano is well aware of this difficulty. In the commentary on Hippocrates's *De alimento* he writes that fish is easier to digest, and thus ultimately nourishes better than pork. The reason is that the flesh of pigs is very nourishing and needs to be cooked in order to become digestible; yet, this is providential, because pork and human meat taste remarkably similar before cooking.[193]

Indirectly, the proximity of certain types of meat to the human body clearly displays what is at stake medically in the choice of a vegetable versus a meat diet: how does the body need to be nourished in order to be preserved for a long time? Is meat more an advantage or a disadvantage if its nutritional value also makes it a difficult food to digest? But the most difficult question of all is perhaps that of accounting for the plants' good nutritional value, given that they are so distant from us. 'Philosopher' mentions the fact that there are physicians who would say that it is impossible to reach old age on a purely vegetable diet, which would render one 'imbecillis' (feeble in body and mind), for lack of fat and blood.[194] At this point in the dialogue Cardano inserts examples of long-lived people who enjoyed a varied, but not overly strict diet, as opposed to the hermit himself. Ficino and his mother are mentioned: Ficino, it is claimed, reached the age of ninety-six, and his mother the impressive age of one hundred and seventeen. Since it remains unclear from which source Cardano has derived this information, it is possible that there may be some irony in 'extending' Ficino's life-span well beyond the modest age he reached, despite his advice in *De vita longa*: sixty-six years.[195]

Of all the medical and philosophical sources discussed in *Theonoston* only one, apart from the references to Porphyry and Plutarch, briefly mentions the advantages of a vegetarian diet, and that is Cardano's own *De sanitate tuenda*, which indirectly supports the hermit's semi-vegetarian choice. Yet the hermit is a religious figure with a Stoic approach: in his attempt to reach the state of *tranquillitas* through abstinence, he reminds the reader of a long tradition of pursuing moderation while also exchanging meat for fish. At the same time the hermit in *Theonoston* shows that he is aware of the importance of medical knowledge, on the basis that intervening in the health and longevity of the body means dealing on a deeper level with the metaphysical value of the human being. This is why medical theories, for instance with regard to the benefits of meat, may be challenged by reasoning on the position of certain vegetarian animals along the chain of perfection. Yet, for the hermit perfection is not a state, but a process of constant readjustments. In Book I of *Theonoston* the hermit acknowledges that some shortcomings, like idleness ('inertia'), and even gluttony ('gula') and lust ('libido'), can be combined with a certain 'tranquillitas' of the soul.[196] Analogously, the striving for the perfect diet remains in process, too, as Cardano negotiates medical and metaphysical concepts.

It is certainly an ironic touch on Cardano's part that the dialogue is interrupted by food being prepared and served, as the philosopher states: 'having said this, we lay down and had supper'.[197] Through this and other interruptions in the dialogue, Cardano constructs the transition from detailed discussion of medical approaches to diet to the exposition of how the hermit adapts these in practice. But it also connects *Theonoston* with previous discussions on food which used the dialogue form in order to raise issues to which no simple answer can be given: Erasmus's 'A Fish Diet' and the dialogue of the monk and the soldier also end with supper.

Before even commenting on the properties of specific foods, 'Citizen' remarks that the food served by the hermit to his guests tastes good. He thus asks whether the hermit always cooks that way, or if is something special for his guests. The supper at the hermitage is thus enjoyable, but it presumably also followed some of the criteria previously discussed in the text: the episode is framed through this narration as an attempt at combining the medical and philosophical evidence previously examined.

The hermit's diet, at least partially, overlaps with Cardano's own: they both eat grilled fish, and favour cockle and tortoise broth. Certain more general aspects are strikingly similar, too, including the description of animals not only as food but also as companions, posing the ethical problem of whether it is legitimate to eat them. The hermit decided not to eat those animals with which he shared life at the hermitage, including the birds that regularly flew above his table, never actually finding themselves on the table as food. Cardano himself writes in his autobiography that he ended up keeping all animals that were given to him, 'kids, lambs, hares, rabbits, and storks. They litter up the whole house'.[198] In the case of Cardano, however, it seems that at least some of those species of animals were at the same time companions as well as (potential) food.[199]

Nevertheless, the hermit and the hermit's *socius* in *Theonoston* remain a model of how a semi-vegetarian diet can lead to a long life; in turn, the hermit's diet is inspired by religious models and by the reading of the 'classics' on vegetarianism, with *On Abstinence* in the foreground. Rather than directly answering Porphyry's question — can a philosopher be healthy? — Cardano has thus shown that 'health' does not simply mean finding medical evidence for how to care for the body in the best possible way: rather, practically achieving good health is instrumental to the aim of extending the lifespan, thus developing the association with the most perfect creatures in the animal world as well as among humans. Health crystallizes as a complex notion at the crossroads of medicine and metaphysics, also building on the religious legacy of the term 'abstinence', as embodied by the figure of the hermit in *Theonoston*. This complex intertwining of different levels in assessing the benefits and dangers of meat-eating explains why Cardano mentions specific examples, successful or unsuccessful, of how diet influences health, and thus the length of the lifespan, instead of enunciating a set of fixed prescriptions. The comparison of specific dietetic examples, as we will see in the next chapter, had been one of Porphyry's strategies too.

Notes to Chapter 2

1. Galen, *Quod optimus medicus sit quoque philosophus*, in *Opera omnia*, ed. by Karl Gottlob Kühn, 20 vols (Leipzig: Cnobloch, 1821–33; repr. 2011), I, 53–63; *The Best Doctor is Also a Philosopher*, in *Selected Works*, trans. by Peter N. Singer (Oxford & New York: Oxford University Press, 1997), pp. 30–34 (p. 33). See the discussion in Teun Tieleman, 'Galen's Psychology', in *Galien et la philosophie: huit exposés suivis de discussions*, ed. by Jonathan Barnes & Jacques Jouanna (Geneva: Librairie Droz, 2003), pp. 131–61.

2. *OA*, 1.2.2; p. 31.

3. Seneca, Letter 108. Latin edn: *Ad Lucilium Epistulae Morales*, ed. by L. D. Reynolds, 2 vols (Oxford: Oxford University Press, 1965), II, 455; English edn: *Selected Letters*, ed. by Elaine Fantham (Oxford & New York: Oxford University Press, 2010), pp. 233–34.

4. Seneca, *Ad Lucilium Epistulae Morales*, II, 455–56; *Selected Letters*, p. 234.

5. *OA*, 1.52.1; p. 51. As pointed out by Clark, Usener listed this as an Epicurean fragment (cf. Epicurus, *Epicurea*, ed. by Hermann Usener (Leipzig: Teubner, 1887), p. 299 (frag. 464)). There is no indication that Epicurus had chosen a vegetarian rather than simply a frugal diet, so Porphyry gives here a specific inflection to the Epicurean reflection on diet. On Porphyry's view of the Epicurean diet as frugal and mostly plant-based, see *OA*, 1.48.3. See also below, Chapter 4, section 8.

6. Thomas Taylor, 'Introduction', in *Select Works of Porphyry, Containing His Four Books on Abstinence from Animal Food*, trans. by Thomas Taylor (London: Thomas Rodd, 1823), p. xi. On Taylor's complex view on the use of animals see James Vigus, 'Adapting Rights: Thomas Taylor's *A Vindication of the Rights of Brutes*', in *Romantic Adaptations*, ed. by Cian Duffy, Peter Howell, & Caroline Ruddell (Farnham: Ashgate, 2013), pp. 41–56.

7. About the rejection of vegetarianism within Aristotelianism and Stoicism see Haussleiter, *Der Vegetarismus in der Antike*, pp. 233–45 & 245–72.

8. *OA*, 1.15. Porphyry means strength in the sense of robustness (*róme*): see Clark, 'Fattening the Soul', p. 43.

9. Catherine Osborne, *Dumb Beasts and Dead Philosophers: Humanity and the Humane in Ancient Philosophy and Literature* (Oxford & New York: Oxford University Press, 2007), p. 232.

10. Diogenes Laertius (*Lives of Eminent Philosophers*, VIII.1), however, considers the possibility that there might have been more than one person named 'Pythagoras': one who recommended meat for athletes, and one who instead encouraged abstinence from meat-eating. On the conflicting reports of Pythagoras's involvement in animal sacrifice see above, Chapter 1, section 1. On Porphyry's interpretation of the diet of the Pythagoreans, and on why Pythagoras did not straightforwardly command vegetarianism see Giuseppe Girgenti's introduction in Porphyry, *Vita di Pitagora*, ed. by Angelo R. Sodano & Giuseppe Girgenti (Milan: Rusconi, 1998), p. 33.

11. This is the interpretation of Gillian Clark, 'Introduction', p. 7.

12. See Porphyry, *Life of Plotinus*, II.3–7; and Clark, 'Philosophic Lives and the Philosophic Life', p. 37.

13. Yet, vegetarianism does not appear to have been generally practiced within Platonism (Plotinus being a major example): Porphyry's stance with regard to the diet appropriate to a (Platonic) philosopher appears to be an exception. But it has been argued that Plato had suggested adopting a vegetarian diet in the *Republic* (see for instance 372a-d; and for a contemporary interpretation see Corinne M. Painter, 'The Vegetarian Polis: Just Diet in Plato's Republic and in Ours', *Journal of Animal Ethics*, 3.2 (2013), 121–32).

14. Dietary regulation is a crucial aspect of the life of ancient philosophers, as discussed by Pierre Hadot, *La Philosophie comme manière de vivre: entretiens avec Jeannie Carlier et Arnold I. Davidson* (Paris: Albin Michel, 2001).

15. For an introduction to debates on health in the Renaissance, focusing especially on the terminology employed, see Guido Giglioni, 'Health in the Renaissance', in *Health: A History*, ed. by Peter Adamson (Oxford & New York: Oxford University Press, 2019), pp. 141–73.

16. See Clark's introduction to Iamblichus, *The Pythagorean Life*, p. xiii. On the differences between Porphyrian and Christian types of asceticism — the former grants food a much more important role than the latter, which also involves other aspects, such as sexuality — see Clark, 'Fattening the Soul', pp. 42 & 46.

17. On Ficino's influence on Cardano with regard to this specific topic, see Nancy Siraisi, *The Clock and the Mirror: Girolamo Cardano and Renaissance Medicine* (Princeton: Princeton University Press, 1997), p. 78.

18. Durling, 'A Chronological Census of Renaissance Editions and Translation of Galen', p. 236.

19. See Siraisi, *The Clock and the Mirror*, p. 256.

20. Galen, *De alimentorum facultatibus*, III.1, in *Opera omnia*, VI, 660; *On the Properties of Foodstuffs*, ed. and trans. by Owen Powell (Cambridge: Cambridge University Press, 2003), p. 114.

21. Galen, *De alimentorum facultatibus*, pp. 660–61; *On the Properties of Foodstuffs*, pp. 114–15.

22. Galen, *De alimentorum facultatibus*, pp. 661; *On the Properties of Foodstuffs*, p. 115: 'Pork is the most nutritious of all foods, and athletes provide a very visible test for this. For when, after identical exercises, they take the same amount of a different food on one day, straightaway on the following day they appear nor only weaker but also obviously less well fed'.

23. The treatise, originally untitled, was called *De esu carnium* upon publication. See the general introduction to this text in Arnau de Villanova, *De esu carnium*, ed. by Dianne M. Bazell, in *Opera medica omnia*, 16 vols (Granada & Barcelona: Publicacions de la Universitat de Barcelona, 1975–), XI (1999), 145–48.

24. Guigues Ier Prieur de Chartreuse, *Coutumes de Chartreuse, introduction, texte critique, traduction et notes par un Chartreux* (Paris: Éditions du Cerf, 1984), p. 234 (Chapter 33: 'De ieiuniis atque cibis'). The *Consuetudines Cartusiae*, written between 1121 and 1128, were first published in 1510 (see ibid., p. 125).

25. James Hogg, 'Carthusian Abstinence', in *Analecta cartusiana: Spiritualität heute und gestern*, 35.14, ed. by James Hogg (New York & Salzburg: Edwin Mellen & Institut für Anglistik und Amerikanistik, 1991), pp. 5–15 (p. 5).

26. David Grumett and Rachel Muers, *Theology on the Menu: Asceticism, Meat and Christian Diet* (Abingdon & New York: Routledge, 2010), esp. p. 99. The foundational text accusing those who abstain from meat completely of heresy is Tertullian's *On Fasting*. The Bogomiles, a heretical group which had a direct influence on Catharism, excluded from their diet all foods which derive (even if indirectly) from a sexual act: not just meat, therefore, but also cheese and eggs (see Francesco Zambon's introduction to *La cena segreta: trattati e rituali catari* (Milan: Adelphi, 1997), p. 37).

27. Bazell, in Arnau de Villanova, *De esu carnium*, pp. 151–52.

28. Ibid., pp. 146 & 149.

29. Ibid., pp. 118–19: 'Sed tamen ad eam [*virtutem*] tunc confortandam et reparandam, non est necessarium ut cibus carnium magis exhibeatur quam alterius alimenti. Quod patet ex eo quod dictum est, scilicet quod deficienti propter hanc causam debetur alimentum velocissime reparans et habundanter virtutem deficientem. Talia vero testantur medici esse vinum et vitella ovorum mediocriter mollia, sic probantes quia nichil habundanter et velocissime potest virtutem vitalem reparare in corde et per consequens in arteriis cunctorum membrorum, nisi potens fuerit velocissime generare spiritus copiosos in membris predictis'; and pp. 121–22: 'Unde patet quod non est necessarium carnes administrare languentibus ad extirpandum / vite periculum, quapropter oppositum asserens profanam invenit novitatem'.

30. On Augustine see above, Chapter 1, section 5.

31. Jean Charlier de Gerson, *De non esu carnium apud Carthusienses*, in *Œuvres complètes*, ed. by Palémon Glorieux, 5 vols (Paris & New York: Desclée, 1960–73), III, 77–95 (see also *Opera omnia*, 5 vols in 4 (Antwerp: Sumptibus Societatis, 1706), II, 715–30). See Palémon Glorieux, 'Gerson et les chartreux', *Recherches de théologie ancienne et médiévale*, 28 (1961), 115–53. Cf. Jole Agrimi, *Poteri carismatici e informali: chiesa e società medioevale* (Palermo: Sellerio, 1992), p. 271; Joseph Ziegler, *Medicine and Religion c. 1300: The Case of Arnau de Vilanova* (Oxford: Clarendon Press, 1998), p. 162.

32. Jean de Gerson, *De non esu carnium apud Carthusienses*, in *Opera omnia*, II, 730: 'Haec est laudabilis et ab indiscretione libera sanctorum Patrum abstinentia, quam etsi peccator et saecularis imitari non valeo, aut non satis volo; veneror tamen in aliis, admiror et colo, venerandam insuper colendamque libens denuncio, et libera voce defendo'.

33. Ibid., p. 718: 'Lex talis de nunquam comedendo carnes est huiusmodi, prout experientia longa

dotrix est. Etenim sub hac Lege et secundum eam Religiosi viri, et disciplinati et de salute sua solliciti, vixerunt usque ad senectam bonam et plenam dierum incolumes in anima et corpore, plus quam in locis aliis plurimis, ubi conceditur esus carnium ad saturitatem. Denique constat eos imitatores esse antiquorum Prophetarum, et Eremitarum Eliae et Elizaei, ac Joannis Baptistae, aliorum quoque Sanctorum Patrum, per Aegyptum olim degentium'.

34. Ibid., p. 719.

35. See also Denis L. Drysdall's introduction to the translation of Erasmus's *De esu carnium / On Eating Meat*, in *The Collected Works of Erasmus*, 89 vols (Toronto, Buffalo, & London: University of Toronto Press, 2015), LXXIII (*Controversies*, ed. and trans. by Denis L. Drysdall), xxvi–xxvii. The revised version of *De esu carnium* was published as *Epistola de delectu ciborum, cum scholiis per ipsum autorem recens additis* (Basel: Froben, 1532). See Marcel Gielis, 'Leuven Theologians as Opponents of Erasmus and of Humanistic Theology', in *Biblical Humanism and Scholasticism in the Age of Erasmus*, ed. by Erika Rummel (Leiden: Brill, 2008), pp. 197–214 (p. 212).

36. The literature on (religious) discipline wih regard to food is vast. Massimo Montanari provides a useful frame of reference to understand the meaning of religious abstinence from meat in the Middle Ages (*Alimentazione e cultura nel Medioevo* (Rome & Bari: Laterza, 1988), esp. pp. 41–51). A seminal study about the religious fasting of women in particular is Caroline Walker Bynum, *Holy Feast and Holy Fast: The Religious Significance of Food to Medieval Women* (Berkeley: University of California Press, 1987). Pierre Hadot (*Philosophy as a Way of Life*, p. 128) considers the role of food restriction from the point of view of the training of the philosopher.

37. Erasmus, *Epistola de interdicto esu carnium*, in *ASD*, IX.1, 46; *De esu carnium / On Eating Meat*, p. 97 (translation modified).

38. *ASD*, I.3, 502; 'A Fish Diet', in *The Collected Works of Erasmus*, XL (*Colloquies*, trans. and annotated by Craig R. Thompson), 684.

39. Glaucoplutus represents Ulrich Zasius, to whom Erasmus wrote on 23 March 1523. The letter, in which Erasmus explains once more his refusal of the roast chicken, was published for the first time in 1574 with the title *Epistola de delectu ciborum in ieiuniis ab ecclesia catholica excusa*: in *The Collected Works of Erasmus*, IX (*The Correspondence of Erasmus: Letters 1252 to 1355*, trans. by R. A. B. Mynors, annotated by James M. Estes), 441: 'A light-winged breath of rumour (false, as I suppose) has reached us here to the effect that you have been taken to court and obliged yourself on the charge that you had procured a roast chicken for my humble self'.

40. See also Erasmus's letter to Zasius (ibid., p. 442), where Erasmus justifies his choice of eggs over the offer of the roast chicken with his desire to leave quickly because of his health problems, which he attributes to 'stones'.

41. On the health risks connected with Lent, and the consumption of fish and vegetables in particular, see David Gentilcore, *Food and Health in Early Modern Europe: Diet, Medicine and Society, 1450–1800* (London & New York: Bloomsbury, 2016), p. 107.

42. *ASD*, I.3, 513; 'A Fish Diet', p. 705.

43. *ASD*, IX.1, 46–47; *On the Eating of Meat*, p. 98.

44. On the discipline of the Carthusians see Hogg, 'Carthusian Abstinence', p. 11.

45. *OG*, VI, 59; *The Best Doctor is Also a Philosopher*, p. 33.

46. Cf. Arnau de Villanova, *De esu carnium*, p. 193.

47. Massimo Montanari, *The Culture of Food*, trans. by Carl Ipsen (Oxford: Blackwell, 1994), p. 78: 'Ecclesiastical rules obliged this "carnivorous" society [...] to abstain from meat for between 140 and 160 days per year. This renunciation which [...] indirectly confirmed the centrality of meat to the diet of the period, had become widespread in Christian culture over the preceding centuries. [...] Abstinence from meat, in fact, figured as a central theme of moral treatises and penitential rule from the first centuries of Christianity. The resulting need for alternative foods led to the great (economic and cultural) success of "substitutes" such as legumes, cheese, eggs and fish'.

48. *ASD*, I.3, 496; 'A Fish Diet', p. 678.

49. For a medical discussion of swapping fish for meat during Lent see Cavallo & Storey, *Healthy Living in Late Renaissance Italy*, p. 215.

50. *ASD*, I.3, 498; 'A Fish Diet', p. 678. On the health hazard connected with slaughtering animals

see John Henderson, 'Public Health, Pollution and the Problem of Waste Disposal in Early Modern Tuscany', in *Interazioni fra economia e ambiente biologico nell'europa preindustriale secc. XIII–XVIII*, ed. by Simonetta Cavaciocchi (Atti della Quarantunesima Settimana di Studi 26–30 aprile 2009) (Florence: Firenze University Press, 2010), pp. 373–82, esp. p. 376: '[a butcher's shop] in itself would have been seen as creating pollution through the release of the corrupt vapours contained in bodies of animals when they were slaughtered'. With special regard to the case of Florence, see Henderson's discussion of the legislation on butchering (p. 380). I consider the place of slaughterhouses in Renaissance narratives of ideal cities in 'Real Animals in Ideal Cities'.

51. *ASD*, 1.3, 499; 'A Fish Diet', p. 680.
52. Galen, *De alimentorum facultatibus*, p. 726 (Book III.29); *On the Properties of Foodstuffs*, p. 142.
53. Hogg, 'Carthusian Abstinence', p. 5.
54. *ASD*, 1.3, 316; 'The Soldier and the Carthusian', in *The Collected Works of Erasmus*, XXXIX (*Colloquies*, trans. and annotated by Craig R. Thompson), 332.
55. Hippocrates, *On Ancient Medicine*, ed. by Mark J. Schiefsky (Leiden: Brill, 2005), esp. pp. 29 & 234. See also Jacques Jouanna, 'Dietetics in Hippocratic Medicine: Definition, Main Problems, Discussion', in his *Greek Medicine from Hippocrates to Galen: Selected Papers* (Leiden: Brill, 2012), pp. 137–53; on the dietetic approach presented in ancient medicine see ibid., p. 146: 'What we call digestion and assimilation is seen by this medical writer as a struggle of human nature, which must overcome the food in order to appropriate it'.
56. See *ASD*, 1.3, 315; 'The Soldier and the Carthusian', p. 330: 'SOLDIER: [...] I marvel you're not turned into a fish. CARTHUSIAN: If men turned into everything they ate, your fondness for pork would have made you a pig long ago'. I discuss the topic of the transformations triggered by food in 'Animals in the Renaissance: You Eat What You Are', in *Animals: A History*, ed. by Peter Adamson & G. Fay Edwards (Oxford & New York: Oxford University Press), pp. 163–86 & 371–76.
57. *ASD*, 1.3, 498; 'A Fish Diet', p. 680.
58. See Ficino, *De vita*, 1.3 (*OMF*, I, 496; *Three Books on Life*, p. 112). On the history of the notion of melancholy see especially Raimond Klibanski, Erwin Panofski, and Fritz Saxl, *Saturn and Melancholy: Studies in the History of Natural Philosophy, Religion and Art* (London: Nelson, 1964) (on Ficino see Part III, Chapter 2.2). Ficino also lists celestial factors (especially the influence of Mercury and Saturn), alongside a natural cause, namely the inward concentration stimulated by studying (*De vita*, 1.4). See Pier Luigi Cabras, Donatella Lippi, & Francesca Lovari, *Due millenni di melancholia: una storia della depressione* (Bologna: CLUEB, 2005). For a general introduction to the crystallization of the conception of black bile as a separate humour see Vivian Nutton, *Ancient Medicine* (Abingdon & New York: Routledge, 2004), pp. 83–84. For an overview of how the conception of melancholia evolved see the anthology *The Nature of Melancholy: From Aristotle to Kristeva*, ed. by Jennifer Radden (Oxford & New York: Oxford University Press, 2000).
59. Ficino, *De vita*, 1.1 (*OMF*, I, 495; *Three Books on Life*, p. 111): 'In the first place, as much care as runners habitually take of their legs, athletes of their arms, musicians of their voice, even so it behooves literary scholars to have at least as much concern for their brain and heart, their liver and stomach — and indeed so much more, in proportion as the latter parts are more excellent than are the former and literary scholars use their parts more frequently and for more important things than the former people do theirs').
60. Ficino, *De vita*, 1 .9 (*OMF*, I, 502–03; *Three Books on Life*, p. 133).
61. Robert Burton's voluminous *Anatomy of Melancholy* (1621) devotes a section to the kind of meats to be avoided in order to prevent melancholia, quoting from Galen, but also from Arnau de Villanova and from Ficino. In particular, Burton follows Galen in condemning the consumption of beef: *The Anatomy of Melancholy*, ed. by J. N. Bamborough, 6 vols (Oxford: Clarendon Press, 2000), I, 212.
62. On this edition see Cavallo & Storey, *Healthy Living*, p. 19.
63. Marsilio Ficino, *De le tre vite*, trans. by Lucio Fauno (Venice: Michele Tramezzino, 1548), sig. *iiiir. Tramezzino also dedicated to Domenico Veniero *Opera utilissima di Arnaldo di Villanuova* (Venice, 1549): this is a *liber regiminis sanitatis* ascribed to Maino Maineri, but in fact deriving

from Arnau's writings. Maineri was accused of plagiarism, and the book was already attributed to Arnau in the early sixteenth century (see on this Margherita Palumbo, 'Maineri, Maino', in *Dizionario Biografico degli Italiani*, ed. by Alberto M. Ghisalberti and others, 85 vols (Rome: Istituto della Enciclopedia Italiana, 1960–2016), LXVII (2006), 595–97. In 1549 Tramezzino also published vernacular versions of two Galenic writings: *A che guisa si possano, e conoscere e curare e infermità dell'animo* and *Delli mezzi che si possono tenere per conservarci la sanità*.

64. See Teodoro Katinis, *Medicina e filosofia in Marsilio Ficino: il 'Consilio contro la pestilenza'* (Rome: Edizioni di Storia e Letteratura, 2007), especially pp. 81–83.

65. Ficino, *De vita*, 'Epistola dedicatoria' (*OMF*, I, 493; *Three Books on Life*, p. 103).

66. Ibid., I.26 (*OMF*, I, 508; *Three Books on Life*, pp. 160–61).

67. Ibid., II.4 (*OMF*, I, 511; *Three Books on Life*, pp. 172–73).

68. These rules include eating moderately humid vegetables and fruits, and rarely milk and fish (see Ficino, *De vita*, II.6 (*OMF*, I, 513; *Three Books on Life*, p. 180).

69. Ibid., II.6 (*OMF*, I, 514; *Three Books on Life*, p. 181).

70. Galen, *De alimentorum facultatibus*, p. 663 (Book III.2); *On the Properties of Foodstuffs*, p. 115.

71. *ASD*, I.3, 498; 'A Fish Diet', p. 680.

72. See Antònia Carré and Lluís Cifuentes, 'Girolamo Manfredi's *Il Perché*: I. The *Problemata* and its Medieval Tradition', *Medicina & Storia*, 10.19–20 (2010), 13–38.

73. Girolamo Manfredi, *Liber de homine* (Bologna: Ruggeri & Bertocchi, 1474), unpaginated: 'Perché la carne porcina è molto viscosa e umida. [...] Adonque el porco, perché è di poco exercitio e movimento, ma sta continue nel luto ripossato, imperò è di molta superfluità e sua carne è molto dura da padire, unde genera assai superfluità. Vero è che ha gran convenienza e conformità con la substantia del corpo nostro, e più che ciascuno altro animale fuora che esso huomo. Imperò quando è digesta è di sangue laudabile e buono nutrimento'. In the modern edition (Girolamo Manfredi, *Liber de homine / Il Perché*, ed. by Fabio Foresti, Anna Maria Nada Patrone, & Anna Laura Trombetti Budriesi (Bologna: Luigi Parma, 1988), p. 75), the last part of the final sentence reads differently: 'Imperho quando è digesta e di sangue laudabile è buono nutrimento'. On Manfredi's use of sources and translations in *Il Perché* see David A. Lines, 'When is a Translation not a Translation? Girolamo Manfredi's *De homine* (1474)', *Rivista di storia della filosofia*, 74.2 (2019), 287–307.

74. Manfredi, *Liber de homine* (1474), unpaginated: 'Li homini adunche che faticano hanno bisogno di notrimento grosso che facilmente per la fatica non se rissolva neache se putrefazza. Imperò el cibo leggiero e delicato è contrario a suo exercitio'.

75. Ibid.: 'E non è cosa nè cibo che più sia conforme al nutrimento dell'homo quanto è la carne humana, se non fusse la abhominatione che la natura ha a quella' (see also Manfredi, *Liber de homine / Il Perché* (1988), p. 75). According to Tommaso Duranti, this statement is the most innovative one in the dietetic section of *Il Perché*, which otherwise follows in the steps of Galen and Hippocrates, while also drawing inspiration from the Pseudo-Aristotelian *Problemata*: *Mai sotto Saturno: Girolamo Manfredi, medico e astrologo* (Bologna: Clueb, 2008), pp. 74–75.

76. Ficino, *De vita*, III.1 (*Three Books on Life*, p. 247, translation modified; *OMF*, I, 532: 'Si volueris ut alimentum rapiat prae caeteris formam cerebri tui vel iecoris atque stomachi, simile quantum potes accipe alimentum, id est cerebrum, et iecur, et stomachum animalium ab humana natura non longe distantium').

77. Ibid., II.6 (*Three Books on Life*, p. 181; *OMF*, I, 514: '[Suis carnes et sanguis] [o]ptimae sunt igitur similibus corporibus, ut rusticis et robustis, corpusque multum exercitantibus'). There was a long tradition of using pigs for vivisection precisely because of the physical similarity with humans. A foundational text is Copho's *De anatomia porci*: the opening of the text explains that sectioning animals is essential in order to understand the hidden, internal anatomy of humans, and that pigs are the animals that most closely resemble humans with regard to the internal disposition of the organs, even if the monkey appears more similar from the outside. See *Collectio Salernitana ossia documenti inediti, e trattati di medicina appartenenti alla scuola medica Salernitana*, ed. by Salvatore de Renzi, 5 vols (Naples: Filiatre-Sebezio, 1852–59), II (1853), 385.

78. Galen, *On the Thinning Diet*, in *Selected Works*, pp. 305–24 (p. 315). On this treatise, which was not known in the West before 1840 (and is thus not included in Kühn's standard edition

of Galen's works), see John Wilkins, 'The Contribution of Galen, *De subtiliante diaeta (On the Thinning Diet)*', in *The Unknown Galen*, ed. by Vivian Nutton, supplement 77 of the *Bulletin of the Institute of Classical Studies* (2002), 47–55. According to Wilkins, *De subtiliante diaeta* can be considered a forerunner of *De alimentorum facultatibus*. On the meaning of 'thinning' see Wilkins, 'The Contribution of Galen', p. 51: 'The adverse humours are to be cut or thinned, though it is not clear to what extent it is blood that is to be thinned. [...] What Galen appears to be thinning is phlegm and possibly bile, whether or not in combination is unclear'. Translating 'thinning' as 'slimming' (see Galen, *La dieta dimagrante*, ed. and trans. by Nino Marinone (Turin: Paravia, 1973)) is thus misleading.

79. On this see Juliana Schiesari, *The Gendering of Melancholia: Feminism, Psychoanalysis and the Symbolics of Loss in Renaissance Literature* (Ithaca, NY, & London: Cornell University Press, 1992), p. 113.

80. On the connection between bile and melancholia see Guido Giglioni's useful account of humoural medicine, and of the different types of bile in particular: 'Medicine', in *Brill's Encyclopaedia of the Neo-Latin World*, ed. by Philip Ford, Jan Bloemendal, & Charles E. Fantazzi, 2 vols (Leiden: Brill, 2014), I, 679–90. Further on humours and digestion in Galen see Owsei Temkin, *Galenism: Rise and Decline of a Medical Philosophy* (Ithaca, NY: Cornell University Press, 1973), p. 17. Celsus also discusses foods which make phlegm (*pituita*) thicker (*crassa*): see Celsus, *De la médecine*, ed. by Guy Serbat, 2nd edn (Paris: Les Belles Lettres, 2003), I, Book II.23.

81. Galen, *The Thinning Diet*, pp. 315 & 308.

82. Burton, *Anatomy of Melancholy*, I, 212. Burton repeatedly refers to the doctor Michele Savonarola (1385–1468) and his opinions regarding the properties of foods. On Savonarola see *Michele Savonarola: medicina e cultura di corte*, ed. by Chiara Crisciani & Gabriella Zuccolin (Florence: SISMEL Edizioni del Galluzzo, 2011).

83. Ficino, *De vita*, II.6 (*OMF*, I, 513; *Three Books on Life*, p. 181 (translation modified)).

84. See ibid., II.6 (*OMF*, I, 514; *Three Books on Life*, p. 181: 'meat which is rather moist is not approved as we have said, nor that which is hard or dry as that of hares or beef-cattle that have gotten too old, but a moderate sort of meat is approved, as that of barnyard cocks, capons, peacocks, pheasants, partridges, perhaps even of young doves, especially if domesticated. Such also are young roebucks and bull-calves, yearling wethers and likewise wild boars. Nor do I reject the suckling kid and fresh cheese. I have indeed omitted small birds, for the frequent use of foods which are too fine is suitable only to the stomach which has no tolerance at all for denser food; but a healthier stomach acquires a fleeting smoke or moisture from these foods').

85. This is the diet drafted in Ficino's *Advice Against the Plague* (see Katinis, *Medicina e filosofia in Marsilio Ficino*, p. 186).

86. Ficino, *De vita*, II.15, where Ficino also praises the proverb 'nothing to excess' (*OMF*, I, 529; *Three Books on Life*, p. 213).

87. Marsilio Ficino, *Predicationes*, ed. by Daniele Conti (Turin, Aragno, 2014), p. 13. See also Conti's introduction, p. li.

88. Guido Giglioni attends to all these different layers and aspects of Cardano's work, in 'Girolamo [Geronimo] Cardano', in *The Stanford Encyclopedia of Philosophy*, ed. by Edward N. Zalta, <https://plato.stanford.edu/archives/sum2019/entries/cardano/> [accessed 23 July 2019].

89. On the dates of Cardano's works see Ian Maclean's introduction to Girolamo Cardano, *De libris propriis: The Editions of 1544, 1550, 1557, 1562 with Supplementary Material* (Milan: FrancoAngeli, 2004). The seminal work on Cardano as a philosopher-physician is Siraisi, *The Clock and the Mirror*.

90. Quotations from Cardano's work are taken from *OGC* if not stated otherwise. Here see Cardano, *De rerum varietate*, Chapter 40 (*OGC*, III, 147[b]): 'Ergo in omnem naturam alimenta mutare possunt homines [...]. Itaque diligenter studendum, quo quis alimento utatur'. This comment is prompted by a discussion of the effects of rabies. I analyse this passage further in 'Animals in the Renaissance', p. 177.

91. Cardano, *The Book of My Life*, trans. by Jean Stoner (New York: Dutton, 1930; repr. 2002), p. 21 (*De vita propria liber*, in *OGC*, I, 5[a]: 'Cruditas praeterea et ventriculi imbecillitas').

92. Cardano, *The Book of My Life*, p. 21 (*De vita propria*, p. 5[a]: 'At ab anno lxxii. supra, coepi

cum aliquid plus comederim, aut biberim, vel importune assumpserim, aut quod parum utile ventriculo, laedi').

93. See on this Siraisi, *The Clock and the Mirror*, Chapter 4.

94. Cardano, *The Book of My Life*, p. 39 (*De vita propria*, p. 8[b]: 'in eo instituto a prima aetate mansi, ut vitae consulerem').

95. Cardano, *In librum Hippocratis de alimento commentaria*, Praefatio (*OGC*, VII, 356: 'Liber enim primum est Divini Hippocratis, Argumentum de Alimento ex quo vitam ipsa constare non dubitamus').

96. Cardano, *De vita propria*, p. 6[b]; *The Book of My Life*, p. 28 (translation modified).

97. Cardano, *The Book of My Life*, p. 29 (*De vita propria*, p. 6[b]: 'Astacorum etiam fluvialium usu oblector, quod mater dum essem in alvo tam avide comederit; item chamis atque ostreis. Praeterea libentius et maiore cum utilitate piscibus quam carnibus vescor').

98. Cardano, *De vita propria*, p. 6[b]: 'Piscibus vescor libentius quam carne, modo boni atque recentes'; *The Book of My Life*, p. 29: 'I eat more freely of fish than of meat, but only wholesome fresh fish'.

99. Dianne M. Bazell points to Arnau's strategies for dealing with the same issue in Arnau, *De esu carnium*, p. 160.

100. On the tradition of medical *consilia* see Siraisi, *The Clock and the Mirror*, pp. 202–04, and pp. 207 ff. on Cardano's own *consilia*, which Siraisi describes as being fully conventional in their structure. See also Anthony Grafton and Nancy Siraisi, 'Between the Election and My Hopes: Girolamo Cardano and Medical Astrology', in *Secrets of Nature: Astrology and Alchemy in Early Modern Europe*, ed. by William R. Newman & Anthony Grafton (Cambridge, MA: MIT Press, 2002), pp. 69–113 (esp. pp. 73–92).

101. Cardano, *Consilia medica* (*OGC*, IX, 97[a] (*Consilium* XIX): 'In hoc aegro est maxima imbecillitas ventriculi, ergo minimus cibus dandus est: sed minimus cibus et parum nutrimentum non potest alere corpus, imo nec mediocriter nutriens, ergo necessarius est cibus maximi alimenti, ut quod detrahitur ex quantitate suppleat qualitas').

102. In *De sanitate tuenda*, Cardano criticizes the fact that Galen seems to judge how well a food nourishes merely on the basis of this distinction between thickness and thinness, without explaining how other parameters (such as the rising of bile) come into play. Cardano distinguishes in this text between five types of bad aliment (*OGC*, VI, 80[a]: 'Porro, ut dixi, Galenus malum alimentum putat, quod vel crassissimum est, vel serosum [...]. Putat solum alimentum vel crassum, vel serosum esse. Quid si biliosum sit? [...] Erunt ergo quinque saltem genera mali alimenti, et singula singulis opposita, sed diversa ratione biliosum, quod lento et pituitoso opponitur, serosum quod terreo, et putridum quod optimo sanguini omnino contrarium est').

103. Galen, *De alimentorum facultatibus*, p. 714 (Book III.26): 'Alimentum sane, quod tum ex hoc, tum ex aliis piscibus provenit, sanguinem gignit consistentia tenuiorem, quam quod ex pedestribus animalibus sumitur, adeo ut non affluenter nutriat, et celerius discutiatur'; *On the Properties of Foodstuffs*, p. 137: 'The nutriment from this and the other fish generates blood that is thinner in composition than that from terrestrial animals, so that it does not give abundant nourishment and is quickly dispersed'.

104. Galen, *De alimentorum facultatibus*, p. 714: 'Laudissimus vero est qui inter hos exacte est medius'; *On the Properties of Foodstuffs*, p. 137: 'The best blood is that produced precisely between these extremes'.

105. Cardano, *Consilia*, p. 97[a] (*Consilium* XIX): 'Ut ergo de singulis dicamus, sciendum est, quod sex sunt differentiae ciborum. Prima est, ut sint boni alimenti, aut mali. Circa hoc dicebat Galenus *tertio de Alimentis: Cibi mali succi sunt, qui nutrimentum dant nimis tenue, aut nimis crassum*'.

106. Ibid., p. 97[a-b], for example: 'Omnia ergo olera et radices sunt mali alimenti, et est regula, quae non patitur ullam exceptionem, quia serosum aut crassum et crudum praebent alimentum; ergo omnia talia sunt vitanda sub forma alimenti. [...] Nam omnia legumina non solum sunt difficilis coctionis, sed difficillimae'.

107. Ibid., p. 98[a]: 'Reliquae non sunt utiles'.

108. Cardano, *Consilia*, p. 65[a] (*Consilium* VIII): 'De cibi autem bonis. Alae omnium avium, quae non degant in aquis, seu quae non habent rostrum latum: inde iecora anserum, gallinarum,

et anatum. Ex alis vero praestantissimae gallinarum indarum, sunt enim candidissimae, lenissimae, friabiles, admodum suaves, atque levissimae, inde etiam gallinis nostris praeferendae. Quadrupedum carnes bonae nullae'. Ficino in *De vita* states that the flesh of young quadrupeds only can be recommended to those who need to keep the rising of black bile in the body under control (*De vita* 1.10).

109. Cardano, *Consilia*, p. 65^{a-b} (*Consilium* VIII): 'pisces fluviorum meliores marinis, minus enim generant melancholiae, minus tamen nutriunt. [...] Cibi autem optimi duo sunt: vitella ovorum et lac, sed lac ei non convenit, quia patitur flatuosam'.

110. See Michael W. Dols, 'Galen and Islamic Psychiatry', in *Le opere psicologiche di Galeno: Atti del terzo colloquio galenico internazionale, Pavia, 10–12 settembre 1986*, ed. by Paola Manuli & Mario Vegetti (Naples: Bibliopolis, 1988), pp. 243–80 (pp. 247–48).

111. Pictorius is the Latinized form of Mahler. On Pictorius see Tillmann Wertz, *Georgius Pictorius (1500–1569/73): Leben und Werk eines oberrheinischen Arztes und Humanisten* (Heidelberg: Palatina Verlag, 2006). Pictorius's works were published in Latin, German, and Italian translations, and were also included in editions of Agrippa's *De occulta philosophia*.

112. See Cardano, *De rerum varietate*, p. 109^b. Cardano mentions Pictorius in the list of authors who quote Cardano himself in their writings (*De vita propria*, p. 46^b). It is noteworthy that Pictorius and Cardano were the two main authors in a 'Werbeplakat' [publicity poster] that the printer Heinrich Petri circulated in 1576 (see Wertz, *Georgius Pictorius (1500–1569/73)*, pp. 64 & 78).

113. Marsilio Ficino, *De studiosorum tuenda sanitate [...] librum, cum Georgii Pictorii [...] scholiis*, in Georg Pictorius, *Opera nova* (Basel: Petri, 1569), pp. 1–93. See Wertz, *Georgius Pictorius (1500–1569/73)*, pp. 108–09. The Basel publisher Heinrich Petri printed Ficino's *Opera* in 1579. See also Stuart Clark, *Thinking with Demons: The Idea of Witchcraft in Early Modern Europe* (Oxford & New York: Oxford University Press, 1997), pp. 277–78.

114. Georg Pictorius, *Dialogi [...] del modo di conservare la sanità: nuovamente dalla lingua latina nella volgar italiana tradotto* (Venice: Bottega d'Erasmo di Vincenzo Valgrisi, 1550). This text is also discussed in Cavallo & Storey, *Healthy Living*, pp. 19–20.

115. On the dual role of food as medicine and nutriment see Pictorius, *Dialogi*, p. 142. On this issue see Nancy Siraisi, *Medieval and Early Renaissance Medicine: An Introduction to Knowledge and Practice* (Chicago: University of Chicago Press, 1990), pp. 121–23.

116. Pictorius, *Dialogi*, p. 32: 'POL: Al pane ne seguita la carne, mostrami o Teofrasto qual sia la migliore. TEO: Galeno e Averroe dicono che la carne del porco, perché la temperatura uguale del caldo e humido è megliore dell'altri, purché il porco non passi l'anno e la carne sia stata alquanti giorni nel sale, acciocché perda la viscosità. Ma chi non si sente bene non è da dargliene, per la tarda concottione che fa nello stomaco, quella de' porcelli piccoli non è così lodata, per esser troppo humida, la carne del bufalo, del manzo, et della vacca sono al tutto contro la sanità quando sono d'animali vecchi, e molto più se tai carni sono secche al fumo, però che sono difficili da smaltire, di cattivo nutrimento, e producano humore maninconico. La carne di vitello e di capretto è lodata da tutti, essendo facile a smaltire, e generando buon sangue; è lodata ancora la carne del castrato giovane, quella del montone è dannata'.

117. See Pictorius, *Dialogi*, p. 35. On Pictorius's dietetics see the references in Albala, *Eating Right in the Renaissance*, pp. 33 & 54.

118. Pictorius, *Dialogi*, p. 129: 'Disse un certo: mi maraviglio come un huomo il quale mangia il pane fatto di buon grano, et le carni di buoni animali, e bee il vino di buona vite, quando, quanto, e come fa bisogno, si possa ammalare e morire'. On this text see Chiara Crisciani, 'Premesse e promesse di lunga vita: tra teologia e pratica terapetica (secolo XIII)', in *Vita longa: vecchiaia e durata della vita nella tradizione medica e aristotelica antica e medievale*, ed. by Chiara Crisciani, Luciana Repici, & Pietro B. Rossi, Micrologus' Library, 3 (Florence: SISMEL, Edizioni del Galluzzo, 2009), pp. 61–86 (p. 76).

119. Cardano, *De subtilitate* (*OGC*, III, 501^b; my translation, but cf. Cardano, *The 'De subtilitate'*, trans. by John M. Forrester, 2 vols (Tempe: Arizona Center for Medieval and Renaissance Studies, 2013), I, 495).

120. Cardano's understanding of magic is relevant here, but I can only refer to further reading on the topic: with specific reference to diet see Siraisi, *The Clock and The Mirror*, p. 75; on the relation

between the notions of magic and sympathy see Guido Canziani, ' "Nihil est quod sapientia ipsa efficere nequeat": Cardano e la magia', *Bruniana & Campanelliana*, 16.2 (2010), 439–50.

121. See Guido Giglioni, 'Medicina e metafisica della vita animale in Cardano', *Bruniana & Campanelliana*, 8.1 (2002), 113–58 (p. 158): 'in natura, come nella storia, regna il conflitto e la violenza — *tyrannis in rebus ipsis constituta*'.

122. Cardano, *De rerum varietate*, p. 147^b: 'Qui ergo ferarum carnibus aluntur et aromatibus, omnes feri et truculenti evadunt; qui oleribus, contra'.

123. Cardano, *De subtilitate*, p. 507^b: 'Animalia fuisse sola, quae aliorum carnibus vescerentur, possibile non fuit: nam altero alterum comedente, nec alio cibo suppetente [...] quantitate primum moles tota animalium et numero minueret, demum etiam imo brevi deficeret. Quod si plantis omnia animalia vescerentur, non adepta fuisset natura perfectionem quoniam sanguis ille, et caro, non ex elementis confractis et optime temperatis consisteret'. My translation, but cf. Cardano, *The 'De subtilitate'*, II, 512. On the teleological structure of nature in Cardano see Guido Giglioni, 'Humans, Elephants, Diamonds and Gold: Patterns of Intentional Design in Girolamo Cardano's Natural Philosophy', *Gesnerus*, 71.2 (2014), 237–57.

124. See Galen, *Mixtures*, in *Selected Works*, pp. 215 & 220. On the notion of the complexion of foods in the Renaissance see Cavallo & Storey, *Healthy Living*, pp. 210–11.

125. Cardano, *Contradicentia medicorum* (*OGC*, VI, 402^b: 'In regimine tamen restaurandi corporis facilius est pinguescere ex cibo assumpto in coena, quam in prandio, et virtutem recuperare, et hoc Galenus voluit et hac causa athletae ad vires et carnem instaurandam, carnium quantitatem immensam in vespere comedebant. Sed horum constitutionem non probat Galenus [...] quinimo et brevis vitae et morbosae illos esse affirmabat').

126. Cardano, *De subtilitate*, p. 501^b: 'Quod si quis luporum carnibus utatur et maxime corde, adhuc evadet longe magis ferus et audax, ac perfidus. Evidentius autem hoc in animalibus quam hominibus, et plantis quam animalibus, quia non aliunde mutantur'.

127. Cardano, *De uno* (*OGC*, I, 277^a: 'Unum bonum est, plura vero malum'). This is of course a Platonic stance: see the introduction in Giglioni, 'Girolamo [Geronimo] Cardano'.

128. Cardano, *De uno*, p. 280^a, where the elephant is coupled with the donkey: 'Asini etiam et elephantes pauciores sunt hominibus, et pauciores etiam generant: rarius enim duos, et nunquam tres elephantes natos, aut asinos vidimus, aut audivimus, legimusve. At homines saepe geminos pariunt, tres nonnunquam'.

129. Ibid.: 'non tamen asini aut elephantes hominibus sunt perfectiores, ut si nihil aliud desit illis, ratio saltem ipsa deest'.

130. Even if Cardano does not simply maintain the idea of a hierarchical structure in nature, with the human positioned at the top of the *scala*, he nevertheless applies a series of criteria through which he develops the distinction between humans and animals. As Guido Giglioni has shown, Cardano does not follow the traditional view of a simple hierarchy in nature, dominated by humans (see 'Man's Mortality, Conjectural Knowledge, and the Redefinition of the Divinatory Practice in Cardano's Philosophy', in *Cardano e la tradizione dei saperi*, ed. by Marialuisa Baldi and Guido Canziani (Milan: FrancoAngeli, 2003), pp. 43–65, esp. p. 53). See further Eckhard Keβler, '*Alles ist eines wie der Mensch und das Pferd*: zu Cardanos Naturbegriff', in *Girolamo Cardano: Philosoph, Naturforscher, Artz*, ed. by Eckhard Keβler (Wiesbaden: Harrassowitz, 1994), pp. 91–114. On human and animal happiness in relation to the place of each creature in nature see Cecilia Muratori, 'From Animal Happiness to Human Unhappiness: Cardano, Vanini, *Theophrastus redivivus* (1659)', in *Early Modern Philosophers and the Renaissance Legacy*, ed. by Muratori & Paganini, pp. 185–200.

131. Cardano, *De subtilitate*, p. 507^b: 'Ob id nullum animal, quod carne non vescatur, sagax est, et prudens, excepto elephante'; cf. Cardano, *The 'De subtilitate'*, II, 512. On the *sagacitas* attributed to dogs in the sceptical tradition see Luciano Floridi, 'Scepticism and Animal Rationality: The Fortune of Chrysippus' Dog in the History of Western Thought', *Archiv für Geschichte der Philosophie*, 97.1 (1997), 27–57.

132. Cardano, *De subtilitate*, p. 550^b; my translation, but cf. Cardano, *The 'De subtilitate'*, II, 639–40 (Forrester translates 'inter pisces, quadrupedia et aves' differently).

133. Ibid., p. 507^b: 'Nam quae carnibus utuntur, sensu proximiora homini sunt quam quae plantis, ut canes, vulpes, cercopitheci, feles, leones, delphini, ursi, aquilae'.

134. Cardano, *In libro Hippocratis de alimento*, p. 467[a]: 'Naturaliter enim unumquodque alimentum tam est gratum quam idoneum fini, ita enim a natura commode comparatum est, ad salutem animalium, ut tam iucundum esset, et tum, quantum, et cum professe posset illis'.

135. The notion that humans have no 'assigned food', unlike herbivores and carnivores, is recurrent in the Renaissance. A very clear example is Della Porta's discussion of food as that which distinguishes humans from all other animals, since the former have a choice in this respect, while the latter do not (see Giovan Battista Della Porta, *De humana physiognomonia libri sex / Della fisionomia dell'uomo*, ed. by Alfonso Paolella, 2 vols (Naples: Edizioni scientifiche italiane, 2011–13), I, 65–66, & II, 76–78). See below, Chapter 3, section 6.

136. See Cardano, *Hyperchen* (*OGC*, I, 287[a]: 'Interim vero cum elementa sint plantis alimentum, animalibus plantae, hominibus animalia, erunt et homines aliis'). Cardano is referring here to the issue of feeding daemons and the practice of sacrifice (on this see above, Chapter 1).

137. Ibid.: 'Idque etiam Platonici affirmant: quare in sanguine erunt, et ex eo nutrientur, foedum, ut nobis videtur, alimentum. Sed et nos cruenta vulnera animalium comedimus, quod Porphyrius reprehendit, et abominatur, tabes enim quaedam est. Et quae aliis abominanda viderentur, usus obtinuit ut cuperemus'.

138. *OA*, I.13.1; p. 36.

139. *OA*, I.31.1 & I.15.1; pp. 36 & 37.

140. On Scaliger (pseudonym of Giulio Bordon) see especially Kuni Sakamoto, *Julius Caesar Scaliger, Renaissance Reformer of Aristotelianism: A Study of 'Exotericae Exercitationes'* (Leiden: Brill, 2016).

141. Maclean has shown how Scaliger's critique (in this case specifically on the issue of the soul's immortality) reveals unexpected twists in Cardano's argumentation (see Ian Maclean, 'Cardano's Eclectic Psychology and its Critique by Julius Caesar Scaliger', in *Transformations of the Soul: Aristotelean Psychology 1250–1650*, ed. by Dominik Perler (Leiden: Brill, 2009), offprint of *Vivarium*, 46.3 (2008), 170–95).

142. On the Cardano-Scaliger controversy see Guido Giglioni's seminal essay 'Scaliger versus Cardano versus Scaliger', in *Forms of Conflict and Rivalries in Early Modern Europe*, ed. by David A. Lines, Jill Kraye, & Marc Laureys, Veröffentlichungen der Bonn University Press (Göttingen: Vandenhoeck & Ruprecht, 2015), pp. 109–30.

143. Julius Caesar Scaliger, *Exotericarum exercitationum liber XV de subtilitate, ad Hieronymum Cardanum* (Paris: Vascosan, 1557), f. 275r: 'Non est igitur elephanto optimum temperamentum ad vivendum diu, quia esset optimum in olea, aut palma, aut ulmo, quae diutius vivunt. An vero temperamentum optimum attribuat suillo generi Galenus, propterea quod humani simillimas carnes illas iudicarit'.

144. See Daniel Schäfer, *Old Age and Disease in Early Modern Medicine* (London: Pickering & Chatto, 2011), esp. Chapter 2.

145. Cardano, *De subtilitate*, p. 524[a]: 'Equidem si ad vitae longitudinem respicimus, camelus proximior est homini quam canis: nam camelus centum quandoque annis vivit, canum vita vigesimo anno terminatur [...]. Cameli quoque musica delectantur, canes minime'; my translation, but cf. Cardano, *The 'De subtilitate'*, II, 561. On the animals' reactions to music, also with reference to camels, see Fadlou Shehadi, *Philosophies of Music in Medieval Islam* (Leiden: Brill, 1995). It is worth remembering, though, that Erasmus mentions the 'dancing camel' as an example of lack of grace: see *Adagia*, in *ASD*, II.6, 66.

146. See Cardano, *De utilitate ex adversis capienda* (*OGC*, II, 164[b]).

147. See Cardano, *De consolatione* (*OGC*, I, 597[a]).

148. Cardano, *De uno*, p. 281[a]. See also Cardano, *De uno / Sobre lo uno*, ed. by José Manuel García Valverde (Florence: Olschki, 2009), p. 22.

149. Aristotle in *On the Length and Shortness of Life* groups the elephant and the human being together as the two longest living creatures among the sanguineous animals that live on land (466a10–15).

150. Scaliger, *Exotericae exercitationes*, f. 327v: 'Elephanto ac Simia nullum essse animal, post hominem, sapientius. Quorum neutrum suapte natura carnivorum est. Culex vero et pulex essent sagacissimi. Purissimo nanque aluntur sanguine'.

151. Cardano, *In librum Hippocratis de aere, aquis, et locis commentaria* (*OGC*, VIII, 10[b]: 'Elephas vivit ducentis saltem annis, multaqua alia animalia feruntur diutius vivere homine: quae omnia

acquam bibunt, et a carnibus abstinent'; and ibid: 'Ergo necessitas est potus aquae, non simpliciter ad vitam, sed vitae longitudinem, nam in omni genere operationis est aliquid necessarium, ad vitam cibus et potus, ad longam autem panis et aqua').

152. See Cardano, *De sanitate tuenda*, p. 80[a]: 'Relinquitur ut vita optima constet fructibus, et δορκλῶτοις, et seminibus, et surculis, talibus enim ut vivunt elephantes, cameli, cervique, quorum vitam constat esse omnium diuturniorem, atque salubriorem, moresque simul concinnos'.

153. Ibid., p. 79[b]: 'Ob idque Plutarchus et Porphyrius, duo disertissimi philosophi, opera scripsisse de non edendis animalibus, praeterea brevioris vitae, nullum enim animal quod carne vescitur est longae vitae'.

154. Scaliger, *Exotericae exercitationes*, f. 327v: 'Ais: "Homo, qui carnibus vescitur, tum maxime volatilium, potuit esse tenuissimae, densissimae, calidissimae, temperatissimaeque naturae"'. Cf. Cardano, *De subtilitate*, p. 550[b]: 'Itaque homo, qui etiam carnibus vescitur, tum maxime volatilium, potuit esse simul tenuissimae, ac densissimae, calidissimae atque temperatissimae naturae'); my translation, but cf. Cardano, *The 'De subtilitate'*, II, 640.

155. Scaliger, *Exotericae exercitationes*, f. 327v: 'Omnia haec tuus homo est, modo carnibus vescatur. Caro igitur haec omnia est. At caro neque entium est tenuissima [...]. Neque tenuior est homo, qui carne vescitur, quam qui lacte, et melle, cum pane'.

156. Ibid., f. 327r: 'Primum igitur radicibus vescentia maiore conatu, laboreque terram fodere coacta, maiore praedita esse sagacitate, necesse est. Quia quod intercedit medium ad odorandum, crassius est, quam iis, quae in aquis aut äere agitant animalia. Tales sunt talpae, lumbrici, cuierae illae, quas sic supra nominabamus, sic semper nominabimus, quoad nos doceas verum nomen. [...] Nihil apibus sagacius, quas ego ad flores e longinquis maxime locis convolare attentius observavi, cum id apud Aristotelem scriptum invenissem. At nobis carnivoris nullus is odor sese offerebat'.

157. Ibid.: 'Caro namque crassa est, et crasse alit. Herbae tametsi crassiores, tamen ex earum subtilissimis partibus confit alimentum'.

158. On the horse see Julius Caesar Scaliger, *In libros de plantis Aristoteli inscriptos commentarii* (Lyon: Rovillius, 1566), f. 118[a].

159. Cardano, *In librum Hippocratis de alimento commentaria*, p. 466[a]: 'Deinde quomodo homines et boves plantis alerentur? [...] Sed et illa multas patitur difficultates, nam primum bos melius nutritur plantis quam carne, et tamen caro est similior. [...] Et etiam homo nutritur melius carne hoedina et pulli quam accipitris aut canis, et tamen caro canis et accipitris est proprior carni humanae, quam hoedina aut pulli. Accidit quod quaedam ex ordine remotiori (ut lactuca) melius nutriunt, quam caro struthii'.

160. Antonio Fracanziano, *In librum Hippocratis de alimento commentarius* (Venice: ex officina Marci de Maria Salernitani, 1566), pp. 21–22. Fracanziano is at the centre of an episode narrated in Cardano's autobiography: Cardano is supposed to have humiliated his colleague by correcting from memory a Greek passage discussed by the professor in front of his students (see Cardano, *De vita propria*, p. 10[a]; *The Book of My Life*, p. 47).

161. Cardano, *In librum Hippocratis de alimento commentaria*, p. 466[a].

162. Cardano, *Contradicentium medicorum libri*, p. 402[b]. An approved method discussed here for strengthening the body is that of eating large meals, including 'a huge quantity of meat' ('carnium quantitas immensa').

163. Cardano, *In librum Hippocratis de alimento commentaria*, p. 478[a].

164. On Scaliger's approach see Guido Giglioni, 'Girolamo Cardano e Giulio Cesare Scaligero: il dibattito sul ruolo dell'anima vegetativa', in *Girolamo Cardano: le opere, le fonti, la vita*, ed. by Marialuisa Baldi & Guido Canziani (Milan: FrancoAngeli, 1999), pp. 313–39.

165. See Julius Caesar Scaliger, *Commentarii et animadversiones in sex libros de causis plantarum Theophrasti* (Lyon: Apud Ioannem Crispinum, 1566), p. 242[a-b].

166. Aristotle in *On the Length and Shortness of Life* uses the example of the date palm as one of the longest-lived beings (466a9–10). In general terms, he claims that plants live longer than animals both because their moisture does not dry out as quickly, and because they have the capability to regenerate themselves (see 467a6–30).

167. Cardano, *De subtilitate*, p. 386[a]. Cf. *The 'De subtilitate'*, I, 115.

168. Manfredi, *Il Perché*, unpaginated: 'Quanto la cosa ha in sé più humido substantiale e conglutinativo tanto dà più nutrimento al corpo. La carne che non è cocta ha il suo humido substantiale. Imperò se padire se potesse saria di grandissimo nutrimento. Ma il stomaco nostro questo non padisse, sì per abhominatione, sì per debilità de virtù digestiva sel non fusso nutrito dal principio del so nasciere. Bisogna adonche che la se cuoca, e quanto più sta al fuoco tanto più il suo humido substantiale se rissolve e se consuma, de che non dà tanto nutrimento' (cf. Manfredi, *Liber de homine / Il Perché*, ed. by Foresti & others, pp. 81–82). On 'umido sostanziale/ umido radicale' see Matteo Motolese, *Lo male rotundo: il lessico della fisiologia e della patologia nei trattati di pesti fra Quattro e Cinquecento* (Rome: Aracne, 2004), p. 289.

169. Crisciani, 'Premesse e promesse di lunga vita', p. 64.

170. Manfredi, *Il Perché*, unpaginated: 'Perché le carne malcocte son più dure che ben cocte. [...] cussì come la carne mal cocta è dura nel tocare, cussì è dura nel digerere perché quello che face a il caldo del fuoco a cuocerla sottigliando sua humidità bisogna che ciò faccia il caldo naturale del stomaco. E questa è la casione che la carne malcocta non se de dare a stomachi debili e a quelli che poco sa faticano, ma a stomachi forti e a quelli che usano molto exercitio' (cf. Manfredi, *Liber de homine / Il Perché*, ed. by Foresti & others, p. 81).

171. Scaliger, *Exotericae exercitationes*, f. 43r: 'Ergo prodest coctio. Est enim quasi maturatio'.

172. Ibid., f. 42v: 'Aethiopes, a veteribus appellati Troglodytae crudis ali carnibus [...]. Quos si velis imitari, liceat'.

173. Cardano, *De sanitate tuenda*, p. 13: 'Verum docebimus infra, vitam longaevam neque carnibus, neque ovis, neque vino constare [...] sed in fructibus terrae, ut pane, amygdalis, pineis, castaneis, aqua cum saccharo'.

174. See Siraisi, *The Clock and the Mirror*, p. 82.

175. The choice of the best foods in fact varies from person to person: Cardano, *De sanitate tuenda*, p. 110[b]: 'Cum necesse sit nutrimentum in nutriti aut nutriendi substantiam converti, illud in primis notandum, non unum esse, idemque omnium particularium ciborum temperamentum'; ibid., p. 111[b]: 'Cibaria ergo quae generaliter laudantur sunt ea, quae optimum praebent alimentum corpori nostro, quae neque crassi, nec glutinosi sunt succi, ex quibus sanguis generatur status mediocris'.

176. Cardano, *Theonoston* II (*OGC*, II, 389[a] & 397[a]).

177. Ibid., p. 382[b].

178. On this see Siraisi, *The Clock and the Mirror*, pp. 79–92, and Anthony Grafton, *Cardano's Cosmos: The Worlds and Works of a Renaissance Astrologer* (Cambridge, MA: Harvard University Press, 1999), p. 183.

179. Alvise Cornaro, *Trattato della vita sobria* (Padua: Percacino, 1558). On Cornaro see Cynthia Skenazi, *Aging Gracefully in the Renaissance: Stories of Later Life from Petrarch to Montaigne* (Leiden: Brill, 2013), pp. 36–42. For a recent English translation of *Della vita sobria* see Cornaro, *Writings on the Sober Life: The Art and Grace of Living Long*, ed. and trans. by Hiroko Fudemoto (Toronto, Buffalo, & London: University of Toronto Press, 2014).

180. Cardano, *De santitate tuenda*, p. 15[b]: 'his Aloysius Cornarius Patritius Venetus pulcherrime respondit, quinimo etiam acerbe arguit delinquentes eo libello, qui in omnium manibus est'. See also Siraisi, *The Clock and the Mirror*, p. 79.

181. See Yves Pélicier, 'Les Nourritures à la Renaissance: essai de typologie', in *Practiques et discours alimentaires à la Renaissance*, ed. by Jean-Claude Margolin & Robert Sauzet (Paris: Maisonneuve et Larose, 1982), and Siraisi, *The Clock and the Mirror*, p. 84. Similarly, the physician Tommaso Rangoni did not recommend a vegetable diet to extend the lifespan: *De vita hominis ultra CXX annos protrahenda* (Venice: [Comin da Trino?], 1550), Chapter 14, which deals with various vegetables that are supposed to make life shorter rather than longer. On this see also Gentilcore, *Food and Health in Early Modern Europe*, p. 115.

182. Cardano, *Theonoston* II, p. 372[b].

183. Cardano, *Theonoston* I (*OGC*, II, 365[b]: 'Tranquillus homo ne animalibus mansuetis negotium facessit: inditio sunt capreoli hi, tum cuniculi, testudinesque neque enim vir tranquillus his miseris animalibus negotium facesset. Et antequam vos venissetis, passeres in mensam involabant, aliaeque aviculae').

184. Ibid.

185. Plato, *Timaeus*, 92b, in *Dialogues of Plato*, trans. by Benjamin Jowett, 4 vols (London & Oxford: Macmillan and Clarendon, 1871; repr. 2011), II, 585: 'The fourth class were the inhabitants of the water: these were made out of the most entirely senseless and ignorant of all, whom the transformers did not think any longer worthy of pure respiration, because they possessed a soul which was made impure by all sorts of transgression; and instead of allowing them to respire the subtle and pure element of air, they thrust them into the water and gave them a deep and muddy medium of respiration; and hence arose the race of fishes and oysters, and other aquatic animals, which have received the most remote habitations as a punishment of their extreme ignorance'.

186. On the dietary choice of the hermit see Giglioni, 'Medicina e metafisica della vita animale in Cardano', p. 137.

187. According to Porphyry the custom of some people to roast fish shows that humans are not by nature raw-eating animals: see *OA*, 1.13; p. 36.

188. See Cardano, *Theonoston* II, pp. 375^{a-b} & 389^b on frying.

189. Ibid., p. 373^b.

190. Ibid., p. 385^b: 'Ille ego cum melle tam ovis vesci solitus erat; panem madefaciebat in iure testudinum, nonnunquam piscium. Edebat et pisces, sed raro, in craticula coctos cum melle, cuius et copiam magnam habebat, et summam gerebat curam, et olus coctum, et lentem quandoque, sed optime coctam'.

191. See ibid., p. 383^a.

192. Ibid., p. 386^a, & 387^a: 'nullus ergo piscis, qui non respirat, bene nutrit'.

193. Cardano, *In librum Hippocratis de alimento commentaria*, p. 466^b: 'De piscibus dixi quod sunt facilioris conctionis, ideo melius exhibent alimentum suilla. Si tamen suilla assimiletur, melius alit, et plus restaurat, ac robur magis addit. Ideo Galenus *septimo Methodi cap. 6* primum dat pisces, post carnem suillam. De carne humana et suilla dico quod ob coctionem fiunt dissimiles, ideo nutriunt, crudae non. Et hoc fecit natura credo, ut species animalium carnivorarum servarentur. Cum enim necesse esset ob generationem, et educationem filiorum, ut simul versarentur, si simile simili nutriretur, cum ratione careant, et eisdem armis utantur, et iisdem moribus praedita sint'.

194. Cardano, *Theonoston* II, p. 377^a: 'Praeterea si cibos non pingues assumere velit solum, ut olera et fructus, imbecillis omnino reddetur'.

195. Ibid., and see Siraisi, *The Clock and the Mirror*, p. 81.

196. Cardano, *Theonoston* I, p. 368^b.

197. Cardano, *Theonoston* II, p. 402^b: 'His dictis discubuimus, cibumque sumpsimus'.

198. Cardano, *The Book of My Life*, p. 53 (*De vita propria*, p. 11^a: '[retineo] animalia dono accepta: haedos, agnos, lepores, cuniculos, ciconias, ut totam defaedarent domum'). For further on Cardano's view on living with animals: Giglioni, 'Medicina e metafisica della vita animale in Cardano', p. 114.

199. See Cardano, *De vita propria*, p. 6^b: 'nihil melius vitulina solida, in olla cocta absque liquore ullo, verum dorso gladiorum diu verberata, inveni'; *The Book of My Life*, pp. 28–29: 'I consider nothing better than firm young veal, beaten tender with the back of a butcher's knife and pot-roasted without any liquors save its own'.

CHAPTER 3

❖

Otherness

3.1. Introduction: Diet and the Horizons of the World

One major event marked the distance between the world of Porphyry and that of his Renaissance readers: the new geographical discoveries. In *On Abstinence* Porphyry often mentions the dietetic habits of human populations that lived beyond the borders of the Roman Empire, showing keen curiosity in the variety of human approaches to diet. The study of dietetic patterns in human societies provided Porphyry with vital information to be used for his vegetarian argument. He addresses questions such as these: what conclusions can be drawn from the comparison of different dietary habits among human populations? What is the connection between the cultural traits of a group and their diet? And finally, is it possible to use such information to define which is the best diet for human beings in general, and specifically for those who pursue philosophy?

Claude Lévi-Strauss remarked that the discovery of the Americas did not so much mark the beginning of a new era as complete the period that had started in the early Renaissance with the rediscovery of ancient Greek authors, including of course Porphyry.[1] The new knowledge about the ancient world thus provided the foundation for interpreting the new travel reports: parallels could be drawn between ancient and modern views of the world, identifying elements of novelty. For Renaissance thinkers, the borders of the known world had shifted as a result of territorial expansion, and the encounter with new groups of human beings rekindled curiosity about the variety of human diets. As we saw in the exchange between Cardano and Scaliger on health, it is significant that references to Porphyry appear in their discussion of the effects of meat, in particular in relation to the question whether meat produces brutality, and whether a plant diet renders the eater meek. While examples considered until now mainly regarded the comparison between herbivores and carnivores among animals, the effects of these two diets on humans are at the centre of Porphyry's concern and, as we shall see in this chapter, this remains the case for Renaissance philosophers who engaged with this topic. Yet while information transmitted by Porphyry entered the Renaissance debate on the advantages and disadvantages of the vegetable diet, Porphyry's examples came to acquire new meaning in a world that had substantially changed its geography.

Porphyry was well aware that diet is in the first instance an expression of the variety of human cultures. What is acceptable to eat and what is not for each human group is determined by cultural factors, including religious practices. As his discussion of religious sacrifice demonstrated, Porphyry knew that the (potentially) vegetarian philosopher lives within a social context that functions according to its own rules, which must be taken into account. At various points in the work he reflects on the similarities or differences between the diet he proposes to Firmus Castricius and other known types of diet. For instance, he points out that Jews avoid eating certain animals, while 'we' (the culture with which Porphyry himself identifies) would not eat creatures such as worms, mice, or dogs. Disgust at eating some foods and not others reflects cultural relativism.[2]

Such considerations are of course very frequent in medical literature as well, and Galen, too, had commented on this issue, using the same example of eating dogs: 'As for dogs and foxes — I have never tasted their meat, since it is not the custom to eat it either in Asia or in Greece, or indeed in Italy. But there are certainly parts of the world where they are eaten'.[3] The availability of foods in different regions and the cultural significance attached to them are factors with a crucial role in medical discussion on the properties of food. The variety of human behaviour with regard to diet means that a physician like Galen would have to guess at the properties of each of those unknown foods.

Porphyry focuses his attention especially on two diametrically opposed dietary options: the strictly vegetarian diet of certain human groups, and a diet based mostly on meat, possibly including even human meat. He uses the criterion of diet to draw distinctions between the traditions and behaviours of human populations that fall into the former or the latter pattern. The comparison between the heavy meat-eaters and the vegetarians thus serves the purpose of demonstrating that there is a clear connection between the food eaten and the level of cultural development. Comparing the two extremes allows Porphyry to emphasize what he believes to be the dangers that humans risk in eating large quantities of meat, while employing the example of the vegetarian (or semi-vegetarian) peoples as positive role models.

One of the chief difficulties in reading *On Abstinence* consists in identifying its sources, including many undeclared direct quotations.[4] For describing the contrast between meat-eaters and vegetarians, Porphyry had a variety of materials at his disposal. Among the main authors whose work appears in long extracts in *On Abstinence* is Plutarch, who devoted particular attention to the role of food within established cultural practices. Eating and not eating flesh are dietary choices that Plutarch views against the background of his conception of what is natural and what is acquired behaviour. As he puts it in *De sanitate tuenda* [Advice About Keeping Well], meat-eating 'has become a sort of unnatural second nature':[5] therefore in order to argue for a different choice, it is of the utmost importance to collect information on the broad variety of dietary practices. Food, in other words, is defined against the backdrop of culture.[6] This is the reason why Plutarch describes the dietary habits of other peoples, linking them to their respective societies and cultures, and drawing prescriptive conclusions as to which populations should be followed as models and which should not. Further, Plutarch associates dietary habits directly with philosophical positions: even if it cannot be said that a specific population drew inspiration for its diet from a certain philosophical school, coupling philosophies and cultures serves the purpose of showing that philosophical positions have direct implications with regard to what is accepted as food and what is not. This is an approach used by Porphyry, too.

According to Plutarch, meat is an unnatural aliment for humans: he believes that this is proven by, among other things, the fact that human groups have learnt to cook and season it, thus covering up the unpleasant characteristics of meat itself, which would otherwise repulse any eater.[7] This, as we saw, is a topic that resurfaced in the Renaissance discussion of raw meat in particular.[8] Intercultural exchange is directly involved in making meat acceptable, for instance through the marketing of Syrian and Arab spices used to prepare meaty dishes.[9] Even if the spices can conceal the natural repulsiveness of meat, Plutarch claims that 'eating flesh' is 'physically against nature', and that it is not a suitable food for nourishing human bodies. Further, he holds that meat has a negative influence not only on the physical but on the spiritual level too. He uses the example of a specific group of people: his own. It is not by chance, he states, that the Bœotians, who are known for eating flesh, are 'spiritually coarse and gross', so brutal that they are even called 'swine', and indeed the term 'Bœotian' became a synonym for 'ignorant' or 'dull'.[10]

Yet, Plutarch does not simply compare meat-eaters to vegetarians: rather, he presses the contrast to its extreme, opposing plant-eaters to those who not only indulge in animal flesh, but even eat their fellow humans.[11] To the anthropophagi, he opposes the followers of Pythagoras and Empedocles, ultimately asking:

> Do but consider which are the philosophers who serve the better to humanize us: those who bid us eat our children and friends and fathers and wives after their death, or Pythagoras and Empedocles who try to accustom us to act justly toward other creatures also?[12]

Presenting this choice between the anthropophagi and the plant-eaters leads Plutarch to ask what humanity itself should be and what it should strive for: is the best embodiment of humanity a vegetarian or an anthropophagus?

Plutarch thus furnishes Porphyry with the view not only that considering and comparing the diets of others is essential for building an argument in favour of vegetarianism, but also that dietary choices can be coupled with specific philosophical positions. This approach informs Porphyry's strategy, as he argues that vegetarianism is the philosophical diet par excellence. Practical comparisons should thus direct Firmus Castricius to follow certain philosophical models, while using the example of the most extreme meat-eaters as a warning.

The present chapter reconstructs the Renaissance afterlives of this opposition. It draws attention to the fact that the anthropophagic populations of antiquity are not the same as those at the centre of Renaissance discussion of contemporary instances of anthropophagy. In the Renaissance, the line dividing cannibalism and vegetarianism is remarkably blurred. The cannibals, as the first part of this chapter shows, function as a mirror to reflect on meat-eating in particular, and on the difference between eating animals and eating humans. The case of positive, vegetarian models, is different: from antiquity to the Renaissance the focus remains essentially on the same groups, and Porphyry played a key role in shaping and transmitting their myths. These are the Indian Brahmans and the

Gymnosophists, but also the Essenes among the Jews, the Egyptians priests, and the Persian Magi — that is to say, groups (mostly Eastern) who abstained from meat, engaged in contemplation, had religious roles, and in some cases were also said to be remarkably long-lived.[13]

The Renaissance encounter with cultural otherness prompted both a comparison with and a reassessment of the models transmitted from antiquity. Anthropophagi and vegetarians are viewed as extreme examples of dietetic 'otherness'. In discussing them, Renaissance philosophers review the evidence for and against meat consumption not just to promote a long, healthy life, but also to encourage certain cultural traits over others.[14] Porphyry provides abundant materials to support such arguments.

3.2. Ancient Anthropophagi and Renaissance Cannibals

The portrait of the Scyths as anthropophagi has a long tradition. Herodotus in his *Histories* comments on their extreme brutality;[15] Pliny states that they are believed to feed on human meat.[16] But Plutarch embeds this information within a philosophical frame, portraying the Scyths as the incarnation of the Stoic theory, formulated by Chrysippus, that it is acceptable to eat the bodies of already deceased human beings, including one's own relatives. For the Stoics, there are no valid arguments against this practice.[17]

Even if he does not directly accuse the Stoics of anthropophagy, as Plutarch had done, Porphyry, too, uses the example of the Scyths, and highlights the connections between philosophical stances and their cultural incarnations in real human groups. Therefore, those who have chosen a vegetable diet are identified by Porphyry with the followers of Pythagoras and Empedocles, siding with Plutarch against the 'meat-eaters' among philosophers, namely Peripatetics, Stoics, and Epicureans.[18]

From Porphyry's point of view, the Scyths are included in the number of human populations that have 'lapsed into savagery or are bestial by nature'. Like Plutarch, he encourages the reader not to draw from their behaviour the wrong conclusions about human nature itself, as 'it is not right for intelligent people to use them to slander human nature'. 'We have not abandoned civilised behaviour towards fellow-humans because of these people', Porphyry points out. Rather, this example should work as a moral warning to 'imitate, not those people who by necessity eat flesh, but those who are pious and inclined towards the gods'.[19] We will see that the key role of 'necessity' in the assessment of anthropophagy resurfaces in the controversy between Girolamo Cardano and Julius Caesar Scaliger on this subject.

Porphyry adds several details regarding the cultures of these dangerous 'anthropophagi'. It is these details that present challenges to Renaissance readers, for whom the boundaries of the known world had changed radically. Both Plutarch and Porphyry choose the Scyths because they were nomads, known for sustaining themselves mainly with meat.[20] The Scyths are thus simply a more radical instance of a general tendency among nomadic people to eat the meat of the animals they hunt, rather than plants, which would mostly need to be cultivated. As Porphyry puts it, nomads and troglodytes 'know flesh food and nothing else'.[21]

Geographically, the Scyths inhabited the territories above the Dead Sea, a vast area of unclear contours, as unclear as the word 'Scyth' itself, which must have been used to cover a variety of nomadic people.[22] The essential feature, from Plutarch's and Porphyry's points of view, is that these people are particularly brutal, and that there is a clear connection between their diet and their behaviour. In this context, the fact that they are depicted as eaters of human meat simply signals an escalation of violence: they are the most brutal among the brutish human groups, they consume huge quantities of meat, and are believed not to stop at animal flesh, but to include the flesh of their fellow human beings as well. It is apparent that Porphyry sees an immediate contiguity between eating animals and eating humans, in a scale of rising brutality.

The fascination with anthropophagy, embodied in a foreign population or as a symbol of extreme violence, persisted up to the Renaissance. But it clearly gained currency in the aftermath of the 'discovery' of the Americas. This is reflected first of all in the language used to talk about it, as the new word 'cannibalism' was created to denote the anthropophagic behaviour of some inhabitants of the New World. Geographically, the 'cannibals' are thus (believed to be) located in some of the islands discovered by Columbus, even if the word then also came to be used also as a synonym for the population of Brazil.[23] As Frank Lestringant has reconstructed, *caniba* derives from *cariba*, a word that the inhabitants of the Lesser Antilles used to describe themselves as brave or bold. Yet, the first Europeans to travel to the Americas attribute to it a very different meaning: a cannibal is a violent anthropophagus, usually depicted as naked or nearly naked, intent on severing parts from human bodies.[24]

One of the first instances of the Italian term *cannibale* is in an account of Columbus's travels based on Peter Martyr's *De orbe novo* and known as *Libretto di tutta la navigazione de re di Spagna* [Booklet on All the Voyages of the King of Spain], composed in 1501 and published in Venice in 1504.[25] In the booklet the word 'cannibal' is employed to refer to a particularly fierce group of natives that is said to raid the areas inhabited by their neighbours, disseminating terror of being caught and eaten.[26] The word is thus introduced in the context of a probable misunderstanding between the Europeans and their interlocutors, a peaceful population, which is supposed to have expressed the fear of attacks by a neighbouring population that would kidnap and eat them.[27] In another report, by Michele da Cuneo (1448–1503), who accompanied Columbus on his second journey, it is instead the cannibals who run away on seeing the Europeans approach, hiding in the mountains of their island.[28] Michele da Cuneo distinguishes between the cannibals (called 'Camballi'), and the peaceful populations, simply called 'Indians', and possibly to be identified with the Arawak of the Lesser Antilles.[29] He thus often refers to 'Indians' and 'cannibals' when comparing the habits of these two substantially different groups.[30]

It is noteworthy that the figure of the cannibal is thus constructed from the very beginning in opposition to that of the non-violent indigenous people: the myths of the cannibal and of the *bon sauvage* have a common root, and the line dividing one from the other is often blurred.[31] This is a well-known debate, but it has not been explored with regard to the dietetic implications, and specifically the intertwining of the two dietetic alternatives under examination here. In both cases, the construction of the myth occurred rapidly from the early sixteenth century, in a combination of observation, imagination, and miscommunication.[32]

The cruelty of the American cannibals in tearing up human bodies became a commonplace: references to their supposed dietetic practice and expertise in butchery appear in numerous literary texts and iconographic material.[33] At the same time, authors added details about their general lifestyle, as well as the description of the geographical areas in which they lived, sometimes before (or without) setting foot in the New World.[34] The encounters with the cannibals are also filtered through the accounts of the anthropophagi of antiquity, which had reached the Renaissance through a variety of recastings. Though historically distinct, anthropophagi and cannibals are thus often imaginatively conflated. Among such re-elaborations, key medieval texts discussing anthropophagy are Marco Polo's *Milione* and an anonymous text that circulated in England and northern France from the second half of the fourteenth century, known as Mandeville's *Book of Marvels and Travels*.[35] There are similarities between the descriptions contained in these two texts, which functioned as 'compasses of the imagination' for Renaissance travellers and writers in reporting on new discoveries.[36] *Il Milione* locates a group of anthropophagi 'above Java minor' ('sopra la Giava minore'), and claims that they eat all sorts of meat, human and animal, and in general are very brutish (thus in accordance with the tradition of the ancient discourses on anthropophagy).[37] *The Book of Marvels and Travels* attributed to John Mandeville also features a discussion of a particularly brutish group of people, or more precisely giants: they 'have no clothing, only animal pelts hanging from them, and they eat no bread, only raw meat; and they drink milk. They have no houses and they would prefer to eat human flesh above any other'.[38] Once again, the characteristics of brutishness are the same: the preference for eating the meat of animals and of humans, especially raw, together with the lack of other signs of civilization, such as wearing clothes.

This tradition of framing anthropophagy continues up to the Renaissance, sometimes intertwining with the new portrait of the cannibal in Renaissance travel literature. Yet, the anthropophagi of antiquity and the 'new' cannibals are entirely different groups of people, and it is important to appreciate this difference in order to understand how the opposition between anthropophagy and vegetarianism acquired new meaning in the Renaissance. The Scyths were a nomadic group located in Asia; the cannibals, instead, natives of the Americas, were believed to inhabit mainly the Antilles, and certain areas of Brazil.[39] But the crucial difference regards their diets, and in particular the question whether there is a natural connection between eating large amounts of animals and the tendency to eat humans as well. Porphyry and his sources would have answered in the affirmative with regard to the Scyths, who are said to indulge in eating meat, including the human kind. But this connection does not seem to apply in the case of the American cannibals — the only meat-eating people legitimately to be defined as 'cannibals', even if the term is used quite freely in Renaissance travel reports to talk about various groups of savage Americans.[40]

Renaissance reports on the diet of the cannibals, unlike the ancient philosophical works, do not assume that a diet heavily reliant on meat might feed a process of brutalization, which might end with eating humans as well. Therefore I distinguish between the use of the general terms (anthropophagy, anthropophagi) and the more specific ones, referring only to the case of the newly-discovered American man-eaters — namely cannibalism and cannibals.

One of the main sources on the diet of the anthropophagi among the American natives is a series of texts attributed to Amerigo Vespucci. The most famous one, which is in the form of a letter addressed to Lorenzo di Pierfrancesco de' Medici, was published with the catchy title *Mundus novus* [New World] in 1504 and circulated also partly due to its inclusion in Giovanni Ramusio's collection *On Navigations and Travels*, with the title *Sommario di due navigazioni* [Report on Two Navigations]. Furthermore, a 'Letter on the Newly Rediscovered Islands' relates four journeys in which Vespucci supposedly participated.[41]

In the (pseudo-)Vespuccian texts, the comments on diet are extensive, and said to be based not simply on direct observation, but on a prolonged period of cohabitation with this population.[42] According to a letter addressed to Lorenzo di Pierfrancesco de' Medici from Lisbon in 1502, the American cannibals 'eat sitting on the ground. Their food consists of many root vegetables and delicious fruits, large amounts of fish [...]. The meat they eat, especially the one eaten commonly, is human flesh'.[43] The report goes on to explain that the natives only rarely go hunting and eat other animals: the woods are inhabited by wild animals of all species, but there are no domesticated animals.[44] The land appears to European eyes to be extremely fertile, with abundant vegetation and fields providing all sorts of vegetables and flowers. The letter compares the view of such a glorious landscape with the terrestrial paradise, thus evoking in European readers a precise image: the islands of the cannibals are like a paradise on earth itself, in which the land provides the majority of the foods.[45]

This account of a 'Cannibal paradise' is not unique, but rather becomes part of a specific representation of the New World.[46] Unlike the anthropophagi of antiquity, the cannibals thus hunt mainly humans, rather than mainly animals. In some reports they even appear to hunt humans exclusively, rather than animals. They are certainly described as cruel, but their cruelty is not directly related to the amount of meat eaten, in contrast to the medical debates reconstructed in the previous chapter.[47]

Furthermore, the travel reports often suggest that the American cannibals are not organized according to a proper social order. Vespucci describes the man-eaters as follows:

> Non tengono né legge né fede nesuna. Vivono secondo natura. Non conoscono immortalità d'anima. Non tengono infra loro beni propi, perché tuto è comune. Non tengono termini di regni o di provincia; non hanno re, né ubidiscono a nesuno: ognuno è signore di sé. Non aministrano giustizia, la quale non è loro necesario.[48]

> [They have no law and no faith. They live according to nature. They do not know the immortality of the soul. They do not have private possessions, because

everything is in common. [...] They do not have a king, they are not subject to anyone: everyone is his or her own master. They have no administration of justice, because it is not necessary to them.]

The representation of the cannibal as an outsider from human society became an established commonplace: the cannibal, as the Aristotelian philosopher John Case (*d.* 1600) put it, is someone who cannot be tolerated within society.[49] Eating human meat is thus viewed as a symbolic attack on the very idea of a human community.

3.3. *Bons sauvages* and Civilized Cannibals: Montaigne

The dietetic practice of the cannibals positioned them at the borders of humanity. The nomadism of the ancient anthropophagi signalled their distance from the civilization of human societies, too.[50] In his famous essay 'On Cannibals' (written 1579–80), Montaigne reflects on the 'amazing distance' ('distance merveilleuse') between 'us' (Europeans) and 'them' (the cannibals), by comparing the traditional view of the ancient anthropophagi with the new travel reports on the inhabitants of the new world.[51] In particular, Montaigne discusses the habits of the Brazilian tribe of the Tupinambá, which are at the centre of a famous account by Hans Staden of his captivity among these Indians, published in 1577: *Warhaftige Historia und Beschreibung eyner Landtschafft der wilden, nacketen, grimmigen Menschfresser Leuthen in der Newenwelt America gelegen* [True History and Description of a Land of the Wild, Naked, Ferocious Anthropophagi Situated in the New World America].[52]

Montaigne emphasizes the crucial role played by the sources on which the portrayals of the anthropophagi, old and new, are founded. With regard to the former, Montaigne, just like Plutarch, mentions the Stoic theory that eating human corpses is, or rather should be, acceptable. Then Montaigne stresses two important distinctions: first, between eating humans dead or alive; and second regarding whether or not eating human flesh should be a means of nourishment. The Stoics, he points out, had been favourable only to the kind of anthropophagy that involves eating human corpses, and exclusively for nourishment. The idea of eating humans alive has a clear symbolic bearing, as Montaigne compares the Europeans' 'cannibalistic' practices of mutual torture and killing, especially within religious conflicts, to the American cannibals' very selective approach, directed at neighbouring populations. Unsurprisingly, the Scyths are Montaigne's main example of ancient anthropophagi. Unlike the American cannibals, Montaigne's Scyths ate human flesh to gain nourishment from it, just as they would have eaten any other type of meat. Montaigne underlines that the cannibals, by contrast, eat humans as an act of vengeance, as a strategy of war, not as part of their diet.[53]

The sources from which Montaigne derives information on the habits of the cannibals are varied and are deployed with ironic twists, including conversations with direct witnesses — one being a simple man who lived with Montaigne, and who is credited with accurate information precisely because of his lack of education.[54] The fact that simplicity is presented as trustworthy reveals Montaigne's scepticism: he asks critically whether civilization is really the opposite of brutishness. The influence of specific travel literature is evident, but Montaigne must have purposefully selected those sources, already mentioned, in which the New World is described almost as a paradise on earth. It has been suggested that Peter Martyr's *De orbe novo*, which served as basis for the already mentioned *Libretto*, was an essential source for Montaigne's essay.[55] In opposition to literature in which the 'Indians' were portrayed as uncivilized barbarians, Montaigne follows instead the reports in which America is not simply a savage place inhabited by human brutes. What we label as 'savagery', explains Montaigne, is simply what we do not know, and those 'cannibals' can be called savage only by understanding *sauvage* as wild, just like wild fruits that are generated naturally, following nature's own course.[56] Thus Montaigne underlines the original naivety of the cannibals, guided by natural laws not yet 'rendered bastard' by European civilization.[57] But Montaigne does not merely expose the fact that a certain view of the cannibals is the result of a European construction: he also uses this very same construction to reflect on the character of the Europeans themselves. These are not just the creators of the myth of the cannibals, but they are the real cannibals, attacking their enemies in the form of their neighbours in the French Wars of Religion. As David Quint puts it, 'Montaigne's admiring description of the cannibals' portrays them as 'perfect upholders of the Stoic bravery to which the French nobility aspires'. The convergence of Stoicism and cannibalism means that, for Montaigne, 'the most valorous nobleman, the most rigid Stoic are no better than cannibals'.[58] It is the European 'cannibals' that have displayed a remarkable lack of pity: they kill without actually eating, but the ritual meaning of slaughtering one's enemy remains the same for the imagined cannibals as for the very real Europeans.

It is noteworthy that the same interplay of perspectives — between that of the supposedly ferocious cannibals and 'our' own — also informs the structure of Voltaire's entry 'Anthropophagi' in his *Dictionnaire philosophique* (published 1764), even if Montaigne is not directly mentioned.[59] Like Montaigne, Voltaire, too, has recourse to direct witnesses of cannibalism in order to approach the myth of the American cannibal. He claims to have had a conversation with a woman who had arrived from Mississippi to Fontainebleau together with three other 'savages': she candidly admitted to having eaten human flesh, justifying her actions by explaining that it is better to eat one's enemy rather than leaving him or her to be devoured by the beasts. '*We* respect the dead more than those who live' is Voltaire's comment.[60] He goes on to explain that if it were permitted to eat one's enemy eventually one would end up eating one's compatriots. But Voltaire seems to suggest that it is the Europeans who would run this risk, not the cannibals, who in Voltaire's presentation, too, restrict themselves to eating defeated enemies. Ultimately, the question is once again who are the real savages and who are the civilized people: the answer is not straightforward, and not just because all populations have been savage in the past, but also because paradoxically the cannibals apply an ethical principle in their choice, while the Europeans do not.[61] If humans are more worthy than animals, it is legitimate to eat a dead enemy rather than leaving it to the beasts, even if in so doing the eater treats humans like any other animal.[62]

Voltaire thus shows, like Montaigne, that the phenomenon of cannibalism challenges a series of boundaries: between 'us' and 'them', between ancient and modern anthropophagi, between humans and animals. With regard to the origin of the 'cannibal myth', the boundary is the well-known one between the representation of the American Indians as 'noble savages' or as the embodiment of brutish humanity. But what must be noted is the fact that dietary assumptions also change accordingly: in the case of the cannibals as they are described by Montaigne, as well as in certain travel literature (for instance Vespucci's letters, Peter Martyr's *De orbe novo*, and the *Libretto*), the consumption of human flesh is presented as exceptional. It has no dietary purpose, but is rather an act of war: these cannibals do not eat humans indiscriminately, they eat enemies.[63] Vespucci's 'Letter on the Newly Discovered Islands' describes this crucial feature in striking terms:

> Mangion poca carne, salvo che carne di uomo, [...] in questo sono tanto inumani che trapassano ogni bestial costume, perché si mangiono tutti e loro nimici che amazzano o pigliano, sì femine come maschi, con tanta efferità che a dirlo pare cosa brutta, quanto più a vederlo, come mi accadde infinitissime volte e in molte parti vederlo. E si maravigliorono udendo dire a noi che non si mangiamo e nostri nemici.[64]

> [They eat little meat, apart from the human type, [...] in this respect they exceed any bestial habit, since they eat all the enemies they kill or catch, both female and male, with such cruelty that it seems an ugly thing just to tell it, and it is even worse to see it, as indeed I happened to witness countless times and in many areas. And they were surprised to hear that we do not eat our enemies.]

When the letter describes these anthropophagi as 'barbarians' ('barbari'), this refers to the cruelty of dealing with their enemies and prisoners, and not to the extensive consumption of animal flesh, as in the case of the barbarian Scyths of antiquity.

Apart from 'episodic cannibalism', the diet of these American inhabitants is not portrayed as the epitome of carnivorous brutishness, as was the life of the Scyths. On the contrary, a different frame of reference is put in the place of the ancient assumption about the remarkable carnivorousness of the anthropophagi. It is the idea that these cannibals live in a sort of earthly paradise, with an abundance of tasty vegetable nourishment. Peter Martyr had claimed that hardly any quadrupeds were actually seen on the cannibals' islands, where no dangerous animal could be found at all, with the exception of the man-eaters themselves.[65] Montaigne does mention that hunting is one of the natives' activities. In any case, the strong emphasis on meat-eating has been replaced by a view of the landscape clearly influenced by biblical images of earthly paradise, that is to say a vegetarian ideal.

The descriptions of the 'new' anthropophagi thus unsettle the firm opposition to the vegetarian diet, offering to Renaissance thinkers an alternative version of anthropophagy. The brutishness of the man-eaters can be interpreted as the innocence that precedes civilization. The cannibals live an uncorrupted, simple life that bears a resemblance to that of biblical figures: they share with Adam the major part of their diet, based on vegetables; and they are said to enjoy exceptionally long lives, like Adam and his descendants before the flood. The lack of restriction imposed by law is of course a classical trait of the Golden Age, for instance as defined in Ovid's *Metamorphoses*.[66] Vegetarianism as the original diet is here an important point of reference, connecting the myth of the Golden Age with biblical representations, and the figure of the cannibal — naive, yet brutal — is constructed at the intersection of these discourses. Can then the cannibals embody an almost vegetarian ideal?

3.4. Vegetarianism, Cannibalism, and the Origin of Humanity: A Cannibalistic Paradise on Earth

Cannibalism and vegetarianism are deeply intertwined in the mythology of humankind's original condition, as is presented in the travel literature on the Americas. In the eyes of the Europeans, America provides a contemporary setting for imagining the Golden Age of humanity. The discussion of sacrifice in Chapter 1 showed that Porphyry believed carnivorism to be the result of the corruption of the original state. Sketching an anthropological evolution of sacrificial practices, Porphyry had explained that the first people turned to sacrificing one another, forgetting all 'holiness', whenever there was a shortage of crops to offer as sacrifice. Therefore human bodies substituted vegetables, marking a sudden shift from a non-violent original state (both with regard to the food and the sacrificial offer) to the supreme violence of sacrificing and eating human beings.[67] Using animals instead of plants is considered to be a later development, preceded by an anthropophagic phase, which immediately followed the initial, vegetarian one. Porphyry had thus constructed a direct continuity from vegetarianism to anthropophagy in the evolution of humanity.

   Further still, Porphyry had discussed the myth according to which Pythagoras had established the vegetarian diet in reaction to such a dangerous turn towards anthropophagy:

> As for saying that long ago Pythagoras took this precaution [i.e. prescribing vegetarianism] in an attempt to stop people eating each other, this is silly. This method was more likely to encourage them, by showing that eating members of one's own species is just the same as devouring the flesh of pigs and cattle.[68]

Porphyry's polemical answer to this rumour aimed at dismissing the objection that Pythagoras' vegetarianism might have been the result of an attempt actually to stop a natural tendency towards anthropophagy in human beings, which would be triggered when other types of food are not available. Vegetarianism, for Porphyry, cannot be presented as a cure for anthropophagy; yet Porphyry's own argumentation tightly links these two apparently opposite diets, showing that they are deeply intertwined in the myth of the origin.

   Porphyry had connected vegetarianism and anthropophagy, when he stated that in sacrifices animals simply came to substitute humans at a later stage, both as offerings on the altar and as food on the plate. But the easiness of this substitution implies a radical question: why is eating humans any different than eating animals? Pythagoras's idea of the transmigration of the souls implied that there would indeed be no difference between eating humans and eating animals, because by eating an animal one would in fact be consuming a creature with a human soul, that is to say, a human. Therefore, Pythagoras's choice of the vegetarian diet was open to the interpretation that stopping humans from eating animals was a means of stopping them from eating humans. As Jonathan Barnes puts it: 'The doctrine of transmigration [...] shows that killing animals is killing people, and that eating animals is eating people; and eating people is wrong'.[69] What is clear is that already for Porphyry discussing anthropophagy is nothing less than essential in order to retrace the origin of the vegetarian diet, and to present vegetarianism as the original ideal.

But first of all, Porphyry connects these two diets on the basis of food availability, asserting the idea that the fall into carnivorism, and into anthropophagy in particular, was triggered by famine and the unavailability of plant food.[70] In order to understand how the connection between vegetarianism and anthropophagy shifted from antiquity to the Renaissance it is thus important to consider not only the differing approaches to the populations involved but also descriptions of the 'setting', namely the landscape of the New World. It is noteworthy that Giovanni Botero (1544–1617) explains the origin of cannibalism with a story that is reminiscent of Porphyry's own account, and indeed ends with a reference to Pythagoras.[71] In the third book of *Le relationi universali* [Universal Reports] Botero narrates the following episode:

> In alcune parti della medesima provincia, persuadendosi d'haver' a sforzare gli Spagnuoli a uscir fuor del paese con la fame, si risolsero di non seminare i lor grani: ma essendo per questa cagione mancato il vitto non tanto a gli Spagnuoli, quanto a lor medesimi, si mangiarono l'un l'altro; e'l paese si desolò. Per un simil mancamento di vettovaglie questi anni passati s'introdusse l'antropofagia nell'Arauco.[72]

> [The inhabitants decided not to sow their grain because they were convinced that they needed to drive the Spaniards out of the country by starving them. But since this caused a shortage of food not just for the Spaniards, but mostly for themselves, they thus ate each other, and the land became empty and deserted. It is because of similar food shortages in the last few years that anthropophagy was introduced in the region of Arauco.]

Botero continues with other examples of anthropophagy, which he describes as a terrible cruelty, and concludes with the rhetorical question: 'What would Pythagoras have said, given that he abhorred the use of animal flesh?'[73] Elsewhere, Botero specifies that the anthropophagi are barbarians not just because they behave differently from other human groups, as in this respect one could say that every population appears to be 'barbarian' to every other: rather, they are barbarians in the sense that they do not follow reason in their savage behaviour.[74] Yet the story of the famine purports to show that anthropophagy can be triggered simply by lack of more suitable food, and as a result of bad strategy in dealing with food supplies.

It is therefore important to note that early travel reports seem to agree in describing the New World as highly fertile and suitable for growing plants and trees, and so not a place where anthropophagy might be rendered necessary by famine. For instance, Vespucci's letter to Lorenzo di Pierfrancesco de' Medici of 1502 from Lisbon, describes that landscape as follows:

Questa terra è molto amena e piena d'infiniti albori verdi e molto grandi, e
mai non perdono foglie e tutti hanno odori soavisimi e aromatici e producono
infinitisime frute e molte d'esse buone al gusto e salutifere al corpo. [...] qualche
volta mi maravigliavo de' soavi odori de l'erbe e de' fiori e de' sapori d'esse
frute e radice, tanto che infra me pensavo esser presso al paradiso teresto.[75]

[This land is very beautiful and full of endless green and very large trees that
never lose their leaves and all smell wonderful and sweet, and produce a truly
infinite amount of fruit and many [types] of them are tasty and healthy for the
body. [...] At times I marvelled at the pleasant smells of the vegetation and of
the flowers, and at the taste of those fruits and roots, so that I thought to myself
that I was in the earthly paradise.]

This is a description that resonates with biblical allusions: 'And out of the ground
made the Lord God to grow every tree that is pleasant to the sight, and good for
food (Genesis 2: 9); and 'I have given you every herb bearing seed, which *is* upon
the face of all the earth, and every tree, in the which *is* the fruit of a tree yielding
seed; to you it shall be for meat' (Genesis 1: 29–30). The biblical lens through
which the Europeans regarded the Americans is also apparent in the remark that
the inhabitants of the New World enjoy very long lives.[76] In the same letter, the
connection between the landscape, the fertility of the soil, and the health of the
inhabitants is clearly emphasized:

Quanto alla disposizione de la terra, dico che è terra molto amena e temperata
e sana, perché di quello tempo andamo per essa, che furono 10 mesi, nesuno di
noi non solo morì ma pochi n'amalarono. Come ho detto, loro vivono molto
tempo e non sentono infermità né pestilenza o di coruzione d'aria, se non di
morte naturale o causata per man di sofocazione. E in conclusione, e medici
arebono cativo stare in ta' luogo.[77]

[With regard to the condition of the land I say that the land is very beautiful
and temperate and healthy, because during the period of our stay, that is to say
10 months, not only did none of us die, but very few became ill. As I said they
[i.e. the inhabitants] live for a very long time and do not experience disease,
plague, or corruption of the air, and die only naturally or by suffocation. And
in conclusion physicians would have a hard time over there.]

By breaking the taboo that humans cannot possibly be viewed as food, the cannibal
— or rather, the European image of this figure — provides a practical example
of earlier medical speculations, exemplarily expressed in Manfredi's comment on
the hypothetical benefits of anthropophagy in *Il Perché / Liber de homine*.[78] Possibly
no other aspect of the cannibals' lives reflects the context of the European literary
tradition more clearly than the assumption about their excellent life expectancy.
Vespucci's *Mundus novus* states that they live one hundred and fifty years and are
rarely ill (when this happens they use herbal medicine).[79] *Mundus novus* lists the
striking features of the newly discovered territories, and the factors that 'are to be
taken into account, namely the temperate air, the good sky, the fertile soil, and
the long lifespan. And this perhaps happens because of the east wind that blows
constantly here'.[80] With regard to food, the text claims that the inhabitants of these
territories eat fish, but hardly any other animals, primarily because they do not go
hunting, and fear the attacks of the wild animals themselves.

Vespucci's descriptions both of climate and food indicate that the New World offers ideal conditions, and indirectly suggest a comparison of its inhabitants to Adam and Eve in the Garden of Eden, enjoying the beauty of the vegetation and a vegetable diet — this, however, is tainted in the case of the American cannibals by the occasional episode of anthropophagy. Moreover, just like Adam in the Garden, the barbarians of the New World are often naked; yet this can be interpreted more negatively as lack of civilization, as indeed Botero suggests in the *Relationi*, remarking that, whether or not they eat human flesh, it is clear that these people are closer to animals than to proper humans because they do not feel shame.[81]

The position of the Garden of Eden on earth had also been at the centre of a long controversy, upon which the travel reports on the new territories also bear.[82] A noteworthy example is the monumental commentary on Genesis by the Jesuit Benedictus Pereira (1535–1610), who discusses questions such as whether Paradise had been below the equinoxial circle, or beyond the ocean, drawing on a variety of sources. In particular it is the conception of a perfectly tempered area of the earth, in between the tropics, which creates a contact point between the Garden of Eden and America (even if the author ultimately supports the theory that Paradise had been in Mesopotamia).[83]

There is also a further important element to the biblical background of the encounter with the people of the New World, and this is the question regarding their origin. While their condition resembles that of Adam, it remains to be proven that they descend from Adam, since the lack of geographical connection between the old and the New World raises the problem of how humans came to inhabit that part of the earth and when exactly that happened. Heirs of Adam with regard to the land they inhabit, the cannibals nevertheless run the risk of being excluded from the status of humanity. Augustine had already queried the status of those living on 'distant islands', explaining that if they are to be considered human then they must also be descendants of Adam.[84]

The other option was to classify them as animals, rather than humans. Renaissance presentations of the brutality of the new 'barbarians' often develop in this direction, for instance when considering whether their lack of (comprehensible) language signifies lack of rationality. This motif appears in various Renaissance travel reports on the encounters with the cannibals, and indeed even the creation of the word 'cannibal', as we saw, derives from linguistic misunderstanding. Peter Martyr suggests that the cannibals might be creatures somewhere between animals and humans: 'feri homines', as he calls them.[85] Vespucci's letter to Lorenzo di Pierfrancesco de' Medici of 1502 features the expression 'rational animals' to denote the human inhabitants of the New World. The emphasis here falls rather on 'animals' than on 'rational', since they are described as naked and without any sense of shame, just like beasts.[86] The question of the cannibals' rationality, or whether they are endowed with *lógos*, is a crucial one if they are to be converted.[87]

At the border between the vegetarian ideal of the earthly paradise and extreme barbarity, the figure of the cannibal thus also affects the understanding of the border dividing humans from animals. The cannibals break the taboo of not eating members of one's own species: choosing humans as food, they appear to lapse into animality, thus prompting the further question of what it means to eat like an animal and what to eat like a human being.

3.5. Cannibals and the Human-Animal Border: Botero and Renaissance Travel Reports

One of the most striking passages in the *Libretto* on Columbus's travels describes a scene of meat-curing. But instead of preparing sausages and ham using the meat of animals, the cannibals use human meat:

> Li garzoni che loro prendeno li castrano, come faciamo noi castrati, perche diventano piu grassi per mazarli, e li homini maturi cosi come li prendeno li amazano, e mangiano, e mangiano freschi le intestini e li extremi membra del copro [sic]. Et resto insalano, e li servano ali soi tempi come faciamo noi.[88]

> [They castrate the boys they catch, just as we castrate animals to make them grow fatter in order to kill them, and they kill on the spot and eat the adult men they catch, and eat their intestines fresh and the extremities of the body. They cure the rest and preserve it for future times, as we do.]

There would not be anything remarkable in a description of curing meat, were it not for the fact that the meat in question is of the human kind. What is noteworthy in this scene is what it reveals about the 'observer', who perceives that an exchange has taken place: the cannibals handle human flesh in exactly the same way the Europeans handle the flesh of animals. The cannibals do not simply eat fellow humans by, for instance, attacking them, and savagely dismembering the parts. Rather, they seem to follow a preparatory method in transforming the flesh into proper food. It is evident that the encounter with the peoples of the New World is filtered through expectations of what is acceptable to eat based on a hierarchical order. Therefore the weight of the narration falls on the horror of putting humans in the place of animals in the most radical situation of all, namely when choosing food.

A similar description is contained in Vespucci's *Mundus novus*, which expands the same image:

> Viddi anche una certa città, nella quale io dimorai forse ventisette giorni, dove le carne umane, avendole salate, erano appiccate alli travi, sí come noi alli travi di cucina appicchiamo le carni di cinghiale secche al sole o al fumo, e massimamente salsiccie e altre simil cose.[89]

> [I saw a certain city in which I stayed maybe twenty-seven days, where cured human meats were hanging from the beams, just as we have cured meats of wild boar hanging from the kitchen beams, dried in the sun or in the smoke, and especially sausages and similar things.]

The text continues by pointing out that the difference in the way in which the Europeans and the 'cannibals' view their respective enemies at war: 'they were amazed that we did not eat the flesh of the enemies, which they say is appetizing and tastes lovely, and they praise it as a delicacy'.[90] The above-mentioned Michele da Cuneo, too, refers to the cannibals' habit of castrating boys, but appears not to be completely sure of the reason: it might be a way of preparing their meat for consumption, but it could also be a way of claiming their women exclusively for their own people.[91] His comments on the cannibals' relationship with the Indians show that he also employs the comparison between humans and animals:

> Li quali Cambali, quando prendeno de dicti Indiani, li mangiano come noi li capreti, e dicano che la carne del garzone è assai migliore che quella de la femina. E di tal carne umana sono ghiottissimi, per ciò che, per mangiare di tal carne, stanno alcuni fora de loro paese sei, octo e dece anni inanti che rimpatriano, e tanto stanno dove vanno, che consumano le isole; e se questo non facessino, li dicti Indiani multiplicarebbero tanto, che copririano la terra.[92]

> [These Cannibals, when they catch said Indians, eat them like we eat goat kids, and they say that the meat of the boy is much better than that of the female. And they very much enjoy human flesh, to the point that in order to eat this meat they remain out of their country six, eight, and ten years before going back, and where they go they remain until they have exhausted the islands; and if they did not do this, the said Indians would multiply to the point of covering the earth.]

The Indians are not only compared to animals, but are treated as such, and this is best exemplified by Michele's understanding of the 'ecological' impact of the cannibals' diets: by eating the Indians, the cannibals mean to stop them from multiplying too much, an argument that is still used today to justify the killing of certain species of animals.[93]

The belief in the existence of certain populations that eat enemies is certainly not new in the Renaissance. It is sufficient to recall Marco Polo's vivid narration of the behaviour attributed to the inhabitants of certain islands:

> Quando prendono qualcuno, che non sia loro amico e che non si possa riscuotere con denari, convitano tutti i loro parenti e amici a casa sua, e fanno uccidere quell'uomo suo prigione e lo fanno cuocere, e mangianselo insieme allegramente, e dicono, che la carne umana è la piu saporita e migliore, che si possa truovar al mondo.[94]

> [When they catch somebody who is not their friend and whom they cannot exchange for money, they invite all their relatives and friends at home, they have the prisoner killed and cooked and they merrily eat him together, and they say that human flesh is the tastiest that you can find on earth.]

Polo's narrations of anthropophagy are mentioned in Botero's discussion of the customs of a population so greedy for human meat that they would make carnage of their fellow humans whenever they desired that particular food. Botero uses the striking word *beccaria* (slaughtering, slaughterhouse), thus suggesting the same perverse substitution of animals with humans.[95] Regarding the habits of those people properly called 'cannibals', Botero again insists on the exchange of humans for animals, and on the distinction among human beings that justifies eating some and not others. Continuing along the same lines as Vespucci, he states that the 'Caribi or Cannibals, bestial populations [...], eat human flesh, raw or preserved, as we do the flesh of pigs. They castrate the boys as we do with chicken, in order to eat them more tender and fatter'.[96] Again, Botero points out that the cannibals 'go hunting for humans as we go for animals'.[97]

Yet the major distinction between friends and enemies complicates the main hierarchical division between humans and all other animals. Porphyry had used the example of the treatment of enemies to argue that killing and eating do not necessarily follow one from the other. In the case of enemies it is certainly legitimate to kill them, but eating them would be 'beyond the bounds of humanity'.[98] The situation, Porphyry argues, is no different in the case of killing and eating animals: it might be legitimate to kill them, for instance in self-defence, but that does not automatically make eating them acceptable. This is the same reasoning used by Porphyry with regard to the connection between sacrificing and eating animals.

There is of course a ritual aspect to the eating of enemies that has a long tradition; indeed this was also behind Montaigne's approach, which involved juxtaposing the image of the cannibal and the ways in which the Europeans kill their enemies.[99] But the context I sketched in the previous sections of this chapter is equally vital for understanding Renaissance interpretations of this particular habit in the case of the new American cannibals. Renaissance thinkers underline the fact that cannibals do not eat human meat indiscriminately, but rather tend to eat enemies, and also that their consumption of animal meat is limited; they also project biblical images on the descriptions of the cannibals' territories. Taken together, these elements operate a notable shift: the main dividing-line with regard to the choice of food becomes the one between friends and enemies, rather than the one between humans and animals. The cannibals, in other words, take a practical approach to the question about human exceptionality, which is clearly in the background of the reports such as Vespucci's letters, which express distress at the substitution of animals with humans as food: by eating their enemies they affirm that there is nothing special about humans in general that would speak against consuming their flesh. Cannibalism itself is nothing but the application within the human group of a form of behaviour — eating members of one's own species — present also in the animal world. This is another way in which cannibalism subverts the clear division between humans and animals: in eating their own kind, the cannibals behave like other species of animals that do not refrain from turning against each other.

In the passage in which he discusses Pythagoras's supposed establishment of vegetarianism as a reaction to anthropophagy, Porphyry had used the term 'allelo-phagi', that is 'those eating their own kind', rather than the more specific 'anthro-pophagi'.[100] The underlying assumption is therefore that Pythagoras intended to stop humans from behaving as other creatures might, rejecting a taboo that is foundational to humanity itself: humans are those animals that do not eat their own kind.[101] From this point of view, anthropophagy is thus only a specific instance of a behaviour that is not unique to humans, but that humans should resist adopting.

Descriptions of anthropophagi as 'bestial' (for instance in Botero's *Relationi*) could suggest not just a generic brutality, but more specifically the fact that those humans technically behave like animals. For humans, breaking the anthropophagic taboo would thus mean renouncing humanity and embracing an animal nature. Botero calls the cannibals 'enemies of humankind', even if he then adds that they could be simply considered 'completely crazy'. In order to be able to communicate with them, and most importantly to convert them to Christianity, 'they must be first rendered capable of rational thinking and of humanity', so as then to 'educate them and instruct them to [follow] virtue and the way of God'. It is significant that Botero compares this procedure to that of taming and domesticating animals, mentioning Aristotle as the authority for the fact that it would be legitimate to use violence in the process.[102] The cannibals are thus animals that have the potential to be 'civilized' and educated to become human. The consumption of human meat is an indicator of this hybrid position. The conversion of the cannibals could be seen as a process by which the border between animality and humanity is crossed once more, as the human lapsed into animality (re)discovers his or her own human nature.[103] Thus the topic of anthropophagy remains central in the conversion of the indigenous people: as Porphyry had already pointed out, Christianity places an act of anthropophagy at the heart of its main ritual.[104] The act of conversion aims to rescue the human soul trapped by brutal behaviour, and yet precisely that behaviour is ritually repeated on the altar when the body of Christ is eaten by the faithful. Converting the brutal cannibals would thus consist in a transition from actual anthropophagy to a sublimated form of it, as bread is eaten in place of a human being.[105]

3.6. Allelophagy, Anthropophagy, and Learning to Eat Like a Human: Botero and Della Porta

A guiding assumption in this discussion of allelophagy, or eating members of one's own species, is that this form of behaviour is common among animals, but exceptional among humans. This is why Botero mentions madness as a possible explanation for the cannibals' behaviour. For Botero there are two ways in which humans can behave like animals with regard to food: one is cannibalism, while the other can be seen as its opposite, namely feeding on what grows spontaneously from the soil, without cultivating it. Both — eating humans and eating wild vegetables — are examples of 'fierezza', that is beastly behaviour.[106] The conclusion is thus that the proper, civilized food for humans consists in the products of agriculture, that is to say in cultivating one's own food. With regard to meat, the distinction falls between eating one's own kind (as beasts sometimes do), and consuming the flesh of other species (appropriate human behaviour). According to this line of thought a human becomes a human by eating animals, the distinction being drawn between consuming the flesh of one's own kind and consuming the flesh of other species. The differentiation between humans and animals crystallizes in the choice of food, to the extent that by eating like animals a human becomes brutal, and vice-versa: the shift in food habits also marks the development of human civilization. Putting it in more medical terms, Botero writes that 'since our complexion takes its quality from nourishment, it follows that from wild food proceed also a wild complexion and nature'.[107]

A contemporary of Botero, Giovan Battista Della Porta (1535–1615) recurs to the same conception of brutality with regard to human nutrition when he lists examples of human groups eating wild vegetation (seeds, twigs, berries). He considers them closer to savagery than civilization. Even the myth of humanity's vegetarian past can be framed in this context:

> Disse Hippocrate che l'huomo potea solo cibarsi di semi, ché così nell'età de' suoi avi era usato a pascersi; né tanto lo disse, penso io, per fuggir molte infermità che da sì vario cibo vengono, quanto per non aver così variabili costumi.[108]

> [Hippocrates said that the human being could feed purely on seeds, that he used to do so in the age of his predecessors. But I believe he said so not as a recommendation to avoid many illnesses that come from such variety of foods, but rather so as not to have such variable habits.]

The extreme dietary variety of different human populations is bewildering, but at the same time food, for Della Porta, is responsible for the identity of human populations, and it is not by chance that he argues for diet as the common denominator even in the case of such a varied human group as the so-called Scyths.[109] In general terms, a population will be as wild as the food that forms its main sustenance.[110] Therefore humans can eat more or less like animals, and Della Porta devotes a chapter of his main work, *Della fisonomia dell'huomo* [On Human Physiognomics], to the topic 'that from the foods that human beings eat it is possible to assume what their habits will be'.[111] Referring to Plato, Della Porta writes that 'human beings, some because of the water they drink, others because of the foods they eat and that the soil produces, have better or worse habits, and those also penetrate into the soul, not just altering the body'.[112] From the point of view of physiognomics, the science which aims to understand the character of the soul by looking at the signs impressed on the body, food is a key agent that by altering the body affects the depths of the soul too.[113] Della Porta explicitly points out the role of geographical variations, referring to particular characteristics of the land; and the central role of the concept of 'habits' in his work serves the purpose of emphasizing the plurality of human nutrition. Thus human populations became examples of the positive and negative effects of food on 'the habits', or behaviour: in the case of the cannibals, their faces, and their foreheads in particular, express for Della Porta cruelty of character.

From this background, Della Porta develops a precise conception of what it means to eat like a human being, rather than like an animal. Unlike animals, he points out, human beings do not turn spontaneously to a specific kind of food, but rather have to choose what to eat, and in choosing their food they also choose the nature they want to assume:

> Gli animali bruti si pascono di un sol cibo: chi di herba, chi di radici, chi di seme di frutti, chi di carne, e però ciascun di loro ha un sol costume. Sol l'huomo di tutti gusta e vuol servirsi, onde ancor non si sa qual sia il suo proprio e peculiar cibo, dal pane e dall'acqua in poi; e però ha varii costumi: piacevoli, selvaggi, indulgenti e ferini.[114]

> [Brute animals feed on one kind of food only, some eat grass, some roots, some fruit seeds, some eat flesh, and yet each of them has one habit only. The human

being is the only one who enjoys and wants to make use of all [types of food], since it is not yet known which is his own proper food, apart from bread and water. Rather, he has a variety of habits, pleasing, wild, indulgent, and feral.]

It is the very possibility of choosing that sets humans apart from all other animals. If the idea of human adaptability is reminiscent of Pico's famous image of the human being as a chameleon, then Della Porta's account of the effect of food attempts a practical approach to finding the human position in the cosmos. The choice of diet becomes a way of increasing or decreasing the distance between humans and animals: a human can feed like an animal, or can opt for food that will support the development of civilized, rather than wild habits. From this point of view, cannibals renounce humanity itself, but so do those humans who only eat a strict vegetable diet consisting of wild plants. The cutting edge in this discourse is civilization.

Botero had suggested a simpler explanation, namely that cannibalism could be the result of madness. He had a famous precedent for this interpretation: Leonardo da Vinci (1452–1519), who had used the general conception of allelophagy as a criterion for pinpointing the human-animal border:

> Nelli animali terressti [...] non si trova animali che mangino della loro spetie se non per mancamento di cerebro (inperò che infra loro è de' matti, come infra li omini, benchè non sieno in tanto numero) [...]; e cquesto none achade se non neli animali rapaci come nella spetie leonina [...] e pardi, partere, cerveri, chatte e simili, li quali alcuna volta si mang[i]ano i figl[i]oli; ma ttu, oltre alli figl[i] oli, ti mangi il padre, madre, fratelli e amici, e non ti bassta questo, che tu vai a chaccia per le altrui isole pigliando li altri omini; e quelli moçando il menbro e li testiculi fai ingrassare e tte lli cacci giù per la tua gola.

> [Among these [i.e. the animals of the earth] there are no animals which eat members of their own species except from want of brains (as there are fools among them as among men, although they are not in so great number) [...]; and this is not the case, except among the beasts of prey, as in the species lion [...] and leopards, panthers, lynxes, cats, and the like, which sometimes eat their young ones; but you eat, besides the young ones, the father, the mother, the brothers, and friends, and this is not enough for you, as you go hunting in foreign islands, catching other men; and these, mutilating their *membrum virile* and their testicles, you fatten and force them down your gullet.][115]

Leonardo is evidently referring to the scenes of meat curing mentioned in the travel literature discussed earlier in this chapter.[116] He uses the powerful image of fattening up humans, and severing their parts, as a way to take the human-animal comparison further, and to argue that in fact humans are unique in their cruelty. Eating members of one's own species, for Leonardo, does not make humans like animals, but rather singles them out as the only creatures that are prone to turning against their own kind out of a sort of inexplicable greed. The human gullet is thus described as an insatiable pit into which humans force their innocent prey — the gate that turns the human being into a 'tomb of all animals'.[117]

A letter by the cosmographer and astronomer Andrea Corsali to Giuliano de' Medici suggests that Leonardo was indeed a vegetarian. The letter was sent from India, and describes the habits of a local vegetarian group, the 'Guzaratti' (i.e. the

Gujarati people), who 'do not eat anything that has blood', and refuse 'to hurt any living being, like our Leonardo da Vinci. They survive on rice, milk, and other inanimate foods'.[118] Their diet, according to Corsali, is responsible for the fact that they were subjugated by the Arabs: he presents the vegetarian diet as an expression of non-violence, and as such it leads, almost inevitably, to lack of military success.[119]

Even if in his notes he does not directly declare his adherence to vegetarianism, Leonardo pinpoints key elements that run through a broader Renaissance debate on the topic, for instance that certain animal species and human populations are seen as positive or negative role models; the comparison between animal and human behaviour in the case of abnormal case studies; and also the connection between meat-eating and cruelty or violence. These are topics that are developed further through an exchange that was examined in Chapter 2, regarding the role of meat in preserving health: the debate between Cardano and Scaliger, to which we now turn again to examine the causes of cannibalism in relation to the human-animal border.

3.7. The Debate on the Causes and Effects of Cannibalism

In 1688 the French scholar and poet Pierre Petit publishes a *dissertatio* in which he promises to investigate the origin and causes of cannibalism, which he calls a monstrosity and deformity.[120] Among Petit's main sources are Cardano and Scaliger. He considers dialogically the explanations that each of them offered for this abnormal human behaviour, placing their debate in a broader context, which involves discussion of ancient sources, including Porphyry, as well as later 'travel literature', such as Peter Martyr and Vespucci.[121] Therefore Petit's *De natura et moribus anthropophagorum* [On the Nature and Habits of the Anthropophagi] is informative both on the sources and the afterlives of Renaissance discourses on cannibalism.

A crucial characteristic of Petit's text is the use of the words 'cannibal' and 'anthropophagus': they feature as synonyms, and Petit combines a variety of traditions in order to sketch a history of man-eating.[122] In so doing, Petit follows one of his sources, Cardano, who had also mixed reports on ancient anthropophagi with those on the 'new' cannibals, intertwining ancient sources with contemporary ones. Cardano was proud of being cited in new travel literature.[123] In *De sapientia* [On Wisdom] he mentions Columbus's journey as the most fitting example for answering the question 'quid nova prosunt?', 'in what way are new things useful?': Columbus discovered the New World because he followed up Aristotle's statement that there is land beyond Africa, in the ocean.[124] Cardano was thus familiar with the new travel literature on cannibals. He underlines the cruelty of all men-eaters across the centuries, tracing the origin of anthropophagy to animosity or hatred ('odium').[125] Yet his main example, when he comes to explain this theory, is not the ancient anthropophagi, but the new ones, called 'Caribbes'.[126] Cardano knew from the statements in the reports from the New World that the cannibals, unlike their predecessors, did not consume large amounts of animals, and that therefore their tendency to eat other humans could not depend on the brutalizing effect of this meat-heavy diet. The anthropophagy of the cannibals thus required a different explanation from that of the ancient populations prone to cannibalism, such as the Scyths.

In *De rerum varietate*, Cardano posits what could be called a primary and a secondary cause for this behaviour. The main reason is indeed 'odium', or desire to annihilate the enemy, hatred directed against other human beings. Yet, Cardano also identifies another cause, which he considers to have preceded in time the rising of the sentiment of hatred, and thus worked as a trigger for cannibalism. This is the lack, in the New World, of animals that could be eaten, such as pigs, or sheep, or cows.[127] As a result, the cannibals had turned to anthropophagy because they could not eat the flesh of other animals, not because they ate too much of it. Reports on ancient anthropophagi, like the Scyths, underlined instead the abundance of edible animals in the territories inhabited by the meat-eaters. Pliny, for instance, had remarked that close to the areas where the Scythian anthropophagi lived, there were deserts populated by a large number of animals as wild as the Scyths themselves: he thus asserted a close connection between the two groups. Beasts and anthropophagi are both considered to be feral, and prone to attack one another.[128]

The abundance or shortage of animals distinguishes new and old anthropophagy, but the sentiment of animosity, or 'hatred', links both groups. Yet even at this level there is a distinction. Cardano states that the cannibals' animosity is not a general form of brutality: it is directed specifically at enemies. This implies that the cannibals differentiate between humans who can be eaten (enemies) and those who should not (one's own group). The animals fall out of the picture entirely. In dietary practices as well, the main difference between animals and humans dissolves, since the cannibals hardly eat any animals, and thus bypass the entire Western discussion on the way in which certain types of animal flesh affect the human eater.

Yet Cardano does underline the effects of food on the character of the cannibals, a topic in which, as we saw, he took a strong interest. He writes that the cannibals have 'such a ferocious, savage and frightful appearance that other human beings are barely able to look at them as captives and dead'. The cause for this is that 'food changes the appearance and nature'. The passage continues with a key sentence, already discussed, regarding the transformative power of food: 'Indeed it is easy to change the behaviour and the shape of living beings through habit and through the type of diet'.[129] The hatred that directs the cannibals' choice of food twists their appearance as well: they do not simply assume feral characteristics, but express a ferocity so intense that it remains visible even on a dead cannibal's body. Furthermore, Cardano appears to assume that anthropophagy is not exactly like any other kind of allelophagy, because human meat is a special aliment. In *De subtilitate* Cardano reports a story originating in Oviedo's *Historia general y natural de las Indias* [General and Natural History of the Indies] (1535), regarding a dog that had been fed human meat and had become both particularly smart and particularly cruel: thanks to this food, he had learnt to distinguish the natives from the Spaniards, and if needed, to kill the former.[130] The power of human meat is thus so radical that it affects even animals that consume it, not only humans. This could explain why, according to Cardano, the appearance of the cannibals is altered so profoundly that the change even persists after death.

To sum up, for Cardano cannibalism might have been triggered by a lack of animal food, yet it was then propelled by the cannibals' animosity, and this consumption of human flesh eventually changed both their outer appearance and their inner nature.[131] This multi-layered explanation was criticized by Scaliger, who posited food scarcity ('inopia', i.e. general scarcity, not just of meat) as the main reason for cannibalism. Petit contrasts the two alternatives: it was either hatred or food scarcity that made humans turn against their kind. In *Exotericae exercitationes*, Scaliger had noted further that animals such as sheep appear not to be present on the cannibals' islands. He adds that even fruit is scarce, and that fish is available but unreachable, because the cannibals have no fishing techniques. Therefore, he concludes, the cannibals eat human meat simply because they could not survive on other food resources.[132] According to Scaliger, human flesh is thus a food like any other. Cardano's more complex account had instead maintained a certain difference between the cannibals and all other human beings: for Cardano, lack of food alone is not enough to turn a human into a cannibal, but the transformation needs the driving force of 'odium', too.[133] For Scaliger, however, anthropophagy can be simply a means to avoid starvation and to survive. It therefore follows that including human meat in the diet is a decisive advantage in certain areas of the earth.

As Petit reminds his readers, the argument of 'inopia' had been used in antiquity to justify episodes of temporary anthropophagic behaviour. Petit reports one of the most famous cases, namely Hannibal's alleged advice to his troops during the expedition to Italy that they should be prepared to eat human flesh in case of emergency. This advice is discussed in the second book of *On Abstinence*, to which Petit refers directly: according to Porphyry, notes Petit, the advice was not intended to brutalize the troops, but simply to provide a last resource to keep them alive.[134] Yet, in Petit's view, Porphyry's explanation of such transitory acts of anthropophagy (or at least of the theoretical permission to commit them) is instrumental to his main aim, namely to convince scholars to avoid all meat.[135] Thus Petit claims that anthropophagy and vegetarianism are closely connected phenomena in *On Abstinence*: Porphyry had tried to soften the story about Hannibal's anthropophagic recommendations in order to show that any form of emergency meat-eating need not become a permanent habit. In *On Abstinence* (II.57), Porphyry had linked the example of Hannibal to his discussion of animal sacrifice: just as eating human flesh as a last resort in wartime does not legitimize eating it in other circumstances, so even if animals must be sacrificed on the altar, it nevertheless does not follow that their flesh should be eaten as well.

Petit is correct in pointing out that Porphyry had used anthropophagy as an argument in favour of vegetarianism by assuming that there might be circumstances that force humans to eat other humans, or to kill animals, and yet that such episodes would not grant ethical legitimation for a continuous practice. From such a perspective, eating members of one's own species is reduced to a practice for survival to which both humans and animals might occasionally resort. Petit himself does not appear to agree with Porphyry: he states that, properly speaking, anthropophagi are those human beings who actively cultivate the 'vicious habit' ('prava consuetudo') of eating human flesh, enjoying it more, and more often, than other kinds of meat.[136] Accordingly, Petit mentions the Scyths as his main example: the American cannibals do not fit into this picture. He thus qualifies Porphyry's interpretation of anthropophagy as based on marginal cases. Lack of other foods may explain transitory anthropophagy, he argues, but is insufficient explanation for the endurance of this habit, including among such different groups as the Scyths and the cannibals.

Petit appears to be fascinated by Cardano and the theory that 'inopia' is not a sufficient explanation for anthropophagy. Yet, he criticizes Cardano for not grasping the major role that daemons play in causing anthropophagy. According to Petit, anthropophagic behaviour must be stimulated by daemonic possession.[137] This implies that anthropophagy is exceptional, and the result of the infiltration into the human being of something quite alien. If daemons are responsible for such brutal behaviour, then humans can retain their humanity, because it is not, or at least not entirely, their fault. Cardano had mentioned the possibility that daemons could play a part in the brutalization of eating human meat: but he had done so only in relation to the exceptional case of the dog eating the Indios, in the story reported by Oviedo.[138]

Elsewhere in his *dissertatio*, Petit suggests the possibility that the propensity to anthropophagy could instead be caused by a disease ('morbus'), a theory that had already been discussed by Daniel Sennert in *De morbis occultis* [On Occult Diseases] (1654).[139] Sennert had mentioned the anthropophagi in relation to the notion that eating members of one's own species (animal or human) caused the spread of syphilis ('lues venerea').[140] Yet, on the relation between syphilis and anthropophagy, Sennert points out a few uncertainties: it would still remain to be explained whether other groups of American people, apart from the anthropophagi, suffered from the disease, and furthermore why anthropophagy was restricted to some groups only.[141] It is nevertheless significant that both Sennert and Petit envisage the possibility that anthropophagy might be linked to diseases, either by encouraging their diffusion, or by being itself akin to a disease.

Cardano himself had wondered how best to interpret the relationship between anthropophagy and physical impairment: is eating human meat the cause of disease, for example due to the fact that the anthropophagus has abandoned the terrain of rationality? Or, conversely, is disease, such as an abnormal rise in black bile, the cause of the fury that leads to anthropophagy?[142] Yet Cardano approaches the issue not from the point of view of pathology, like Sennert, but as part of his investigation of the effects of food. For Cardano, the anthropophagus displays an excess of viciousness and bestiality that is present, in some form, in all human beings and that can be sharpened by his choice of food, whether or not it is triggered by lack of other foods ('inopia') in the first place.[143] In turning against their own kind, cannibals act as other animals also (occasionally) do: it might be a brutal form of behaviour, but in Cardano's view it is nevertheless a natural one.[144] Therefore observing the habits of other people, including the cannibals, can function as a warning, both regarding the bestializing result of famine, and the fact that food and character go hand in hand. This is the strategy that Petit had uncovered in Porphyry: certain portrayals of cannibalism can promote the opposite, namely the vegetarian diet. In the case of the exchange between Cardano and Scaliger, comparing the diets of different populations also raises a key question: which people are a good example for the Europeans, and which are rather a cautionary warning?

3.8. Choosing Between Cannibals and Vegetarians: Cardano, Scaliger, and the Afterlives of Their Controversy

The comparison between carnivorous and vegetarian animals, as we saw in Chapter 2, leads Cardano to discuss the human being's position in the food chain, and to ask whether an association with the former or with the latter group be more desirable from various points of view. In *De rerum varietate* Cardano applies the same reasoning to the diets of human populations, too, mapping the human world according to dietetic differences. Here Cardano maintains that the nature of the human being is inherently changeable and in particular capable of being adapted to resemble the natures of a variety of animals. Humans can be as fierce as tigers or snakes, as violent as wolves, as strong and cruel as lions, as timid as hares. Strikingly, even the quality of 'humanity' is derived from comparison with the animal world, as Cardano states that some human beings are 'humane' ('humanus'), like lambs.[145] Then Cardano proceeds to draw conclusions with regard to human populations, making direct connections between ancient and contemporary societies: the Scyths, the Parths, the Scots, and the Spaniards are fierce, and the 'anthropophagi, who are now called cannibals' represent the pinnacle of violent behaviour.[146] All these populations are more akin to wild beasts than to gentle, humane animals. Cardano thus offers a spectrum of dietary possibility, which establishes parallels in the animal world, while also promoting assessment of positive and negative examples among humans.

Cardano acknowledges that food is only one element in explaining the variations in character among human populations. Another crucial factor is geographical position, and thus climate, as pointed out in the reports on the New World and in the discussion on the causes of cannibalism. In particular, Cardano holds a combination of food and climate responsible for the varying life expectancies of humans.[147] At the beginning of *De sanitate tuenda* he addresses the question of the role of air in influencing the length of human lifespan, thus approaching from the point of view of human geography a topic that he considers from a medical angle as well. He explains that inhaling and exhaling implies a movement, and movement creates heat: therefore it seems that it is air, which, as he puts it, 'makes our bodies dry'.[148] As a consequence, the characteristics and quality of the air will play a key role, and different regions of the earth will accordingly support or impede the long continuation of human life. Cardano explains that while the Garamantes (an African tribe) rarely reach the fortieth year of life, Indians can enjoy lives of one hundred and twenty years or longer.[149] These are not, as for Michele da Cuneo, the non-anthropophagic natives of the Americas, but inhabitants of India who are 'meek' ('mansueti'), thus closer to animals such as the lamb. And indeed, like the lamb, they are vegetarian.

Using the same strategy as he employed in *De subtilitate*, Cardano compares species of animals with human groups. In *De sanitate tuenda* vegetarian animals such as the elephant, the deer, and the camel are coupled with one particular Indian group: the Brahmans. Cardano explains that plants in general live longer than animals, and that among animals, the vegetarian ones live longer than the carnivorous ones. Among humans, the Brahmans, who are located in one of the regions with the best type of air and are vegetarians, enjoy the longest lives, as opposed to tigers, panthers, and presumably the humans who eat like them:

> Et nostra aetate Brachmanes Indi, licet gaudeant tenuiore et meliore aëre, plus tamen nobis et aliis vivunt, quod neque carnibus, nec piscibus, nec vino utuntur. Haec enim omnia violentiam vitae afferunt. Ergo et inter homines qui fructibus, veluti nucum genere et aqua vescuntur, longioris vitae multo erunt, cum purius alimentum sumant. Verisimileque est, ut quemadmodum potum optimum ubique terrarum communicavit Deus aquam optimam, pluviam scilicet, ita et cibum, qui fructibus, arundinibus, melleque constat.[150]

> [And in our time the Brahmans in India, although they enjoy a more subtle and better air, live longer than us and other people because they do not eat meat or fish, and do not drink wine. Indeed, they say that these are offences to life. Therefore, also among humans those who eat fruits, and nuts and water, will have much longer lives by taking a purer aliment. And this is probable, for just as God provided excellent water as an excellent drink everywhere on the earth, that is rain, thus also food, which consists of fruits, plant stems, and honey.]

The purity of the air explains how the Indians are able to maintain the original humidity of their bodies, thus slowing the process of drying out, that is of ageing. The choice of food adds a further element: the Brahmans do not take nourishment from any living creature, and also avoid drinking wine, underlining the fact that refraining from meat-eating is part of a general attitude of abstinence. Lastly, Cardano adds a religious element when he states that the Brahmans follow the diet originally indicated by God himself, who provided simple water, plants, and honey for human nutrition. In this respect, the Brahmans' approach to food appears as an ideal, as they eat a diet similar to the one that the Bible attributes to human beings before the flood, before they started sacrificing and eating animals.

To find a positive example of a human population, Cardano looks East, not West: this is a model that has strong roots in Porphyry, whom Cardano often mentions in relation to the Indians. According to Porphyry, the Brahmans inhabit a region which is made particularly fertile by the Ganges River. Those who live in the mountains follow a vegetarian diet, including milk alongside fruit and vegetables; those living directly by the river appear to follow a completely plant-based diet comprising fruit, vegetables, and rice. This diet is not simply the result of geographical features, which enable agriculture as opposed to the nomadic lifestyle. Porphyry presents it also as the dietetic expression of the Brahmans' philosophical view and as directly linked to their religious practice: 'To eat other food, or even to touch animate food, is thought equivalent to the utmost impurity and impiety. This belief is revealed to them in their worship of the divine and their piety towards it'.[151] The vegetarian diet is therefore an essential aspect of the Brahmans' approach to attaining wisdom and to worship.

Following Porphyry, Cardano presents the long-lived, vegetarian Indians as the opposite pole to the negative examples of brutish, anthropophagic populations. Yet, Cardano's references to the Brahmans emphasize the problem of pinning down this opposition. What is ultimately at stake is the value of meat, not only for nutrition but in its full spectrum of cultural implications. Whereas in the discussion of the effect of meat on health and intelligence Cardano appeared to reach the conclusion that meat is necessary, considerations about human geography lead him to a different conclusion: the human populations which consume predominantly vegetable food are more prone to philosophical speculation and are wiser than the meat-eaters.

This contradiction did not escape Scaliger's careful eye: in *Exotericae exercitationes* he points out that there is an inconsistency between Cardano's theory about meat and what can be observed in human behaviour. Comparison between the eating habits of different people would, he maintains, raise questions about the benefits of meat that Cardano had listed when comparing the alertness of the carnivorous animals to the physical and mental slowness of the herbivores. Cardano's argumentation regarding the alleged necessity of meat poses the problem of explaining not just the deviant behaviour of the cannibals, but also why the Indian Brahmans, who avoid meat entirely, should be a good model. On a purely physical level, if meat is the best aliment and promotes intelligence, then why are meat-eaters brutal, cruel, and arguably closer to wild beasts than to rational humans?[152] And conversely, how can the connection be explained between the Brahmans' wisdom and the food they eat?

Scaliger, too, mentions the Scyths as example of heavy meat-eaters, and Eastern populations as examples of plant-eaters, thus opposing the anthopophagi to Eastern vegetarians, just as Cardano had done. But Scaliger uses this contrast to show that Cardano's position is built on an inconsistency regarding the alleged benefits of meat-eating:

> Itaque Septentrionales barbaros, Scythas, Sarmatas, Islandos, Lituanos, multa vescentes carne, crasso obsitos ingenio, stupidos, bardos videmus. Aegyptios, Syros, Assyrios, Chaldaeos, longe omnium sapientissimos. [...] Percurres etiam Brachmanum et Gymnosophistarum mores.[153]

> [Indeed the northern barbarians, Scyths, Sarmatians, the populations of Iceland and Lithuania, who eat a lot of meat, appear to be slow witted, dull and stupid. The Egyptians, Syrians, Assyrians, Chaldaeans, are by far the wisest of all. [...] Consider the habits of Brahmans and Gymnosophists.]

According to Scaliger, the differences among human populations demonstrate that meat is responsible for bestiality. He considers climate indirectly responsible as well, as the barbarians he mentions live in colder regions of the earth and the wise people in warmer ones. Climate and diet are intertwined causes, but diet is the one in which humans can actively intervene, at all latitudes. This is why Scaliger insists that Cardano misunderstood the link between meat and behaviour: examples drawn from both the animal world and human populations show us that the dangers of meat-eating outnumber the benefits. Yet, by reference to the Brahmans and the other wise people Scaliger draws a substantial distinction between the case of animals and that of humans. The kind of 'intelligence' he attributes to those sages is not equivalent to the smartness, or perceptiveness ('sagacitas') that Cardano ascribed to the carnivores. Rather, Scaliger connects a vegetarian diet to the development of philosophical insight, of wisdom ('sapientia'), thus opposing not only carnivorous to vegetarian humans, but brutish human beings to sages, philosophers, and religious figures. He stresses the fact that Galen and Diogenes Laertius 'rarely mention meat in the foods of the illustrious men'.[154]

Despite his overtly critical efforts, Scaliger thus follows in the tradition of Porphyry here in maintaining that a plant-based diet supports philosophical thought. Scaliger makes clear that what is at stake in choosing to eat a carnivorous or a vegetarian diet is not only the association with different groups of animals (as discussed in Chapter 2), but also, and more importantly, the assessment of what makes human life different from animal life. In other words, the alternative that Scaliger sketched is between a philosophical life and a savage one.

For European readers, the controversy between Cardano and Scaliger ultimately related to the problem of positioning themselves within the spectrum of human behaviours in a geographically expanded known world. Should Europeans view themselves as being closer to the Scyths, the Indians, or the puzzling new American anthropophagi? Among the European populations, Cardano had mentioned the Scots and the Spaniards as negative examples of violent populations. In the case of the Spaniards, this raises the question that Montaigne had addressed in 'On Cannibals': who are the truly savage people, the American natives or the European invaders?

Cardano and Scaliger's controversy on the dietary aspects of human geography continued in a dialogue that draws upon those two authors as main sources: Giulio Cesare Vanini's *De admirandis naturae reginae deaeque mortalium arcanis* [On the Marvellous Secrets of Nature, Queen and Goddess of the Mortals], composed between 1615 and 1616.[155] Vanini devotes an ample section of the work to the problem of 'how food can hinder sound habits'.[156] The text is constructed as an exchange between the character Alexander, who mainly poses the questions, and Julius Caesar, who replies.[157]

With regard to the connection between food and habits, Julius Caesar explains that food is absorbed through digestion, penetrating into the subtlest part of the blood, eventually becoming 'almost a kind of air' ('aëris prope species') that reaches the heart and the lungs. It is then transformed into very thin matter, a vital spirit flowing through the arteries. Finally, it spreads to the brain, where it generates animal spirits, which are in turn responsible for the habits of a person.[158] At the same time, the air one breathes penetrates into the bloodstream via the lungs. Therefore, the quality of the air can have a direct impact on the body: in particular, 'dark air' ('aër tenebricosus'), a kind of polluted air, can cause the mind to be affected by 'absurd fantasies', and to commit evil deeds. Climate and diet are thus closely connected in the way that they influence the innermost workings of the body.[159]

The idea that food deeply affects the nature of a being has a long history, part of which has already been discussed above. But Vanini goes a step further, linking this understanding of the power of food to intercultural comparisons. If moral goodness and corruption derives from food, then it is possible to explain with a direct assertion of cause and effect that 'the Tartars are cruel because they drink the blood of horses', an example derived from Cardano.[160] The Scots are also mentioned, and the two discussants cannot decide whether the English are also fierce because they eat, or rather used to eat, huge amounts of semi-raw meat. The specific link between meat and cruelty is clear: 'blood increases blood, and anger is blood being ignited'.[161]

In this way, positing an alternative between fierce and meek populations also implies choosing between bodily strength and weakness, if meat consumption is identified as the cause of both brutishness and strength. At the centre of Scaliger's reply about the character of human populations there was also a division into classes, or professions, as he distinguished between the cultivation of knowledge on one side (Egyptians, Assyrians, Persians) and activities that require the exercise of the body on the other (for instance the care of herds in the case of nomadic people). Vanini picks up on this contraposition when, in *De admirandis*, he explains through Julius Caesar:

> Quare vilissimi homines, ut nautae, aurigae, baiuli, vectores etc., ubique pessimi sunt, feroces, inhospitales, nullo tanguntur metu, nulla Religionis reverentia, propterea quod crassiori utuntur cibo, qui crassum sanguinem, densos ac turbu-lentos efficit spiritus, quare et incrassatam illi habent conscientiam mentemque densissimis vitiis offuscatam.[162]

> [The most ordinary people, such as sailors, charioteers, porters, carriers etc., are everywhere the basest, ferocious, inhospitable, untouched by fear, without respect for religion, and this happens because they eat fatter food, which produces fat blood, and dense and agitated spirits, and for this reason they have a thick, fat consciousness and a mind obfuscated by a dense multitude of defects.]

The case of the sailors' brutishness is particularly revealing: meat was commonly preserved with salt, and indeed the character Julius Caesar states that all sailors are irascible and inhumanely fierce ('immanes') because they eat salty foods. Examples of savage behaviour are thus not only to be found in distant lands, as the European sailors are portrayed as being no less brutish than the barbarians of the new and old worlds. This is an explanation that links firmly character and diet into a deterministic model — and this is precisely why Julius Caesar hastens to add that no attempts should be made to cure either melancholy or moral dissolution by changing dietary habits, because the Church's sacraments are the only cure.

It is noteworthy that Vanini uses the same adjective, 'crassus' [thick], that Scaliger had employed in highlighting the distance between vegetarian and meat-eaters among both animals and humans: meat, according to Scaliger, provides thicker nourishment than plants, and thus it thickens the mind as well.[163] This refers to the medical theory that while plant food is light because it is relatively poor in nutrients, meat can be very nutrient-dense, ranging, as we saw, from more digestible kinds to the most dense and indigestible forms (pork and human meat). In *Contradicentia medica*, Cardano had compared lettuce and meat in terms of their similarity to the blood's thickness: lettuce, but also other vegetarian foods like bread and beets, are very dissimilar to blood, and require a long series of transformations before their nutrients can be released. In this sense they are not thickening. Yet, an abundance of blood, as both Scaliger and Vanini point out, could have a dulling effect on the mind itself: this would explain the stupidity not only of certain populations in general, but of all those who rely on a meaty diet to support their physically demanding activities. From geographic and cultural distinctions, this explanation moves the focus to the effect of dietary choices within each community, in the old as in the new world.

Vanini lists a variety of side-effects ascribed to the 'thickening diet': an obtunded mind and fierceness of habits are associated with lack of fear and disregard for religion. The latter two aspects may derive directly from Cardano. In Book 18 of *De subtilitate*, dedicated to the discussion of miraculous events, Cardano had suggested that bodily strength and feelings such as fear are inversely proportional: the stronger a human being the less he or she is susceptible to imagination, and hence to fear. Cardano mentioned both anthropophagi and Scyths as examples, explaining that apparitions, which depend on the fervid imagination of the subject, seem not to occur in their cultures, because they are 'very strong' ('fortissimi'). This strength derives from their habits, and primarily their diet: this implies that food that thickens the blood makes the mind less capable of a range of experiences, lowering its capacity for imagination. The mind becomes sharper and more perceptive when the food is 'thin', and Cardano mentions as an example that witches use a range of herbs to heighten their perceptions.[164] Furthermore, Cardano believes that apparitions are frequent in Egypt, Ethiopia, and India: once again, climate and geography overlap with diet, since heat and a less powerful constitution both seem to contribute to experiencing apparitions.

In Vanini's *De admirandis*, too, the powerful effect of foods on the eater's imagination is the culminating point of the exchange between Alexander and Julius Caesar. This section of the dialogue ends with the scene of an afternoon luncheon being served. The discussion is thus interrupted by the staging of its outcomes, as had also occurred with the luncheon prepared by the hermit in Cardano's *Theonoston*. In *De admirandis*, the menu is a simple, vegetarian one: eggs with saffron, accompanied by lemonade.[165] Julius Caesar specifies that according to Hippocrates eggs are very nutritious, and that therefore they will be excellent for regaining strength after a tiring philosophical dispute.[166] Eggs are not meat, but are close enough to it that they still retain sufficient nutritional power: quoting Hippocrates, Julius Caesar calls them 'chicken milk' ('pulli lac'). The role of the imagination comes into play when the method of cooking the eggs is explained. The boy serving the eggs claims that he cooked them partly with fire and partly with the force of his own heat. To Alexander's objection that this does not seem likely, the boy replies that according to Avicenna it would be possible to knock a camel down by the force of the imagination: it should thus certainly be possible to cook eggs by the same method.

The meal that concludes the discussion of the danger of meat is thus a vegetarian one, prepared by drawing on the positive force of imagination, resulting in an amicable conclusion to the conversation, rather than one based on animal flesh, which presumably would instead have stimulated feelings of anger in the discussants. Alexander and Julius Caesar are involved in philosophical discussion: they are no brutish manual workers. The Renaissance re-elaboration of the myth of the oriental sages, to which Cardano and Scaliger refer, is in line with the Porphyrian view, in that vegetarianism is strongly associated with philosophical speculation. The next section examines how a specific group of sages — the Indian Brahmans — came to be viewed as the alternative to the brutality of meat-eating, and of cannibalism in particular.

3.9. The Figure of the Brahman from Antiquity to the Renaissance

The figure of the Brahman, just like that of the Renaissance-period cannibals and of the ancient anthropophagi, is the result of a construction out of a variety of sources and has a long tradition, becoming in the Renaissance a standardized model of the virtues of vegetarianism.[167] Yet, the difficulty in pinning down exactly who the Brahmans are, and how their profile was formed, begins from the linguistic point of view. Porphyry presents them as a 'branch' of those 'wise about the gods, whom the Greeks habitually call "gymnosophists"', literally 'the naked sages'.[168] There is therefore at least a certain overlap between the terms 'Brahman' and 'gymnosophist': a Brahman is also, more generally, a gymnosophist. In Pliny's *Natural History* the naked sages of India called gymnosophists were described as sitting in permanent meditation, their eyes fixed on the sun: they supposedly spent their lives in contemplation and in the pursuit of wisdom, and then ended them voluntarily on a burning pyre.[169] Strabo (63 BC–*c.* AD 23) in his *Geography* tells the story of a gymnosophist called Calanus, whom Alexander the Great had met: he, too, had died on the pyre, after having lived a simple, abstinent life — an example also related by Plutarch.[170]

An extremely sober way of life, dedication to contemplation, and a certain retreat from society are the three main characteristics of these Indian sages. Their myth had been initially shaped by narrations of Alexander the Great's expedition to India, which included his fictional encounter with Dindimos, the king of the Brahmans.[171] A speech by Dindimos about the Brahmans' life-style features in one of the main encyclopedias of the Middle Ages, the *Speculum maius* [The Great Mirror] by the Dominican Vincent of Beauvais (*c.* 1190–1264). 'We, the Brahmans,' says Dindimos, 'lead a simple and pure life, we do not want any more than what our nature requires'. Their diet consisted mainly of fruit, milk, and river-water.[172]

This portrayal developed in the West by way of comparison and contrast with Christianity. While the Brahmans were often mentioned throughout the Middle Ages as an example of virtue, early critics of Indian wisdom had stressed the fact that their 'virtue' is very different from that which should be cultivated by Christians.[173] Most notably, Tertullian in his *Apologeticum* [Apology] mentions the habits of the

Brahmans only in order to defend Christians, directly comparing the two groups on the basis of the above-mentioned description of Brahmans and gymnosophists: 'For we are not Brahmans, naked sages of India [Gymnosophists], forest-dwellers, exiles from life. We remember that we owe gratitude to God, the Lord, the Creator. We reject no fruits of His labours'. Tertullian uses the example of Brahmans and Gymnosophists with the intention of stressing, by way of contrast, the approach of Christians to life within society, including the specific aspect of diet. Picking the fruits of God's labour implies — as Tertullian asserts immediately after the latter quotation — making use of all centres of social exchange and encounter, such as 'the forum' and the 'meat-market'.[174] Christians, Tertullian claims, are not abstinent Indians, who in refusing to eat animals ultimately choose exile from life itself. Rather, they do not impose restrictions on the goods that the Creation offers: they practice moderation, but not the exaggerated abstinence of those so-called wise men. Tertullian's position is thus close to that of Augustine, discussed above in Chapter 1: Christians do not abstain from buying meat at the market, because God created animals in order to sustain human life in a number of ways, and this includes their use as food. Tertullian treats vegetarianism as representative of the Brahmans' detachment from life in society; the Christians' omnivorous diet, on the other hand, reflects their involvement and social commitment.

In his *Preparatio evangelica* Eusebius makes explicit another important link with regard to the Brahmans' diet: he states that Pythagoras himself had studied with the Indian Brahmans, thus creating a connection between the Indian sages and Pythagoras, Plutarch's model of a vegetarian philosopher.[175] This notion paved the way for the use of the terms 'Pythagorean' and 'Brahman' as synonyms. This education with the Brahmans would have taught Pythagoras the value of scrupulous control of the intake of food and drink, in the context of a generally non-violent mode of life, in which philosophical speculation and pious contemplation play a leading role. The *Preparatio evangelica* was an important source for Renaissance authors reflecting on the habits of the Brahmans. Polidoro Virgili (1470–1555) refers directly to it in *De inventoribus rerum* [On the Inventors of Things], in which he discusses the diets of Egyptian and Indian sages:

> Cheremon Stoicus, de vita antiquorum Aegypti sacerdotum scribens, narrat eos ex eo tempore quo coepissent divino cultui deservire carnibus et vino abstinuisse. Ovum quoque pro carnibus vitavisse et lac, eorum alterum carnes liquidas alterum sanguinem esse dicentes colore mutato. Brachmanae apud Indos, teste Eusebio libro 6 *De praeparatione evangelica*, nihil animatum edebant.

> [Writing on the life of the ancient Egyptian priests, Cheremon the Stoic says that they abstained from meat and wine once they began to devote themselves to worshipping the gods. They also avoided eggs and milk too as if they were meat, saying that the one was liquid flesh and the other blood with its colour changed. The Brahmans in India would eat nothing living, according to Eusebius in Book 6 of the *Preparation for the Gospel*.][176]

It is remarkable that this passage follows from a discussion of the origins of animal sacrifice, which Virgili traces back to those of Abel and his descendants. Moving on from animal sacrifice, he then proceeds to relate various opinions on the beginning of human consumption of meat, implicitly applying the same line of reasoning as Porphyry in the first book of *On Abstinence* in considering animal sacrifice and meat-consumption as different facets of the same question. Virgili writes that according to St Jerome: 'No one ate meat in Saturn's time — that golden age when everything poured from the soil — but all lived on the grain and fruit that grew up naturally from the earth'.[177] The Egyptian sages and the Brahmans thus appear still to be living as if the Golden Age had never ended. It is noteworthy, too, that Virgili does not place the emphasis simply on meat-eating, but on abstaining from anything that derives from a living organism (in the case of the Egyptian sages), or on avoiding ingesting anything that has life in it (in the case of the Brahmans). The fertility of the soil is thus key to the provision of food in both cases, and that is why the land inhabited by the Brahmans must be similar to the earth of the Golden Age.

For this reason, the exact location of the Brahmans had been a matter of debate in both older and newer travel reports circulating in the Renaissance. The identification of India with the Garden of Eden had already gained currency in maps at least since the eighth century.[178] One of the most influential medieval narrations that addresses this matter is the abovementioned *Book of Marvels and Travels*, which contains a description of a peaceful, vegetarian society, living on a 'fine, large and fertile land', which 'some people call the Island of Brahmins and some [...] The Land of Faith. A great river runs through it'.[179] 'Brahmins' is used here as synonym for Brahmans to indicate the highest cast, the priests, in Hindu society. But both the meaning and the terminology varies greatly, adding up to the unclear contours of these figures in Mandeville and in this period in general. Mandeville refers to Brahmans or Brahmins as priests, or more generally philosophers. He characterizes them as extraordinarily virtuous people, who 'eat and drink in such a sensible manner that they live for a very long time and many of them die without sickness, it's just that nature fails them in old age'.[180] Climatic conditions and diet, he claims, directly influence the virtuousness of these people. Mandeville furthermore notes the absence of diseases, which is a direct consequence of the Brahmans' simple choice of vegetable food. Marco Polo's *Il Milione* echoes Mandeville's description of the Brahmans — called, in the twelfth-century vernacular version of the text 'bregomanni' — as one of the longest-lived people on earth, because they practice abstinence, which involves eating little and especially refraining from killing living creatures for food. The text even adds that they also avoid consuming anything that is green because 'they say that it has a soul'. The plants' sap is thus equated to the blood in animals: just as religious prescriptions require that the blood of animals be drained before meat can be eaten (as in Judaism and Islam), so these 'bregomanni' wait until plants are completely dry before consuming them.[181]

Renaissance compilations further repeated and transmitted this portrait of the Brahmans. For instance, the ethnographic work *Omnium gentium mores, leges et ritus* [The Customs, Laws, and Rites of All People] by Johann Böhm (*c.* 1485–c. 1533), published in Italian in 1542 as *I costumi, le leggi et l'usanze di tutte le genti*, contains a long section on the Brahmans and Gymnosophists.[182] This was also reprinted in one of the most popular compilations of varied information, or *selve*, namely the Italian version of Pedro Mexía's *Silva de varia lección*, expanded by Francesco Sansovino with the addition of a fourth part in 1564.[183] This account of the Brahmans circulated broadly thanks to the various editions and translations of these works, and thus had a significant impact.

Böhm had compiled his work by drawing information from classical sources (such as Herodotus and Pliny) and those of the Renaissance (such as Niccolò Perotti and Enea Silvio Piccolomini). Notably, it did not include a discussion of America and of the new discoveries, but focused only on the traditional three areas of Asia, Europe, and Africa.[184] The preface narrates the story of human civilization, focusing firmly on the topic of eating. Originally, humans drank milk, and ate fruit and the produce of the earth, but often food was not sufficient and therefore they attacked each other, and were also attacked by animals. Then, with the introduction of commerce, they started to deal more peacefully with each other, learning to talk and leaving 'their barbarian and brutish nature' behind.[185] The result was that they started to abstain from killing each other and from eating human meat, a habit they had acquired presumably through the fight for survival. The preface also refers to the Chaldeans, Magi, Brahmans, and Gymnosophists of India and the Egyptian priests as 'very wise men' ('huomini sapientissimi'), presenting them as models of virtue.[186] The history of civilization is thus presented as a process by which humans turned away from brutish anthropophagy towards more virtuous dietetic behaviours, of which the sages named above are the leading examples.

It is thus not surprising to find a long account of the Brahmans' life in the section on Asia. Here again, the Brahmans are considered a branch of the Gymnosophists, and described in accordance with the tradition: they 'lived naked (as the name suggests), and wandering about in the wilderness they philosophized from morning till evening, staring with fixed gaze at the form of the burning Sun'. Among them, the Brahmans

> Vivevano pura e schiettamente, senza appetire strane cose, e esquisite, perché non desideravano se non quello di che la natura si contenta, intanto che veniva ad essere facile il viver loro [...] ma contentandosi di quel che la terra senza essere molto afflitta e tormentata da gli uomini produce.[187]

> [Lived in a simple and straightforward manner, without craving peculiar and refined things, because they did not desire anything other than what satisfies nature, so that their life was easy [...]. They were satisfied with what the earth produces without being vexed and tormented by human beings.]

Since they only ate what was necessary to sustain the body, 'they not only did not experience many diseases and illnesses that we have, but they did not even know their names. They were thus always healthy'.[188] Böhm does not directly mention Porphyry but just like Porphyry's ideal of a vegetarian philosopher, Böhm's Brahmans neither eat meat nor engage in sacrifice:

> Non ammazzavano gli innocenti animali per fare sacrificio a Dio, perché dicevano che Iddio non accetta i sacrificii di coloro che sono imbrattati di sangue, ma che si diletta più tosto del culto che con mani pure gli si fa: e la preghiera, ch'esce mediante la lingua, è sufficiente a placarlo.[189]

[They did not kill innocent animals to offer them in sacrifice, because they said that God does not accept sacrifices that are stained with blood. Rather, he delights in the worship offered to him with clean hands. Prayer, uttered with the tongue, is sufficient to placate him.]

Böhm's depiction of the virtuous Brahmans immediately precedes a section, based mainly on Herodotus, on the habits of the Scyths, known for drinking the blood of their war victims.[190] The contrast between the peaceful vegetarian Indians, and the barbarians inclined to anthropophagy is not an invention of Böhm: in Mandeville, too, the description of the anthropophagi and that of the vegetarian Indians appear consecutively. After discussing the island of the anthropophagic giants, Mandeville then presents further islands, including the one inhabited by the vegetarian Brahmans. Yet, as we saw in previous parts of this chapter, the contrast between anthropophagi and vegetarians turns into a more complex process of hybridization in the Renaissance, when the cannibals' life is often presented almost as a vegetarian ideal, and their land is described in similar terms to the fertile area of India in which the Brahmans live. The geographical displacement of the Renaissance anthropophagi — no longer in the area inhabited by the ancient Scyths, but now in the new 'East' of the Americas — certainly contributed to the notable change in the descriptions of the land and climate of the anthropophagi's territories.

The idea of the Brahmans' virtue reached Renaissance readers through classical and medieval sources, but it then remained a term of comparison for approaching new discoveries, as well as for placing European (and more specifically, Christian) habits within a broader frame. Admiration went hand-in-hand with scepticism as well, reflecting contemporary resonance of the controversy about the nature of the Brahmans' virtue. A clear example appears in a collection of Jesuit reports, published in 1552, where the suggestion is made that the Brahmans' dietary professions are hypocritical: 'These Brahmans claim that they do not eat meat, but only dairy products and vegetables, yet I hear that secretly they eat anything'.[191] Here, meat represents a pleasurable food, one that the Brahmans are supposed to renounce, in order to practice abstinence. Yet, if this strict renunciation is not genuine, and they indulge indiscriminately, the Brahmans transform from a positive, modern, semi-divine mythological figure, into a vile form of humanity, whose life is based on a lie. This potential for reversal is significant because, among philosophers, admiration and scepticism regarding the Brahmans life often overlapped, as will now be discussed.

3.10. The Vegetarian Virtues of the Brahmans

Porphyrius de voto disputans inquit praestantissimos quosque apud omnes gentes sapientiae studio votis incubuisse, quales apud Indos Brachmanae, apud Persas magi, similesque apud Graecos Chaldaeosque fuerint. Haec ille. Neque eos simulasse putandum, qui tum perpetuis operibus, tum vitae periculo vitae sanctimoniam confirmarunt.

[In discussing prayer, Porphyry says that in all nations the men who excel most in the study of wisdom devote themselves to prayers: among the Indians such were the Brahmans, among the Persians the Magi, and the like among the Greeks and Chaldeans. This is what Porphyry says. And one must not suppose that these men, who confirmed their life's sanctity both with everlasting works and at their own mortal peril, were just pretending.][192]

In Book 14 of the *Theologia platonica*, Ficino cites the authority of Porphyry in order to answer an objection by the followers of Lucretius, namely that 'religion does not derive from natural deliberation but from the corruption of our complexion'. Ficino argues that, on the contrary, it is evident that the most pious groups of human beings are formed of 'clever and wise' men who worship God. All the examples he mentions are of Eastern sages, those discussed by Porphyry in Book 4 of *On Abstinence*. Ficino underlines that the sources provide no reason to doubt the truthfulness of this portrait, which indicates that reservation and sarcasm about the habits of these allegedly pious people must have circulated well before the account mentioned in the Jesuit *Avisi*.

In *De christiana religione* [On Christian Religion] Ficino refers directly to *On Abstinence* to support the view that Judaism played a key, worldwide role in spreading divine wisdom, underlining the continuity of revelation throughout history.[193] Ficino has in mind a passage from Book 4 (§ 11), where Porphyry describes the habits of the Essenes, known for their abstinent life: Ficino calls them the 'Philosophers of the Jews'. He then adds the opinions of other authorities, including the ancient Greek historian Megastenes (*c.* 350–190 BC), author of a work on India, who claimed that the Indian Brahmans, too, were of Jewish descent.[194]

Ficino was deeply affected by the myth of the Brahmans, which combines a regimen for achieving health with an emphasis on the speculative attitude of the Brahmans. Yet, both in the *Theologia platonica* and in *De christiana religione* Ficino omits Porphyry's actual aim in mentioning these groups of sages. When introducing the philosophical strands of Judaism, Porphyry remarks that they 'consistently abstained from many animals'; when presenting the Syrians and the Brahmans, their dietetic abstinence is also the central issue.[195] Given Ficino's cautious view of the use of meat from a medical point of view, especially in *De vita*, as discussed in Chapter 2, it is not surprising that he avoids linking the vegetarian diet of the Brahmans to their religious piety. Nevertheless, it is significant that he sides with those who appreciated the moral virtue and religious insight of these Eastern groups, even if he omits to mention the connection with diet, which was at the core of one of his main sources — Porphyry.

This view somewhat resembles that of Cardano, who also stresses the religious piety of the Brahmans. Yet, Cardano is more open to discussion of the role of diet in this context. Cardano seeks to connect the Brahmans' abstinent diet with the aspect that, as we saw earlier, he considers crucial in the choice of food, namely its impact on the extension of the lifespan. Furthermore, for Cardano, the location of the land of the Brahmans is at least as influential as their diet in accounting for their extraordinarily long lives. Since Cardano considers the length of a creature's life an indication of its position on the scale of living beings, the Brahmans' success at extending human life is to him the most appealing detail about these Indian sages.

While simple life forms have the shortest lives, more perfect ones have longer lives: the Brahmans are in this respect among the most perfect of humans beings.

In *Commentarii in Hippocratis de aere, aquis et locis* [Commentaries on Hippocrates's 'On Air, Waters, and Places'], Cardano estimates that some Indians even reach one hundred and fifty years of age.[196] In *De subtilitate* he acknowledges that not everywhere in India will the climatic conditions be so favourable to the extension of human life. But where it is warm, the air is kept thin and pure by winds and waters, and where religious prescriptions indicate a vegetarian diet, there the conditions are ideal for achieving a long life.[197] Cardano thus suggests that it is the combination of vegetable food and the quality of the air that accounts for the exceptionally long lives of certain Indians, and specifically the Brahmans.

Like Ficino, Cardano, too, stresses the element of religious piety. But unlike Ficino, he emphasizes the role of their dietary practices in promoting it. Conversely, he also associates lack of piety with the diet that is most different from the Brahmans' vegetarianism, namely anthropophagy: the character of the hermit in *Theonoston* portrays the Scyths and anthropophagic populations — and 'in our times the Epicureans' — as impious.[198] This is another contact point with Ficino, who had upheld the Brahmans as a model of virtue in opposition to Lucretian Epicureanism.[199] At the end of the second book of *Theonoston*, the character of the 'philosopher' sums up the various positive qualities that Cardano attributes to the Indian sages by presenting them as a vegetarian ideal, stressing that the avoidance of wine and meat promotes their long lives.

As seen in section 8 above, Scaliger highlighted a possible inconsistency in Cardano's argumentation: how can Cardano combine praise of the properties of meat, and of the meat-eaters' intelligence, with the example of the Indian Brahmans, who are among the most pious, sage, and long-lived people on earth? Cardano does not address this impasse directly, but from his treatment of the Brahmans two possible solutions can be developed. First, Cardano would have presumably emphasized the link between climate and diet: it would not be possible to follow the same vegetarian diet of the inhabitants of fertile India in every part of the world; and furthermore an unfavourable climate might cause the attempt to extend lifespan to fail despite a vegetable diet. Second, Cardano's argumentation appears to be close to Porphyry's in that he takes into account the fact that humanity is diverse, and that no diet would be likely to fit all populations, or all professions. Cardano was aware of the conflicting evidence about meat, and regarded the example of the Brahmans, as raised by Scaliger in his attack, particularly highly.

Cardano was not the only philosopher to remain at least partly undecided on this matter, praising the vegetarian virtues of the Brahmans without recommending in unequivocal terms that their example should be followed. In 1576, the year of Cardano's death, Antonio Persio, well known for his subsequent edition of Telesio's short essays (*Varii de naturalibus rebus libelli*, 1590), published his *Trattato dell'ingegno dell'huomo* [Treatise on Human Intellection]. Persio discusses the example of the Brahmans' diet in the context of a strongly naturalistic interpretation of the connection between the care of the body and the promotion of intellectual capabilities. Persio defines *ingegno* as the act of generating or procreating (*ingenero*) a certain virtue 'just as when a human being is generated, a certain virtue and shrewdness is enclosed in the semen'.[200] The whole process of generation is considered in strongly materialistic terms: Persio argues that in the cases both of a female animal and of a woman, there exists a connection between the mother's imagination and the beauty as well as intelligence of the progeny (a theory with a long tradition).[201] When enumerating the features of an agile intellect, or *ingegno*, Persio reminds the reader that the term 'sagacity' is used to refer to hunting dogs, such as bloodhounds, which are particularly skilled in finding their prey and even in reconstructing its movements.[202] The difference between human and animal sagacity is merely one of quantity, not of quality: the spirit — a material substance on which the level of *ingenium* directly depends — is more subtle and mobile in humans than it is in animals. Having a thinner, more delicate skin and more supple flesh gives humans an advantage over animals with regard to the level of *ingegno*, but it also accounts for differences within the human race. Humans are thus far superior to animals, as according to Persio the latter merely have 'particles' of *ingegno*.[203]

Since the level of *ingegno* depends directly on material, natural factors, the problem of how to achieve wisdom depends on the question of how to care best for the body's health.[204] This is precisely the background for Persio's discussion of the Brahmans:

> All'utero segue il latte della balia [...]. Fornito il lattare, viene il manicare, il quale richiede non minor avvertenza, perché secondo gli alimenti nudritivi son sani o non sani, così cagionano spirito sottile, o non sottile. Di che ne parlò Galeno a disteso, né tacerò che intorno a gli alimenti io trovo dispareri infra valent'huomini, de' quali chi loda la carne, et chi no; et que' del no, hanno alcune ragioni dalla lor parte, et per essempio dicono che alcune nationi le quali usano la carne bramosamente, sono d'ingegno grossolano come scithi, islandi, lituani et altri barberi settentrionali; et alcun altre che non l'usano, o pure di rado l'usano, per prova hanno mostrato sempre ingegno svegliato come egitii sirii, assirii, et caldei, che hanno avuti savissimi huomini, et / chi porrà mente alle vite de brachmani, de' ginnosophisti, et de' propheti, sentirà che il loro cibo si fu per l'ordinario di latte, miele, fighi, et uva passa. In somma chi cerca per dovitia di ragioni in questo sentimento, potrà leggere i quattro libri compilati da Porphirio, per titolo, *Dello astenersi da gli animali*.[205]

> [After the womb follows the wet nurse's milk [...]. After lactation comes eating, which requires no less care because according to whether the aliments are healthy or unhealthy they produce subtle or unsubtle spirit. Galen wrote at length about this, and I will not fail to say that I find conflicting opinions regarding this topic among excellent men: some of them praise meat, others do not, and those who do not have some good reasons on their side. For instance they say that the populations who eagerly indulge in meat have a thick *ingenium* [i.e. are slow witted], like Scyths, the inhabitants of Iceland, Lithuanians, and other northern barbarians; and some other populations who do not eat it, or eat it rarely, have always displayed as a proof an awakened *ingegno*, like Egyptians, Assyrians, Chaldeans, who had very wise men among them. And whoever considers the lives of brahmans and gymnosophists, and of the prophets, will know that their food usually consisted of milk, honey, figs, and raisins. All in

all, one seeking a wealth of proofs about this opinion can read the four books
written by Porphyry, entitled *On Abstinence from Animals.*]

It is easy to recognize the same main arguments and even formulations used
by Scaliger against Cardano: Persio and Scaliger refer to the same list of people
with thick *ingegno*, as well as of those with an awakened *ingegno*.[206] Persio further
highlights the relationship between the purity of the air and the level of intelligence
of human populations: the people of Bœotia were said to be rough because of
the thick air they breathed, while thin air makes subtle minds, and that is why
physicians and philosophers have claimed that in this way the body influences the
mind.[207] In line with the classical tradition, he also points out the philosophical
lineage in which the Brahmans stand, as teachers of Pythagoras.[208] Ficino, too,
had referred to the same lineage of philosophical sages in the *Theologia platonica*,
listing 'the Magi of the Persians, the Egyptian Priests, the Hebrew prophets, the
Orphic, Pythagorean, and Platonic philosophers, and the ancient theologians of
the Christians' among those who are 'ingeniosi et sapientes', and worship God.[209]

Despite the fact that Persio stands in this tradition in appreciating the Brahmans'
diet, he ultimately concludes that the examples given above reflect 'extreme
opinions', to which he prefers a third one, namely moderation. This is the medical
way, and indeed Persio mentions Galen, who distinguished between types of meat
that promote health (such as some birds, chicken, and veal) and those which on
the contrary should be avoided.[210] Persio thus contrasts the effects of the Indians'
abstinent life with the instructions of Galenic medicine, transposing the promises
of health and wisdom on a natural, entirely materialistic basis. The Brahmans fail
here to become a model from a medical point of view. Once again, they remain a
fascinating but distant example, which need not be followed strictly by westerners,
who live in a different climate, too.

Almost a century later, the Dutch physician Vopiscus Plemp (1601–71), Professor
at Leuven and correspondent of Descartes, used the same ethnographic examples:
the 'northern Scyths, Sarmatians, inhabitants of Iceland, and the Lithuanians, who
eat a lot of meat, are stupid', while 'Syrians, Egyptians, Assyrians, Chaldeans, who
live solely on fruit, are sharp, shrewd, clever, and perspicacious'.[211] Like Persio and
Ficino before him, he opts for a medically-based diet, which restricts but does not
entirely eliminate the consumption of meat. Yet, Plemp's reasons are not only of
a medical nature: he also mentions the influence of society on diet. For instance,
invitations to dinner often lead to being presented with a plate of meat — a prospect
that according to Plemp makes it difficult to adhere to the 'austere, hard, and rigid
life' of the vegetarian models.[212]

Even though frequently viewed as a positive model, the Brahmans nevertheless
fail to become a plausible alternative for Renaissance philosophers — either because
the climatic conditions in which they live cannot be reproduced in the West, or
because the busy lives of Europeans appear too far from the Brahmans' contemplative inactivity. Their vegetarian virtues — longevity, piety, philosophical insight
— appear to remain unachievable, rather than working, as Porphyry had envisaged,
as practical aims that would prompt the philosopher to follow in their steps.

Notes to Chapter 3

1. Claude Lévi-Strauss, *We Are All Cannibals, and Other Essays*, trans. by Jane Marie Todd (New York: Columbia University Press, 2016), p. 73

2. This is an aspect which is still very prominent in contemporary discussion on vegetarianism. Why do certain populations (e.g. Europeans, Americans) find it acceptable to eat veal but not dog meat? See for instance Melanie Joy, *Why We Love Dogs, Eat Pigs, and Wear Cows: An Introduction to Carnism* (San Francisco: Conari Press, 2010).

3. Galen, *On the Thinning Diet*, p. 315. On Galen and dietetic relativism see Peter Garnsey, *Food and Society in Classical Antiquity* (Cambridge: Cambridge University Press, 1999), p. 84.

4. See Clark, 'Introduction', pp. 19–20; Bouffartigue and Patillon, 'Introduction', pp. xxvi–xxxiv.

5. Plutarch, *Advice on Keeping Well (De sanitate tuenda)*, in *Moralia*, trans. by Frank Cole Babbitt and others, 15 vols (Cambridge, MA: Harvard University Press; London: Heinemann, 1927–2004), II, 265 (132a). This passage is commented upon by Stephen T. Newmyer, *Animals, Rights and Reason in Plutarch and Modern Ethics* (New York: Routledge, 2006), p. 89.

6. The cultural history of food is of course a major strand of contemporary food studies: see for instance *A Cultural History of Food*, ed. by Fabio Parasecoli & Peter Scholliers, 6 vols (Oxford: Berg, 2012).

7. See the example of Diogenes eating a raw octopus in Plutarch, *On the Eating of Flesh* I, 995d (in *Moralia*, XII, 554–55).

8. This practice is also called 'omophagia': see Angelo Tartabini, *Cannibalismo e antropofagia: uomini e animali, vittime e carnefici* (Milan: Mursia, 1997), p. 5.

9. Plutarch, *On the Eating of Flesh* I, 995d, pp. 552–53.

10. Ibid., 995e, pp. 554–57. See 'Bœotian' in *OED*.

11. Plutarch, *On the Eating of Flesh* II, 998a, p. 571.

12. Ibid., 997e, p. 569.

13. André-Jean Festugière, 'Sur une nouvelle édition du *De vita pythagorica* de Jamblique', *Revue des Études Grecques*, 50 (1937), 470–94 (p. 476), notes that this is 'un genre littéraire bien connu à l'époque hellénistique: la peinture idéalisée des castes sacerdotales ou de confréries religieuses des peuple barbares, Égyptiens [...], Juifs [...], brahmanes de l'Inde [...], gymnosophistes des bord du Nil'. See also Bouffartige and Patillon, 'Introduction', p. xxxii.

14. On the association between anthropophagi and vegetarians in Renaissance literature see Cecilia Muratori, 'Pitagora tra i cannibali: dieta e ordine dei viventi a partire dalla letteratura rinascimentale sul nuovo mondo', in *Bestie, filosofi e altri animali*, ed. by Felice Cimatti, Stefano Gensini, & Sandra Plastina (Milan: Mimesis, 2016), pp. 143–60.

15. On Herodotus's portrait of the Scyths, especially in Book IV of the *Histories*, see François Hartog, *The Mirror of Herodotus: The Representation of the Other in the Writing of History*, trans. by Janet Lloyd (Berkeley, Los Angeles, & London: University of California Press, 1988), pp. 19–30; on their diet, especially their supposed habit of drinking blood, see p. 168; on their violence see p. 188. Rosalind Thomas (*Herodotus in Context: Ethnography, Science and the Art of Persuasion* (Cambridge: Cambridge University Press, 2000), p. 64) draws attention to the fact that Herodotus describes different groups of Scyths with partly different habits. On the Scyths and the history of cannibalism see also Kelly L. Watson, *Insatiable Appetites: Imperial Encounters with Cannibals in the North Atlantic World* (New York & London: New York University Press, 2015), p. 33: 'The endurance of the Scythian reputation for cannibalism [...] reveals how whole groups of people were conflated into artificial categories and how the differences between them were minimized. The category of Scythian encompasses a rather poorly defined group of people inhabiting a region whose boundary was equally vague'. Watson has also pointed out a circular argument in portraying the Scyths as anthropophagi: 'These accusations [of anthropophagy] also constrained ways of thinking about cannibalism in the ancient Mediterranean world, for if Scythians were cannibals, then one knew what a cannibal was: a Scythian. This kind of circular logic will be repeated throughout the Middle Ages and the early modern period' (ibid., p. 32). As I explain in this section, I believe it is important to differentiate between the words 'anthropophagus' and 'cannibal', refraining from defining groups such as the Scyths as cannibals.

16. Pliny, *Natural History*, VI.20.
17. According to Katja Maria Vogt, 'theses about incest, anthropophagy, and so on illustrate how, for the Stoics, no type of action is generally forbidden' (*Law, Reason and the Cosmic City: Political Philosophy in the Early Stoa* (Oxford & New York: Oxford University Press, 2008), p. 23).
18. *OA*, I.3.3; p. 32.
19. *OA*, IV.21.6; p. 118.
20. But see Herodotus's testimony about the possibility that the Scyths might have been settled cultivators: *Histories*, IV.5.3 (see also Hartog, *The Mirror of Herodotus*, pp. 20–21).
21. *OA*, I.5.1; p. 32.
22. See for instance Tamara Talbot Rice, *The Scythians* (London: Thames & Hudson, 1957), p. 21.
23. Frank Lestringant, 'Le Nom des "Cannibales" de Christophe Colomb à Michel de Montaigne', *Bulletin de la Société des Amis de Montaigne*, 17–18 (1984), 51–74 (p. 61). Lestringant has studied the genesis and the diffusion of the word 'cannibal', considering that reports relate travels in a variety of areas, often generating geographical confusion. That this confusion should be mirrored also on the level of dietetic speculation is understandable from this context. On Brazil in particular see Lestringant, *Mapping the Renaissance World: The Geographical Imagination in the Age of Discovery* (Cambridge: Polity Press, 1994), Chapter 3. On the appearance of cannibals on maps see Surekha Davies, *Renaissance Ethnography and the Invention of the Human: New Worlds, Maps and Monsters* (Cambridge: Cambridge University Press, 2016), Chapter 3.
24. See exemplarily the illustrations by Theodor de Bry, based on Staden's *Wahrhaftige Historia*, discussed in Michiel van Groesen, *The Representations of the Overseas World in the De Bry Collection of Voyages (1590–1634)* (Leiden: Brill, 2008), pp. 182–88.
25. *Libretto de tutta la navigatione de re de Spagna de le isole et terreni novamente trovati*, ed. by Angelo Trevisan (Venice: [n. pub.] 1504; facsimile reprint with an introduction by Lawrence C. Wrote (Paris: Libraire ancienne Honoré Champion, 1929)). See *European Americana: A Chronological Guide to Works Printed in Europe Relating to the Americas 1493–1776*, ed. by John Alden, 6 vols (New York: Readex Books, 1980–88), I (1493–1600), 8; and *L'umanista aronese Pietro martire d'Anghiera primo storico del 'nuovo mondo': Atti del convegno Arona 28 Ottobre 1990*, ed. by Roberto Cicala & Angelo L. Stoppa (Novara: Interlinea edizioni, 1992).
26. *Libretto de tutta la navigatione*, ed. by Trevisan, Chapter 5: 'Et se lementavano li poveri homini che non altramente sono vexati da questi canibali, come fere selvatiche da tigri et leoni'. See also Cristoforo Colombo, *Diario di bordo: libro della prima navigazione e scoperta delle Indie*, ed. by Gaetano Ferro (Milan: Mursia, 1985), p. 104: 'Dice che tutta la gente che ha trovato fino ad oggi ha una grandissima paura di quelli di *Caniba* o *Canima*'.
27. Peter Martyr of Anghiera, *De orbe novo Decades 1: Oceana Decas*, ed. by Brigitte Gauvin (Paris: Les Belles Lettres, 2003), I.12: 'Canibales' and 'Caribes' are used as synonyms.
28. On Michele da Cuneo see Antonello Gerbi, *Nature in the New World: From Christopher Columbus to Gonzalo Fernández de Oviedo*, trans. by Jeremy Moyle (Pittsburgh, PA.: University of Pittsburgh Press, 1985), Chapter 5.
29. Cristoforo Colombo and others, *Prime relazioni di navigatori italiani sulla scoperta dell'America. Colombo — Vespucci — Verazzano*, ed. by Luigi Firpo (Turin: UTET, 1966), p. 49.
30. Ibid., p. 64: 'dicti Camballi sono òmini più feroci e più acuti che non sonno dicti Indiani'. Michele da Cuneo emphasizes the wild sexuality of the cannibals: see Guido Abbattista, 'Trophying Human "Otherness": From Christopher Columbus to Contemporary Ethno-ecology (Fifteenth-Twenty First Centuries)', in *Encountering Otherness: Diversities and Transcultural Experiences in Early Modern European Culture*, ed. by Guido Abbattista (Trieste: Edizioni Università di Trieste, 2011), pp. 19–41.
31. Montaigne's essay *On Cannibals* (which I discuss below in this chapter, section 3) notably blurs the line between the *bon sauvage* and the cannibal. On the construction of the myth of the American savage see Giuliano Gliozzi, 'La scoperta dei selvaggi', in his *Differenze e uguaglianza nella cultura europea moderna*, ed. by Anna Strumia (Naples: Vivarium, 1993), pp. 82–105.
32. Alison Coudert, 'The Ultimate Crime: Cannibalism in Early Modern Minds and Imaginations', in *Crime and Punishment in the Middle Ages and Early Modern Ages: Mental-historical Investigations of Basic Human Problems and Social Responses*, ed. by Albrecht Classen & Connie Scarborough (Berlin & Boston: De Gruyter, 2012), pp. 521–54.

33. On the proliferation of representations of cannibalism as related to the construction of identity see Hannah Chapelle Wojciehowski, *Group Identity in the Renaissance World* (Cambridge: Cambridge University Press, 2011), p. 94.

34. See for instance the account of the islands of the cannibals in Nicola Scillacio's *Delle isole del mare meridiano e indiano recentemente scoperte*, ed. by Osvaldo Baldacci (Florence: Olschki, 1992), p. 70.

35. See Sir John Mandeville, *The Book of Marvels and Travels*, trans. by Anthony Bale (Oxford & New York: Oxford University Press, 2012), pp. 78–79, and introduction, p. xxvi. Marco Polo, *Il Milione: edizione del testo toscano ('Ottimo')*, ed. by Ruggero M. Ruggieri (Florence: Olschki, 1986), p. 247. On the differences and similarities between Polo's and Mandeville's descriptions of anthropophagy see Merrall L. Price, *Consuming Passions: The Uses of Cannibalism in Late Medieval and Early Modern Europe* (London & New York: Routledge, 2003), p. 13.

36. Nicola Bottiglieri, *Nel verde mare delle tenebre: viaggi reali e immaginari nei secoli XIV e XV* (Rome: Edizioni Associate, 1994), p. 67. Yet I agree with Joan-Pau Rubiés that it is reductive to regard Polo's and Mandeville's accounts as simply fantastical (Joan-Pau Rubiés, *Travel and Ethnology in the Renaissance: South-India through European Eyes, 1250–1625* (Cambridge: Cambridge University Press, 2000), p. 36).

37. *I viaggi di Marco Polo, gentiluomo veneziano*, in Giovanni Battista Ramusio, *Navigazioni e viaggi*, ed. by Marica Milanesi, 6 vols (Turin: Einaudi, 1978–88), III, 260: 'quelli che abitano ne' monti sono come bestie, però che mangiano carne umana, e generalmente ogni sorte di carni monde e immonde'.

38. Mandeville, *The Book of Marvels and Travels*, p. 113. On Mandeville and cannibalism see also Carlo Ginzburg, *The Cheese and the Worms: The Cosmos of a Sixteenth-century Miller*, trans. by John & Anne C. Tedeschi (Baltimore: Johns Hopkins University Press, 1980), pp. 41–46.

39. I leave aside the problem of the speculations regarding the actual connection of 'East and West'. See Marica Milanesi, 'Arsarot o Anian? Identità e separazione tra Asia e Nuovo Mondo nella cartografia del Cinquecento (1500–1570)', in *Il nuovo mondo nella coscienza italiana e tedesca nel Cinquecento*, ed. by Adriano Prosperi & Wolfgang Reinhard (Bologna: Il Mulino, 1992), pp. 19–78 (esp. p. 26).

40. Therefore it is also important to pay attention to the vocabulary to avoid confusion: Clark (*OA*, 1.23.2; p. 39) translates αλληλοφάγοι (literally: 'those who eat their own kind') with 'cannibals', but the frame of reference for the two terms is not the same. Bouffartigue and Patillon translate it with 'anthropophages' (Porphyry, *De l'abstinence*, I, 10).

41. See Milanesi's introduction to *Due navigazioni di Amerigo Vespucci*, in Ramusio, *Navigazioni e viaggi*, I, 657–58.

42. Vespucci, 'Lettera a Lorenzo de Pierfrancesco de' Medici del 1502 da Lisbona', in *Il mondo nuovo di Amerigo Vespucci: Vespucci autentico e apocrifo*, ed. by Marco Pozzi (Milan: Serra e Riva, 1984), p. 79 (§ 8): 'Molto travagliai ad intendere loro vita e costumi, per che 27 dì mangiai e dormì' infra loro. E quello di loro conobbi è el seguente apresso'.

43. Ibid., p. 80 (§ 9): 'Mangiano a sedere in su la terra. Le loro vivande sono molte radice d'erbe e frute molto buone, infinito pesce [...]. La carne che mangiano, masime la comune, è carne umana'.

44. Ibid., p. 79 (§ 7).

45. Ibid. (§ 6).

46. See *Sommario di Amerigo Vespucci fiorentino, di due sue navigazioni, al magnifico M. Pietro Soderini* [...], in Ramusio, *Navigazioni e viaggi*, I, 670–81. See also the usage of Vespucci's reports and the idea of 'irdisch Paradiß' in Sebastian Franck, *Weltbuch: Spiegel und Bildtnis des gantzen Erdtbodens* (Ulm: Varnier, 1542), p. ccxxv^v.

47. Vespucci, 'Lettera a Lorenzo de Pierfrancesco de' Medici del 1502 da Lisbona', p. 81 (§ 14): '*Item* son gente belicosa, e infra loro molti crudeli'.

48. Ibid., p. 79 (§ 9).

49. John Case, *Speculum quaestionum moralium* (Frankfurt am Main: Basse, 1589), p. 273: 'Sed ut carnifices et anthropophagi, qui humano sanguine delectantur, non sunt tolerandi in civitate, ita rosa sine spina, id est, nimia indulgentia sine severitatis virgula in bene administrata republica florere non debet'. On Case see Charles B. Schmitt, *John Case and Aristotelianism in Renaissance England* (Kingston & Montreal: McGill-Queen's University Press, 1983).

50. On cannibalism and civilization see Cătălin Avramescu, *An Intellectual History of Cannibalism*, trans. by Alistair Ian Blyth (Princeton: Princeton University Press, 2009), esp. Chapter 7.

51. Michel de Montaigne, 'Des Cannibales', in *Essais*, ed. by André Tournon, 3 vols (Paris: Imprimerie nationale, 1998), I, 356. On Montaigne's possible encounters with 'cannibals' in France see Philippe Desan, 'Le Simulacre du Nouveau Monde: à propos de la rencontre de Montaigne avec les Cannibales', *Montaigne Studies*, 22 (2010), 101–18 (this issue of *Montaigne Studies* is entirely devoted to *Montaigne et le Nouveau Monde*). For a recent discussion, see Timothy J. Reiss, 'Montaigne, the New World, and Precolonialisms', in *The Oxford Handbook of Montaigne*, ed. by Philippe Desan (Oxford & New York: Oxford University Press, 2016), pp. 196–214. On the use of the word 'cannibales' in French see Lestringant, 'Le Nom des "Cannibales"', p. 61.

52. The text was republished accompanied by Theodor de Bry's famous engravings: see Hans Staden, *Hans Staden's True History: An Account of Cannibal Captivity in Brazil*, ed. and trans. by Neil L. Whitehead and Michael Harbsmeier (Durham, NC: Duke University Press, 2008), p. lxxii; and van Groesen, *The Representations of the Overseas World*, pp. 182–83. On Staden see Annerose Menninger, *Die Macht der Augenzeugen: Neue Welt und Kannibalen-Mythos, 1492–1600* (Stuttgart: Steiner, 1995), p. 68 ff.

53. Montaigne, *Essais*, I, 350.

54. Ibid., pp. 342–43.

55. Stelio Cro, *The Noble Savage: Allegory of Freedom* (Waterloo, ON: Wilfrid Laurier University Press, 1990), p. 15; and, 'Antiquity, America and the Noble Savage', in *The Classical Tradition and the Americas: European Images of the Americas*, ed. by Wolfgang Haase & Reinhold Meyer, (Berlin: De Gruyter, 1994–), I.1, 379–418 (p. 397).

56. Montaigne, *Essais*, I, 344: 'chacun appelle barbarie ce qui c'est pas de son usage. [...] Ils sont sauvages de même que nous appelons sauvages les fruits que nature de soi et de son progrès ordinaire a produits'. On Montaigne's critique of civilization see André Tournon, *Montaigne: la glose et l'essai* (Lyon: Presses universitaires de Lyon, 1983), pp. 220–21.

57. Montaigne, *Essais*, I, 345: 'Les lois naturelles leur commandent encores, fort peu abâtardies par les nôtres'. See *America in European Consciousness 1493–1750*, ed. by Karen Ordahl Kupperman (Chapel Hill: University of North Carolina Press, 1995), especially the essay by David Quint, 'A Reconsideration of Montaigne's Des cannibales', pp. 166–91.

58. David Quint, *Montaigne and the Quality of Mercy: Ethical and Political Themes in the Essais* (Princeton: Princeton University Press, 1998), pp. 91–92 & 99.

59. Voltaire, *Dictionnaire philosophique ou la raison par l'alphabet*, in *Les Œuvres complètes* (Oxford: Voltaire Foundation, 1968–), XXXV (ed. by Christine Mervaud), 344–50. Paul J. Smith, 'Montaigne in the World', in *The Oxford Handbook of Montaigne*, pp. 287–305 (p. 294).

60. Voltaire, *Dictionnaire philosophique*, p. 346: '*Nous* respectons plus les morts que les vivants' (my emphasis). On Voltaire's appreciation of Porphyry see Larue, *Le Végétarisme des Lumières*, pp. 189–95.

61. Voltaire appears to follow the tradition according to which anthropophagy started simply out of necessity: Voltaire, *Dictionnaire philosophique*, p. 347: 'C'est la superstition qui a fait immoler des victimes humaines, c'est la nécessité qui les a fait manger'.

62. Ibid., p. 347: 'L'habitude de se nourrir de ce qu'ils avaient tué, fit aisément qu'ils traitèrent leurs ennemis comme leurs cerfs et leurs sangliers'.

63. See Tartabini, *Cannibalismo e antropofagia*, p. 79.

64. Vespucci, 'Lettera di Amerigo Vespucci delle isole nuovamente trovate in quattro suoi viaggi', in *Il mondo nuovo di Amerigo Vespucci*, ed. by Pozzi, p. 139 (§ 18).

65. Peter Martyr of Anghiera, *De orbe novo*, I.16 (p. 27) and X.4 (p. 223): 'In insulis haudquaquam neque unum quidem [animal], mitia sunt omnia insularia, praeter homines in plerisque, uti iam diximus, qui humanarum sunt carnium heluones, Caribes sive Canibales dictos'. On later, eighteenth-century speculations on the differences between the animals found in Europe and those in the Americas see Gerbi, *The Dispute of the New World*, pp. 3–5.

66. Ovid, *Metamorphoses*, trans. by Frank Justus Miller, revised by G. P. Goold, 6 vols (Cambridge, MA: Harvard University Press, 1916), I, 8–9 (Book I.89–90): 'Aurea prima sata est aetas, quae vindice nullo, | sponte sua, sine lege fidem rectumque colebat' ('Golden was that first age, which, with no one to compel, | without a law, of its own will, kept faith and did the right').

67. *OA*, II.27.1–2 & II.27.6; pp. 65–66.

68. *OA*, I.23.2; Clark's translation amended in order to avoid the use of the term 'cannibalism' as a translation for αλληλοφαγία.

69. Jonathan Barnes, *The Presocratic Philosophers* (London & New York: Routledge, 1979), p. 97.

70. See also Julia Marvin, 'Cannibalism as an Aspect of Famine in Two English Chronicles', in *Food and Eating in Medieval Europe*, ed. by Martha Carlin & Joel T. Rosenthal (London: Hambledon Press, 1998), pp. 73–86 (but note that 'cannibalism' is here a terminological anachronism).

71. I have discussed the presentation of vegetarianism in Botero in 'Pitagora tra i cannibali'.

72. Giovanni Botero, *Le relationi universali* (Venice: Angelieri, 1596), part 4, Book III, p. 44.

73. Ibid.: 'Che haverebbe detto qui Pitagora, che detestava l'uso della carne de gli animali?'

74. Ibid., p. 43: 'Diciamo dunque che Barbari si debbono stimare quelli le cui maniere e costumi si dilungano straordinariamente dalla dritta ragione, il che aviene o per fierezza d'animo, o per ignoranza, o per rozezza di costumi'.

75. Vespucci, 'Lettera a Lorenzo de Pierfrancesco de' Medici del 1502 da Lisbona', pp. 78–79 (§ 6).

76. One exception is Michele da Cuneo, who suggests that all American natives (both cannibals and Indians) might be in fact short-lived (Colombo and others, *Prime relazioni di navigatori italiani sulla scoperta dell'America*, p. 65).

77. Vespucci, 'Lettera a Lorenzo de Pierfrancesco de' Medici del 1502 da Lisbona', p. 82 (§ 16). See also p. 81: 'Sono gente che vivono molti anni, perché secondo le loro suvensioni molti uomini v'abian conosciuti che tengono infino a 4 sorte di nipoti'.

78. See above, Chapter 2, section 3.

79. Vespucci, *Mundus novus / Sommario*, in *Il mondo nuovo di Amerigo Vespucci*, ed. by Pozzi, p. 105 (see also Ramusio, *Navigazioni e viaggi*, I, 676).

80. Ibid.: 'Queste sono le cose che ho ritrovate appresso di loro che è da farne qualche stima, cioè l'aere temperato, la bontà del cielo, il terreno fertile e la età lunga; e ciò forse aviene per il vento di levante che quivi di continuo spira'.

81. Botero, *Le relationi universali*, part 4, Book III, p. 47.

82. A seminal work on the geographic position and representation of Paradise is Alessandro Scafi, *Maps of Paradise* (London: British Library, 2013).

83. Benedictus Pereira, *Commentariorum et disputationum in Genesim tomi quatuor*, 4 vols (Lyon: Iunta, 1594–1600), I, 298: 'regio Americana, volgo dictus novus orbis, inter duos tropicos interiacens, plerisque locis temperata est'. On the temperate zone see *La cartografia europea tra primo Rinascimento e fine dell'Illuminismo: Atti del convegno internazionale 'The Making of European Cartography'*, ed. by Diogo Ramada Curto, Angelo Cattaneo, & André Ferrand Almeida (Florence: L. S. Olschki, 2003), p. 121.

84. Cf. *DCD*, xl.2, 483 (Book xx.21) ('et emissurum ex illis salvatos in gentes diversas et in longinquas insulas, quae non audierunt nomen eius neque viderunt eius gloriam'), & 142 (Book xvi.9) on the question whether there exist human beings on the 'opposite part of the earth'.

85. On 'savage men' see Concetta Cavallini, 'La Description de l'animal sauvage dans les *Navigationi e Viaggi* de Giovanni Battista Ramusio', in *L'Animal sauvage à la Renaissance (Colloque international organisé par la société française d'étude du xvie siècle et Cambridge French Colloquia, 3–6 septembre 2004)*, ed. by Philip Ford (Cambridge: Cambridge French Colloquia, 2007), pp. 345–56 (p. 350).

86. See Vespucci, 'Lettera a Lorenzo de Pierfrancesco de' Medici del 1502 da Lisbona', p. 79 (§ 8).

87. On the status of these indigenous people in relation to the question of their animality and the possibility of their conversion see Erica Fudge, *Perceiving Animals: Humans and Beasts in Early Modern Culture* (Urbana & Chicago: University of Illinois Press, 2002), pp. 20–21. The topic is addressed repeatedly in *New World Encounters*, ed. by Stephen Greenblatt (Berkeley, Los Angeles, & Oxford: University of California Press, 1993). A main source on the debate on the conversion of the Indians is José de Acosta, *De natura novi orbis libri duo. Et de promulgatione Evangelii apud Barbaros, sive de procuranda indorum salute, libri sex* (Cologne: Mylius, 1596). See also Watson, *Insatiable Appetites*, Chapter 4.

88. *Libretto de tutta la navigatione*, ed. by Trevisan, Chapter 5. I have discussed this passage from the perspective of how food affects the human-animal border in 'Animals in the Renaissance', pp. 163–64.

89. I quote from the vernacular version printed by Ramusio as *Sommario di due navigazioni*: Vespucci, *Mundus novus / Sommario*, ed. by Pozzi, p. 105 (cf. also Ramusio, *Navigazioni e viaggi*, i, 675).

90. Ibid.: 'anzi si maravigliavano grandemente che noi non mangiassimo della carne de' nimici, le quali dicono muovere appetito ed esser di maraviglioso sapore, e le lodano come cibi soavi e delicati.' See also Vespucci, 'Lettera delle isole nuovamente trovate', in *Il mondo nuovo di Amerigo Vespucci*, p. 139.

91. Colombo and others, *Prime relazioni di navigatori italiani sulla scoperta dell'America*, p. 50.

92. Ibid., p. 64.

93. This is the case with the argument in favour of killing kangaroos in Australia. See for example: Michael Charles Tobias & Jane Gray Morrison, *Why Life Matters: Fifty Ecosystems of the Heart and Mind* (Berlin: Springer, 2014), p. 238.

94. *I viaggi di Marco Polo, gentiluomo veneziano*, in Ramusio, *Navigazioni e viaggi*, iii, 254.

95. Botero, *Le relationi universali*, part i, Book ii, p. 127: 'habitatori d'asprissime montagne, dalle quali discendendo nelle pianure de' Lai per desiderio di carne humana (della quale sono ingordissimi), ne fanno strage miserabile, e horribile beccaria. Marco (s'io non mi inganno) Polo chiama il paese de i Gueoni Cangigù'. Botero is talking about some inhabitants of Siam.

96. Ibid., part i, Book vi, p. 221: 'Caribi, o Cannibali, popoli bestiali. Mangiano carne humana fresca, e salata, come noi porcina. Castrano i fanciulli come noi i polli, per mangiarseli più teneri e più grassi'.

97. Ibid., part i, volume 2 (*Delle isole sino al presente scoverte*), Book iii, p. 39: 'Isole di Caribi. [...] Mangiano carne humana e vanno alla caccia degli huomini come noi delle fiere'.

98. *OA*, ii.2.1; p. 87.

99. On the ritualism of cannibalism see Piero Camporesi, *Bread of Dreams: Food and Fantasy in Early Modern Europe*, trans. by David Gentilcore (Cambridge: Polity Press; Chicago: University of Chicago Press, 1989), pp. 51–52.

100. *OA*, 1.23.1, 39. Clark does not differentiate between *anthropophagia* and *allelophagia* and translates both with 'cannibalism'. Taylor (*Select Works of Porphyry, Containing His Four Books on Abstinence from Animal Food*, p. 16) translates with 'anthropophagites'.

101. For a discussion of the moral implications of eating one's own kin, see Amber Carpenter, 'Eating Your Own: Exploring Conceptual Space for Moral Restraint', in *Ethical Perspectives on Animals in the Renaissance and Early Modern Period*, ed. by Dohm & Muratori, pp. 21–45.

102. Botero, *Le relationi universali*, part 4, Book iii, p. 47: 'Ma perche non tutti i popoli sono d'una dispositione, capacità, non è anco bene l'ammaestrarli, e l'insegnarli tutti a un modo. Co' cannibali, divoratori di huomini, e con altri che mangiano indifferentemente carne humana si può procedere come contra nemici del genere humano, o come contra matti furiosi; e si debbono render prima capaci di ragione e d'humanità, e poi addottrinarli e instruirli nella virtù, e nella via di Dio. [...] Anche Aristotele dice che simil gente si debbono pigliar come fiere, e domar per forza'. On the link between brutality, lack of civilization, and conversion for Botero, see Davies, *Renaissance Ethnography and the Invention of the Human*, p. 226.

103. Reports often specify the gender of the cannibals, highlighting the cruelty of female cannibals in particular: Vespucci, 'Lettera delle isole nuovamente trovate', pp. 164–165 (§ 56) (also *Di Amerigo Vespucci fiorentino lettera prima, drizzata al magnifico M. Pietro Soderini [...]*, in Ramusio, *Navigazioni e viaggi*, i, 661–62). I have discussed this aspect in 'Pitagora tra i cannibali', pp. 157–60.

104. See the introduction to Staden, *Hans Staden's True History*, p. xxxii: 'the native practice of ritual cannibalism became the mirror of theological dispute over the meaning of Christian Eucharist'. See further Neil L. Whitehead, 'Sacred Cannibals and Golden Kings: Travelling the Borders of the New World with Hans Staden and Walter Ralegh', in *Borders and Travellers in Early Modern Europe*, ed. by Thomas Betteridge (Abingdon: Routledge, 2017), pp. 169–85.

105. On the plan to convert the American Indians, starting with Columbus see Wojciehowski, *Group Identity in the Renaissance World*, p. 85. On the impossibility of converting the cannibals see Frank Lestringant, 'The Philosopher's Breviary: Jean de Léry in the Enlightenment', *The New World*, special issue of *Representations*, 33 (Winter, 1991), 200–11.

106. Botero, *Le relationi universali*, part 4, Book iii, pp. 43–44, on the four different degrees of 'fierezza'.

107. Ibid., part 4, Book III (1596), p. 44: 'perche la complession nostra prende qualità del nutrimento, segue che da nutrimento selvativo procede anche complessione e natura selvatica'.
108. Della Porta, *Della fisionomia dell'uomo*, p. 77 (1.21). (I quote the Italian version of this work.)
109. Ibid.: 'Disse ancora nel *Libro dell'aria, acque e luoghi* che però i Sciti avevano un medesimo viso et il medesimo costume, perche si pascevano de' medesimi cibi e bevevano le medesime acque'.
110. Ibid.: 'sono genti dure, inospitali e di selvaggi costumi, come il lor cibo'. Della Porta refers to the Hilophagi of Ethiopia, who allegedly ate raw twigs and tree trunks.
111. Ibid., p. 76: 'Che da gli alimenti di che l'uomo si pasce se possano congetturar i costumi'.
112. Ibid.: 'Platone nel libro delle *Leggi* dice che gli huomini, altri per l'acqua che bevono, altri per i cibi che mangiano, che produce quel terreno, sono peggiori e migliori di costumi; e che quelli penetrano ancora nell'anima, non solo alterano il corpo'. Cf. Plato, *Laws*, 747d-e, in *Dialogues of Plato*, IV, 266: 'Some places are subject to strange and fatal influences by reason of diverse winds and violent heats, some by reason of waters; or, again, from the character of the subsistence which the earth supplies them, which not only affects the bodies of men for good or evil, but produces similar results in their souls'.
113. I have discussed the originality of Della Porta's method of physiognomics, and also its consequences with regard to the body-soul compound in 'From Animal Bodies to Human Souls: Animals in Della Porta's Physiognomics', *Early Science and Medicine*, 22.1 (2017), 1–23.
114. Della Porta, *Della fisionomia dell'uomo*, p. 77 (1.21).
115. Leonardo da Vinci, *Quaderni d'Anatomia*, ed. by Ove C. L. Vangensten, A. Fonahn, & H. Hopstock, 6 vols (Christiania: Jacob Dybwad, 1911–16), II, 30 (f. 14r).
116. On Leonardo's sources see Edmondo Solmi, *Scritti vinciani* (Florence: La Nuova Italia, 1976), pp. 290–91 (in particular on the possibility that Leonardo had read an edition of the travel report attributed to Vespucci). See also p. 219 on Leonardo's acquaintance with Gonzalo Fernandez de Oviedo, author of the *Historia general y natural de las Indias*.
117. Leonardo da Vinci, *Quaderni d'Anatomia*, II, 30 (f. 14r): '[la] tua gola, colla quale tu ai tentato farti sepultura di tutti li animali'. On Leonardo's attitude towards animals see Giorgio Vasari, 'The Life of Leonardo da Vinci, Florentine Painter and Sculptor (1452–1519)', in *Lives of the Artists*, trans. by Julia Conaway Bondanella and Peter Bondanella (Oxford & New York: Oxford University Press, 2008), p. 74: 'he took special pleasure in horses as he did in all other animals, which he treated with the greatest love and patience. For example, when passing by places where birds were being sold, he would often take them out of their cages with his own hands, and after paying the seller the price that was asked of him, he would set them free in the air, restoring them to the liberty they had lost'.
118. Andrea Corsali, *Lettera di Andrea Corsali allo Illustrissimo Signore Duca Iuliano de Medici, Venuta Dell'India del Mese di Octobre Nel MDXVI* (Florence: Stefano di Carlo da Pavia, 1516), sig. a4r: 'Infra Goci e Rasigut, o vero Carmania, è una terra Cambaia dove Indo fiume entra in mare, è habitata da gentili chiamati Guzaratti: sono grandissimi mercanti. [...] non si cibano di cosa nissuna tenga sangue e non consentono infra loro nuocere a nissuna cosa animata come el nostro Leonardo da Vinci. Vivono di risi, lacte, e altri cibi inanimati'. The letter is mentioned in Leonardo da Vinci, *The Notebooks*, ed. by Jean Paul Richter, 2 vols (New York: Dover Publications, 1970), II, 130. See Carlo Vecce, 'In margine alla prima lettera di Andrea Corsali (Leonardo in India)', in *Ai confini della letteratura: Atti della giornata in onore di Mario Pozzi, Morgex, 4 maggio 2012*, ed. by Jean-Louis Fournel, Rosanna Gorris Camos, & Enrico Mattioda (Turin: Aragno, 2014), pp. 67–81. Vecce lists a series of sixteenth-century sources on the vegetarian diet of the Gujarati people, including the *Itinerary* by Ludovico di Varthema (p. 75).
119. Corsali, *Lettera*, sig. a4r: 'Per essere di questa natura sono stati subiugati da Mori'. In the same letter, Corsali also mentions the 'Brahmins', and underlines the fertility of the terrain (sig. a2v).
120. Pierre Petit, *De natura et moribus anthropophagorum dissertatio* (Utrecht: Rudolph Zyll, 1688), p. 6.
121. Ibid., pp. 25 & 23.
122. Ibid., p. 24: 'Anthropophagi frequentes in novo orbe'. See especially p. 7, where Petit explains that ancient sources use both the word *anthopophagia* and the less common *androphagia*. See the same discussion in Fortunio Liceti, *De feriis altricis animae nemeseticae disputationes* (Padua: Varisco,

1631), in particular Disputatio v. See also ibid., pp. 8–9, on the mythology of the anthropophagic giants of antiquity.

123. Cardano, *De vita propria*, p. 46; *The Book of My Life*, pp. 250–54.

124. Cardano, *De sapientia*, ed. by Marco Bracali (Florence: Olschki, 2008), p. 12. See the comment on this passage from Cardano's *De sapientia* in João de Barros, *Decada primeira da Asia* (Lisbon: Rodriguez, 1628), f. 57r.

125. On anthropophagy and the passions see Avramescu, *An Intellectual History of Cannibalism*, especially pp. 98–100.

126. Cardano, *De rerum varietate*, p. 336[b]: 'Quid igitur miremur Anthropophagos, quos Caribbes vocant, in quibus odium (ut dixi) initium dedit consuetudini'.

127. Ibid., p. 337[a]: 'nam ibi nullum quadrupes erat animal, cuius caro suavis esset gustui, non sues, boves, pecudes, caprae, cervi, equi, asinive. Ob inopiam igitur hanc eo progressi sunt'.

128. Pliny, *Natural History*, 10 vols, trans. by William H. S. Jones, Harris Rackham, & E. H. Warmington (Cambridge, MA: Harvard University Press; London: Heinemann, 1938–62), II, 377 (Book VI.20): 'This is the country of the Cannibal Scythians who eat human bodies; consequently the adjacent districts are waste deserts thronging with wild beasts lying in wait for human beings as savage as themselves'.

129. Cardano, *De subtilitate*, pp. 632[b]–33[a]: 'Similiter referunt anthropophagos, Caribes a quibusdam, ab aliis Canibales, adeo truculento ac torvo et terribili esse aspectu, tum truci, ut homines caeteri captivorum et mortuorum vix aspectum sustinere queant [...]. Cibus igitur mutat aspectum et naturam [...]. Facile est igitur consuetudine et victus genere mutare mores ac formam animantium, tum etiam proprietates eis mirabiles adiicere'; my translation, but cf. Cardano, *The 'De subtilitate'*, II, 889.

130. Cardano, *De subtilitate*, p. 525[b].

131. Thus Avramescu (*An Intellectual History of Cannibalism*, p. 21) is only partly right when he states that: 'In the sixteenth century, Cardano is the first to explain the anthropophagy of the savages of the New World based on an economic argument. The Indians end up eating human flesh, he argues, because the land is poor and because the animals they can hunt are few'.

132. Scaliger, *Exotericae exercitationes*, f. 335v: 'Canibales hominivori sunt, quia insulas habent vacuas pecore et frugibus. Piscari nesciunt, carent instrumentis. Humano igitur venatu vitam trahunt, ex alieni cibi inopia'.

133. Cardano also associates anthropophagy with rejection of piety, comparing ancient anthropophagi to early modern Epicureans: *Theonoston* I, p. 308[a].

134. Petit, *De natura et moribus anthropophagorum*, p. 95. Piero Vettori, the first to edit and publish the Greek original of *On Abstinence*, refers to the same episode narrated by Porphyry in his *Variarum lectionum libri XXV* (Florence: Torrentino, 1553), p. 199. I have discussed these references in 'Medical and Ethical Aspects of Vegetarianism'.

135. Petit, *De natura et moribus anthropophagorum*, p. 96: 'Et verisimilius ibi Porphyrium servire proposito illi suo quo carnium omnium usum ne dum humanarum, studiosis interdicit: fortasse etiam talem infamiam ab Annibale pene populari suo [...] amoliri voluit'.

136. Ibid., p. 60.

137. Ibid., p. 81: 'concedo sententiam, quae Diaboli instinctu et maleficio corruptas hominum mentes in hanc consuetudinem comendi viscera humana consensisse proponit'.

138. Cardano, *De subtilitate*, p. 525[b]: 'vel usui, vel daemonum auxilio'.

139. Daniel Sennert, *Practica medicina*, 6 vols (Wittemberg: Mevius, 1648–54), VI, 139. On Sennert's *Practica medicina* and the understanding of the spreading of diseases (especially syphilis) see Joel A. Klein, 'Daniel Sennert and the Chymico-atomical Reform of Medicine', in *Medicine, Natural Philosophy and Religion in Post-Reformation Scandinavia*, ed. by Ole Peter Grell & Andrew Cunningham (Abingdon & New York: Routledge, 2017), pp. 20–37 (pp. 28–29).

140. Sennert, *Practica medicina*, VI, 139: 'Deinde sit ut, si animal sui generis animalium carnibus nutriatur, pustulis et doloribus corripiatur, et pilorum casum patiatur: tamen quaestio adhuc esset, an morbus iste sit ipsissima lues Venerea, talisque, qui per contagium, et praecipue Venerem, in alios transferri possit'.

141. See also the reference to the cannibals in Girolamo Fracastoro's poem on syphilis (*Syphilis sive morbus gallicus* (Basel: Bebel, 1536), sig. C6v).

142. Cardano, *Problemata naturalia* (*OGC*, II, 646^b).

143. Cardano, *Proxeneta seu De prudentia civili* (*OGC*, I, 407^b): 'Quum vero mortalium genus adeo pravum sit, animisque alii viperinis, alii vulpinis, certe qui paucissimi (ut dixi) qui humanitatis aliquid retineant, sed prorsus omnes ferini sint, licet alio atque alio modo feritatem illam suam explere nitantur'. See also ibid., p. 408^a.

144. In *De subtilitate* Cardano mentions the example of fish and mice that display this allelophagic behaviour, eating members of their own species (p. 653^a).

145. Cardano, *De rerum varietate*, p. 146^b.

146. Ibid., p. 147^a.

147. For on overview of debates on the influence of climate see *Governing the Environment in the Early Modern World: Theory and Practice*, ed. by Sara Miglietti & John E. Morgan (Abingdon & New York: Routledge, 2017).

148. Cardano, *De sanitate tuenda*, p. 31^b: 'ideo aër corpora nostra exsiccat'.

149. Ibid.

150. Ibid., p. 25^b. I take 'cum genere' in the 1663 edition to be a typographical error for 'nucum genere' (as in *De sanitate tuenda* (Rome: Zanetti, 1580), p. 20), and I translate accordingly with 'nuts'.

151. *OA*, IV.17.5; p. 113.

152. The idea that meat promotes smartness is echoed by Michele da Cuneo, who remarks on the fact that the cannibals are fiercer but also smarter ('acuti') than the Indians (Colombo and others, *Prime relazioni di navigatori italiani sulla scoperta dell'America*, p. 64).

153. Scaliger, *Exotericae exercitationes*, f. 327r.

154. Ibid.: 'Galenus aliquot locis, Laertius perpetuo instituto virorum illustrium vitas narrant. Raro carnes in eorum cibis commemorant'.

155. See Francesco Paolo Raimondi, 'Monografia introduttiva', in Giulio Cesare Vanini, *Tutte le opere*, ed. by Francesco Paolo Raimondi, Luigi Crudo, & Mario Carparelli (Milan: Bompiani, 2010), p. 73.

156. Giulio Cesare Vanini, *De admirandis naturae reginae deaeque mortalium arcanis*, in *Tutte le opere*, p. 1334: 'quid alimentum obest morum integritati?'

157. Despite the name, Julius Caesar is not simply to be considered the personification of the author himself. The dialogical persona allows Vanini to stage not just his own opinions, but a learned debate based on intertwining earlier Renaissance sources. The way in which the two characters in the dialogue argue by employing other philosophers' theories, and even words, was considered plagiarism by Luigi Corvaglia in his *Le opere di Giulio Cesare Vanini e le loro fonti*, 2 vols (Milan: Società Editrice Dante Alighieri, 1933–34). In the case of *De admirandis*, this accusation is the result of misunderstanding Vanini's aims in using his sources. By making Alexander and Julius Caesar employ passages from Cardano and Scaliger, Vanini reopens their controversy, and develops dialogically a series of outcomes. Cardano's *De subtilitate* is one of the main sources from which Vanini derives material: for an overview of the 'plagiarism affair' see Raimondi, 'Monografia introduttiva', pp. 59–108.

158. Vanini, *De admirandis*, p. 1334.

159. Ibid., p. 1332.

160. Ibid., pp. 1336 & 1762. The reference is to Cardano, *De rerum varietate*, p. 14^a.

161. Vanini, *De admirandis*, p. 1336: 'Sanguis sanguinem adauget, ira vero sanguinis accensio'.

162. Ibid.: I translate *vilis* as 'ordinary', 'base', rather than as 'vile', 'despicable', as Raimondi and Crudo do. I believe it refers to simple, ordinary professions that are based on sheer bodily strength.

163. See above, Chapter 2, section 6.

164. Cardano, *De subtilitate*, p. 653^a.

165. Vanini, *De admirandis*, p. 1338.

166. Ibid., p. 1340.

167. Tristram Stuart, *The Bloodless Revolution: Radical Vegetarians and the Discovery of India* (London: Harper Collins, 2006), has reconstructed the influence of the myth of the Indian sages from the seventeenth century onwards.

168. *OA*, IV.17.5; p. 113.

169. See Pliny, *Natural History*, VII.2 & VI.22

170. Strabo, *Geography*, XV.I.64; Plutarch, *Life of Alexander*, Chapter 65.

171. Marc Steinmann, *Alexander der Große und die 'nackten Weisen' Indiens: der fiktive Briefwechsel zwischen Alexander und dem Brahmanenkönig Dindimus* (Berlin: Frank & Timme, 2012). See also Ambrose, *The Brahman Episode: St. Ambrose's Version of the Colloquy between Alexander the Great and the Brahmans of India*, Edited from a Vatican Manuscript, trans. by S.V. Yankowski (Ansbach: Wiedfeld & Mehl, 1962).

172. Vincent of Beauvais, *Speculum maius*, 4 vols (Venice: Nicolini, 1591), III, 102r^a: 'Nos bragmani, ait, simplicem et puram vitam ducimus, nihil volumus habere plus nisi quantum nostra natura exigit [...], corpora de foliis arborum operimus, de quorum fructibus ea reficimus, lac comedimus, et aqua de fluvio bibimus'. The leader of the Brahmans is here called 'Dandamus'.

173. Thomas Hahn, 'The Indian Tradition in Western Medieval Intellectual History', *Viator*, 9 (1978), 213–34 (p. 213). On the hostility of several Church Fathers towards the Brahmans see Hahn, 'The Indian Tradition in Western Medieval Intellectual History', p. 217; but some, like Saint Ambrose and Saint Jerome, were more favourable: see ibid., p. 218.

174. Tertullian, *Apology*, trans. by Gerald H. Rendall (Cambridge, MA: Harvard University Press; London: Heinemann, 1931), p. 191 (Book XLII.1–2).

175. On the Renaissance reception of Eusebius's *Praeparatio* see above, Chapter 1, sections 2, 3, and 4. On the broader context of the association between Brahmans and Pythagoreans see Eva del Soldato, 'Bramani e colori tra Ficino e Campanella', *Rinascimento*, 41 (2001), 315–25.

176. Polydore Vergil [Polidoro Virgili], *On Discovery*, ed. and trans. by Brian P. Copenhaver (Cambridge, MA: Harvard University Press, 2002), pp. 384–05. On Chaeremon see below, 'Epilogue'.

177. Vergil, *On Discovery*, pp. 384–05: 'Carnes autem sub Saturno, hoc est, in aureo seculo cum omnia humus funderet, nullum comedisse sed universos vixisse frugibus et pomis quae sponte terra gigneret'.

178. Hahn, 'The Indian Tradition in Western Medieval Intellectual History', p. 222.

179. Mandeville, *Book of Marvels and Travels*, p. 115, and on the inhabitants of this land: 'good, honest men who follow a fine faith and lifestyle. Even though they are not Christian, by natural law they are full of excellent qualities. They eschew all sinfulness, all vice, and all malice, as they are not jealous, proud or covetous, and they are not lecherous or gluttonous, and they only do unto other men as they would have done unto them'.

180. Ibid., p. 116.

181. Polo, *Il Milione*, pp. 267–68: '[I bregomanni] non mangiano carne né beono vino, e istanno in molta grande astinenza e onestade, e non toccherebbono altra femmina che la loro moglie, né non ucciderebbono veruno animale, né non farebbono cosa onde credessono aver peccato. [...] Questi bregomanni vivono più che gente che sia al mondo, perché mangiano poco e fanno grande astinenza. [...] E ancora vi dico che costoro non ucciderebbono veruno animale di mondo, né pulce né pidocchi né mosca né veruno altro, perché dicono ch'egli hanno anima: però sarebbe peccato. Ancora non mangiano veruna cosa verde, né erba né frutti, infino tanto ch'egliono sono secchi, però che dicono che hanno anima'.

182. Johann Böhm, *Gli costumi, le leggi et l'usanze di tutte le genti, raccolte qui insieme da molti illustri scrittori*, trans. by Lucio Fauno (Venice: Tramezzino, 1542). On Böhm (also Boemus) see Margaret T. Hodgen, *Early Anthropology in the Sixteenth and Seventeenth Centuries* (Philadelphia: University of Pennsylvania Press, 1964), pp. 131–43, and Diego Pirillo, 'Relativismo culturale e "armonia del mondo": l'enciclopedia etnografica di Johannes Boemus', in *L'Europa divisa e i nuovi mondi: per Adriano Prosperi*, ed. by Massimo Donattini, Giuseppe Marcocci, & Stefania Pastore, 3 vols (Pisa: Edizioni della Normale, 2011), II, 67–77.

183. Pedro Mexía, *Selva di varia lettione di Pietro Messia Spagnuolo, da lui divisa in tre parti, alle quali s'è aggiunta la quarta di Francesco Sansovino* (Venice: de' Cavalli, 1564). The *Silva* was published for the first time in Seville in 1540. It had an extensive reception in Italian, including various editions with added new sections. On Sansovino's expansion of Mexía's *Selva*: Paolo Cherchi, *Polimatia di riuso: mezzo secolo di plagio (1539–1589)* (Rome: Bulzoni, 1998), p. 76.

184. On the possible reasons for this choice see See Giuliano Gliozzi, 'Il selvaggio americano e l'idea di progresso', in *Differenze e uguaglianza nella cultura europea moderna*, pp. 192–209 (pp. 192–95).

185. Böhm, *Gli costumi, le leggi et l'usanze di tutte le genti*, sig. *6v: 'spogliandosi de loro istessi de la lor barbara e fiera natura, cominciarono ad astenersi da l'uccidersi l'un l'altro, dal mangiare le carni humane, da le rapine'.

186. Ibid., sig. a1r. A certain overlap between 'Brahman' and 'gymnosophist' had continued throughout the Middle Ages; both became a model of virtue, and it is to this tradition that Böhm refers here. See Hahn, 'The Indian Tradition in Western Medieval Intellectual History', p. 213; and Marianne O'Doherty, *The Indies and the Medieval West* (Turnhout: Brepols, 2003), p. 45.

187. Böhm, *Gli costumi, le leggi et l'usanze di tutte le genti*, f. 47v. Cf. the same section on the Brahmans in Pedro Mexía, *Della selva di varia lettione, di Pietro Messia, ampliate e di nuovo rivedute per Francesco Sansovino* (Venice: Polo, 1574), f. 346r–v.

188. Böhm, *Gli costumi, le leggi et l'usanze di tutte le genti*, f. 47v: 'e di qua era poi, che non solo non sapevano, che cosa si fussero tanti morbi, e tante diverse infirmità c'habbiamo noi, ma non ne sapeano ne anco i nomi. Stavano dunque sempre sani'.

189. Ibid., f. 49r. Cf. *OA*, II.34.2; p. 69.

190. Böhm, *Gli costumi, le leggi et l'usanze di tutte le genti*, f. 52v.

191. *Avisi particolari delle Indie di Portugallo ricevuti in questi doi anni del 1551 & 1552* (Rome: Dorico & Bressani, 1552), p. 162.

192. Ficino, *Platonic Theology*, IV, 301–02 (Book XIV.10).

193. On this see Cesare Vasoli, 'Il *De christiana religione* di Marsilio Ficino. Parole chiave: religione, sapienza, profezia, vita civile, ebrei', *Bruniana & Campanelliana*, 13.2 (2007), 403–28 (esp. p. 419).

194. Ficino, *De christiana religione* (OMF, I, 29–30): 'Porphyriusque idem in libro de Responsis adducit Apollinis oraculum, in quo continetur quod inclyta valdeque sancta gens Hebraea prae caeteris novit, recepit et tradidit veram sapientiam, optimum Dei cultum, vitamque beatam. Praeterea in libro de abstinentia religiosos quosdam, philosophosque Iudaeorum, quos Essaeos vocant, tantis prosequitur laudibus ut eos ante alios omnes et prophetas, et sanctos et divinos ostendat. [...] Megastenes insuper Brachmanas Indiae philosophos a Iudaeis asserit descendisse'.

195. *OA*, IV.11.1; p. 108. See also *OA* IV.15 & IV.17.

196. Cardano, *In librum Hippocratis de are, aquis, et locis commentaria*, p. 10ᵃ (*Lectio VI super Tex. III*): 'nam et Gentiles hodie in India quod vino, carnibus, et his quae ex carne fiunt, prorsus abstineant, quemadmodum ovis, lacte, caseo, butyro, piscibus, prope centum quinquaginta annos vivunt'. In *Theonoston* II (p. 400ᵇ) Cardano mentions reports on Eastern India (including Strabo), stating that human life in those areas could reach 130 years.

197. Cardano, *De subtilitate*, p. 560ᵇ: 'Non tamen semper, nec ubique in India tam diuturnam vitam invenire licebit. [...] Locus ille calidus, ideoque tenuem habet aërem et purum, propter ventos, cum in littore maris sit: ob aquas etiam minime siccus. Victus autem ob idolorum cultum, absque vino, carnibusque, praecipue vaccinis, ex fructibus constat ob coeli temperiem praestantissimis, saccaroque'.

198. Cardano, *Theonoston* I, p. 308ᵃ.

199. Like Ficino, Cardano also mentions the Essenes next to the gymnosophists: Cardano, *Theonoston* I, p. 370ᵇ.

200. Antonio Persio, *Trattato dell'ingegno dell'huomo*, ed. by Luciano Artese, *Bruniana & Campanelliana*, Supplementi, Testi, 2 (Pisa & Rome: Serra, 1999), p. 27: 'Dicesi dunque dal verbo ingigno, che vale ingenero, come se volesse dire, in procreando, od in generando pianto a dentro dalla cosa che procreo, o genero una certa virtù, perché quando si genera l'huomo, va inchiusa nel seme una certa virtù, et agume, che si dirà. [...] noi per ingegno intendiamo propiamente quella parte dello spirito per la quale siamo atti a comprendere le cose'. Therefore I prefer to render *ingegno* simply with 'intellection' rather than 'wit' (as translated by Miguel Ángel Granada, '"Spiritus" and "anima a Deo immissa" in Telesio', in *Bernardino Telesio and the Natural Sciences in the Renaissance*, ed. by Pietro Daniel Omodeo (Leiden: Brill, 2019), pp. 33–50 (p. 43)) or 'genius' (Ulrich Pfisterer, 'Animal Art/Human Art: Imagined Borderlines in the Renaissance', in *Humankinds: The Renaissance and its Anthropologies*, ed. by Andreas Höfele & Stephan Laqué (Berlin: de Gruyter, 2011), pp. 217–43 (p. 225)); see also Raphaële Garrod and others,

Logodaedalus: World Histories of Ingenuity in Early Modern Europe (Pittsburgh, PA: Pittsburgh University Press, 2018), pp. 53–56.

201. Persio, *Trattato dell'ingegno dell'huomo*, p. 66. See *Imaginationen des Ungeborenen/Imaginations of the Unborn: Kulturelle Konzepte pränataler Prägung von der Frühen Neuzeit zur Moderne/Cultural Concepts of Prenatal Imprinting from the Early Modern Period to the Present*, ed. by Urte Helduser & Burkhard Dohm (Heidelberg: Winter, 2018).

202. Persio, *Trattato dell'ingegno dell'huomo*, p. 29.

203. Ibid., pp. 43–44 & p. 48; see also p. 32.

204. Persio adds a 'disclaimer' that his view of *ingegno* would not invalidate the religious opinion that humans also possess a mind infused in them directly by God (p. 86). This is a well-known issue: see on this Germana Ernst, 'L'analogia e la differenza: uomo e animali in Campanella', in *The Animal Soul and the Human Mind*, ed. by Muratori, pp. 209–25; and in the same volume Cecilia Muratori, 'The Earth's Perilous Fertility: Telesio on Spontaneous Generation and the Continuity of Living Beings', pp. 131–51.

205. Persio, *Trattato dell'ingegno dell'huomo*, pp. 41–42.

206. Cf. Scaliger, *Exotericae exercitationes*, f. 327r.

207. Persio, *Trattato dell'ingegno dell'huomo*, p. 71: 'perché i beoti per l'aria grossa portavano voce d'esser grossolani, et melloni. [...] così l'aria tenue crea sottili ingegni, et la grossa poco sottili, per qual cagione forse i medici e' philosophanti han detto gli animi seguire la temperatura del corpo, la quale temp[e]ratura serbando le leggi dell'aria, aviene che lo 'ngegno alle istesse leggi sia sottoposto'.

208. Ibid., p. 54.

209. Ficino, *Platonic Theology*, IV. 301 (Book XIV.10). On the references to the Orphic tradition in Ficino (and also in Pico) see Walker, 'Orpheus the Theologian and Renaissance Platonists', on the fact that Renaissance syncretism emerged out of the combination of 'ancient, pre-Platonic, religious tradition, including Orpheus, the Chaldaean Oracles and Pythagoras' (p. 104). The legacy of the individual strands was therefore often indistinguishable. On Ficino and the Chaldaen Oracles see Ilana Klutstein, *Marsilio Ficino et la théologie ancienne: oracles chaldaïques, hymnes orphiques — hymnes de Proclus* (Florence: Olschki, 1987).

210. Persio, *Trattato dell'ingegno dell'huomo*, p. 42: 'Delle quali opinioni amendune estreme temprandone una terza, quella stimerò per la più vera, et non discorderò con Galeno, da cui sono approvate le carni di buon sugo come di certi uccelli, galline, et altri, et di certi quadrupedi come vitelli, et altri, et il simile dell'herbe, et come che monti assai l'usar cibi dilicati, et eletti, et di buon sugo, non pertanto, cerca non minor riguardo che non si faccia un rimescolamento di cibi di diversi humori, posto che tutti sieno buoni, et perfetti; e sì come credo che quasi tutti conoschinlo, così non credo che l'osservino molti, et è pur cosa a cui dovrebbono intendere i savi huomini, et gelosi della salute dell'anima, et del corpo'.

211. Vopiscus Fortunatus Plemp, *De togatorum valetudine tuenda commentatio* (Brussels: Foppens 1670), p. 157: 'Septentrionales Scythas, Sarmatas, Islandos, Lituanos multam vorantes carnem stupidos, hebetes, obtusos esse observamus: Syros, Aegyptios, Assyrios, Chaldaeos fructibus fere victitantes, acutos, acres, solertes ac perspicaces'.

212. Ibid.: 'Nos nihilominus austeram illam, duram, rigidamque vitam non probamus, qui inter homines agitamus, et urbana tractamus negotia, subindeque ad convivia nos invitari sinimus, et concidimus, carnesque appositas temperanter adsumimus; quod vitio caret'.

CHAPTER 4

❖

Rationality

4.1. Introduction: The Renaissance Roots of the *querelle de l'âme des bêtes*

Rationality and food are connected in a twofold way: does the choice of food reveal the rationality or irrationality of the eater? But also: can a rational being legitimately be consumed and become food? The first question, as seen in the previous chapter, surfaced in Renaissance debates dealing with the characteristics of eaters such as the American cannibals and the Eastern Brahmans. This chapter is devoted instead to the second one. In Book 3 of *On Abstinence*, Porphyry discusses a variety of arguments for and against the view that animals are rational. As is the case with the other topics already considered — sacrifice, health, and dietetic plurality — Porphyry is interested in the practical outcomes: if animals are rational, would the philosopher make an ethical choice in deciding to eat them nonetheless?[1] In Renaissance philosophical literature, this topic is probably the one most frequently associated with Porphyry's name, and references to his view that animals partake in rationality are almost ubiquitous.

In scholarship to date, the sixteenth- and seventeenth-century debates on the ethical consequences of attributing rationality to animals have been neglected in favour of exploring the famous developments of the controversy that started with Descartes and that extended well beyond, into the eighteenth century. The so-called *querelle de l'âme des bêtes* gained currency as a debate among supporters and critics of the Cartesian theory according to which animals do not possess a 'mind' (*mens*), and are thus to be considered incapable of rational thought.[2] Animals — as Descartes claims in the *Discours de la méthode* — are not merely less endowed with reason than humans are: they are completely devoid of it.[3] Yet, Descartes had specified that the absence of a mind in animals did not, in his view, imply depriving them of a soul, understood as the life principle. As he pointed out to Henry More, he talked of 'cogitation, not of life or sensation', adding, 'I do not deny life to any animal, as far as I establish that this consists only in the heat of the heart'.[4] Yet, it remained ambiguous whether or not this position ultimately meant that animals had to be considered as incapable of sensation, as well as of thought, or if it remained possible to attribute to them the capability of experiencing sensation without that of processing such sensations at the level of rational thinking. The answer to this depends on the understanding of the interdependence of rationality and sensation — a topic which, as we will see in this chapter, was debated throughout the Renaissance, well before Descartes's controversial statements on the nature of animals.[5] Can animals be considered as completely devoid of rationality, but still able to perceive and respond to sensory impulses? Or rather is a certain degree of rational thinking always involved in the process of sensation? Indeed, can rationality be conceived as present in varying degrees, or is it either fully present or fully absent?

At least partially ignoring Descartes's own specification that 'mind' and 'soul' are not synonymous, the *querelle* led to an international debate on whether or not animals could be viewed as soulless machines. If 'animal souls are banished', as Denis Des Chene aptly puts it, 'old questions take a new turn: life must be redefined'. The result was the view that 'Descartes' animal-machine, perhaps the most influential image of the living in the new science, has no life'.[6] Descartes would have protested against this way of putting it, as he protested against Henry More accusing him of turning animals into machines or statues deprived of both life and sensation.[7] But precisely this comparison of animals and machines became the cornerstone of the *querelle*. Marin Mersenne (1588–1648) for instance famously compared the reactions of an animal to the ticking of a clock; Thomas Willis (1621–75) in *De anima brutorum* [On the Soul of Animals] stated that the soul of animals resembled an hydraulic musical instrument, whose mechanics follow a set of rules. The rational soul of humans, on the other hand, resembles for Willis a musical instrument played by a proper musician.[8]

The ethical implications of the *querelle* were evident already to Descartes and his contemporaries. In a letter to Descartes, Henry More expressed his anxiety for the 'destiny of animals', if they are considered to be machines.[9] From a Cartesian point of view, even if animals were endowed with a basic capability of sensual response, the absence of a consciousness would make killing them legitimate and guilt-free.[10] This practical outcome is the result of the conviction that in order to feel, a living being must be conscious of those sensations, which is only possible due to the presence of a mind.[11] Therefore if an animal does not feel in the proper sense of the word, no suffering is caused by its slaughter. To More's accusation that his position was 'cruel', Descartes replied sharply that his view was kind to humans, rather than cruel to animals.[12] The reason is that it would finally liberate humans from a longstanding philosophical prejudice that causes feelings of guilt about killing animals (even if, it seems, the guilt would not necessarily stop the butchering, but would just make one feel uncomfortable about it). Descartes calls this the 'Pythagorean superstition', referring to the idea of the transmigration of souls as an explanation for how rational souls could inhabit animal bodies.[13] If this were the case, killing an animal would not be substantially different from killing a human being. Descartes thus claims to be the first to have argued successfully against a key tenet in the history of philosophical vegetarianism: that if animals are rational, it is unlawful to kill them.

This is the argument at the centre of the present chapter. It can be traced back to a certain interpretation of Pythagorean metempsychosis, one thoroughly discussed in Porphyry's *On Abstinence*. The emphasis on the ground-breaking modernity of

Descartes's position, highlighting how Descartes represented a turning point in the rise of a 'modern' approach to the human-animal distinction, has often been the result of overlooking the legacy of earlier philosophical traditions.[14] What this narrative neglects is that throughout the Renaissance the attribution of rationality to animals was intensely debated, and that these debates even included discussion of the extreme position that animals might be deprived of sensation *and* rationality, a position that is still too often assumed to originate with the Cartesian theory and its aftermath.

This chapter will now focus on two conceptual areas related to the key topic of animal rationality. It will show that Renaissance philosophers did take into account the ethical consequences of attributing rationality to animals, or of depriving them of it. Porphyry is commonly mentioned as a key source for such debates, and the two main areas this chapter will explore are central in *On Abstinence*. These are, first, the question whether animal language is a primary indication of animal rationality; and second, the continuity of sensation and rationality, and its implications not only for animal rationality but also for extending sensation to the vegetable world. This last issue was crucial in Porphyry's presentation of vegetarianism as a viable option for the philosopher, and it had a particularly heated revival in the Renaissance, with authors such as Tommaso Campanella addressing directly the supposed fallacies of Porphyry's argument on this point. Methodologically, the chapter considers the Renaissance debate on animal language with a dual interface, both in relation to its sources (primarily Porphyry) and to its aftermath, thus bridging the still common historiographical gap between Renaissance and post-Renaissance discussions of animal nature.

Renaissance readers of *On Abstinence* refer to Porphyry as a leading example of a philosopher who attributed rationality to animals, alongside Plutarch and Pythagoras.[15] Ficino, among the first to translate *On Abstinence*, already selected animal rationality as a key argument from Porphyry's text (it occupies a large section of Book 3).[16] As Fay Edwards has convincingly demonstrated, Porphyry's approach is dialogical in nature, as he responds to the views of those who consider animals to be irrational, that is to say mainly the Stoics. He thus reviews the main tenets of the Stoic definition of *lógos* in order to assess whether or not those criteria lead by necessity to the exclusion of animals. For Porphyry, the outcome is decisive in view of the connection between justice and rationality: if justice is due only to rational creatures, as the Stoics had claimed, then animals can be eaten without committing a crime.[17] This is why Porphyry enters Stoic territory in trying to demonstrate that animals do possess *lógos*, both in the sense of uttered speech (*lógos prophorikós*) and of internal speech (*lógos endiáthetos*). With regard to the former, Porphyry employs the argument of 'linguistic relativity' in order to claim that all sound voiced by the tongue expresses *lógos*, whether it is a human language unknown to the Greek, or the different voices of animals. This is one of the arguments most often linked to Porphyry in the Renaissance: just as humans do not understand languages other than their mother tongue, unless they have studied them, so it is not surprising that they would not understand the languages of other animal species, unless they have learnt them through careful observation of and co-habitation with such animals. All in all, Porphyry concludes that 'animals which have a voice share in *lógos*'.[18] Sharing in *lógos* implies the idea of a gradation, rather than a stark alternative between presence and absence of *lógos*, as Descartes would assume. Like the Stoics, Descartes used the example of the parrot to stress that animals do not possess meaningful language at all.[19]

With regard to internal *lógos*, or the capability of inner reflexion, Porphyry follows the same path and argues in favour of drawing a distinction among living creatures in terms of more or less, rather than presence or absence.[20] Porphyry's point of reference in this context is Aristotle. Aristotle's writings on animals are used as evidence for attributing to animals a whole series of capabilities and passions that explain certain behaviours: for instance, animals are said to be able to plan in advance, to make decisions to their own advantage, to teach each other and to have memory.[21] Porphyry repeatedly appeals to experience as a guide to understanding animal behaviour.[22] Human language is simply one of many variations of meaningful utterance, as can be learned by becoming familiar with the specific modes of expression in the animal world.[23]

The fact that Porphyry refers to Aristotle on animal rationality, against the Stoics, is particularly relevant in light of the Renaissance reception. As we will see, the debate on the border dividing sensation from rationality in Aristotelian psychology is often the frame within which the discussion of ethical consequences with regard to the treatment of animals takes place. The question at the centre of the debate is whether being capable of sensation necessarily entails at least a certain capability of organizing those sensations at a higher, (proto-)rational level. In other words, is sensation without any rational thinking possible? Porphyry answers in the negative:

> There is no way that the taking and pursuit of useful things, and rejection and avoidance of destructing and harmful things, which are consequent on perception, can be present in creatures which do not by nature reason and judge and remember and attend.[24]

The very same dilemma is also in the background of the seventeenth-century *querelle*: the advocates of the theory of the animal-machine give the same answer as Porphyry — sensation and rationality cannot be separated — but argue that that is precisely why animals must be deprived of both.

Porphyry's discussion of animal rationality is, as mentioned above, as much a reply to the Stoics as it is an interpretation of Aristotle. He addresses a crux in Aristotelian psychology, that is the distinction between animal and human souls on the basis of the interaction of sensation and rationality. Richard Sorabji maintains that Aristotle is responsible for the great divide between rational humans and irrational animals, a divide that never closed.[25] Porphyry was acutely aware of this outcome of Aristotelian psychology, and of its consequences at the level of ethics: therefore he refers to Aristotle's zoological works in order to emphasize the capabilities of animals and stress the continuity with humans.[26] Rather than strict adherence to a specific view of animal rationality, and of what this involves, Porphyry points out the impossibility of separating rationality from sensation, and *lógos* (both as internal and external speech) from the absence thereof. This is why he states that Aristotle, Plato, Empedocles, Pythagoras, and Democritus in fact agreed in granting animals participation in *lógos*, deliberately underplaying the differences between their specific understandings of what *lógos* actually means.[27]

This approach explains also why Porphyry mentions Pythagoras and the idea of transmigration in this context. Porphyry notably does not commit to the belief that souls can transmigrate into animal bodies, because this could be understood as an argument against as much as in favour of vegetarianism.[28] It is true that, in general terms, the cycle of transmigration entails the principle that all living beings are connected, since a soul can inhabit any body: it thus provides a kind of egalitarian view, based on a certain homogeneity of all forms of life.[29] But if transmigration is seen as a kind of punishment, as in the Platonic version, then for a soul it can only be a disadvantage to be trapped in an animal body: thus killing the animal and freeing the soul, making it available for a new cycle of transmigration, can be seen as a virtuous action.[30] The fact that in this interpretation all souls would be rational ones transmigrating into animal bodies — bodies which are considered less able to host such souls than human ones — becomes yet another element in favour of killing (and potentially eating) animals.[31] Thus, when Porphyry lists Pythagoras among those who, correctly, granted to animals at least a certain degree of rationality, he means to refer to the general principle that rationality cannot be considered an absolute barrier dividing humans from animals, rather than to express support for metempsychosis in particular.

Porphyry also uses the topic of metempsychosis to introduce another corollary about animal rationality, one that was to enjoy a particularly rich Renaissance afterlife: if souls can transmigrate into any life form, then would it not become potentially unlawful to kill plants as well, since a vegetable body could also host a rational soul? And if this is the case, would it not become impossible for humans, or at least for philosophers, to nourish themselves in any lawful way, without being plagued by guilt (as Descartes would put it)? Porphyry's answer to this puzzle relies once more on the understanding of the realms of sensation and rationality. Porphyry insists on their connection in the case of animals, but stresses that plants, on the other hand, are devoid of both. An argument that seems to worry Porphyry is the following: if plants and animals are inhabited by the same souls, and one were to argue that it cannot be impious to kill plants, since eating them is necessary for human sustenance, then killing animals should not be considered impious either. The only viable solution, for Porphyry, is to consider plants entirely incapable of sensation, and thus of having preferences. If that is the case, he argues, it is impossible to harm a plant, and the philosopher does not behave unjustly when preparing salad for dinner. Plants remain, quite simply, outside of the territory of justice.[32]

There are nevertheless passages in *On Abstinence* in which Porphyry involves plants indirectly in the sphere of justice. For instance, Porphyry suggests that there is a difference between taking just part of a plant, such as an apple from a tree, and uprooting the entire plant, as in the case of a lettuce. But he does not discuss this in detail, because he repeats that eating vegetables is a kind of harm permitted by God for one's survival, and he likens it to drinking water and even to milking a sheep.[33]

Moreover, even if the plant is not technically harmed, especially when one avoids uprooting it all, it can still be harmful for the eater to choose foods not according to need but to pure gluttony. This remains a key point for Porphyry throughout *On Abstinence*: the health of the eater (in terms both of his soul and of his body) is the cornerstone of his argumentation.[34] Yet, Porphyry seems to claim that there is a fortunate convergence of conditions in the case of plants: plants do not feel, humans do not even need to kill the entire plant in order to use it for nourishment, and the vegetarian philosopher can actually survive on them without having to eat meat.

Such a view prompted a series of questions in Renaissance readers: how can we be sure that plants do not feel? If sensation and rationality are intertwined in terms of 'more or less' in the case of animals and humans, how can it be explained that plants do not partake in the least in this gradation of the soul's faculties? If it should be proven that plants do prefer certain conditions and avoid others, can Porphyry's position that they do not take part in sensation and thus remain outside of the territory of justice be defended? Moreover, is the use of plants by humans completely harmless for the environment, regardless of whether a section or the entire plant is used? And can humans really survive on plants only?

The following sections will consider answers to such questions given by Renaissance thinkers, spanning from sixteenth-century debates on animal language (especially Girolamo Fabrici D'Acquapendente and Michel de Montaigne), to contemporaries of Descartes (here Tommaso Campanella and Pierre Gassendi are in the foreground). This broad timeframe will enable us to retrace the continuity of the debate on animal rationality and animal language, going beyond the historiographical assumption that a swift change of scenery occurred with Descartes. A crucial aspect that provides continuity is that Renaissance philosophers contrasted and sometimes combined the views of Aristotle and of Porphyry on language and rationality, using the negotiation of Aristotelianism with Porphyry's view, in order to measure the distance between humans and animals.

4.2. Animal Voice and Animal Speech: Fabrici D'Acquapendente on Aristotle and Porphyry

According to Porphyry, the dietetic volte-face of his friend Firmus Castricius is also a change of philosophical party: from a philosophy that supports vegetarianism, such as the philosophy of Pythagoras and Empedocles, to the side that does not, including Aristotelianism, Stoicism, and Epicureanism. Depriving animals of rationality, for Porphyry, is the main single reason for a specific ethical approach, namely one that justifies the exploitation of animals. Yet, his interpretation of Aristotle on this point is ambiguous. On the one hand, Porphyry is well aware that Aristotelians are not famous for practicing vegetarianism; on the other, he seeks to win Aristotle to his side when arguing that animals in fact share in *lógos*, placing him next to Pythagoras and Empedocles (and Plato and Democritus) in that respect.[35]

In the first book of the *Politics*, Aristotle had famously stated that 'the human being is the only animal who has the gift of speech (*lógos*)'.[36] All other animals express their pain and pleasure through voice (*phoné*), but only the human being articulates the voice into speech. The main indication that humans have speech and not just voice is a political and ethical one: humans live in society, and can distinguish good from evil. The animals' voices, on the other hand, remain outside the territory of ethics. When Porphyry claims that Aristotle is on his side in acknowledging that animals share in *lógos*, he is probably using the term *lógos* in the broad sense of 'intelligence', rather than as a specific term for language.[37] Elsewhere Porphyry has recourse again to the authority of Aristotle to state that animals are more or less wise according to the sharpness of their perceptions, thus indicating that they should not be excluded from sagacity altogether.

It is not surprising that Renaissance authors juggle the dual legacy of Porphyry and Aristotle on animal language. Girolamo Fabrici D'Acquapendente, a professor of anatomy in Padua and author of *De brutorum loquela* [On the Language of Non-Human Animals] (1603), follows in Porphyry's wake in interpreting Aristotle's theory of language in terms of gradation, rather than assuming an absolute boundary dividing human language from animal voices. Just as for Porphyry, the topic of animal language has for Fabrici broad implications with regard to how to grasp the human-animal difference. Studying animal language, for Fabrici, amounts to nothing less than investigating philosophically the nature of animals: through language, it is possible to understand animality.[38]

Porphyry's *On Abstinence* is Fabrici's key source in arguing that animal voices are in fact languages, in the sense that they are articulated voice.[39] To the objection that animals produce sounds but do not have a proper language, Fabrici replies that if a creature is capable of articulating the voice as many animals do, then it displays a capability for language.[40] The capability to articulate the voice is an important feature that humans and several animal species have in common; the difference consists in the fact that human language is articulated in letters, while the articulations of animal languages are varied. By comparison with human language, animal languages are simpler, as they are not based on combinations of letters, syllables etc.[41] But for Fabrici it is clearly a matter of more or less, rather than of all or nothing. It is therefore the same capability in both cases, only differentiated by degrees of complexity.

Loquela expresses the passions ('affectus animi') felt by a creature, and can therefore be more or less clear and multifaceted, according to how the creature feels.[42] The degree of complexity will depend on the variety of animal species, rather than on the differentiation between human and non-human animals. Fabrici applies a naturalistic approach, which he supports, beginning from the preface, by referring to Aristotle's zoological works:[43] there is no other natural-philosophical topic on which Aristotle has written more copiously, he points out. Fabrici thus anchors the investigation of the nature of animals within what could be termed 'biological Aristotelianism'.[44]

This approach, for Fabrici, brings Porphyry in unison with Aristotle.[45] From this point of view of biological gradation among animal species, Porphyry only made explicit what Aristotle had put in more cautious terms. For instance, Fabrici quotes a passage from Theodore Gaza's translation of *De historia animalium* [On the History of Animals] where Aristotle states that articulated voice is *almost* like the 'language' of animals — 'language' being *diálektos* in Greek (a word often used to mean the specific language of a country or a group of people), and *locutio* (meaning 'speech', 'discourse') in Latin translation.[46] Fabrici interprets this to mean that, according to Aristotle, animals are straightforwardly capable of language. Fabrici knows that Aristotle, in the same chapter of *De historia animalium*, had stated that the human being is the only creature who possesses language (again, *diálektos*), but he considers this to mean that only human language is formed of letters, not that animals are deprived of the capability of talking altogether.[47] In this sense, Aristotle and Porphyry are interpreted as sharing essentially the same view, namely that animals talk, despite the fact that Porphyry unambiguously argues in favour of attributing *lógos* to animals, while Aristotle is more cautious about the identification of animal voices with the power of speech.

Porphyry is mentioned by Fabrici as the main authority on animal language.[48] Fabrici considers him the pinnacle of an entire tradition of philosophers who attributed language to animals, following primarily in the footsteps of Aristotle. Fabrici argues that if language expresses emotions, speaking and being capable of knowing (that is to say, possessing a *cognoscens facultas*) must also go hand in hand:

> Si loquela homini data est, non solum ad disciplinas edocendas capescendasque, sed etiam communiter, ut aliquid alteri significetur: bruta, quae cognescente facultate et ipsa praedita sunt (et, ut Porphyrius ex Aristotele, Platone, Empedocle, Pythagora, Democrito affirmat, rationis quoque capacita), cur erunt hac ipsa privata?[49]

> [If language is given to the human being not only for learning and apprehending disciplines, but also, generally, for signifying something to someone else, why should animals be deprived of it, given that they possess the faculty of knowing (and, as Porphyry, following Aristotle, Plato, Empedocles, Pythagoras, Democritus, says, that they are also capable of reasoning)?]

Fabrici quotes extensively from Book 3 of *On Abstinence*: animals modulate their voice according to their emotions, and the situations they are living in — from the cries they let out when they are scared, to the specific modulations that signify invitations to eat, or provocations to fight.[50] Language thus expresses emotions of various kinds, which are considered by Fabrici, as well as by Porphyry, as signs that animals, too, are capable of knowing, that they are intelligent — in other words, that they partake in some degree of rationality.

With a quotation from Cicero, Fabrici adds that only the human being is capable of thinking beyond the present moment, imagining future consequences or recalling past events, while animals have only a very dim cognition of past and future. In this respect, the human being can be called the only rational creature.[51] Yet, it is clear that this view is a pragmatic simplification of a complex gradation of being: the difference can be seen as one of degree rather than of kind. Rationality is conceived in this context as a very practical capability that allows the human to understand the deeper fabric of reality, and thus to dominate better his own environment.

The connection between the emotions, their expression, and the intelligence that regulates the animals' responses remains the pivotal point of this understanding of animal language. In order to understand the languages of different animal species it is necessary to grasp the relationship between a specific call and the intention that lies behind it. If we watch carefully, we see easily that animals talk. Only by patiently observing animal behaviours can one learn the meaning of specific sounds, which will then appear to the trained ear as modulated voice, that is to say, as language.[52] Fabrici notably refers to the examples given by Porphyry in *On Abstinence* of sages who had claimed to be able to understand the conversations of animals: the legendary prophets Melampus and Tiresias, and the Pythagorean philosopher Apollonius of Tyana (first century AD).[53] These are examples of human beings with exceptional capabilities: their understanding of animal languages resembles prophecy. But from a purely methodological point of view, the reference serves the purpose of relativizing the strict human-animal division. Rather than reasoning in terms of human languages versus animal languages, these three sages stand for the possibility of dividing languages into two different groups: those known to the speaker versus those unknown. Therefore, the examples prompt the question regarding the qualitative difference between unknown human languages and unknown animal languages: just as a Greek might not be able to understand an Indian, so a human might not be able to understand a horse. Yet, just as it is possible for a Greek person to learn Sanskrit, so it might be theoretically possible also to learn the language of another animal species. In this context, Fabrici brings Aristotle once more into unison with Porphyry, by interpreting the famous passage in *On the Soul* about the voice of the lyre as proof that everything and every species has its own voice: the lyre's music is like a language, even if in the case of inanimate things this can only be said metaphorically.[54]

Fabrici employs another reference to the third book of *On Abstinence* (III.3) to point precisely to this issue: even among human languages, those that are unknown to us sound as unintelligible as animal languages. But Fabrici pushes Porphyry's argument towards a strongly relativistic outcome, stating that humans argue according to 'human law', and animals according to the law that the creator and nature have given them. But there is an important difference between human and animal languages. For Fabrici, human language is both natural (with reference to the use of letters) and artificial (with regard to locution and actual speech), and this explains the great variety of languages within the human species. Animal language, on the other hand, is purely natural and therefore Fabrici believes that there exists only one language for each animal species.[55] For instance, there would only exist one canine language: all dogs therefore understand each other.

In his 'An Apology for Raymond Sebond' ['Apologie de Raymond Sebond'], Montaigne — a contemporary of Fabrici (they were born in the same year) — takes the argument about the inability of humans to understand animals even further. Montaigne refers to the same sages (with the addition of Thales), and may even have Porphyry in mind as a main source;[56] but he draws a more daring conclusion from this material.[57] Rather than appealing to a difference in natural 'laws' to justify the fact that humans and animals do not understand each other, he poses a question in terms of fault: whose fault is it that we and the animals cannot communicate with each other? Here too, Montaigne gives an ethical twist to the argument of relativity, as in the case of his discussion of cannibalism considered in the previous chapter. He compares human inability to understand animals to the inability of the French to understand the Basques, or indeed troglodytes. For Montaigne, the relativity of human languages becomes a basis for suggesting that animals and humans are on an equal footing when it comes to mutual understanding, or lack thereof. Ultimately, the fact that animals are usually considered to be devoid of certain capabilities, including that of speech, is due to human vanity: humans arbitrarily consider themselves to be the judges of the intelligence, or the brutishness, of other creatures.

While Fabrici concluded that the dissimilitude between human and animal voices ultimately explains why we do not understand them, and vice versa, Montaigne, instead, underlines that on the contrary we do, more or less, understand what animal voices signify, and the animals, conversely, appear to grasp the essence of our utterances. Furthermore, Montaigne points out that communication across species takes place regularly in nature: humans should therefore not be tempted to group animal languages under one simple heading, as the opposite of human language, because such languages exist in a huge variety, as different from each other as human languages are from each of them.[58] Again, Montaigne emphasizes the ethical aspect of this differentiation, as he writes that common animal-human relations — expressing aggression, or seeking protection — make clear that successful communication always takes place between 'us' and 'them'. The fact that this division exists is a sign of the damage that human vanity has caused: the animals are the humans' 'brothers and companions', and communication with them, Montaigne implies, need not be considered impossible.[59] With reference to Plato's *Statesman*, Montaigne writes that the capability to communicate with animals was key to the happiness of humans in the mythical age of Cronos (which, incidentally, was also a vegetarian age).[60]

In Fabrici's *De brutorum loquela*, the multiple references to Porphyry serve the purpose of eroding the simple division of humans versus animals, replacing it with a more fluid distinction between 'us' and 'them' — where 'us' is the group of talkers who understand each other, and 'them' comprises everyone else. The animal-human border is thus replaced by a multiplicity of borders dividing human communities from each other, and also from other animal species. Implicit in both Fabrici's and Montaigne's arguments is the question which became the fulcrum of the later *querelle de l'âme des bêtes*, namely: what is it that animal languages express? Do they only reveal the presence of feeling (preferences, fear, pain), or also of rational thought? Depending on the answer to this question, animal language can become a tool to establish, or to question, the human-animal hierarchy, including at the ethical level.

4.3. Hierarchies of Language and Reason: Are Talking Animals Humans?

Porphyry's example of the sages who could communicate with animals is also mentioned in a book devoted to various forms of language, and which features a large section on the languages of animals: the *Discorso sopra tutti li parlari* [Discourse on All Kinds of Speech] by Girolamo Giovannini da Capugnano, first published in 1604. A Dominican, Giovannini's engagement with the topic of the human-animal differentiation is twofold: on the one hand, he published in the *Discorso* his own reflections on the distinction between human language and animal languages; on the other, he was active as a censor, and in this role he 'corrected' a work in which animals speak in order to defend the superiority of the animal to the human condition, namely Giovan Battista Gelli's *Circe* (1549).[61] Giovannini da Capugnano's engagement with the topic of animal language, even if not particularly original, is therefore indicative of the broader context in which this debate unfolded, with special regard to the religious implications of granting animals the ability to talk.

Like Fabrici, Giovannini juggles the authorities of Aristotle and Porphyry in order to point to the similarities and to the differences between human and animal languages. His position is strongly inflected by his religious standing. He claims that it is God's plan that animals do not speak like humans, because God endowed the human being only with the gift of talking ('parola').[62] Furthermore, God gave to each animal species its own language, because if all animals were to speak the same language, meek animals would more easily be attacked by the predators (presumably because the use of the common language would give rise to misunderstandings, and for instance the sheep would be led into the company of wolves).[63]

Giovannini assumes that human language is a divine gift to humankind. There are two main differences that make human language more complex than animal languages: humans have a tongue which is unlike any other tongue in terms of muscles and mobility; and the human mind can make use of the tongue to utter anything it can think of.[64] These are issues that Fabrici had also raised, and indeed Giovannini appears to lean substantially not just on Fabrici's interpretation, and on the sources he quotes in *De brutorum loquela*, but even on his very words.[65] Giovannini, like Fabrici, concedes that 'animals, beasts, and the birds, have a certain way of talking, that they understand', and the whole chapter devoted to this topic is 'borrowed' from Chapter 1 of *De brutorum loquela*.[66] Fabrici refers to the same passage from *On the Soul* also used by Fabrici to support the theory that other creatures beyond humans should be considered as able to talk, since even the lyre can be said metaphorically to have a voice.[67] He also refers to Aristotle's *Historia animalium* (IV.9) and the *De generatione animalium* (V.7) to acknowledge the differences between human and animal languages, appealing to the authority of Aristotle, according to whom 'talking [*favellare*] is proper to humans only'.[68]

Yet, Giovannini adapts Fabrici's text at a key point, where Fabrici had used the authority of Porphyry and Plutarch to argue that animals can talk. In Giovannini's hands, Fabrici's argument is now twisted in favour of a qualitative difference between humans and animals. Further, while Fabrici had sought to harmonize

Aristotle and Porphyry on the topic of animal language, Giovannini ultimately sides rather with Aristotle than with Porphyry.[69] Paraphrasing Fabrici, Giovannini agrees with Porphyry that animals have their own languages, even if humans usually do not understand them:

> Porfirio e Plutarco vogliono che ne gl'irrationali sia un certo favellare. Non è dubbio (per fondamentare questo pensiero) che molti di loro, come di continuo si vede, parlano e altri fanno certe voci per dimostrare gli effetti suoi, il ch'è argomento c'hanno gli organi a proposito per questi effetti. E cosi havendo eglino la voce significante, che ne negherà che 'l suo parlare non habbia alcun significato, di cui la voce è materia? E se gli huomini con la voce articolata, ponno isfogarsi, e mostrare questi affetti naturali, d'onde farà che nelle belve e ne gl'uccelli non si trovi questo aiuto ancora, havendo la voce e gli articoli, o variandola in mille modi?[70]

> [Porphyry and Plutarch claim that irrational creatures are capable of a certain kind of talking. As one sees all the time, it is beyond doubt (to substantiate this idea) that many of them talk, and emit certain voices to express their feelings, and this demonstrates that they have organs that are suitable for this. And thus since they have a meaningful voice, who will deny that their talking has meaning, of which voice is the matter? And if humans can express themselves with an articulated voice and display these natural affects, how should beasts and birds not possess this aid, since they have voice and articulation, and can modulate in a thousand ways?]

Giovannini follows Fabrici, yet avoids overstressing the authority of Porphyry and Plutarch: he does not translate Fabrici's comment that 'reason, too, agrees with these authorities'.[71] The motive for Giovannini's distance from Fabrici's text on this point is revealed a few lines further, when Giovannini completely subverts Fabrici's meaning by adapting the sentence in which Fabrici had pointed out that animals 'are endowed with a kind of cognitive faculty (*cognoscens facultas*) (and as Porphyry, following Aristotle, Plato, Empedocles, Pythagoras, Democritus, says that they are also capable of reasoning)'. Instead, Giovannini unequivocally affirms the following:

> Non voglio dire con Empedocle, Pitagora e con Democrito, che questi bruti sieno capaci di ragione; ma soggiungerò che come noi rationali habbiamo il modo per palesare l'interiore affetto, non c'è scropolo a dire, che questo sia concesso a gl'irragionevoli, che convengano con noi stessi in havergli.[72]

> [I do not want to say, with Empedocles, Pythagoras, and Democritus, that these brutes are capable of reason. But I will add that as we rational beings can show the inner affects, there is no hesitation in saying that this is granted also to the irrational ones, which converge with us in this respect.]

Despite his agreement with Porphyry (and with Fabrici) that animals are capable of language, Giovannini is careful to set boundaries to the animals' range of expression. In particular, he underlines that there is no connection between being able to talk and being rational: animals can talk, but remain irrational. For Giovannini, acknowledging the fact that they are able to show their emotions does not make them any more capable of thinking rationally. All they can bring to expression with their languages are their sentiments, and not complex rational thought. In this respect, Giovannini does not follow Porphyry. To him, animal language is not proof that rationality can be present in a creature in varying degrees.

Yet, Giovannini does follow Porphyry (in Fabrici's interpretation) in emphasizing the relativism of languages: just as humans speaking different languages might not be capable of understanding each other — and yet each language is meaningful — so animal languages appear to humans to be meaningless simply because they do not understand them.[73] But then Giovannini distances himself from the idea that certain humans might be able to understand animal language, as in the case of the sages mentioned by Porphyry. He even adds that those who claim to be able to decipher them either lied or must have been possessed by the devil.[74]

Giovannini sketches a kind of evolution from animal to human language which children undergo when they learn to speak: at first, babies only emit cries, then they begin to articulate syllables, and then finally combine these into words. Humans thus acquire speech in stages, growing out of the simple sounds they make when they are first born, and developing a complex, human language.[75] This understanding of the development of human language exemplifies the intrinsic ambivalence of Giovannini's approach: he maintains that human language is more complex than animal languages, yet the difference is not simply a quantitative but also a qualitative one, since human language also marks an unbridgeable distance between humans and animals, a distance set by God. Giovannini lists examples transmitted by ancient and modern authors which prove that animals talk.[76] But at the same time he holds to the idea of a radical difference between humans and animals.

Giovannini's extensive borrowing from Fabrici makes his approach to animal language at least *prima facie* contradictory, as he incorporates Fabrici's (and Porphyry's) idea that animals talk, and yet inserts in this framework the conception of a radical difference between human and animal language, based on the assertion that humans only are rational and that their language is a divine gift.[77] He must explain why, once it is granted that animals speak, their languages, unlike human languages, are not expressions of an activity of thought. Giovannini reasons *ad absurdum*: if animals were rational, they would be equal to humans. Therefore, they must be considered talking but still irrational creatures:

> Non ponno gli animali ragionare per un'altra causa, seguitando per necessità che bisognarebbe che intendessero quel che dicono, e in consequenza c'havessero l'intelletto, e così non più irragionevoli ma huomini farieno; e mancherebbe al mondo un ordine di cose, e un grado nell'essere [...] e se quelli del sensitivo parlassero com'è detto si porrebbero tra gli umani.[78]

> [There is another reason why animals cannot ratiocinate, namely because it would follow by necessity that they would understand what they say, and consequently that they had intellect, so that they would not be irrational any more, but humans; and the world would lack an order of things and a gradation of being [...], and if those that belong to the sensitive [realm] were to speak, they would, as mentioned, be included in the same group with humans.]

By linking speech and rationality, as Porphyry had done, the hierarchy of the world is shaken: animals and humans would be placed on the same level. Giovannini, instead, wants to preserve the hierarchical order, which he considers to be God's plan. But it is significant that rather than adducing philosophical arguments in favour of the separation of language and rationality, Giovannini simply appeals to the moral and religious importance of the hierarchy that such a separation preserves.

Before Giovannini, this same argument to justify human superiority had been used by an author who enjoyed a particularly prominent afterlife during the years of the *querelle de l'âme des bêtes*: Gómez Pereira. In *Antoniana Margarita* (1554), Pereira argued that 'if animals were equal to us in sensation, by necessity it should be inferred that there is nothing peculiar to us humans, which is not shared with them'.[79] Since granting that humans and animals are equal in feeling may lead to the conclusion that animals, too, must be able to perform rational thinking, at least in some degree, Pereira argues that the only way to preserve the distance between us and them is by depriving them not only of reason, but of sensation as well. A radical gap must be assumed, even if it cannot be fully justified philosophically, because if one attempts a more subtle differentiation it becomes ultimately impossible to draw a clear line between the capabilities shared with animals, and those that are proper to humans only. With a move more radical than Giovannini's, Pereira thus claims not only that animals do not speak, and are not rational, but also that they do not feel.[80] Therefore their sounds must not be considered as indicative of rational thought: those sounds do not even show that they experience natural affections, which Giovannini, following Porphyry, had instead granted to them.

Pierre Bayle (1647–1706) dedicated a famous article of his *Dictionaire* to Pereira's theory that 'brute animals are machines'.[81] According to Bayle, Pereira cultivated a taste for philosophical paradoxes, and in that spirit he set out to overturn the established doctrine regarding the animal soul, namely that animals are sentient. He reports that prior to Pereira, the debate regarded the attribution or privation of rationality to animals, but sensation was taken for granted.[82] Bayle's article thus turns into a discussion of the two most radical positions on the animal soul: that it is neither rational nor sensitive, or that it is both sensitive and rational. Most ancient philosophers, for Bayle, actually agreed that the animal soul is rational: the examples he mentions largely overlap with those given by Fabrici (and Giovannini) in the footsteps of Porphyry, namely Empedocles, Pythagoras, Plato, and Plutarch.[83] Among them, Bayle highlights Porphyry as the philosopher who put forward the most favourable view of the soul of animals: 'he granted to them not only reason but also the faculty for making their reasoning understood; he believed that the human being does not surpass animals in anything other than possessing a more refined reasoning power'.[84] Therefore, Pereira stands in the article as the polar opposite of Porphyry.

In assessing Porphyry's arguments in favour of animal rationality, against Pereira's paradoxical conclusions, Bayle refers to Porphyry's use of Aristotle. As already considered in the previous section, Porphyry claimed that he had Aristotle on his side when granting reasoning powers to animals. Bayle evaluates the situation by quoting at length the discussion of Porphyry's position by the Jesuit professors at the University of Coimbra (the 'Conimbricenses'), drawing attention in particular to the example of the sages Tiresias and Melampus, mentioned in *On Abstinence*.[85] The Coimbrans, Bayle points out, argued that Porphyry essentially misunderstood Aristotle, who had maintained a qualitative difference between the rational soul of humans, and the soul of brutes: the latter would possess only an 'imitation of reason', not reason proper.[86] The difference between human speech (*sermo*) and animal voice (*vox*) was key to the Coimbrans' argument that humans only can be said to be rational.[87] Bayle, on the other hand, is inclined to agree with Porphyry's interpretation that the difference between the animal and the human soul can be seen in terms of gradation rather than of radical difference: humans can think better, that is to say, more subtly than animals, partly because they possess organs that facilitate this activity, as compared to those of animals.[88] This is an argument that, as we will see later in this chapter, resurfaces in one of the main Renaissance critical engagements with Porphyry: that of Tommaso Campanella.

In support of a gradual transition between animal and human rationality, Bayle cites the example of children and the mentally disturbed, who have the same kind of soul as all other humans, and yet have weaker reasoning powers than many animals. Bayle continues his analysis of animal rationality in a companion article to the one on Pereira, dedicated to 'Rorarius'. A hundred years after its composition, the booklet written by the diplomat and scholar Girolamo Rorario (1485–1556), entitled *Quod animalia bruta saepe ratione utantur melius homine* [Animals Often Reason Better than Humans], became famous for its claim that animals partake in rationality.[89] It was published for the first time by the libertine Gabriel Naudé in 1648, with an important modification to the title: Naudé dropped the adverb 'often' (*saepe*), turning a cautious statement into a bold one — animals use reason better than humans not just 'often', but generally.[90] Rorario's text combines a variety of sources (notably Plutarch), with anecdotal knowledge of the capabilities of animals. As Marcialis has noted, the key point of the text, written in the form of a dialogue, is that it presents rationality as a method, a capability, rather than an 'essence'.[91] This means that rationality is not anchored to the essence of a soul as an inborn quality, but can be defined as a set of abilities. Therefore, examples of animal behaviour can be used as proof that animals can perform tasks usually linked to human rationality, including the ability to talk. If animals are found to have memory, a desire to learn, and a strong ability to think (*ingenium*), then why should they not be considered capable of communicating with each other?[92] Communication is presented here as yet another feature of a loose concept of rationality that can be modulated according to 'more or less' on the scale of beings.

Just as he presents Porphyry as the opposite of Pereira, so Bayle views Rorario as the opposite of Descartes. Thus he constructs two lines of tradition: one that understands the difference between humans and all other animals as a matter of gradual differentiation; and the other that assumes a qualitative, unbridgeable divide between them. For Bayle, the examples of animal capabilities, recounted by Rorario and in the tradition of Plutarch and Porphyry,[93] not only stand against Descartes's theory (or 'sentiment', as Bayle calls it), but also cause an 'extreme embarrassment' to the Peripatetics.[94] The latter would object to the Cartesian comparison of animals to automata, and yet insist that animals do not possess reasoning power. Bayle comments that instances of animal behaviour such as those reported by Rorario would remain 'absolutely inexplicable according to the hypothesis of the Aristotelians', that hypothesis being that animals have a soul capable of sensation (including memory and, in most cases, imagination), but not rationality.

The recognition that animals have language provides the main foundation for the argument that they must be considered as partaking in rationality, too: if animals talk, they express internal feelings. Rorario provides examples of talking animals as well, mentioning also the traditional example of Apollonius of Tyana, who could understand the language of sparrows.[95] Rorario asks rhetorically why we should not assume that animals understand each other in their own languages. If animals are considered capable of talking, the human-animal difference must be conceived in terms of gradation of rationality.

On the other hand, holding to the uniqueness of human rationality, Giovannini has to distinguish between the languages of animals and those spoken by humans: he excludes any possibility that animal languages might express rationality. In separating language from rationality, the hierarchy could be maintained. In his annotations to Gelli's *Circe*, Giovannini remarked in even clearer terms on the animals' lack of proper language.[96] This was particularly important given that it was a commentary on a story in which the animals talk with human tongues, and argue that the animal condition can be superior to the human one. Inspired by Plutarch's *Bruta animalia ratione uti* [Animals Use Reason], Gelli had staged a dialogue between Circe, Odysseus, and various companions of Odysseus, transformed into animals by the sorcerer.[97] Published in the 1509 *editio princeps* of Plutarch's *Moralia*, *Bruta animalia ratione uti*, also known as *Gryllos* from the name of Odysseus's main interlocutor, a Greek turned into a pig by Circe, contributed to making Plutarch the ambassador of animal rationality, next to Porphyry. Plutarch's fictional dialogue between Odysseus and Gryllus thus presents animals as rational by giving them a voice to argue for themselves.

Giovannini argues that a talking animal is potentially a threat to the human-animal hierarchy, by commenting as follows on the first dialogue in the *Circe*:

> A gli huomini soli e non ad altri animali è concesso il parlare dalla natura, perché questi continuamente discorrendo producono sì poderose cose, che molto disdicevole sarebbe che stessero celate, e non fossero comuni. [...] una penosa servitù mi parrebbe il dover stare noi fermi in compagnia senza poter dire o intendere il pensiero del vicino, e non si potrebbe governare il mondo, sedendo nel trono della ragione ornata di scienze e d'arti senza manifestare il pensiero interno. Ora gli animali di tutte queste cose essendo privi, non tengono bisogno di così fatto dono.[98]

> [Nature has granted speech to humans only, and to no other animal, because by continuing to talk humans produce wondrous things [...]; it would seem to me a painful slavery having to be still while in the company of others, without being able to express or understand the thought of one's fellow human being, and the world could not be governed, sitting on the throne of reason, adorned

by sciences and arts, without being able to express one's one internal thinking. Now, since all animals are deprived of these things, they do not need such a gift.]

In place of the balance that he maintains in his *Discorso*, where animals are deemed capable of talking but not of rational thought, here Giovannini holds a simpler, clear-cut position: animals do not think and do not talk. The human-animal hierarchy reappears at the practical level, too, in the assertion that humans govern the world with their rational talk. Giovannini's position in this text could be explained by the desire to clarify that Gelli's talking animals do not subvert the human-animal hierarchy: if the transmutation of humans into animals could appear to blur the line between the two, Giovannini's remark serves the purpose of underlining that humans and animals are qualitatively different, and that no gradation of thinking, or talking abilities, can exist between them. Giovannini thus does not side here with Plutarch and Porphyry, as he at least partially does in his *Discorso*.

Porphyry and Aristotle are the two points of reference in measuring the distance dividing humans from all other creatures, and Giovannini's argumentation is particularly interesting in that it tends to combine the two, but ultimately reinforces, against Porphyry, a clear hierarchy of human dominion. The most thorough engagement with the ethical consequences of the Porphyry-Aristotle alternative is that of Tommaso Campanella, who analyses the impact that the topic of rationality has on the choice of human diet in particular. From a 'parasitic' kind of engagement with the topic of animal language (as Giovannini's writing has been labelled), we now turn to one of the most original responses to *On Abstinence* in the Renaissance.[99]

4.4. With Porphyry, Against Aristotle: Campanella (and Telesio) on Animal Rationality

> Quapropter Porphyrius, Lactantius Firmianus, Osius Cardinalis, Plinius, Valla, Plutarchus, Virgilius, Ovidius, et meliores philosophi brutis rationem concedunt. Nos autem inferimus illis oportere alterum genus animae tribuere supra sensitivum [...].[100]

> [Therefore Porphyry, Lactantius Firmianus, Cardinal Hosius, Pliny, Valla, Plutarch, Virgil, Ovid, and the best philosophers grant rationality to animals. We, too, conclude that it is necessary to attribute to them another kind of soul beyond the sensitive one [...].]

Campanella's main target is the Aristotelian conception of the soul: while 'Aristotle ignorantly attributes sagacity to animals, but not rationality', Porphyry, on the other hand, is included in the list of those philosophers who rightly argued that animals must partake in rationality as well.[101] The main error of the Peripatetics, for Campanella, is their insistence on separating sensation from rationality: if animals are granted sensation, then it becomes impossible to prove that they do not combine, recollect, and elaborate their sensations to form rational thoughts. Campanella argues instead in favour of the unity of the soul. He dedicates the first chapters of his *Metaphysica* to demonstrating that all these actions — feeling, remembering, imagining, ratiocinating — must be seen as belonging to one and the same soul. In two steps, Campanella first argues that memory cannot be different from sensation and that 'the same soul remembers and feels', and then adds that the soul that imagines is the same as the one that feels, remembers, and ratiocinates. The images that occur in sleep, for instance, are just reverberations of previous sensations, and would thus be impossible without those sensory experiences.[102]

Campanella lists examples taken from the observation of animals to support this interpretation. Against Aristotle, it is necessary, claims Campanella, to attribute both memory and imagination to animals, because we observe that they learn to flee what is harmful and to seek purposefully what is advantageous to them. Aristotle had famously stated in *On the Soul* that a few creatures, such as the earthworm, the ant, or the bee, might be devoid of the capacity to imagine ('phantasía').[103] But this, for Campanella, is impossible, because 'imagination is present in all animals, since the impression produced by the objects persists in all, and according to it they pursue or flee'.[104] He rejects Aristotle's idea that certain animals, such as the fly, do not possess memory by stating that we can observe how flies must have memory of what they ate, since they return to the food.[105] The fact that not all animals comply with human discipline and that they seem not to be able to learn, is not sufficient reason to deny them the ability to feel, imagine, and remember. The lives of animals are shaped by their possession of a soul which can perform all these tasks, and thus ensure their preservation. Just as Porphyry had done, Campanella lists examples of animal behaviour that demonstrate that they ratiocinate too: the dog hunting the hare, for instance, chooses the fastest way to reach its prey, calculating where its path will cross that of the hare; the crab, when trying to eat the flesh of a mollusc, is careful to insert a little stone in between the valves, so that its feet will not be caught inside the shell, if the mollusc suddenly closes its valves.[106]

In his list of the best philosophers, those who attributed rationality to animals, Campanella includes only two modern figures: Lorenzo Valla (1406–57) and Cardinal Stanislav Hosius (1504–76). Valla claimed that the tradition that views animals as irrational is based on a wrong interpretation of *álogos*, which simply meant 'without speech', rather than 'without reason'.[107] Hosius is often mentioned by Campanella with regard to the idea that rationality is a red herring in pinning down what distinguishes animals from humans. Both for Campanella and for Hosius, the claim that animals are rational does not imply that they are on all accounts equal to humans. As we will see, a differentiation persists — one that has a noticeable impact at the ethical level, as it is the foundation for human dietary practices.

Campanella does not mention among the best philosophers his main modern ally for his attack on Aristotelian psychology: Bernardino Telesio. In *De rerum natura iuxta propria principia* [On the Nature of Things According to its Own Principles], Telesio had also argued that all animals possess the ability to reflect on their sensation to form judgements whether to pursue or avoid something: 'Indeed reason and the inclination to avoid ill and seek good, which is present in animals, all this derives from those things that were previously perceived and that adhered to the spirit'.[108] Sensation, as for Campanella, is the foundation for ratiocination, and since animals are capable of feeling, they cannot be excluded from the sphere of rationality, even if the subtlety of their reasoning may vary. Ratiocination is anchored in sensation because what a creature feels remains impressed in a material substance that Telesio calls 'spirit', and that flows within the brain's ventricles: these impressions provide the basis for future thoughts. Both in animals and in humans, this process is the same, and it is explicitly a material one.[109]

Against Aristotle, Telesio showed that if sensation and rationality are to be considered entirely separate, this leads to a multiplication of the faculties of the soul, to bridge the gap that has been created between the two.[110] Aristotle's treatment of imagination ('phantasía'), and his uncertainty as to whether all animals are endowed with it, is for Telesio such an example of an unnecessary complication caused by the stubborn desire to preserve the distance between sensation and rationality. Imagination should function as a bridge connecting sensation and rationality, but in fact the opposite is true: it keeps sensation separate from thinking by inserting a new faculty, which, in Aristotle's view, most but not necessarily all animals possess.[111] Later developments of Aristotelian psychology show this same process at work: for instance, Avicenna's *vis aestimativa* is yet another insertion that ultimately separates the creatures considered to be endowed with it from those supposedly deprived of it.[112] Rather than clarifying how thoughts are formed from sensations, Aristotelian psychology, for both Telesio and Campanella, postpones the solution, repeating the problem ad infinitum by adding steps to bridge an unbridgeable gap — unbridgeable, because it is created by the very approach of Aristotelian psychology, which emphasizes the subdivision of tasks rather than the actual functioning of the faculties together.

Campanella thus agrees with Telesio that all these faculties must be seen as integrated within a conception of the soul as one and the same. But from this it follows that rationality does not fundamentally differ from sensation and imagination, and that therefore it is not justifiable to exclude animals from reasoning altogether.[113] Telesio concludes that 'the substance that feels in humans, thinks, too; and the other animals are not entirely devoid of rationality'.[114] Arguing in terms of absolute distinction of the faculties is untenable; the alternative consists in assuming a gradation, whereby rationality is not the prerogative of the human being, but is present in varying degrees among animals, too. In place of the binary of rational versus irrational, Telesio thus suggests that the capability to think rationally is a matter of 'more or less': humans can think better than animals, but this does not imply that animals are completely irrational. They cannot be, because of the constant interplay of sensation and rationality.

For Campanella, the observation of animals is the decisive proof that Telesio is right about their capabilities, and not Aristotle. In his *Syntagma*, Campanella recollects that he turned to reading Telesio in search of answers to philosophical questions that he had not been able to find in the writings of the Peripatetics, even after scrutinizing all the Greek, Latin, and Arab commentators on Aristotle.[115] As

Germana Ernst has explained, what Campanella finds in Telesio is a way out of bookish knowledge, and a philosophical method that does not ignore nature and the value of direct experience in favour of abstract speculations.[116] Applied to the issue of understanding the difference between humans and animals, Telesio's method allows Campanella to account for everything that animals can do. In *Del senso delle cose e della magia* [On the Sense of Things and on Magic], Campanella indulges in a long discussion of animal capabilities. We observe that horses learn to jump upon our command, monkeys can be taught to play, bees find their way home: these examples show that animals have memory. They can also recollect past events, can live in organized societies (as bees do, for instance), and in some instances, such as in the case of elephants, they can make agreements with humans and can even learn human language.[117] If one were to object that animals learn all these capabilities simply by repetition, Campanella replies that humans, too, learn crafts through practice. The appeal to the concept of 'instinct' to draw a line between animal and human instances of the same behaviour, is not useful either, in Campanella's view: ultimately, what is meant by instinct is an impulse which demonstrates that animals know what to expect in certain situations.[118] For Campanella, the examples of animal behaviour reveal that animals 'syllogize', inferring from what they know that which is not known yet: for instance a dog 'argues' (in the sense of *argomentare*) when it guesses from a smell the origin of it.[119]

With regard to animal language, Campanella employs the same argument regarding linguistic relativity used by Porphyry, and later by Fabrici d'Acquapendente and Montaigne. In *Del senso delle cose*, Campanella writes that we can be sure that the cries made by animals are 'voice', as we see that birds and cattle call each other. The reason we do not understand the meaning of their voices is that those languages are as foreign to us as the languages of distant human people. As an example, Campanella presents his own encounter with a foreign animal: 'I saw in Naples a Polish dog that did not understand the Neapolitans at all, apart from those who spoke Polish'.[120] Thus Campanella claims that (certain) animals will learn to understand the specific human language, or languages, spoken to them. The fact that they cannot pronounce words as we do has an anatomical explanation: 'they do not have organs similar to ours'. Similarly, a horn cannot sound like a bell, and a person who stammers cannot talk fast.[121] Parrots are an exception: their palate is concave, like the human one, and that is why they can pronounce words.[122]

As mentioned above, the parrot's ability to talk is used by Descartes precisely to argue that animals cannot speak: parrots only imitate, without understanding the connection between sound and meaning which is the true foundation of language. Campanella, on the other hand, establishes an indissoluble connection between thinking and talking, and claims that animal languages are meaningful in their own ways: 'all talk in their own language, argue, and understand'.[123] Animal behaviour is, again, key in Campanella's explanation. We observe, he claims, that animals are capable of grasping universals, not just particulars. For instance, a dog will form the concept of 'human', and will be able to recognize the similarity between its owner (Peter), and all other men. Proof of this is that the dog at first growls when it sees a human approaching, but then starts wagging its tail when it recognizes that the figure is actually a friendly human it knows — Peter.[124] Animals proceed like children in their learning, as they first become used to the 'universal' (human being), and then the 'particular' (Peter), since children, too, will call every man 'father' before being able to distinguish between their own father and all other men.

The fact that humans are normally incapable of understanding the languages of animals is therefore an optical illusion: from our human position, animal voices remain unintelligible, but we should not come to the conclusion that they are per se meaningless: 'The other animals appear to us as devoid of thinking, language, and judgment; but all partake in it, some more and some less, as it happens that among us humans some seem to be beasts, and Aristotle indeed said that we do not all have intellect'.[125] As in the debate on the nature of the cannibals presented in the previous chapter, Campanella stresses the human-animal similarity by breaking up the uniformity of the two groups — that of humans, and that of animals. Certain humans appear to be brutish, and all human communities are foreign to each other, as language and culture go hand-in-hand in forming a barrier that often prevents mutual understanding.[126] Language, as an indicator of rationality, is no longer the distinctive marker of humanity.

4.5. With Aristotle, Against Porphyry: Campanella (and Telesio) on Animal Irrationality

> Quapropter absque dubio in brutorum animis, si est prudentia, est etiam ratio, non tamen dicuntur animalia rationalia (licet Plinius et Plutarchus et Porphyrius et alii contendant esse rationalia et Osius Cardinalis) quoniam ratio illorum est adeo exilis, ut tale nomen vix mereatur, nec tamen, licet ratione sint donata, erunt eiusdem cum homine.[127]

> [Therefore without doubt if there is practical wisdom in the souls of animals, there is also rationality. And yet animals are not said to be rational (even if Pliny and Plutarch and Porphyry and others, including Cardinal Hosius, maintain that they are rational), since their rationality is so weak that it hardly deserves that name, and even if reason should be granted to them, it will not be the same as the human one.]

The terminology used by Campanella in this passage might seem surprising: there must be rationality ('ratio') in animals, yet they cannot be said to be rational ('rationalia'). At the basis of the controversy on animal rationality, Campanella sees a terminological issue. The Aristotelians got lost in a maze of distinctions, in their attempts to keep sensation separate from rationality. As we saw in the previous section, Campanella declared their arguments void, mainly on the basis of the results of direct observation. Humans share with animals capabilities such as remembering, calculating and inferring, abstracting universals, and even talking. But it remains to clarify two aspects: whether these capabilities exhaust the meaning of rationality, or, on the contrary, whether being rational could involve further facets; and, if the latter should be the case, whether humans are rational in a different sense from animals — in other words, whether there is a qualitative difference between humans and all other animals.

In this passage from one of the books of his *Theologia* [Theology], Campanella does indeed reach the conclusion that animals are not rational in the same way as humans are. Here, he stresses the fact that animals' rationality is weaker than the human version. But it is not simply a matter of gradation, or rather, it seems that Campanella feels justified in drawing a distinct line between animal and human rationality because the former is so weak that it does not deserve the name of rationality after all.

In arguing along these lines, Campanella again follows in Telesio's footsteps. Telesio, too, had first stated that 'there is no doubt that all animals or most of them possess a certain faculty of ratiocination or of judgment, as we will say, and of recollection'.[128] Then, however, he had specified that only humans can be called 'rational' in the proper sense of the word. This might be the reason why Campanella did not include Telesio among the philosophers who attributed rationality to animals in the passage already quoted from the first book of the *Metaphysica*. Unlike Porphyry, mentioned by Campanella as one of those 'best philosophers' who saw animals as rational, Telesio first attributes rationality to animals, but then proceeds to specify that a qualitative difference persists between the rationality of humans and of animals. This difference consists in the fact that in animals ratiocination depends entirely on the body, more precisely on the material substance that Telesio calls 'spirit', and which resides in the ventricles of the brain. In humans, on the other hand, ratiocination results from the combination between the material spirit and an immaterial soul infused by God. Therefore it is not just a matter of 'brain power' that differentiates animal from human ratiocination: the immortal soul changes the kind of rational thinking that humans are able to perform, and thus marks a qualitative difference.

How exactly the material spirit and the immaterial soul are supposed to cooperate to originate human rational thought is difficult for Telesio to explain: on the one hand, the human being appears like a hybrid, with a material spirit and an immaterial soul; animals, on the other hand, possess a material spirit that is remarkably capable of performing cognitive tasks without the presence of the immaterial soul.[129] The first edition of the text, *De natura* [On Nature] (1565), does not contain any references to the immaterial soul, which enters the scene for the first time in Chapter 31 of the first book in the second edition of 1570.[130] Also, it is noteworthy that Telesio inserts cautionary reminders about the divine soul of humans whenever arguments in *De rerum natura* threaten to blur the line between humans and animals.[131] In a manuscript version composed before the final, 1586 version of *De rerum natura*, Telesio had stated unequivocally that 'the faculty of ratiocination cannot belong to an incorporeal substance [...] but (as it is said) it has to be attributed to a completely corporeal substance and to the spirit, which resides in the ventricles of the brain'.[132] In the last version of *De rerum natura*, by contrast, Telesio is careful to stress the immateriality of the rational soul of humans by explaining how his view might be reconciled with Aristotle's on this point:

> Si quidem rationalis anima ea Aristoteli ponatur, quae singulis hominibus a Deo creata infunditur, nihil est quod cum homine disputemus; nobiscum enim facit, incorpoream penitusque impartibilem eam statuens; at si illam intelligat, quae belluis inesse et a qua duci videntur [...], ab eo plane dissentimus.[133]

[If Aristotle were to conceive as rational soul the one which is created by God and infused in each individual human being, we would have nothing to dispute about with him; indeed he would proceed like ourselves, considering it incorporeal and completely indivisible; but if he should mean the one which is present in the beasts and by which they seem to be guided [...] we plainly dissent from him.]

Here Telesio employs a conception of 'rational soul' which radically separates humans from animals; he invokes Aristotelian psychology as combinable with this view. It is debatable whether this passage should be read rather as a cautionary statement (deflecting suspicion of materialist heresy), than as presenting a philosophically stringent conception.[134] It is significant that, as noted, Telesio first introduces this explanation in the last edition of the *De rerum natura* (1586). This suggests that the idea of a human soul, immaterial and infused by God, was at the very least not part of Telesio's initial philosophical plan.[135] But the key point, which Campanella criticizes, is the doubling of 'rationality' that it presents: human rationality depends on an immortal, divine substance, which enhances the activity of the material spirit and expands the range and quality of what it can think; Telesio considers animal rationality, on the other hand, to be completely different, dependent solely on the body and thus limited in its action.

For Campanella, humans can think better than animals, because they have a purer, more lucid 'spirit', that is the material substance already discussed by Telesio. Furthermore, the spirit is made more subtle by the presence, in humans, of a divine mind: Campanella uses the term 'mens', 'mind', rather than 'anima', 'soul', as Telesio had done. In this way, Campanella can argue that animals partake in all those capabilities that the Peripatetics attributed to the rational soul (remembering, inferring, arguing), while at the same time stressing that in humans there exists a completely different level of ratiocination, dependent on the immortal mind. Campanella thus combines a gradation of certain rational capabilities, with a radical difference at a higher level of rationality, which is the mind. This enables him to argue that the common definition of animals as 'irrational' is after all correct:

> Ma perché [gli animali] poco discorrono più di quel che veggono e sentono presente, e l'uomo discorre a molte altre simili cose e azioni e figure e virtuti e vizii e negozii nell'istesso tempo, sì per le migliori celle interiori, sì per lo spirito più puro, lucido, nobile, e per l'affinamento che esso spirito ha nel conoscere dalla mente immortale in lui involta [...] è avvenuto che l'uomo si dica razionale e discorsivo, e non i bruti, ma solo sensitivi, non perché non discorrano, ma poco; come anco le piante perché sentono poco non son dette animali. E così parleremo noi.[136]

[But since [the animals] ratiocinate little more than on what they see and feel at that moment, and human beings ratiocinate further on many similar things and actions, figures, virtues, vices, and affairs at the same time, because they have better internal ventricles, and both because the spirit is purer, more lucid and noble, and because the spirit is made more subtle in the action of knowing by the immortal mind enfolded in it [...] therefore it occurred that the human being is called rational and ratiocinating, and not the brutes, who are called only sensitive, not because they do not ratiocinate, but little. And we, too, will talk like this.]

Gradation and radical differentiation are intertwined: humans can think more subtly than animals, but this difference ultimately creates a radical divide, because the spirit and the mind work together in the case of humans. Their association gives rise to a kind of rationality on a different scale from its animal counterpart. The Latin version of the text, *De sensu rerum et magia*, states that humans have mental rationality, but calls the animal kind of rationality 'sensitive rationality'.[137] In contrast with humans, animal rationality has clear boundaries, both with regard to the input that it is capable of processing (the immediate information derived from sensations), and also to its breadth of operation. This is partly the result of the way in which the material spirit can move inside the human brain, which occurs more freely than in animals. Furthermore, the immaterial mind allows humans to think beyond the kind of ratiocination that matter can perform.

In the *Metaphysica* Campanella defines the animal-human border as follows: 'we grant to the brutes spontaneity, not freedom, reason and sensory (not mental) intellect, which indeed does not deserve the name of intellect but of estimative faculty'.[138] It is the conception of rationality that forms the pivot of Campanella's explanation: animals can be considered rational, if by rationality is meant those capabilities that primarily pertain to the realm of sensation; but compared to the 'mental rationality' of humans, animals appear irrational. It is a matter of viewpoint: Campanella can both agree with Porphyry that the examples of animal behaviour listed in *On Abstinence* demonstrate the possession of the kind of rationality that derives from sensation; and with Aristotle that animals are not rational in the proper sense of the word.[139] There is a qualitative difference, then, but the line of demarcation is not where the Peripatetics drew it: this line does not coincide with the difference between pure sensation and the organization of sensations into ratiocination. Animals, for Telesio and Campanella, perform the latter kind of thinking on a daily basis.

Since Campanella does not agree with Aristotle on the meaning of rationality, it remains to explain what are the specific functions of mental rationality that Campanella attributes to humans only.[140] First of all, the mind makes human thinking free, and not merely spontaneous. As Germana Ernst aptly put it: for Campanella 'freedom consists in the examination of what is uncertain', and this is what animals are not capable of doing.[141] Whenever an animal examines a situation — as for instance the dog deciding which way to go to catch the hare — the deliberations are always dictated by the calculation of a benefit, and are shaped by the present, immediate circumstances, including passions (for instance, the hunger that leads the dog to the fastest trail). This is why, according to Campanella, animals remain devoid of free will. The mind, on the other hand, makes humans capable of thinking well beyond the present circumstances, of judging a situation regardless of immediate benefit, and even of choosing what is not in the person's best interest, if there are higher, more complex benefits to be attained. Connected with this freedom of thought is the capacity to be religious, a human prerogative that derives

from the possession of a mind, and that according to Campanella is different in kind
from the pseudo-religious behaviour displayed by certain animals.

Another author in Campanella's list of the 'best philosophers' who attribute
reason to animals, Cardinal Hosius, had insisted that the human being is the only
religious animal, a view that Campanella shares, acknowledging his agreement
with the cardinal on this point. According to Hosius, the main point of distinction
between humans and other animals is 'not reason [*ratio*], not speech [*oratio*], not
practical wisdom [*prudentia*], not anything else, but religion only, which separates
us from them'.[142] Campanella explains that the human predisposition to religion
derives from the possession of a mind, because to the mind 'more divine gifts are
suited' than to the corporeal spirit.[143] Even if, for Campanella, animals may display
a kind of veneration — as when elephants kneel before the moon, an example
that Campanella takes from Pliny — still, humans only are properly religious.[144]
In *Atheismus triumphatus* [Atheism Conquered], Campanella thus concludes that
animals can be said to be religious only metaphorically, an interpretation that he
claims to be consistent with the views of Hosius, Lactantius, Plutarch, and Porphyry
on the capabilities of animals.[145] On the other hand, 'the specific operation of the
mind infused by God is the contemplation of divine things and religion, and this is
the difference from brutes, as Chrysostomus and Hosius attest, not reason'.[146]

Campanella claims that his interpretation of animal rationality allows him to
avoid the mistake of the Aristotelians, which consisted in disregarding the role of
observation in assessing what animals can do; this is a mistake that can be corrected
by following the opinion of Porphyry and his successors on the capabilities of
animals that display rational behaviour. But he does not agree with Porphyry
that rationality is entirely a matter of gradation. At the same time, Campanella
also believes that his view rectifies another error, one that became popular in the
years of the *querelle de l'âme des bêtes*, but that (as we have seen) had already been
circulating before Descartes: the view that the only way to avoid having to grant
rationality to animals, thus annihilating every difference between humans and
animals, is to declare them devoid not just of rationality, but of sensation as well.
Campanella writes:

> Dunque non si deve dire che l'istinto divino le guidi, ma il proprio senso; e a
> tanto son trascorsi questi savii che par che tolgano il senso, non solo a gli enti
> tutti, ma anco alle bestie, perché si credono, donando a loro discorso sensitivo,
> donargli anco mente d'arbitrio libera come ha l'uomo, e non veggono quanta
> differenza ci è tra la mente umana e questo senso commune.[147]

> [Therefore, we should not state that divine instinct guides them, but their own
> sense. And these sages went so far that it seems that they deprive not just all
> things but even beasts of sensation, because they believe that by granting them
> sensitive ratiocination, they grant them also a mind endowed with free will,
> like that which the human being has, and do not grasp what difference there is
> between the human mind and this common sense.]

This is, as we saw, the position of Gómez Pereira, who deprived animals of both
sensation and rationality because it seemed to him that feeling and thinking were

deeply entangled: therefore, either both are granted to animals, or both are denied. In the Latin version of this chapter from *Del senso delle cose*, Campanella refers directly to the Spanish theologian Domingo de Soto (1495–1560), who in his *De iustitia et iure* [On Justice and Right] had argued that brute animals are subjected to natural law, and thus act instinctively, not freely, like the human being.[148] A Dominican, like Campanella, Soto repeatedly denies that animals participate in rationality, to any degree: the possession of reason is that which marks the radical difference between the world of animals, ruled by instinct, and the world of human beings, who tend to the good and are capable of voluntary actions.[149] In Campanella's eyes, Soto's insistence on animals' instinctual behaviour thus provides an example of the philosophical mistake discussed in the above quotation, which essentially consists in preferring to argue against experience rather than granting that animals partake in rationality, for fear that in so doing the border dividing humans from animals would be demolished.

Domingo de Soto's view is strongly rooted in the Thomistic tradition.[150] Like Thomas Aquinas, Soto draws ethical conclusions from his human–animal differentiation (in Soto's terms, the opposition of rationality versus instinct). In the *Summa contra gentiles*, Aquinas had argued that the more imperfect creatures are made for the sake of the more perfect ones.[151] In practice, this means that 'elements exist for the sake of mixed bodies; these latter exist for the sake of living bodies, among which plants exist for animals, and animals for men. Therefore, man is the end of the whole order of generation'.[152] There is a clear hierarchical order in the creation, and the human being is placed at the top, and is entitled to make use of all animals — for instance as nourishment or as a source of materials for clothing.[153] Soto repeats Aquinas's scheme, but stresses the practical consequences of this hierarchy: he explains that the human being has dominion over creation, including the right to eat other creatures (which is not an offence). The animals, by contrast, do not have dominion over what they make use of — for instance, the sheep has no dominion over grass.

Despite their divergence regarding the human-animal distinction, Campanella develops ethical guidelines that bear some similarity with those of Soto. The animals share in rationality, for Campanella, but this is not, as it was for Porphyry, sufficient reason for abstaining from eating them. As we will now see, animal rationality becomes for Campanella the foundation for his argument that humans should not abstain from using animals, including as food.

4.6. Killing Plants and the Right to Kill: Sozzini, Pucci, and Campanella

In arguing in favour of vegetarianism, Porphyry had made cautious use of the idea of gradation. He had argued that rationality (*lógos*) is present in varying degrees in animals, but he had not viewed sensation as a matter of gradation. Plants, for Porphyry, are entirely incompatible with *lógos* and do not share in the least in sensation. On the ethical level, this means that no justice is due to plants, but that justice is due to animals. Campanella considers this view to be inconsequential and untenable. Just as he had pointed out the similarities between human and animal behaviour, so he stresses that plants, not unlike animals, share in the essential desires for self-preservation and for avoiding everything that could endanger their survival. Therefore he interprets the flourishing of a plant as an attempt to extend its lifespan, just as animals reproduce to achieve the same aim; leaves and thorns, meanwhile, are almost the equivalent of an animal's claws or teeth: instruments of self-defence.[154] Since it is necessary to think in terms of continuity and gradation when considering the human-animal difference — at least when dealing with capabilities such as ratiocination, and excluding the mind, which only humans possess — so also the border between animals and plants must be viewed as equally permeable.

Campanella even pursues the idea of continuity beyond the realm of plants: sensation streams throughout creation, and reaches everything, including stones. All in all, Campanella claims that 'in everything there is flight from and hatred of death and love of life'.[155] This dual impulse, a desire to preserve one's own life and escape death, is at the basis of what Campanella calls the 'sense of things'. 'Even stones and plants have sensation' is the bold statement presented in *Del senso delle cose*, 'but compared to brute animals they seem insensible'.[156] It is, once again, a matter of perspective: animals share in rationality, but seem irrational compared to humans, and equally plants and stones share in sensation, but appear incapable of it if compared to creatures who are very responsive to their surroundings, namely the animals. The very categories of 'plant' or 'animal' are open to misunderstanding, for Campanella, if they are interpreted too strictly: the oyster and the elephant, for instance, are both 'animals', yet the former hardly looks like an animal if compared to the latter.[157]

Of course, an animal, a plant, and a stone will not feel in the same way. Campanella explains the great range in intensity of sensation by reference to the spirit, and the way in which it can move inside a body. In animals, the spirit is subtle, very mobile, and free to stream through the nerves: this spirit is the soul of the creature.[158] But the actual degree of subtlety and mobility varies both among animals and among humans:[159] some will be endowed with a quicker and subtler spirit than others, but in general terms humans have particularly strong intellectual capabilities, such as memory and reasoning ('memoria e discorso').[160] In plants, on the other hand, the spirit is thicker, and does not move with the same agility, therefore it is less capable of performing all those tasks that are connected with being endowed with very subtle perception. The bodily conformation of stones makes it even harder for the spirit to move and create sensation — but that does not mean that they are completely deprived of it.[161] The fact that even stones must share in sensation is necessitated by the recognition that animals feel. Since nobody can seriously doubt that animals feel (as Campanella repeatedly states)[162] and since 'sense is not born out of nothing, it is necessary to say that the elements feel'.[163] Therefore sensation is a matter of gradation: everything that is made of elements partakes in it, including 'the sky, the earth, and the world'.[164]

Unlike Porphyry, Campanella believes that the key to understanding the world and the creatures that inhabit it is the recognition of how sensation works. The kind of rationality that animals share with humans is itself a refined form of sensation, as it ultimately depends on the agility of the spirit in the body. Campanella also calls this shared rationality 'sensitive reasoning' ('discorso sensitivo'), to distinguish it from the divine reasoning that derives from the possession of a mind. Therefore the fact that animals share in rationality is for Campanella a consequence of the pervasiveness of sensation in the cosmos. It is inconceivable to him that the recognition of animal rationality should not go hand-in-hand with viewing the entire creation as sharing in sensation, to varying degrees.[165] Campanella even calls plants 'immobile animals' to underline, against the Aristotelian tradition, that sensation is not the prerogative of animals only.[166] Yet that was exactly Porphyry's view: he considers plants incompatible with sensation, despite granting animals a share in rationality.

Campanella makes the continuity of sensation throughout nature the foundation for a different kind of ethics from those of Porphyry. Guido Giglioni's thesis that 'a discussion about the moral status of animal life boils down to assessing the scope and boundaries of sentience in nature' perfectly fits the case of Campanella and Porphyry.[167] In Book 10 of his *Theologia*, Campanella explains that it is legitimate to kill and eat animals. Following a strategy already used by Porphyry in *On Abstinence*, he subdivides his explanation into two parts: first, he argues that it is legitimate to kill animals that are dangerous to humans, an action that Porphyry, too, had justified. But then he proceeds to claim that it is legitimate for humans to kill animals for their own benefit, even when it is not a matter of self-defence.

> Occidere animalia etiam crimen visum est Pythagoricis, et hoc tempore Bracmanis Orientalis Indiae. Sed cum alia sint nobis infesta, ut pulices, serpentes etc., procul dubio licet non solum cavere, sed occidere, ne laedant, sic docente natura. De non infestis rationes et Pythagorae et Porphyrii Plutarchi non convincunt, cum palam sit bruta esse propter hominem, et eorum carnes utiliores esse caeteris cibis tanquam nobis natura propinquiores. Crudelitas tamen non est, sed usus iuris naturalis: alioquin et plantas procul dubio sensu praeditas manducare non liceret.[168]

> [The Pythagoreans back then, and the Indian Brahmans nowadays, believed it a crime to kill animals. But since some are a plague to us, such as fleas, snakes etc., without doubt it is legitimate not just to avoid them, but also to kill them, so that they won't cause damage, as nature teaches us to do. Regarding those that are not dangerous, the reasons adduced by Pythagoras, Porphyry, and Plutarch, are not convincing, because it is clear that animals are there for the sake of the human being, and their flesh is more beneficial than other foods as it is closer to our nature. Therefore this is not cruelty, but the exercise of natural right. Otherwise it would not be legitimate to eat plants either, since without doubt they are endowed with sensation.]

This page from a section dedicated to the types of damage that are caused to the body (*De iniuriis contra corpus*) contains a summary of the main points in favour of vegetarianism, together with Campanella's confutations. It addresses the topic of vegetarianism indirectly, by explaining when killing is justified. The cornerstone of Campanella's argument against vegetarianism is a combination of two main ideas. First, it is part of the natural design of the world that the least noble creatures should support the lives of the most noble: 'everything has a purpose: that of plants is clearly to be eaten by animals, and animals are for each other. Indeed they are all made for humans to be used or for training'.[169] Second, everything in the universe feels and acts in similar ways, pursuing self-preservation.

Like Thomas Aquinas and Soto, Campanella views the creation as oriented towards the human being, who is therefore allowed to make use of other creatures as resources. Considering this conception from a medical point of view, Campanella agrees with the theory that the best food for a creature is what is closest to it — a popular theory with a rich tradition, as we saw in Chapter 2. Ultimately, Campanella denies that killing animals constitutes a cruel act on the basis of his understanding of pansensism: if everything feels, killing animals cannot be viewed as cruel because killing anything that feels would be cruel in that case. Therefore, it would be illegitimate to kill plants, too, for plants are not just picked, or harvested, but truly slaughtered just like animals. Augustine had mockingly called the vegetarian Manicheans 'killers of pumpkins' ('cucurbitarum homicidae'), a caricature repeated by Soto, who quotes Augustine.[170] For Campanella, everyone who eats plants is indeed a killer, which he does not mean as an (ironic) accusation of wrongdoing, but as a simple fact. Campanella's reasoning seems to be that where every action is cruel, no particular action truly is. If by 'cruelty' one understands inflicting unnecessary pain on a creature capable of feeling, then killing for food is not cruel because any eating involves snatching life from an entity that strives to retain it. Therefore inflicting that pain is necessary, because every creature that eats, including humans, supports its own life by depriving others of theirs.

Cardinal Hosius, whom Campanella appreciated for his view of animal rationality, argued along the same lines in the section of his *Confessio catholicae fidei Christiana* on the commandment 'Do not kill' ('non occidere'). According to Hosius, this refers solely to the prohibition against killing human beings, 'because if whatever is alive should not be killed, vegetables and plants live as well. Therefore it will not be legitimate to pluck a twig, or eat vegetables'.[171] This, for Hosius, is evidently an absurd consequence of the application of the injunction 'do not kill' beyond the boundaries of humanity. Hosius emphasizes that when God gave to the human being 'everything that moves and lives' as food, he must have meant both animal and vegetable nourishment. Hosius's reasoning hinges on the assumption that both animals and plants are alive, without making any distinctions about the way in which plants and animals live. Similarly, Campanella argues in terms of the common ground shared by plants and animals, and it is on this basis that the ethical consequence is drawn: humans are permitted to eat both.

Campanella goes beyond Hosius in arguing in favour of the necessity of eating plants and animals, and views the life of the whole world as a constant practice of reciprocal eating. He uses the verb 'to eat' even to refer to the action of the magnet that attracts the iron: 'But I saw that the magnet eats and nourishes itself upon iron fibres, which are similar but less perfect than itself; and thus the human being eats animals'.[172] Campanella renders with vivid language the suffering of the food in the process of being eaten.[173] The food chain therefore embraces everything, including metals and stones, and eating is the very foundation of life:

> E ognuno cerca, per conservarsi, il magnare; e per la sua vita il lupo uccide le pecore e ogni innocente animale, la pecora uccide l'erbe e arbori, e altri animali gli altri; e l'uomo uccide tutti per suo commodo.[174]

> [And each seeks eating for self-preservation; and the wolf kills the sheep and every innocent animal for its own life, the sheep kills plants and vegetation, and animals kill each other; and the human being kills all for his own benefit.]

The use of the adjective 'innocent' is telling: it appears tempting to view the carnivore, namely the wolf, as the ruthless killer of peaceful, meek animals, such as the sheep. Campanella subverts this assumption, however, by stating soon afterwards that the sheep itself is a killer — of plants. Therefore the superficial distinction between predators and prey is replaced by a chain in which every creature plays both roles: exemplarily, the sheep is the victim of the wolf, but also the predator of plants.

Campanella's position on this point is remarkably similar to that of the religious reformer Fausto Sozzini (1539–1604) who, in his exchange with Francesco Pucci (1543–97) on the state of Adam before the Fall, argued that eating always involves killing, and food is always something dead.[175] Pucci, imprisoned alongside Campanella under the Roman Inquisition, had argued instead that before the Fall Adam had been immortal and had consumed 'immortal food' from the Tree of Life.[176] Sozzini objected that it was not possible that Adam could eat and digest food if that food was not meant to sustain his life — and in that case he could not have been immortal, but must have been a mortal human being relying on food for sustenance, just like his descendants.[177]

Pucci's reply to this objection hinged on the difference between plants and animals: animals cry when pain is inflicted upon them and resist any attempts to deprive them of their lives with all their might. Plants, on the other hand, do not put up resistance, an observation that leads Pucci to claim that plants even offered themselves gladly to Adam as food, because they did not feel any pain. It is significant that Pucci, like Porphyry, underlines that 'seeds, fruits, and vegetables lack sensation': therefore when they are eaten they undergo a transformation, rather than a proper death, as animals do.[178] Just like Porphyry, Pucci suggests that plants do not have a soul ('anima vivens'), as animals do, and that this difference has an ethical bearing. Furthermore, Pucci underscores the fact that the whole plant does not necessarily die when parts of it are consumed, an aspect that Porphyry, too, had emphasized. Pucci even compares picking a plant to shaving the hair of the earth: the plant is not killed, but simply 'shaved' by grazing animals (or by vegetarian humans) and will regrow, at least in some cases.[179] Therefore, according to Pucci, Adam could eat plants without letting death enter the Garden of Eden, a place without violence and without murder. Just as a mother feeds her babies at the breast, so nature feeds its creatures by offering plants and seeds. Ultimately, Pucci claims that it is perfectly conceivable that Adam could have consumed food in the Garden of Eden, and still be immortal, untouched by the cycle of life and death that characterizes the food chain after the Fall. Adam must have been a vegetarian.[180]

Arguing in a similar vein to Campanella, Sozzini had objected to this view that eating without killing is simply not possible: if Adam ate at all before the Fall, then he must have killed to obtain his nourishment. Sozzini sarcastically pointed out that Adam would not (according to Pucci's view) have been able to eat plants that need to be completely uprooted in order to be consumed: 'therefore, if you are to be believed, before the Fall it was not permitted to uproot and eat the roots of onions, garlic, parsnips, radishes, carrots, turnips, and of many plants of the same kind, whose principal use in foods consists in the root'.[181] Also, Sozzini had remarked that the fact that we do not hear the cries of plants when they are picked does not mean that they do not suffer — an argument that is remarkably in line with that of Campanella.[182]

The passage from Campanella's *Theologia* on killing for food continues with a brief discussion of the origins of vegetarianism, presented not only in the Bible, but narrated also by poets like Ovid in the myth of the Golden Age. The example of the diet of the first humans could be seen as an argument in favour of drawing a line between eating plants (the food given by God to mankind in Genesis 1: 29) and eating animals. It is on the basis of this difference that Pucci presented vegetarianism as the original diet, one not based on cruelty and exploitation: 'before the original sin, the animals did not devour one another, as we see now, but had plants and seeds as their food, which the earth, their mother, abundantly supplied'.[183] The vegetarian animals, like the sheep, are for Pucci almost a physical reminder of what mankind has lost: they still nourish themselves as if they were in the Garden of Eden.[184] Yet, Campanella interprets the apparent prohibition against eating flesh in Genesis 9: 4 ('but flesh with the life thereof, *which is* the blood thereof, shall ye not eat') to mean that only flesh with raw blood should be avoided. The reason, once again, lies in the principle that one becomes what one eats, and by eating the blood of an animal, a human being ingests the creature's passions too, because they reside in the blood. It will be sufficient to cook any flesh to avoid this dangerous consequence of meat-eating.[185] The myth of biblical vegetarianism is thus refuted as a basis for drawing a substantial distinction between plants and animals, and Campanella adds that 'we have a declaration of natural right from God in Genesis 1 and 9, where he gives us vegetables, and everything that moves as food'.[186]

'Natural right' thus replaces the idea that killing for food is cruel. In the *Ethics* of 1623, Campanella explains the difference between dominion ('dominium') and right ('ius'): when a creature uses its strength to overcome another creature that is less powerful than itself, it dominates; but when any creature, regardless of its position in the cosmos and of its strength, fights to preserve its own life, it exercises a natural 'ius'. A human being who seizes upon a fish to eat it, is an example of 'dominium'; but the fish that seeks to escape the net is acting according to its right, in the sense of 'ius'. A doubling of viewpoint occurs here: the human being has a right to kill the fish, and the fish has also a natural right to try to survive. These opposing rights are Campanella's alternative to labelling the act of slaughtering animals (and plants) as cruel.[187]

Looking as though through a microscope into the minute workings of the natural world, Campanella finds the same structures of dominion and of right to survive repeated at all levels. At the same time, putting the world itself under the lens of an imaginary telescope, he declares that the earth is in fact a huge animal, plagued by creatures that inhabit and exploit it — namely humans and animals — just like the worms that populate the interiors of various animals, and that hurt their hosts by painfully clinging onto their viscera. The double perspective of micro- and macrocosm is used to sublimate the idea of cruelty: can humans be called cruel for moving on the surface of the earth, or the worms for burrowing inside the viscera of a bigger animal, or the fish for eating the worm, or the wolf for eating the sheep? In place of cruelty, Campanella employs the idea of natural necessity. The human being becomes an eater, like all other animals, but one who kills by a right given to him by God himself, and who is more skilled and more powerful than most.[188]

Positioned at the very top of the chain, the human being is not simply portrayed as the crown of creation — in the terms in which Thomas Aquinas had put it — but also as the ultimate killer: while other creatures tend to occupy a precise position in the food chain, the characteristic of humans is that they can potentially use almost everything as their food. As we saw in the previous chapter, Della Porta also viewed dietetic flexibility as peculiar to human beings: while all other animals have a specific food that nature has assigned to them — meat for the wolf, grass for the sheep — humans can choose what to eat. But Della Porta and Campanella draw different conclusions from this starting point. For Della Porta, by choosing what to eat, the human being selects which habits to reinforce in his or her character, for instance becoming more or less feral, or sober, or self-indulgent. For Campanella, on the other hand, the possibility to eat anything is the natural expression of human dominion over creation. Humans are not only capable of exploiting other creatures (for instance by using instruments such as the knife to subdue them), but they also have a right to do so. The way in which humans can master a number of disciplines and use tools is proof of the fact that human *ingenium* is incomparably better than the *ingenium* with which the animals are endowed. Humans thus rightly stand at the centre of creation, and model it to suit their needs.[189]

But there is a notable difference: human dominion over animals is granted by God. The human being may kill 'according to God's concession, for food, to defend himself and so that [the animals] won't harm him'.[190] Even if man is not actually the creator of animals, nor of plants — and Campanella implies that an agent possesses absolute power only over something they have created — the human being's position in creation both justifies and necessitates his use of other creatures. It justifies it, because the use of animals and plants is seen as grounded in the Bible; and it necessitates it, because the human animal is fully dependent on other creatures for survival. As Campanella puts it in *De senso delle cose*, the human being is born naked, but in a short time he 'defeats all animals, he dresses in their skins, eats their flesh, tames and rides them, arms himself with their weapons, and employs their force as his own'.[191] Campanella thus intertwines different orders of explanation — biblical and philosophical — to give shape to his ethical approach to eating. The biblical aspect is that God grants humans a right to kill; and this is supported by philosophical investigation, because an analysis of sensation proves that everything feels, including plants.

But for Campanella this does not imply that human behaviour should know no boundaries in exploiting other creatures. In his short utopian narrative, *La città del Sole* [The City of the Sun], he demonstrates how his ethics, propounded as an alternative to Porphyry's vegetarianism, could take shape. The life of the citizens in the City of the Sun, called 'Solarians', encapsulates for Campanella the practical conclusions of his philosophical discussion of the pervasiveness of sensation in nature.

4.7. The Defeat of the Brahmans: Campanella's *La città del Sole*

The City of the Sun is not a utopian place in the sense of an impossible fantasy.[192] It is rather a vision of philosophical ideas offered as applicable in the practical realm and presented in the form of a narration. Written originally in Italian, the short, philosophical dialogue *Civitas Solis* was published for the first time in Frankfurt in 1623 as an appendix to Campanella's encyclopedic *Philosophia realis*, which comprises theories of morals, economics, and politics. Over a decade later, Campanella still considered the text as a practicable philosophical vision, and was apparently seeking a way to realize it, since the dedicatory letter of *De sensu rerum* to Cardinal Richelieu ends with a reference to the City of the Sun, 'that I sketched and that is to be built by you', as Campanella writes.[193]

What the poets sang as the 'Golden Age', the prophets foresaw as 'New Jerusalem', and the philosophers envisaged as the perfect state, is for Campanella not to be interpreted as a metaphor, then, but as a genuine possibility, a plan to be pursued.[194] In a text written in prison, defending himself against the accusations regarding the role he had played in a planned conspiracy in Calabria in 1599 (*Secunda delineatio defensionum*), Campanella compiled a list of biblical loci suggesting that the new realm is to be built here on earth. The idea of a peaceable kingdom is conveyed by images such as these: 'the lion will eat straw', or 'wolves will pasture with lambs'.[195] The violent aspects of eating seem to be replaced by a traditional vision in which the original, biblical vegetarianism is regained. In other works, too, such as the *Ecloga in nativitatem Delphini*, Campanella envisages a future of prosperity that critics have linked to the idea of the City of the Sun.[196] The *Ecloga*, composed for the birth of Louis XIV, the future *Roi Soleil*, suggests a peaceful, bright future to come, by evoking the biblical image of the lamb that will lie next to the wolf (Isaiah 11: 6): 'that the lambs may not fear the wolf, nor the herd the lion'.[197]

Yet, when Campanella turned to drafting the contours of the City of the Sun, the idea of a peaceful, vegetarian state proved incompatible with the principles of Campanella's philosophy, which serve as the framework for the conception of the city. The distance between the ideal of perfect peace, and the regulated exploitation of animals in *La città del Sole* is a good example of how Campanella balances utopian ideals with a very practical attitude: the City of the Sun is intended as an 'exemplum' of a perfect state, for which it is worth striving even if it may be strictly unattainable in reality.[198] As we will now see, in Campanella's City of the Sun the sheep has every reason to be afraid not just of the wolf, but especially of humans.

The exploitation of animals plays a key role in Campanella's utopia: the City of the Sun is not a biblical, vegetarian paradise. Its model is not the peaceful ideal of Francesco Pucci, who viewed vegetarian animals almost as a guide to regaining what Adam lost through the Fall. A much closer example is Thomas More's *Utopia*, where precise guidelines are provided with regard to the citizens' diet and the use of animals.[199] At the market of Utopia, all sorts of foods are offered: not just vegetables, fruit, and bread, but also fish, and the meat of both birds and other animals. Yet, for the slaughtering of animals special regulations are in place, because butchering is viewed as a problematic action, which introduces violence into an otherwise peaceful community. Animals are to be slaughtered outside the city by running water, where the blood and all impurities can be washed away. Furthermore, and most importantly, the citizens themselves may not kill the animals, but must delegate this job to the slaves: the reason is that the action of killing is potentially unsettling on a social level, because it extinguishes a person's natural feeling of mercy.[200] A printed, marginal comment to the text warns that 'from the butchery of cattle we have learned to cut the throats even of men', suggesting that from killing animals one might easily slide into killing humans, by losing a sense of the distinction.[201] By practicing a lack of mercy towards animals, the citizens might also forget mercy towards their fellow human beings: therefore, a series of precautions are in place to limit the destructive potential of slaughtering.

Unlike in Utopia, the killing of animals is not under such strict control in the City of the Sun. There are no slaves in the city, so the citizens themselves are in charge of slaughtering animals (with the exception of the useful ones: oxen and horses).[202] Indeed, in the *Theologia*, Campanella includes the job of the butcher among the activities that 'have an appearance of evil, but are not actually evil', such as hunting.[203] In this text, hunting is viewed as necessary in order to obtain meat for consumption: Campanella claims that God himself has thus given humans permission to use the meat of animals. Here, Campanella even plays down the ethical impact of killing in the case of certain animals, such as fish, 'which are not properly slaughtered, but simply extracted from water':[204] this is surprising, because Campanella had already ruled out the possibility that killing any animal might be a cruel and thus unlawful act, both because of the theory of pansensism, and because it is God's plan that animals are to be used. Whether or not fishing strictly constitutes killing should therefore make no difference in terms of the moral status of human actions.

Hunting is allowed in the City of the Sun as training to prepare the citizens for war.[205] Therefore the utility of this activity goes well beyond the need to kill animals for food. The exploitation of animals is thus integrated at many levels in the life of the Solarians. Unlike the Utopians, the Solarians do not handle the killing of animals with unease, by trying to limit its impact on the city and displacing it to distant areas as was the case in Utopia. Notably, More's Utopians 'regard hunting as the meanest part of the butcher's trade' and 'unworthy of free men', because 'this desire of looking on bloodshed, in their estimation, either arises from a cruel disposition, or degenerates finally into cruelty through the constant practice of such brutal pleasures'.[206] In the City of the Sun, instead, the citizens' behaviour is guided by their philosophical view of nature. In particular, the necessity of killing is philosophically grounded in the conception of sensation and it provides the foundation for the exploitation of animals and plants:

> Or essi mangiano carne, butiri, mèle, cascio, dattili, erbe diverse, e prima non volean uccidere gli animali, parendo crudeltà; ma poi, vedendo che era pur crudeltà ammazzar l'erbe, che han senso, onde bisognava morire, consideràro che le cose ignobili son fatte per le nobili, e magnano ogni cosa.[207]

> [Now, they eat meat, butter, honey, cheese, dates, a variety of vegetables, and at first they had not wanted to kill animals, as it seemed cruel; but then, seeing that it was also cruel to kill plants, which have sensation, and that therefore one would have had to die [of hunger], then they considered that the things that are not noble are made for the noble ones, and they eat everything.]

Campanella does not simply list what the Solarians eat, but in just a few lines he argues that the choice of food results from the philosophy embraced. The diet of the Solarians changed in accordance with a modification in the citizens' philosophical view of nature. While originally the Solarians maintained that there is a difference between animals (as capable of feeling) and plants (as deprived of it), they later on came to the conclusion that this position — which is the foundation of Porphyry's vegetarianism — is untenable. Therefore, the City of the Sun had been a vegetarian state upon foundation; but a change in philosophy brought with it a change in diet.

This philosophical conversion is more precisely defined as an evolution from the philosophy of the Eastern Brahmans to a pansensistic view, Campanella's own philosophy. The protagonist, namely the Genovese sailor, states that the founders of the City had been 'Pythagorean Brahmans', even if they did not believe in one of the typical tenets ascribed to the Indian Brahmans, namely the transmigration of souls. This is in line with Campanella's conviction that 'it is a bestiality to believe that fleas and mosquitos should resuscitate in glory', a belief that he attributed not only to 'many Indians', but also to a 'Florentine learned man', who is in all probability to be identified with Francesco Pucci.[208] Campanella reasons in purely practical terms: given how many creatures die every day, the whole earth would not be sufficient for recreating so many bodies. Like Campanella, the Solarians-Brahmans do not believe in the reincarnation of the souls, but they did initially practice vegetarianism, like the 'Indians'.

In his depiction of the Solarians, Campanella deploys some of the mythological traits attributed to the Brahmans (as the previous chapter has shown, these contributed greatly to the Renaissance discussion of vegetarianism). He shows the same fascination with the figure of the Eastern Brahman that emerged also in the writings of Cardano, Scaliger, or Persio. In La città del Sole , the Solarians are also said to live exceptionally long lives — at least one hundred years, and occasionally up to two hundred — and to be learned and wise.[209] In line with the tradition that goes back to Eusebius's *Praeparatio evangelica*, the Brahmans are, for Campanella, 'Pythagorean', and therefore vegetarian. The crucial difference is the choice of food: the Solarians are Brahmans who have been convinced by the arguments that Campanella himself presents in *Del senso delle cose*, and thus have started to view plants as endowed with sensation. Since they consider eating any being capable of sensation to be cruel, the cruelty of killing is presented as a necessity for survival: as it is not possible to abstain from both plants and animals, then the Solarians decided that eating both was philosophically sounder than just choosing to eat plants. Campanella's Solarians are therefore omnivorous.

The same objection that Campanella raised to the Brahmans' vegetarianism also appears in a later seventeenth-century *disputatio* entirely devoted to the Pythagorean teaching of vegetarianism: the *Dogma pythagoricum de abstinentia carnium* (1668) by Michael Bohn, chaired by the Leipzig professor Anton Günther Heshuius.[210] The text, which makes abundant use of Porphyry, poses the question in these terms: if animals are considered rational because the same 'spirit' flows through the whole world, how could it be legitimate to eat vegetables and other plants?[211] Both Heshuius/Bohn and Campanella express a certain sympathy for the Brahmans' vegetarianism, but they both opt for a conscious omnivorism. Heshuius/Bohn mention Cardano's view on the sagacity of carnivores, and conclude that it is the abuse, rather than the simple use of meat that should be avoided.[212] Campanella, too, warns against both excesses of abstinence and of indulgence in meat. In the *Theologia*, fasting and abstinence are an instrument to contrast vices, as if one would try to straighten a stick by bending it first in the opposite direction.[213] If the abstinent diet is one extreme, the other extreme is the voracity of the habitual meat eater, which might even reach the vicious excess of anthropophagy.[214] In the City of the Sun, a similar kind of moral adjustment occurs: the Solarians' original vegetarianism is presented as a form of unjustified extremism that is later corrected by a conscious omnivorism based on philosophical pansensism. Campanella thus describes the philosophical process that led the Solarians to that particular choice of diet, rather than just reporting the final outcome.

The dietetic view expressed in *La città del Sole* ultimately coincides with that which Campanella presented in a poem: 'I do not care about the pain of plants and of animals killed for my supper'.[215] Campanella's own explanation of the poem uses the comparison between micro- and macrocosm already discussed, which allows him to penetrate into the minute workings of nature before zooming out on the life of the whole world seen as a giant animal. He likens the plants and animals eaten for supper to the worms inside the belly of a human being: we kill them and we do not hear their prayers. But the humans are themselves like worms in the belly of the world, to which they cause pain, even if, in turn, they are also at its mercy. In a vertiginous role-reversal, God is seen as almost like a belly, inside which everything is constantly subjected to a process of mutation, resembling a digestion of all beings: 'God is everything, and enjoys the fact that things are transformed inside him without being annihilated'.[216] The death of creatures is included in this cycle of life. The fact that vegetables and animals become food for humans is therefore part of an inevitable process, which is painful for the creature that is eaten, but not cruel if seen in relation to the whole within which this takes place.

The Genovese sailor answers the question about the diet and the length of the lifespan of the Solarians by quoting the principle that 'first, one has to consider the life of the whole, and then of the parts'.[217] Applied to the organization of the city, this means that what matters is the good balance of the whole state: the pain suffered by plants and animals in being transformed into food is irrelevant from the wider perspective. In particular, the Solarians' solution to the choice of diet in a pansesistic world is to 'eat by rotation', including all types of food on their menu: 'once they eat meat, once fish, and once vegetables, and then they go back to meat by rotation, so as not to weigh on and exhaust nature'.[218] Campanella does acknowledge that plants and animals do not feel with the same degree of intensity: just as humans have stronger ratiocination than animals, so animals feel more subtly than plants, because of their physical constitution. Yet, he does not modulate this differentiation at the level of ethics, for instance by including on the menu of the citizens more frequently plants than animals, so as to spare the latter too much suffering. He does not engage in any 'utilitarian' calculations of the creatures' suffering. The Solarians aim at what we would now call the ecological sustainability of the city.

The medical conditions of the citizens are also taken into account when choosing the specific menus. In the *Ethica*, Campanella explains that the plants and animals suitable for human consumption are those that do not differ too greatly from human nature, a medical theory with a long tradition: Campanella refers the reader to his own work on medicine (*Medicinalia*).[219] He specifies that human meat is excluded from the menu — but elsewhere he remains agnostic on the question of whether eating human flesh is permissible in cases of absolute necessity.[220] Just as the Solarians-Brahmans decided that since it was impossible to abstain from both plants and animals, as that would lead to death, then killing both was legitimate, so Campanella writes that the consumption of meat is allowed even on days when it is prohibited by the religious calender, if one otherwise risks starvation.[221] Would then anthropophagy also be legitimate when the alternative is starvation? Campanella's caution on this point is likely due to the fact that humans are in his view unlike all other creatures, and it is that qualitative difference that impedes the assimilation of human flesh with all other food. In any case, this is an extreme and rare scenario.

There are medical and moral constraints to the consumption of meat, but Campanella's Solarians condemn the abuse, and not the controlled intake of animal flesh. Furthermore, this varied diet is adaptable according to the age or physical condition of the eater: in the City of the Sun, the elderly consume lighter food than the young. In line with the tradition in which Porphyry, too, stands, Campanella explains that those who exercise their body extensively should eat denser food than those who use mostly their intellect (*ingenium*), and for whom light (though not necessarily plant-based) food is the best.[222] Food intake should thus be regulated by medical considerations.[223]

The trajectory of the Solarians from vegetarianism to omnivorism brings back to mind the dietetic change of Porphyry's friend, Firmus Castricius, whose conversion to carnivorism prompted the writing of *On Abstinence*. Just as Porphyry suggests in the case of Firmus, for the Solarians, too, a change in philosophical school underpins the dietetic volte-face. But Campanella uses a Porphyrian argument against Porphyry, showing that it is the philosophical necessity of animal rationality that ultimately compels a preference for omnivorism over vegetarianism. Like other philosophers who were both interested in Porphyry's arguments and also fascinated by the example of the Brahmans, such as Cardano, Campanella presents a limited consumption of meat as a better option than Porphyry's vegetable diet. *La città del Sole* seeks to demonstrate the potential advantage of such an omnivorous diet if it were implemented in practice.

With few exceptions, the arguments presented by Porphyry in *On Abstinence* thus seem to have been more philosophically engaging to Renaissance philosophers than they were completely convincing. The last philosopher to be considered in this book, Pierre Gassendi, is a notable exception.

4.8. Gassendi's Vegetarian Epicurus, and the Legacy of Porphyry

In a letter to Gassendi, Campanella praised him for having countered the cloudy philosophy of Aristotle, but accused him at the same time of having sided with an equally hazy one — that of Epicurus.[224] What is at stake, for Campanella, is the view of nature: following Epicurus, it is impossible to regard the world as governed by reason, and not by chance. Yet Campanella writes to Gassendi that he understands the entire structure of the universe as shaped by 'the first virtue', that is to say by God, as can be observed in the functioning of organisms.[225]

The ethical implications of Campanella's conception of the world as a whole in which the creatures are designed to sustain each other have been discussed above. The ethical aspects of Gassendi's Epicureanism are not raised in the two philosophers' correspondence, which addresses mainly astronomical topics, alongside Campanella's critique that Epicureanism is incompatible with religion.[226] But Gassendi did reflect on the kind of dietetic choices that Epicurean ethics implies, and, most importantly, did so by endorsing Porphyry's view of Epicurus. While Campanella considered that he had overcome Porphyry's ethical appeal through his own theory of pansensism, for Gassendi Porphyry's *On Abstinence* contains convincing arguments in favour of vegetarianism. Furthermore, Gassendi believes that Epicurus and Porphyry stand in the same line of tradition in endorsing the vegetarian diet. The followers of Epicurus, he argues, should be convinced to become vegetarian.

Like Campanella, Gassendi is also critical of Aristotelian psychology, and sides with those philosophers who attribute reason to animals. In the overview of Book 5 of his collection of selected anti-Aristotelian lectures, the *Exercitationes* (1624), Gassendi had promised to 'give back reason to brute animals', adding in explanation: 'I do not in any way divide intellect and imagination'.[227] This book was never published, as Gassendi abandoned the project after the first two volumes.[228] But in the following years, when he turned to expounding Epicurus's philosophy, Gassendi often turned to a key source, which enlisted animal rationality as an argument in favour of vegetarianism: Porphyry's *On Abstinence*. Porphyry is for instance invoked in the section on physics in *Syntagma philosophicum* [Philosophical Compendium] devoted to animal voice ('De voce animalium'). Here Gassendi claims that the question whether or not animals talk is ultimately a question of terminology: human speech ('humana locutio') is unique; but animals, too, have an articulated voice, which is also a kind of *locutio* — dogs have canine language, and horses equine language. Referring to Book 3 of *On Abstinence*, Gassendi argues that if animals have external discourse ('sermo externus'), then they will also have internal discourse ('sermo internus'). Gassendi, too, uses the argument of linguistic relativism mentioned in *On Abstinence* and revived, among others, by Campanella: we cannot understand other species just as we (for example French speakers) cannot understand Chinese people.[229]

Gassendi therefore shares common ground with Porphyry as well as with Campanella regarding the human-animal difference. Unlike Campanella, however, Gassendi does follow Porphyry on the ethical terrain, too. He does so by using Porphyry as a channel for interpreting Epicurus as a vegetarian philosopher. What Gassendi mainly found in Porphyry was a view of Epicureanism as a philosophy that promoted a sober, frugal way of life, grounded in moral principles, and conducive to good health. First in his *Animadversiones* [Reflections] (1649), and then in the posthumously published *Syntagma philosophicum* (1658), Gassendi included long sections from Book 1 of *On Abstinence*, in Greek with a facing Latin translation.[230] In *On Abstinence* (1.48–53), Porphyry had explained that, contrary to the common assumption that pleasure and abstinence pursue different aims, Epicurus and his followers ate a very simple, vegetarian diet, consisting mainly of cereals and fruit. Such a diet is beneficial both for the soul (which avoids an endless, distressing search for elaborate pleasures) and for the body (because a simple, vegetable diet is more suitable to preserve health and avoid sickness). Gassendi includes these long extracts in a section devoted to the advantages of a simple life, which in *Syntagma philosophicum* belongs to a chapter 'On Happiness' ('De felicitate') of the *Ethics* section.[231] Here Gassendi agrees with Porphyry that the Epicureans choose such a simple lifestyle that they naturally abstain from meat as something unnecessary and potentially dangerous for the body-soul balance.[232]

In *Syntagma philosophiae Epicuri* [Compendium of the Philosophy of Epicurus] (1649), Gassendi employs some of the same material from Porphyry, this time shaping it into the form of a discourse by Epicurus himself. Meat — Epicurus argues in Porphyry's terms — impedes health rather than promotes it.[233] Furthermore a carnivorous diet is more costly and complicated to arrange than a vegetarian one, because meat-eaters will need to eat both meat and vegetables, while the vegetarians require only the latter.[234] Speaking in the first person, Epicurus concludes this section of the *Syntagma philosophiae Epicuri* on 'continence against gluttony' ('De sobrietate adversus gulam') by saying that he was happy to eat just the produce of the field.[235]

In *De vita et moribus Epicuri* [On the Life and Habits of Epicurus] (1647), Gassendi lists various sources in support of this interpretation of Epicurus's mode of living and diet.[236] According to Diogenes Laertius, Epicurus was content with a diet of bread and water; Diocles, cited by Laertius, calls him 'very frugal'; and Plutarch confirms that he ate a sort of bread made with oil and milk, and pulses. A quotation from *On Abstinence* completes the picture of a vegetarian Epicurus, who ate cereals and fruits.[237] Gassendi's interest in the vegetarian diet is therefore to be understood in the context of Epicureanism; Porphyry is the lens through which he views Epicurus's dietetic practice.

But beyond the practice of frugality, there are further points that Gassendi advances in favour of vegetarianism. In a long letter to Jan Baptist van Helmont (July 1629), Gassendi seeks to demonstrate that the consumption of meat is not natural for humans. This is a reply to an *Exercitatiuncula* that Helmont had sent him, following conversations on the subject that they had had in Brussels. While Helmont had argued that humans are natural carnivores, Gassendi on the other hand intertwines traditional arguments with his own view that humans are instead born to eat a vegetarian diet. We have already encountered some of these arguments in previous chapters: that meat needs to be cooked and prepared to be suitable for human consumption (as Plutarch emphasized); that meat is more difficult to digest than vegetables, and thus causes fattening; and that vegetables are no less nourishing than meat, even if vegetarian animals can be nourished by meat as well.[238] This latter point reflects Gassendi's belief that habit is key to diet: a sheep can become accustomed to eating meat (an example based on a 'true story'), just as humans have accepted that meat is on our menu, even if we are not carnivores by birth.[239] To substantiate this claim, Gassendi invokes the anatomical argument still used in discussions on vegetarianism today: humans do not have the long, sharp teeth of tigers, lions, or wolves. They have instead the short and broad teeth that animals like goats, sheep, horses, or oxen also possess: these teeth are evenly distributed in the mouth, and are thus ideal for chewing vegetables, but are a rather unsuitable tool for tearing apart raw meat.[240] This is an argument derived from Plutarch. Combining anatomical with theological considerations, Gassendi also reminds his opponent that humans were vegetarian in the Garden of Eden — an argument that, as we saw, had already been employed by Francesco Pucci against Fausto Sozzini.[241]

Yet, there is one objection raised by Helmont to which Gassendi responds with unease, as is evident from the tortuous answer he delivers. This regards his own dietary practice, for Gassendi was not a vegetarian. His explanation of his own consumption of meat involves the concept that plays a central role in the letter to Helmont, that of 'habit':

> Hinc, quia sentio mihi posse obiici, 'cur non igitur ipse plane a carnibus abstineam, frugibusque solum et frugibus vescar', excusare me posse videor ex inducta consuetudine. Natura quippe in iam adultis ita videtur immutata, ut adventitius ille habitus sine aliquo detrimento minime posse tolli videatur. Quamquam fateor si sapuero, et usum carnium sensim deserens ad ipsa almae telluris dona memet sensim deflexero, non haerere me, quin et constantiore sanitate fruar, et vireis quoque ingenii vegetiores experiar.[242]

> [Since I feel that it could be objected to me, 'why do you not abstain completely from meat yourself, and eat only vegetables?', I think that I can justify myself out of acquired habit. Indeed, in adults, nature appears to have been altered

to such an extent that the added habit can hardly be removed without causing some damage. Yet, I recognize that, if I will be reasonable and gradually turn to the gifts of nourishing earth, progressively putting an end to the consumption of meat, I have no doubt that I will enjoy better health, and that I will also experience a strengthening of intellectual powers.]

Habit leads humans to believe meat an essential food for them, yet Gassendi argues from anatomical evidence as well as theological and philosophical reasoning that this is not the case. But it is also because of habit that a full conversion to vegetarianism appears to Gassendi almost impossible in adults, to whom meat-eating has become second nature. Gassendi does not specify the kind of damage that a radical change of diet could cause if an adult were suddenly to become vegetarian. Nevertheless, he does admit that a slow reduction in meat intake, to the point of complete abstinence, could only bring advantages, for both general health and the functioning of the brain in particular.

Gassendi himself was most likely not a heavy meat eater. In his 1737 biography of the philosopher, Joseph Bourgerel writes that Gassendi rarely ate meat, preferring frequent consumption of vegetables.[243] The source for this statement is *De vita et moribus Petri Gassendi* [On the Life and Habits of Pierre Gassendi] by Gassendi's friend, Samuel Sorbière.[244] According to Sorbière, Gassendi led the life of an anchorite, frugal in the extreme. He did not drink wine, but warm herbal tea; 'he consumed meat rarely, vegetables more often', and in line with Epicurus's own habit, he ate a kind of bread softened in broth, twice a day.[245] Gassendi's conversion to vegetarianism was therefore complete on the theoretical level, but only partial on the practical one. Even assuming that his intake of meat was limited, he was not strictly speaking a vegetarian, and the admission in his letter to Helmont shows that he clearly perceived the difference between following a completely vegetable diet, and a form of moderate carnivorism.[246]

Porphyry proves to be a key source for Gassendi: *On Abstinence* provided the philosophical context for re-interpreting Epicurean diet in terms of frugality rather than gluttony and indulgence.[247] Yet, the dichotomy between philosophical convictions and personal practice separates Gassendi from Porphyry, who had energetically argued that if not everyone, then certainly the philosopher should be a vegetarian. For Gassendi, Porphyry's philosophical arguments are stringent, and yet something as prosaic as habit accounts for his adherence to an omnivorous diet. The philosopher thus set the conceptual basis for a progressive refinement of his diet, tending towards a vegetarian future, which was finally to harmonize his dietetic practice with his philosophical convictions. Adherence to vegetarianism is postponed, but belief in Porphyry's conception of this diet as the one appropriate for philosophers remains a source of hope that eventually philosophical wisdom will prevail even over the shackles of habit.

Notes to Chapter 4

1. As Osborne puts it (*Dumb Beasts and Dead Philosophers*, p. 228): 'When Porphyry tries to show that animals are intelligent or rational [...] these issues get their importance [...] from the need to show that we ought not kill them'.

2. See on this Maria Teresa Marcialis, 'La questione dell'anima delle bestie ovvero la razionalità senza soggetto', *Rivista di Storia della Filosofia*, 48.1 (1993), 83–100; and Claudia Stancati, 'Oltre Descartes: linguaggio e pensiero degli animali tra XVII e XVIII secolo', in *Macchine e vita nel XVII e XVIII secolo*, ed. by Francesca Bonicalzi (Florence: Le Monnier, 2006), pp. 113–40. See further on this topic *Corpus — Revue de Philosophie*, 16–17 (1991), special issue entitled *Sur l'âme des bêtes*; and *De l'animal-machine à l'âme des machine: querelles biomécaniques de l'âme (XVIIe–XXIe siècle)*, ed. by Jean-Luc Guichet (Paris: Publications de la Sorbonne, 2010).

3. René Descartes, *Discours de la méthode & essais* (*Œuvres*, VI, p. 58): 'Et cecy ne tesmoigne pas seulement que les bestes ont moins de raison que les hommes, mais qu'elles n'en ont point du tout'. On Descartes's 'paradox' of the animal-machine see Thierry Gontier, *De l'homme à l'animal. Paradoxes sur la nature des animaux: Montaigne et Descartes* (Paris: Vrin, 1998), p. 166.

4. René Descartes, letter to Henry More (5 February 1649) (*Œuvres*, V, 278): 'Velim tamen notari me loqui de cogitatione, non de vita, vel sensu: vitam enim nulli animali denego, utpote quam in solo cordis calore consistere statuo'.

5. See especially Descartes's *Discours de la méthode*, part V. For discussion of Descartes's position see especially John Cottingham, 'A Brute to the Brutes?'.

6. Dennis Des Chene, *Life's Form: Late Aristotelian Conceptions of the Soul* (New York: Cornell University Press, 2000), p. 12.

7. Henry More, letter to René Descartes (11 December 1648) (*Œuvres*, V, 243): 'utpote de animantium fato sollicitus, acumenque tuum non subtile solum agnosco, sed chalybis instar rigidum ac crudele, quod uno quasi ictu universum ferme animantium genus vita ausit sensuque spoliare, in marmora et machinas vertendo'.

8. Marin Mersenne, *Traité de la voix et des chants*, in *Harmonie universelle* (Paris: Cramoisy, 1636), p. 79: 'l'on peut dire qu'elles [les bestes] n'agissent pas tant comme elles sont agitees, & que les objects font une telle impression sur leurs sense, qu'il leur est necessaire de la suivre, comme il est necessaire que les roües d'une horloge suivent le poids ou le ressort qui les tire'. Thomas Willis, *De anima brutorum quae hominis vitalis ac sensitiva est, exercitationes duae* (London: Wells and Scott, 1672), p. 99: 'Et quidem videtur *homo* organo priori similis, in quo *anima rationalis* musici pulsantis vicem sustinet, quae scilicet spiritus animales regens ac dirigens, inferioris animae facultates pro libitu disponit, ac ordinat; verum *anima brutis* vix sui, aut facultatum suarum moderatrix, propter fines ei necessarios, plures actionum series, eas tamen velut harmoniae modulos, ab alterius generis organo hydraulico scilicet productos, lege quadam ac norma regulariter praescriptas, et fere semper ad idem determinatas instituit'. Both examples are discussed by Marcialis, *Filosofia e psicologia animale*, p. 30. Against the theory that animals resemble such devices see Marianus Brockie ['Praeses'] and Friedrich B. Stelle ['Respondens'], *Tractatus philosophicus de anima brutorum quo asseritur illam esse materialem, sensu et perceptione contra cartesianos praeditam; cogitatione vero et ratiocinio adversus quosdam neotericos, destitutam* [...] (Erfurt: Werther, 1715), p. 39.

9. More to Descartes (11 December 1648) (*Œuvres*, V, 243).

10. Descartes to More (5 February 1649) (*Œuvres*, V, 278–79). In 'Henry More on Human Passions and Animal Souls', in *Emotional Minds*, ed. by Sabrina Ebbersmeyer (Berlin: De Gruyter, 2012), pp. 209–26, I show that despite his rejection of Descartes's position, Henry More's ethical stance on the killing of animals is not substantially different from the Cartesian one. See also my ' "In Human Shape to Become the Very Beast!" Henry More on Animals', *Cambridge Platonism*, ed. by Sarah Hutton, special issue of *British Journal for the History of Philosophy*, 25.5 (2017), 897–915.

11. See Descartes, *Meditationes de prima philosophia* (*Œuvres*, VII, 426: 'Responsio ad sextas objectiones'), where Descartes states that he does not deny that animals live and have a corporeal soul ('neque enim id quod vulgo vocatur vita, nec anima corporea, nec sensus organicus, brutis a me denegatur'), but that they are not capable of *cogitatio*.

12. Descartes to More (5 February 1649) (*Œuvres*, V, 278–79): 'Sicque haec mea opinio non tam

crudelis est erga belluas, quam pia erga homines, Pythagoreorum superstitioni non addictos, quos nempe a criminis suspicione absoluit, quoties animalia comedunt vel occidunt'.

13. See also the reference to metempsychosis in Descartes, *Meditationes*, p. 426.

14. Dennis Des Chene has reconstructed the novelties and continuities between Descartes's position on physiology and late Aristotelianism: *Physiologia: Natural Philosophy in Late Aristotelianism and Cartesian Thought* (Ithaca, NY, & London: Cornell University Press, 1996), esp. p. 393.

15. For an overview of Renaissance debates on animal language, with reference to the circulation of Porphyry as well, see Stefano Gensini, ' "E io in Napoli vidi un cane polacco...": ancora sui linguaggi animali, da Gesner a Campanella', *Bruniana & Campanelliana*, 23.2 (2017), 639–49.

16. See above, Chapter 1, section 6.

17. Max Pohlenz, *Die Stoa: Geschichte einer geistigen Bewegung* (Göttingen: Vandenhoeck & Ruprecht, 1992), p. 137: 'Von der Gemeinschaft der Vernunftwesen sind selbstverständlich die Tiere ausgeschlossen, und gegenüber den Pythagoreern und ihren Gesinnungsgenossen, die aus religiösen Gründen den Fleischgenuß verboten, haben die Stoiker nachdrücklich den Satz verfochten, daß es keinerlei rechtliche oder sittliche Bindung gegenüber dem Tiere gebe'. For an overview of ancient debates on animal language see Maria Fusco, 'Il linguaggio degli animali nel pensiero antico: una sintesi storica', *Studi filosofici*, 30 (2007), 17–44.

18. *OA*, III.3.3; p. 81.

19. Descartes, *Discours de la méthode*, p. 57: 'les perroquets peuvent proferer des paroles ainsi que nous, & toutefois ne peuvent parler ansi que nous'. Pohlenz, *Die Stoa.* p. 84: 'Die Tiere haben zwar eine Stimme, aber keine Sprache, die als Organ der Dianoia die Dinge bezeichnet [...]. Auch der Papagei hat [...] nur eine "Gleich-als-ob-Sprache" '.

20. See especially *OA*, III.7.1; p. 84.

21. On Porphyry's use of sources, and here especially of Aristotle, see Bouffartigue and Patillon, 'Introduction', p. xxviii.

22. See for instance *OA*, III.5.6; p. 83.

23. Adriana Cavarero (*A più voci: filosofia dell'espressione vocale* (Milan: Feltrinelli, 2003), p. 19) has argued in this regard that the sphere of 'voice' is broader of that of 'word', and that giving primacy to the latter is one of the vices of logocentrism.

24. *OA*, III.21.6; p. 93. See also III.21.9; p. 93: 'every creature that has perception must also have thought'.

25. Richard Sorabji, *Animal Minds and Human Morals: The Origins of the Western Debate* (Ithaca, NY: Cornell University Press, 1995), p. 7: 'I want to show what a crisis was provoked when Aristotle denied reason to animals'. See also p. 12: 'In denying animals reason, Aristotle intends to deny them the capacity for true or false thought and belief'. I reconsider the trajectory from Aristotle to contemporary ethics in 'The Aristotelian Carnivore: The Ethical Afterlives of Aristotle's Theory of Animal Irrationality', *Revue des sciences religieuses*, 93.3 (2019), 257–79.

26. The difference between Aristotle's approach to the human-animal divide in *On the Soul* and in the zoological works has been addressed by several critics: see recently Patrizia Laspia, 'Aristotele e gli animali', in *Bestie, filosofi e altri animali*, ed. by Cimatti, Gensini & Plastina, pp. 17–35; and Devin Henry, 'Aristotle on Animals', in *Animals: A History*, ed. by Adamson & Edwards, pp. 9–26.

27. G. Fay Edwards ('The Purpose of Porphyry's Rational Animals: A Dialectical Attack on the Stoics in *On Abstinence from Animal Food*', in *Aristotle Re-Interpreted: New Findings on Seven Hundred Years of the Ancient Commentators*, ed. by Richard Sorabji (London & New York: Bloomsbury, 2016), pp. 263–89) argues that Porphyry does not believe himself that animals are rational, but only means to prove that according to the Stoic definition of *lógos*, they should be considered as such. I agree about the dialogical nature of this section of *On Abstinence*, but I understand Porphyry's discourse not as solely centered on the discussion of Stoic *lógos*. In my view, the main issue at stake for Porphyry is the impossibility of separating rationality from sensation, and thus the impossibility of dividing rational from irrational creatures, and ultimately of founding a theory of justice on such premises. See further G. Fay Edwards, 'Irrational Animals in Porphyry's Logical Works: A Problem for the Consensus Interpretation of *On Abstinence*', *Phronesis*, 59.1 (2014), 22–43.

28. But see André-Jean Festugière, 'Une source hermétique de Porphyre: l'"Egyptien" du *De Abstinentia* (II, 47)', *Revue des Études Grecques*, 49 (1936), 586–95, who claims that Porphyry's adherence to the doctrine of transmigration into animals is essential to explain why malevolent daemons or souls might inhabit animal bodies and thus affect those who eat animal flesh (pp. 587–78); see also Heinrich Dörrie, 'Kontroversen um die Seelenwanderung im kaiserzeitlichen Platonismus', *Hermes*, 85 (1957), 414–38. See also the useful summary of the evidence, mostly against considering Porphyry a supporter of the involvement of animals in metempsychosis, in Bouffartigue and Patillon, 'Introduction', pp. li–lii.

29. On this, see Urs Dierauer, *Mensch und Tier im Denken der Antike: Studien zur Tierpsychologie, Anthropologie und Ethik* (Amsterdam: B. R. Grüner, 1977), p. 21: 'In der rein naturphilosophischen Seelenwanderungstheorie wird kein principieller Vorgang der menschlicher gegenüber der tierischen Existenz sichtbar. Vielmehr zeigt sich hier auf besonders eindrückliche Art die Homogenität aller Lebewesen'.

30. Cf. Plato, *Timaeus*, 92b.

31. *OA*, 1.19.2; p. 38: 'For their return to humanity would be quicker, and having the bodies eaten would not engender distress in the souls, because they would have got rid of the bodies'. Festugière ('Une source hermétique de Porphyre', p. 587) wrongly claims that Porphyry mentions the theory of metemsomatosis only once (IV.16), and neglects the passage above, as well as the important 1.6.3 (p. 33), where Porphyry uses the term μεταμόρφωσις.

32. *OA*, 1.6.3 & 1.18.1; pp. 33 & 38.

33. *OA*, III.18.4–5; p. 90.

34. But I would not go as far as G. Fay Edwards in saying that the state of the soul of the eater is the only criterion that matters in the choice of food ('The Purpose of Porphyry's Rational Animals', p. 274). It seems to me that Porphyry is trying to demonstrate that vegetarianism can bring the state of the soul into balance with other aspects, such as caring for one's physical health, but also avoiding the suffering of others.

35. See *OA*, III.18.4–5 & III.6.7; pp. 90 & 84.

36. Aristotle, *Politics*, 1253a10, in *The Complete Works*, trans. by Jonathan Barnes, 2 vols (Princeton: Princeton University Press, 1984), II, 1988 (translation modified).

37. Clark's explanation (*OA*, p. 168) is consonant with this view.

38. Girolamo Fabrici d'Acquapendente, *De brutorum loquela*, in *De locutione / De brutorum loquela*, ed. by Stefano Gensini & Michela Tardella (Pisa: ETS, 2016), p. 138: 'Ne rem inutilem vobis proponi putetis, Lectores candidi et benevoli, cum de brutorum loquela agere constituo. Haec enim non alia est quam philosophia, quae animalium naturas investigat'. For an overview of Fabrici's works on language see Stefano Gensini and Michela Tardella, 'Language in Humans and in Other Animals: Fabrici d'Acquapendente Between Medicine and Philosophy', *Theoria et Historia Scientiarum*, 13 (2016), 17–33.

39. Fabrici, *De brutorum loquela*, p. 142: 'Extat primum Aristotelis auctoritas libro IV *De historia animalium* capitulo 9, quae loquelam animalium his verbis ponit: "At vero vox explanata quam esse quasi locutionem vel brutorum dixeris"'.

40. See ibid., p. 148. Gensini rightly points out that Fabrici even blurs the boundary between *locutio* and *loquela*, using them occasionally as synonyms in arguing that animals do possess language: 'Il *De brutorum loquela* di Fabrici d'Acquapendente', *Bruniana & Campanelliana*, 17.1 (2011), 163–74 (p. 165); Gensini responds here to Cunningham, who, on the contrary, translated *De brutorum loquela* as *On the Vocal Communication of Brutes* in order to underline the gap between human and animal language, between *locutio* and *loquela*: Andrew Cunningham, 'Fabricius and the "Aristotle Project" in Anatomical Teaching and Research at Padua', in *The Medical Renaissance of the Sixteenth Century*, ed. by A. Wear, R. K. French, & I. M. Lonie (Cambridge: Cambridge University Press, 1985), pp. 195–222 (p. 204).

41. Fabrici, *De brutorum loquela*, p. 156: 'Conveniunt quidem primo homines et caetera animalia, quod ambo loquelam habeant et articulos efforment, ut dictum est. Sed in eo differunt, quod hominum articuli litterae sunt, brutorum alii atque alii. Item conveniunt, quod tam homines, quam bruta per articulorum compositionem loquelam faciant; sed variant, quod brutorum loquela simplicior, hominum vero magis composita est. Haec enim ex litteris, syllabis, dictionibus et oratione constat'.

42. Ibid., p. 176.
43. Gensini and Tardella's introduction to Fabrici, *De brutorum loquela*, p. 8; and p. 138.
44. Ibid., p. 10.
45. On Fabrici's interpretation of Aristotle's and Porphyry's theories of language see Gensini, 'Il *De brutorum loquela* di Fabrici d'Acquapendente'.
46. Aristotle, *History of Animals*, 536b11–13. See also 536b5 where Aristotle claims that people who are deaf from birth have a voice (*phoné*) but not language (*diálektos*). See on this Stefano Gensini, 'Locutio in hominis fabrica: il contributo di Girolamo Fabrici d'Acquapendente', in *Traguardi e prospettive nelle scienze del linguaggio: riflessioni con Federico Albano Leoni*, ed. by Francesca M. Dovetto, Valeria Micillo, & Elda Morlicchio (Rome: Aracne, 2012), pp. 165–96 (p. 173).
47. Aristotle, *History of Animals*, 538b1–2. See Fabrici, *De brutorum loquela*, p. 146.
48. Fabrici recurs to Porphyry at key points of the argumentation: Fabrici, *De brutorum loquela*, pp. 140, 142, 144, 154, 160.
49. Ibid., p. 144.
50. Cf. *OA*, III.4–5; pp. 82–83.
51. Fabrici, *De brutorum loquela*, pp. 196–98. Cf. Cicero, *De officiis*, ed. and trans. by Walter Miller (Cambridge, MA, & London: Harvard University Press, 1913), p. 13 (Book 1.4): 'But the most marked difference between man and beast is this: the beast, just as far as it is moved by the senses and with very little perception of past or future, adapts itself to that alone which is present at the moment; while man — because he is endowed with reason, by which he comprehends the chain of consequences, perceives the causes of things, understands the relation of cause to effect and of effect to cause, draws analogies, and connects and associates the present and the future — easily surveys the course of his whole life and makes the necessary preparations for its conduct'.
52. Fabrici, *De brutorum loquela*, p. 192.
53. Ibid., p. 140. As Clark points out, the classical passage on Apollonius's communication with the animals is Philostratus's *Life of Apollonius*, IV.3 (*OA*, p. 165). On Apollonius's asceticism, including the choice of a vegetarian diet, see Haussleiter, *Der Vegetarismus in der Antike*, pp. 299–313. On the tradition of animal speech in Greek antiquity, see Dierauer, *Mensch und Tier im Denken der Antike*, pp. 32–33.
54. Fabrici, *De brutorum loquela*, p. 154, which refers to *OA*, III.3; pp. 81–82. See Aristotle, *On the Soul*, II.8 (420b6–9): Aristotle had stated that only animate things can possess a voice, and that inanimate things have a voice only by analogy (καθ' ὁμοιότητα); Fabrici gives the statement a different tone by turning the phrase round and claiming that, 'per similitituden', all things have a voice according to Aristotle.
55. Fabrici, *De brutorum loquela*, p. 158.
56. Michel de Montaigne, 'Apologie de Raymond Sebond', in *Essais*, II, 192: 'Ce n'est pas gran merveille si nous ne les etendons pas, aussi ne faisons-nous les Basques et les Troglodytes. Toutefois aucuns se sont vantés de les entendre, comme Apollonius Thyaneus, Melampus, Tirésias, Thalès, et autres'. On the *Apology* see Tournon, *Montaigne*, pp. 228–56 (on the human-animal comparison see p. 239).
57. Montaigne, *Essais*, II, 192: 'C'est à deviner à qui est la faute de ne nous entendre point, car nous ne les entendons non plus qu'ellles nous'.
58. Ibid.: 'Il nous faut remarquer la parité qui est entre nous. Nous avons quelque moyenne intelligence de leur sens, aussi ont les bêtes du nôtre, environ à même mesure. Elles nous flattent, nous menacent et nous requièrent, et nous elles'.
59. Ibid., p. 191: 'C'est par la vanité de cette même imagination [...] qu'il se trie soi-même et sépare de la presse des autres créatures, taille les parts aux animaux, ses confrères et compagnons, et leur distribue telle portion de facultés et de forces que bon lui semble'. On this passage, in the broader context of the *Apology*, see Gontier, *De l'homme à l'animal*, p. 65.
60. Plato, *Statesman*, 272b–c (*Dialogues of Plato*, III, 551): 'If having this boundless leisure, and the power of discoursing not only with one another but with the animals, they had employed these advantages with a view to philosophy, gathering from every nature some addition to their store of knowledge; — or again, if they had merely eaten and drunk, and told stories to one another, and to the beasts; in either case, I say, there would be no difficulty in answering the question'.

61. On Giovannini as censor see Ugo Rozzo, 'Italian Literature on the Index', in *Church, Censorship and Culture in Early Modern Italy*, ed. by Gigliola Fragnito, trans. by Adrian Belton (Cambridge: Cambridge University Press, 2001), pp. 194–222 (pp. 218–19); Elena Pierazzo, 'Un intellettuale a servizio della Chiesa: Girolamo Giovannini da Capugnano', *Filologia & critica*, 23 (1998), 206–48. On Gelli's *Circe* in context of the debate on the human-animal differentiation see: Cecilia Muratori, 'Better Animal than Human: The Happy Animal and the Human Animal in the Renaissance Reception of Aristotle', in *Die nackte Wahrheit und ihre Schleier. Weisheit und Philosophie im Mittelalter and früher Neuzeit. Studien zum Gedenken an Thomas Ricklin*, ed. by Christian Kaiser, Leonhard Maier, & Oliver Schrader, Dokimion 42 (Münster: Aschendorff, 2019), pp. 477–97.

62. Girolamo Giovannini da Capugnano, *Discorso sopra tutti li parlari* [1604] (Venice: Barezzi, 1622), p. 85: 'vedendosi che né gli uccelli, ne le bestie, né i pesci hanno il favellare, dobbiamo credere, che ciò sia fatto bene'. Both in the 1604 and 1622 editions this text is preceded by Agnolo Firenzuola (1493–1543), *Consigli de gli animali, cioè ragionamenti civili*.

63. Ibid., p. 102: 'Con infinita sapienza ha fatto Dio, che ogni specie habbia la sua lingua, imperciò che se si ne trovasse una sola, si confonderebbono le specie, e facilmente la pecora ai lupi, il lepre al cane, l'uccello all'avoltoio inavedutamente andrebbe'.

64. Ibid., p. 101: 'la lingua nostra è mobile per li muscoli, e servendo la mente, che in un battere d'occhio quasi scorre per tutto il mondo, e fino in Cielo, onde bisogna che sia molto presta'. See also p. 9: 'Molti animali, uccelli e pesci, hanno lingua, e li serve solamente per mangiare, nel quale officio a noi ella è di bisogno somigliantemente'.

65. See e.g. Fabrici, *De locutione*, in *De locutione / De brutorum loquela*, p. 88. In the 1595 amended edition of Anton Francesco Doni's *Zucca*, Giovannini claimed not to have dealt with Fabrici's work at that point; this must have changed once Fabrici published *De locutione* (1601) and *De brutorum loquela* (1603): Anton Francesco Doni, *La zucca, espurgata e corretta da Girolamo Giovannini da Capugnano* (Venice: Zanetti and Presegni, 1595), dedication to Virginio Orsini, Duca di Bracciano, sig. a5r: 'Avvertiscovi nondimeno che io non ho mai comentato i libri della notomia del Vesallio, né postilato quelli del Valverde, né tampoco stropicciato il rasoio, e i feretti dell'Eccellentiss[imo] Tagliacozzo, né dell'Acquapendente'.

66. Giovannini, *Discorso sopra tutti li parlari*, pp. 97–100: 'Che gli animali, le fere, e gli uccelli hanno un certo suo parlare ancora da lor conosciuto'. Cf. Fabrici, *De brutorum loquela*, pp. 140–54. The first part of the chapter follows Fabrici's text; the second part (from p. 99; cf. Fabrici, *De brutorum loquela*, p. 148), is abridged. On Giovannini's 'borrowing' from Fabrici see Pierazzo, 'Un intellettuale a servizio della Chiesa', esp. p. 234.

67. Giovannini, *Discorso sopra tutti li parlari*, pp. 97–98.

68. Ibid., p. 99: 'Mi direte che Aristotile, a cui tanto si crede, vuole che'l favellare proprio sia dell'huomo, e lo scrive nella sua istoria Istoria de gli Animali, e dalla generatione loro; ma io non dissi che questo parlare sia linguaggio fatto da loro con Lettere, e questo è dell'huomo solo'. A note in the margin refers to Book IV.7 of *Historia animalium*, but IV.9 is a better fit.

69. See also ibid., pp. 91–92, where Giovannini quotes Porphyry's *Life of Pythagoras*: 'Nella vita di Pittagora (dice Porfirio) che varcando il fiume Caucaso, in compagnia d'assai persone, dalle acque s'udì uscire: *Salve Pithagora*'.

70. Ibid., p. 98. Cf. Fabrici, *De brutorum loquela*, p. 144.

71. Fabrici, *De brutorum loquela*, p. 142: 'His auctoritatibus, ratio quoque astipulatur'.

72. Giovannini, *Discorso sopra tutti li parlari*, p. 98.

73. Ibid., p. 100. Cf. Fabrici, *De brutorum loquela*, pp. 152–53.

74. Giovannini, *Discorso sopra tutti li parlari*, pp. 107–08: 'Che Tiresia, Melampo e il Thianeo intendessero gli uccelli e gli animali, giudico che sia menzongna, overo che fosse opra del Demonio, e son cose che non hanno fondamento per l'auttorità di chi le scrive, trovandosi che gli autori n'hanno finte assai altre come queste'.

75. Ibid., p. 101.

76. Ibid., pp. 91–96.

77. Most likely, Giovannini would have not considered his appropriation of Fabrici as an instance of plagiarism. He notably claimed in the dedicatory letter of his amended edition of Doni's *Zucca*,

that this revised work could now almost be considered to be his own: Doni, *La zucca*, dedication to Virginio Orsini, Duca di Bracciano, sig. a3r: 'quasi mia [fatica] hora dir si può, e non del Doni'. Similarly, he claims that he also appropriated Niccolò Franco's *Dialoghi piacevoli* (which he retitles, after his interventions, *Dialoghi piacevolissimi*): Niccolò Franco, *Dialoghi piacevolissimi* (Venice: Salicato, 1590), f. *3r. On Giovannini's appropriations see Ugo Rozzo, *Le letteratura italiana negli 'Indici' del Cinquecento* (Udine: Forum, 2005), pp. 116–17.

78. Giovannini, *Discorso sopra tutti li parlari*, p. 86.

79. *Gómez Pereira's 'Antoniana Margarita': A Work on Natural Philosophy, Medicine and Theology*, ed. by José Manuel García-Valverde & Peter Maxwell-Stuart (Leiden: Brill, 2019), p. 194: 'si bruta in sentiendo nobis paria | essent, exinde necessario inferendum nihil proprium nobis hominibus esse, quod illis commune non esset'; my translation, but cf. ibid., p. 195. See also p. 196: 'Bruta ergo si in sentiendo paria nobiscum sunt, eodem modo fugere, aut aemulari amicos aut inimicos debent, prout et nos: ergo affirmare mentaliter alteros amicos, aliosque inimicos coguntur dicere, qui praefatam similitudinem brutorum et hominum ponunt'. On Pereira's theory see Javier Bandrés and Rafael Llavona, 'Minds and Machines in Renaissance Spain: Gómez Pereira's Theory of Animal Behavior', *Journal of the History of Behavioral Sciences*, 28 (1992), 158–68; and Lorenzo Bianchi, 'Rorario tra Naudé e Bayle', in *Bruniana & Campanelliana*, 17.1 (2011), 175–84.

80. Descartes stated that he did not read *Antoniana Margarita*. See the letter to Mersenne of 23 June 1641, in Descartes, *Œuvres*, III, 386: 'Ie n'ay point vû *Antoniana Margarita*, ny ne croy pas auoir gran besoin de les voir'.

81. Pierre Bayle, *Dictionaire historique et critique*, 5th edn, 4 vols (Amsterdam: Brunel and others, 1740), III, 650: 'Mais ce qu'il y eut de plus surprenant dans ses Paradoxes, fut qu'il enseigna que les bêtes sont des machines, & qu'il rejetta l'ame sensitive qu'on leur attribue'.

82. Ibid., p. 653: 'Je remarquerai que Vossius ne connoissoit point d'Auteur, qui avant Pereira eût soutenu que les animaux ne sentent point'.

83. Ibid., p. 652.

84. Ibid., 'Je ne pense pas qu'il y ait des Philosophes qui aient parlé plus avantageusement de l'ame des bêtes que Porphyre. Il leur a donné, non seulement la Raison, mais aussi la faculté de faire entendre leurs raisonnements; & il a cru que leur language a été intelligible à quelques personnes, & que l'homme ne les surpasse qu'en ce qu'il possede un raisonnement plus raffiné'.

85. See *Commentarii Collegii Conimbricensis Societatis Iesu, in octo libros Physicorum Aristotelis Stagiritae*, 2 vols (Lyon: Buysson, 1594), I. 331 (Book II.9, quaestio 3): 'An brutae animantes solo natura instinctus in fines suos ferantur'.

86. Ibid., p. 335, with references to Aristotle's *History of Animals* and to the *Metaphysics*: 'Quod autem asserebat Porphyrius ex Aristotelis doctrina colligi existimasse illum bruta ratione pollere, falsum est; nisi rationem sumat pro rationis imitatione, quam solam brutis quibusdam Aristoteles attribuit tum loco citato de historia animalium, tum I. Metaph., cap. I. Quod item addebat Porphyrius, bruta inter se colloqui, et a quibusdam intelligi, non ita est, etsi ita esse crediderit quidam ex Hebraeis doctoribus'. Cf. Bayle, *Dictionaire*, III, 652: 'Ceux qui rapportent ces termes ne conviennent pas qu'Aristote soit cité bien à propos (35): ils prétendent qu'il n'accorde aux bêtes qu'une image, ou qu'une copie de raison; & ils se moquent de ce prétendu langage intelligible à Tiresias, & à Melampus, &c. sur quoi ils remarquent qu'un Rabin a suivi l'erreur de Porphyre, & qu'il a cru que Salomon entendoit le même langage'.

87. *Commentarii Collegii Conimbricensis Societatis Iesu, In octo libros Physicorum Aristotelis Stagiritae*, I, 335.

88. Bayle, *Dictionaire*, III, 652: 'On pourrroit donc croire qu'Aristote ne reconnoissoit qu'une différence du plus au moins entre l'ame de la bête, & celle de l'homme, c'est-à-dire, que la difference des organes faisoit, selon lui, que l'ame de l'homme raisonnoit subtilement, & facilement, & que celle de la bête ne raisonnoit que d'une façon confuse'.

89. On the story of this text see Aidée Scala, *Girolamo Rorario: un umanista diplomatico del Cinquecento* (Florence: Olschki, 2004), Chapter 4. On its dating see Marcialis, *Filosofia e psicologia animale*, p. 52; on the existent manuscript and the editions see Scala, *Girolamo Rorario*, pp. 115 & 299. In Gabriel Naudé and Guy Patin, *Naudaeana et Patiniana* (Amsterdam: van der Plaats, 1703), p. 250, the date of the first edition is indicated as 1642 rather than 1648. This is likely the source of the reference to a 1642 edition in both contemporary and eighteenth-century literature. See for

example: Lorenzo Bianchi, 'Sorbière's Scepticism: Between Naturalism and Absolutism', in *The Return of Scepticism: From Hobbes and Descartes to Bayle*, ed. by Gianni Paganini (Berlin: Springer, 2003), pp. 267–82 (p. 277); Christian Hennings, *Geschichte von den Seelen der Menschen und Thiere* (Halle: Gebauer 1774), p. 443. In the chapter 'Whether animals are merely machines' ('Ob die Thiere blosse Maschinen sind?') Hennings mentions Rorarius as counterexample to Cartesian automatism, and in favour of his own theory that animals share in feeling and thinking. See further Paul Oskar Kristeller, *Studies in Renaissance Thought and Letters*, III, 637.

90. On Naudé's edition of Rorario see also Paul Oskar Kristeller, 'Between the Italian Renaissance and the French Enlightenment: Gabriel Naudé as an Editor', *Renaissance Quarterly*, 32.1 (April 1979), 41–72 (p. 50).

91. Marcialis, *Filosofia e psicologia animale*, p. 51.

92. Girolamo Rorario, *Quod animalia bruta ratione utantur melius homine* (Paris: Cramoisy, 1648), pp. 105–06: 'Quod si belluae ingenio pollent, memoria vigent, discendi desiderio accenduntur, et nostras in primis voces imitandi, cur non credere debemus habere etiam quo se mutuo intelligant?'

93. Bayle mentions Plutarch's *De sollertia animalium*: *Dictionaire*, IV, 77.

94. Ibid., p. 76: 'C'est dommage que le sentiment de Mr. Des Cartes soit si difficile à soutenir, & si éloigné de la vraisemblence'; and ibid.: 'Prouvons donc seulement que les Péripatétisme se trouve dans un embarras extréme, quand il faut donner raison de leur [i. e. des animaux] conduite'.

95. Rorario, *Quod animalia bruta ratione utantur melius homine*, p. 106.

96. Giovannini's annotated version was very successful, and was reissued five times: see Rozzo, *La letteratura italiana negli 'Indici' del Cinquecento*, pp. 116 & 270.

97. Plutarch's fable inspired several Renaissance re-elaborations. See Barbara Kuhn, *Mythos und Metapher: Metamorphosen des Kirke-Mythos in der Literatur der italienischen Renaissance* (Munich: Fink, 2003).

98. Giovan Battista Gelli, *La Circe* (Venice: Bonibelli, 1595), f. 10v.

99. Pierazzo, 'Un intellettuale a servizio della Chiesa', p. 234.

100. Tommaso Campanella, *Universalis philosophiae seu metaphysicarum rerum [...] libri 18* [*Metaphysica*] (Paris: D. Langlois, 1638), Part I, p. 55[b] (Book I.6, art. 6).

101. Ibid., pp. 54[b]-55[a]: 'Ergo imperite Aristoteles animalibus dat prudentiam, quibus negat rationem'. On animal *prudentia* see George Klubertanz, *The Discoursive Power: Sources and Doctrine of the 'Vis Cogitativa' According to St. Thomas Aquinas* (Carthagena: Messenger Press, 1952), pp. 34–35.

102. Campanella, *Metaphysica*, Part I, p. 54.

103. Aristotle, *On the Soul*, 428a8–11 (in *The Complete Works of Aristotle*, I, 680): 'That imagination is not sense is clear from the following considerations: Sense is either a faculty or an activity, e.g. sight or seeing: imagination takes place in the absence of both, as e.g. in dreams. Again, sense is always present, imagination not. If actual imagination and actual sensation were the same, imagination would be found in all the brutes: this is held not to be the case; e.g. it is not found in ants or bees or grubs'.

104. Campanella, *Metaphysica*, Part I, p. 54[a] (Book I.6, art. 5): 'Ad alteram rationem dico, cunctis animalibus inesse phantasiam, quoniam in omnibus perseverat illata passio ab obiectis, et secundum illam sectantur aut fugiunt'.

105. Ibid., p. 52[a-b] (1.6, art. 4): 'Ergo falso Aristoteles separat memoriam a sensu, et imprimit eam sensorio. Sed et sensus et memoria a sensorio separanda erant. Quando autem docet muscas non memorari, ergo esse aliud a sentire: nil forsan dixit, nam et ipse muscae memoriam habent eorum quae manducarunt, et revertuntur ad pastum'.

106. Ibid., p. 55.

107. Lodi Nauta, 'From an Outsider's Point of View: Lorenzo Valla on the Soul', *Vivarium*, 46.3 (2008), 368–91 (p. 381), with reference in particular to Valla's gloss on Quintilian (Lorenzo Valla, *Le Postille all''Institutio Oratoria' di Quintiliano*, ed. by Lucia Cesarini Martinelli & Alessandro Perosa (Padua: Antenore, 1996), p. 70). Bayle mentions Valla, too, as one of the moderns who attributed rationality to animals (*Dictionaire*, IV, 79). Bayle's reference to Valla is derived from Gerardus Joannes Vossius, *De origine ac progressu idolatriae* (Frankfurt: Wächtler, 1668), p. 940 (Book III.41), who contrasts the opinion of Valla and others, including Porphyry, with that of Pereira.

108. Bernardino Telesio, *De rerum natura iuxta propria principia*, ed. by Luigi De Franco, 3 vols (Cosenza: Casa del libro; Florence, La Nuova Italia, 1965–76), III, 204 (Book VIII.10): 'Nam quae animalibus ratio quodque malum vitandi bonaque sectandi inest studium, id omne ex iis, quae pridem percepta sunt cognitaque et quae spiritu haesere, inest'.

109. Telesio uses the word 'spirit' in the singular, not in the plural, as had been common in medical literature. On this see Guido Giglioni, 'Spirito e coscienza nella medicina di Bernardino Telesio', in *'Virtù ascosta e negletta': la Calabria nella modernità*, ed. by Germana Ernst & Rosa M. Calcaterra (Milan: Franco Angeli, 2011), pp. 154–68 (pp. 158–59). On Telesio's notion of sentience see Guido Giglioni, 'The First of the Moderns or the Last of the Ancients? Bernardino Telesio and Sentience', *Bruniana & Campanelliana*, 16.1 (2010), 69–87.

110. Telesio, *De rerum natura*, ed. by De Franco, III, 190 (Book VIII.8).

111. Aristotle's distinction between two kinds of *phantasia* is further proof of this multiplication of faculties (Aristotle, *On the Soul*, 434a6–9, p. 690): 'Sensitive imagination, as we have said, is found in all animals, deliberative imagination only in those that are calculative: for whether this or that shall be enacted is already a task requiring calculation; and there must be a single standard to measure by, for that is pursued which is greater. It follows that what acts in this way must be able to make a unity out of several images'). In Richard Sorabji's view, Aristotle had to 'compensate for the denial of reason and belief to animals' by expanding the perceptual content of animal minds (*Animal Minds and Human Morals*, pp. 17–20).

112. On Avicenna's *vis aestimativa* (*wahm*) see: Dag Nikolaus Hasse, *Avicenna's 'De anima' in the Latin West: The Formation of a Peripatetic Philosophy of the Soul 1160–1300* (London & Turin: The Warburg Institute & Nino Aragno Editore, 2000), pp. 127–53; Robert E. Hall, 'Intellect, Soul and Body in Ibn Sīnā: Systematic Synthesis and Development of the Aristotelian, Neoplatonic and Galenic Theories', in *Interpreting Avicenna: Science and Philosophy in Medieval Islam. Proceedings of the Second Conference of the Avicenna Study Group*, ed. by Jon McGinnis (Leiden: Brill, 2004), pp. 62–86 (pp. 65–68).

113. Campanella, *Metaphysica*, Part 1, p. 54[a] (1.6, art. 6): 'Rationem vero a sensu et phantasia non differre realiter in fundamento'.

114. Telesio, *De rerum natura*, ed. by De Franco, III, 226 (Book VIII.14): 'Substantiam, quae sentit in homine, ratiocinari; et animalia reliqua ratiocinationis non prorsus experta esse'.

115. Tommaso Campanella, *Sintagma dei miei libri e sul corretto metodo di apprendere*, ed. by Germana Ernst (Pisa & Rome: Fabrizio Serra, 2007), pp. 32–34.

116. Germana Ernst, *Tommaso Campanella: The Book and the Body of Nature*, trans. by David L. Marshall (Berlin: Springer, 2010), p. 7.

117. Tommaso Campanella, *Del senso delle cose e della magia*, ed. by Germana Ernst (Rome & Bari: Laterza, 2002), pp. 85–86. Cf. Tommaso Campanella, *De sensu rerum et magia* (Paris: Bechet, 1637), pp. 83–84. Campanella often composed both Italian and Latin versions of his works. In the case of *De sensu rerum* / *Del senso delle cose*, he wrote the original draft of this text in Italian (1590–92); the Latin translation was then printed in 1620 (see the overview in Germana Ernst, 'Campanella, Tommaso', in *The Stanford Encyclopedia of Philosophy*, ed. by Edward N. Zalta , <https://plato.stanford.edu/archives/fall2014/entries/campanella/> [accessed 15 August 2019]). I only quote from the Latin version when it is worth comparing the Latin and Italian terminology. These works, and many others by Campanella, are available online in the invaluable *Archivio dei filosofi del Rinascimento*, <http://www.iliesi.cnr.it/atc> [accessed 14 September 2019].

118. Campanella, *De sensu rerum*, p. 84: 'Dicunt instinctu naturali, at instinctus est impulsus praevidentis sapientiae'. *Del senso delle cose*, p. 87: 'Dicono che sia istinto; ma l'istinto è impulso di senso antevedente il bisogno'.

119. Campanella, *Del senso delle cose*, p. 87: 'Dicono che imparano per l'uso; ma pur noi con l'uso tutte l'arti apprendiamo'. *De sensu rerum*, p. 84: 'Dicunt tamen illa discere assuefactione. At nos etiam assuefactione artes discimus'.

120. Campanella, *Del senso delle cose*, pp. 87–88: 'Siamo certi che tra loro ci è voce, e che si chiamano gli augelli e giumenti; dunque hanno discorso, ma noi non intendiamo la loro lingua perché né anco quella de' Tedeschi, né de' Cataini intendemo, perché ognuno pronunzia al verso suo; e li cani che tra noi vivono e le scimie ben imparano la lingua nostra, perché portati in paesi lontani

216   RATIONALITY

non intendono l'altrui lingua, e io in Napoli vidi un cane polacco che non intendeva niente li napoletani, se non quei che li parlavano in lingua polacca'. *De sensu rerum*, pp. 84–85: 'necesse est eas uti voce, et se invicem iumenta et aves vocitare. Ergo discursus habent, at nos ipsarum linguam non percipimus, quoniam nec Polonorum, aut Indorum percipimus; omnes enim suo pronunciant quisque modo. Canes tamen nobiscum viventes et simiae bene addiscunt linguam nostram; nam in alias delati regiones linguam accolarum non intelligunt. Vidi Neapoli canem Polonum nil percipere linguam Napolitanam, nisi loquentis Polonice'. See Gensini, '"E io in Napoli vidi un cane polacco..."', p. 641.

121. Campanella, *Del senso delle cose*, p. 88: 'Vero è che non ponno pronunziare quel che vogliono, perché non hanno gli organi simili alli nostri, come noi non possiamo fare di cetera trombetta, né col corno il suono della campana, né che il balbuziente parli speditamente; ma i pappagalli che hanno concavo il palato, come l'uomo, alquanto, ben imparano molte parole'. *De sensu rerum*, p. 85.

122. See also Tommaso Campanella, *Epilogo magno (1598)*, ed. by Carmelo Ottaviano (Rome: Reale Accademia d'Italia, 1939), p. 474.

123. Ibid.: 'tutti parlano nel loro linguaggio et discorrono et intendono'.

124. Campanella, *Metaphysica*, Part I, p. 55.

125. Campanella, *Del senso delle cose*, p. 88: 'Così paion gli altri animali a noi esser senza discorso e favella e giudizio; ma tutti n'hanno chi più e chi meno, come tra noi avviene che molti paion bestie, e Aristotile però disse che non tutti abbiamo intelletto'. *De sensu rerum*, p. 85: 'Ita videntur alia nobis animalia absque discursu et iudicio, sed omnia pollent ratione, alia magis, alia minus; sicut inter nos evenit, quod multi homines videntur bestiae. Idcirco Aristoteles dixit non omnibus inesse intellectum'.

126. Campanella, *Del senso delle cose*, p. 88; *De sensu rerum*, 85.

127. Tommaso Campanella, *De homine (Inediti theologicorum liber IV)*, ed. by Romano Amerio, 2 vols (Rome: Centro internazionale di studi umanistici, 1960–61), I, 52.

128. Telesio, *De rerum natura*, ed. by De Franco, III, 228 (Book VIII.14): 'animalia omnia aut pleraque quadam ratiocinandi vel existimandi, ut dicemus, commemorandique facultate donata sint, ambigi non potest'.

129. See Guido Giglioni's account of these key issues in his introduction to Bernardino Telesio, *De rerum natura iuxta propria principia libri ix (Naples 1586)*, anastatic copy with an introduction and index by Guido Giglioni (Rome: Carocci, 2013), pp. xx–xxvi.

130. Bernardino Telesio, *De rerum natura iuxta propria principia, liber primus, et secundus, denuo editi (Naples 1570) / Opuscula (Naples 1570)*, anastatic copy of the exemplar in the Biblioteca nazionale di Napoli, with an introduction and index by Roberto Bondì (Rome: Carocci, 2013), p. 22: 'Nec vero de humana etiam anima id dictum existimet quis, quam a Deo ipso in singula hominum corpora infusam esse'.

131. See Roberto Bondì, *Introduzione a Telesio* (Rome & Bari: Laterza, 1997), p. 79.

132. Telesio, *De rerum natura*, ed. by De Franco, III, 552 (Book V.40): 'ratiocinandi facultas incorporeae substantiae attribui non potest [...] sed (quod dictum est) corporeae omnino substantiae et spiritui omnino attribuenda est, in cerebri ventriculis residenti'.

133. Ibid., II, 446 (Book V.40).

134. *De rerum natura* was placed on the *Index librorum prohibitorum* together with *Quod animal universum ab unica animae substantia gubernatur. Contra Galenum*, and the essay 'De somno' (Bernardino Telesio, *Varii de naturalibus rebus libelli*, ed. by Luigi De Franco (Florence: La Nuova Italia, 1981), p. xxxvii of De Franco's introduction).

135. I have argued elsewhere (Muratori, 'The Earth's Perilous Fertility') that the appearance of the immortal soul on the stage goes hand-in-hand with Telesio's reformulation of the theory of spontaneous generation, which from the first to the last version of Telesio's main work, is increasingly displaced into the background. This is noteworthy because spontaneous generation is potentially materialistic; animals (including humans) can be formed out of matter, granted certain climatic conditions.

136. Campanella, *Del senso delle cose*, p. 88; cf. *De sensu rerum*, p. 85: 'Aut quia parum discurrunt ultra quod vident et sentiunt praesens, homo vero discurrit ad multa similia entia et actiones,

et figuras, et virtutes, et vitia, et negotia, eodem in tempore cum ob meliora organa interiora, tum ob spiritum puriorem, lucidiorem et nobiliorem, et ob perfectionem, quam spiritus habet a mente immortali ipsi indita, [...] evenit, ut homo dicatur rationalis, non autem bruta, non quia non ratiocinentur, sed parum; sicuti nec plantae vocantur animalia, quoniam sentiunt parum; ita et nos loquemur'.

137. Campanella, *De sensu rerum*, p. 85: 'Sed hominem rationalem mentalem intelligimus, bruta vero ratione sensitiva donamus, quam D. Thom. vocat aestimativam'. As Gensini ('"E io in Napoli vidi in un cane polacco..."', p. 649) has pointed out, the specification about the sensitive rationality of animals is absent from the Italian version of the text.

138. Campanella, *Metaphysica*, Part I, p. 58^b (Book I.6, appendix): 'Brutis ergo spontaneitatem, non libertatem, rationem et intellectum sensualem, non mentalem, qui nec nomen intellectus sed aestimativae tantum mereatur, nos agnoscimus'.

139. See Aristotle, *On the Soul*, 414b18–19, p. 659: 'Certain kinds of animals possess in addition the power of locomotion, and still others, i.e. man and possibly another order like man or superior to him, the power of thinking and thought'.

140. See Germana Ernst, '"Nascosto in ciclopea caverna": natura e condizione umana in Campanella', in *Il neoplatonismo nel rinascimento*, ed. by Pietro Prini (Rome: Istituto della enciclopedia italiana, 1993), pp. 65–81; and 'L'analogia e la differenza', pp. 209–25.

141. Germana Ernst, '"Sol libertà può farci forti, sagaci e lieti": comunità e libertà in Campanella', *MORUS — Utopia e Renascimento*, 8 (2012), 175–91 (p. 189).

142. Cf. Stanislav Hosius, *Confessio catholicae fidei christiana, Petricoviensis Synodi a D. Stanislao Hosio Cardinale Episcopo Varmiensi conscripta*, in *Opera omnia hactenus edita* (Venice: Nicolini, 1573), 'Prœmium', sig. c2r: 'Quid igitur esse dicemus, quo maxime discerni possint homines a pecoribus? Non ratio, non oratio, non prudentia, non alia quaecunque, sed sola est religio, quae nos ab illis discernit'.

143. Campanella, *De homine*, I, 44: 'Ipsa tandem religio homini naturalis adeo ut per illam a brutis solum separemur, teste Chrysostomo et Osio Cardinali, attestatur inesse homini mentem diviniorem, quam sit corporeus spiritus, cui bona diviniora conveniant'.

144. Tommaso Campanella, *Atheismus triumphatus* (Rome: Zannetti, 1631), p. 53. Cf. Pliny, *Natural History*, Book VIII.1. See on this see Ernst, 'L'analogia e la differenza', p. 212.

145. Campanella, *Atheismus triumphatus*, p. 53: 'Itaque habent quodammodo religionem, prophetiam, medicinam, militarem, rempublicam (et ut Lactantius, Osius, Plutarchus, Porphyrius, aliique asserunt, sensualem discursum, quem S. Thomas vocat aestimativam) sed ita valde inferiores nostris, quod debent vocari metaforice, quippe relatio his est omnibus ad praesentem modo vitam'. Note the similar formulation in Campanella, *De sensu rerum*, p. 85.

146. Campanella, *De homine*, I, 56: 'propria operatio mentis a Deo infusae est contemplatio divinorum et religio, secundum quam a brutis secernitur, teste Chrysostomo et Osio, et non fit per rationem'. See also *De homine*, II, 124: 'Quapropter licet Osius Cardinalis et theologi multi dent brutis prudentiam et rationem, sicuti plerique ex Patarinis et alii, non tamen brutorum ratio est ex propria libertate ductuque, sed obiectorum sic moventium'.

147. Campanella, *Del senso delle cose*, p. 19; *De sensu rerum*, p. 16.

148. Domingo de Soto, *De iustitia et iure libri decem* (Antwerp: Nutium, 1569), f. 10r: 'Homo aliter in suum finem tendit quam bruta, utpote qui se in finem libere movet per eius cognitionem, rationis ductu; bruta autem nulla se ratione agunt, sed aguntur naturali instinctu: ergo homo non movetur lege naturae, sed tantum bruta'. On Soto's justification of the human use of animals, considered both in relation to Aquinas and Campanella see Muratori, 'The Aristotelian Carnivore'.

149. Domingo de Soto, *De iustitia et iure*, f. 10v.

150. Merio Scattola, 'Naturrecht als Rechtstheorie: die Systematisierung der "res scholastica" in der Naturrechtslehre des Domingo de Soto', in *Die Ordnung der Praxis: neue Studien zur Spanischen Spätscholastik*, ed. by Frank Grunert & Kurt Seelmann (Tübingen: Max Niemeyer Verlag, 2001), pp. 21–47 (p. 22).

151. Aristotle stated that plants are made for animals, and animals for humans: *Politics*, 1256b16–20 (in *The Complete Works of Aristotle*, ed. by Barnes, II, 1992): 'In like manner we may infer that, after

the birth of animals, plants exist for their sake, and that the other animals exist for the sake of man, the tame for use and food, the wild, if not all, at least the greater part of them, for food, and for the provision of clothing and various instruments'. See on this also Mario Vegetti, *Il coltello e lo stilo* (Milan: Il Saggiatore, 1996), p. 192.

152. Thomas Aquinas, *Summa contra gentiles*, trans. by Vernon J. Bourke and others (New York: Hanover House, 1955–57), III, 87 (Chapter XXII.7–8). Cf. the Latin text in Thomas Aquinas, *Summa contra Gentiles*, in *Opera omnia iussu edita Leonis XIII P.M.*, vol. 14 (Rome: Garroni, 1926), p. 53: 'Sunt ergo elementa propter corpora mixta; haec vero propter viventia; in quibus plantae sunt propter animalia; animalia vero propter hominem. Homo igitur est finis totius generationis'.

153. Cf. Aristotle, *Politics*, 1265b15–20.

154. Campanella, *Del senso delle cose*, pp. 97–98; *De sensu rerum*, p. 94.

155. Campanella, *Del senso delle cose*, p. 97: 'in ogni cosa trovasi la fuga e odio della morte e amor della vita'. *De sensu rerum*, p. 93: 'Atque in omnibus fugam odiumque mortis amoremque vitae comperimus'.

156. Campanella, *Del senso delle cose*, p. 105: 'Hanno pur le pietre e le piante senso, ma rispetto alle belve paiono insensate'. *De sensu rerum*, p. 102.

157. Campanella, *Del senso delle cose*, p. 105: 'l'ostraga, rispetto all'elefante, par che non sia animale'. *De sensu rerum*, p. 102.

158. Campanella, *Metaphysica*, Part 3, p. 130^b (Book XIV.1), 'anima tenuis substantia est per nervos discurrens'. On this passage see Guido Giglioni, 'Life and its Animal Boundaries: Ethical Implications in Early Modern Theories of Human Animation', in *Ethical Perspectives on Animals*, ed. by Dohm & Muratori, pp. 110–37 (p. 125).

159. Campanella, *Del senso delle cose*, p. 77: 'Vero è che molti animali hanno più senso che memoria, e così tra gli uomini, e son quelli che hanno lo spirito sottile assai e caldo, li quali subito percipeno la passione d'ogni cosa'. *De sensu rerum*, p. 75.

160. On the pathological ways in which the spirit can be affected see Guido Giglioni, 'La magia e i poteri dell'immaginazione', in *I vincoli della natura: magia e stregoneria nel Rinascimento*, ed. by Germana Ernst & Guido Giglioni (Rome: Carocci, 2012), pp. 63–78 (pp. 74–75). Cf. the conception of 'spirit' according to Telesio: spirit is heat enclosed in a body (Telesio, *De rerum natura*, ed. by De Franco, II, 570 (Book VI.20)). I investigate the physical paradoxes deriving from this conception in 'Of Rivers Changing their Course and of Animals Born in Foundries: Paradoxes in Telesio's Natural Philosophy', in *Sense, Affect and Self-preservation in Bernardino Telesio (1509–1588)*, ed. by Guido Giglioni & Jill Kraye (Berlin: Springer, forthcoming).

161. Campanella, *Del senso delle cose*, p. 12: 'E tutti quelli animali che hanno spirito sciolto dentro le cavità, hanno memoria e discorso; e non le piante, per essere ottuso'. *De sensu rerum*, p. 9.

162. See Campanella, *Del senso delle cose*, p. 85: 'Che tutti gli animali sentano, nessuno dubita'. *De sensu rerum*, p. 83.

163. Campanella, *Del senso delle cose*, p. 3: 'Or se gli animali, per consenso universale, hanno sentimento, e da niente il senso non nasce, è forza dire che sentano gli elementi'. *De sensu rerum*, p. 1.

164. Campanella, *Del senso delle cose*, p. 3: 'Sente dunque il cielo e la terra e il mondo'.

165. Campanella, *Metaphysica*, Part 1, p. 49 (Book I.6, art. 2): 'omnia entia participio sensus praedita aliquo esse: proptereaque suo quodam naturali modo sentire, si servari debeant'.

166. See, for example, Campanella, *Del senso delle cose*, p. 103; *De sensu rerum*, p. 99.

167. Giglioni, 'Life and its Animal Boundaries', p. 112.

168. Tommaso Campanella, *Delle virtù e dei vizi in particolare (Inediti theologicorum liber X)*, ed. by Romano Amerio, 4 vols (Rome: Centro internazionale di studi umanistici, 1976–88), III, 44.

169. Campanella, *De homine*, I, 12: 'Vidimus enim quod omnium rerum est aliquis finis, plantarum videlicet ut vescantur bestiae, bestiarum altera alteri est finis: omnes tamen sunt propter homines ad utilitatem vel exercitium'.

170. Augustine of Hippo, *Contra Faustum*, VI.4, in *Corpus scriptorum ecclesiasticorum latinorum*, XXV.1, ed. by Zycha, p. 288. Cf. de Soto, *De iustitia et iure*, f. 137v. On this see also Muratori, 'The Aristotelian Carnivore'.

171. Hosius, *Confessio catholicae fidei Christiana*, f. 149r: 'Nam si quicquid vivit occidendum non est, vivunt et herbae, vivunt et plantae. Non ergo fas fuerit virgultum vellere, aut herbis etiam vesci'.

172. Campanella, *Del senso delle cose*, p. 21: 'Ma io pur vidi che mangia la calamita e si nutrica di limatura di ferro, come di suo simile men perfetto; e così l'uomo mangia gli animali'. *De sensu rerum*, p. 18.

173. Lina Bolzoni, 'Conoscenza e piacere: l'influenza di Telesio su teorie e pratiche letterarie tra cinque e seicento', in *Bernardino Telesio e la cultura napoletana*, ed. by Raffaele Sirri & Maurizio Torrini (Naples: Guida, 1992), pp. 203–39 (pp. 237–38).

174. Campanella, *Del senso delle cose*, p. 96; and see *De sensu rerum*, p. 93: 'et cibum omnia quaeritare, ut enim servet vitam lupus occidit pecudes, omniaque animalia innocentia. Pecus occidit herbas et plantas, aliaque animalia; homo vero omnia in sui commoditatem'.

175. Francesco Pucci and Fausto Sozzini, *De statu primi hominis ante lapsum disputatio*, ed. by Mario Biagioni (Rome: Edizioni di storia e letteratura, 2010), p. 89 (Sozzini: 'Fausti Socini copiosa refutatio'): 'quamvis illis Deus tamquam instrumentis utatur ad vitam in inferioribus aut gignendam aut propagandam, sicut etiam cibis, id est rebus mortuis'. For a detailed discussion of this topic in the *Disputatio* between Sozzini and Pucci see Cecilia Muratori, '"Inter hominem & bruta nulla est similitudo": die Bestimmung der Grenze zwischen Mensch und Tier in *De statu primi hominis ante lapsum disputatio*', in *Religiöser Nonkonformismus und Frühneuzeitliche Gelehrtenkultur: akademische Netzwerke und Formen praktizierter Toleranz*, ed. by Friedrich Vollhardt (Berlin: Akademie Verlag, 2013), pp. 127–47; and 'La caduta dell'uomo e la sofferenza degli animali nella Disputatio tra Francesco Pucci e Fausto Sozzini', *Bruniana & Campanelliana*, 17.1 (2011), 139–49.

176. Cf. Pucci and Sozzini, *De statu primi hominis ante lapsum disputatio*, p. 9 (Pucci: 'Francisci Puccii Florentini argumenta decem pro immortalitate rerum'), and p. 41 (Pucci: 'Confutatio dogmatis de mortalitate rerum').

177. Ibid., p. 23 (Sozzini: 'Responsio Fausti Socini'): 'An non tota humana corporis fabrica cibo ad eius conservationem opus fuisse manifeste arguit? Cur enim ventriculum, cur iecur et venas, cur intestina habuisset si concoqui et digeri ad ipsius nutritionem, crassioribus et inutilibus partibus expulsis, cibus in eo non debuisset?'.

178. Ibid., p. 33 (Pucci: 'Confutatio dogmatis de mortalitate rerum'): 'Nam semina, fructus, et herbae sensu carent, et tamen tantum abest ut illa mutatio sit in illis appellanda mors, ut sit potius eorum vita, et id potissimum videntur expetere, cum laetissima se offerunt edentibus'. On this see also Biagioni's introduction, ibid., p. xxvi.

179. Ibid., p. 34: 'Nam sicut nos sine huius vitae detrimento barbam et capillum nobis tonderi patimur, sic herbae et plantae ab animantibus tondebantur, nec aliquid tamen simile morti illis contingebat'.

180. The poet Percy Bysshe Shelley will go as far as stating that meat-eating *was* the Fall: 'A Vindication of Natural Diet', in *Selected Poetry, Prose and Letters*, ed. by A. S. B. Glover (London: Nonesuch Press, 1951), pp. 900–14 (p. 900): 'I hold that the depravity of the physical and moral nature of man originated in his unnatural habits of life. [...] The allegory of Adam and Eve eating of the tree of evil, and entailing upon their posterity the wrath of God, and the loss of everlasting life, admits of no other explanation, than the disease and crime that have flowed from unnatural diet'.

181. Pucci and Sozzini, *Disputatio*, p. 78 (Sozzini: 'Fausti Socini copiosa refutatio'): 'Ergo, si tibi credendum est, ante hominis lapsum, non licebat caepas, allia, pastinacas, raphanos, daucos, napos et id genus permultas herbas, quarum praecipuus in cibis usus in radice consistit, eradicare et earum radicibus vesci'.

182. Ibid., p. 76 (Sozzini: 'Fausti Socini copiosa refutatio'): 'Certe Francisce, si herbarum gemitus exaudire posses, cum interdum ad usum animantium radicitus extirpantur et convelluntur aut discerpuntur ac quodammodo dilaniantur, non ita diceres'.

183. Ibid., p. 43 (Pucci: 'Confutatio dogmatis de mortalitate rerum'): 'bestiae ante peccatum non vorabant se invicem, ut nunc videmus, sed habebant herbas et semina, quibus vescebantur, quae terra earum mater abunde subministrabat'.

184. Ibid. (Pucci: 'Confutatio dogmatis de mortalitate rerum'): 'vides habitas fuisse a piis immundas eas quae non permanserunt in fide et in primo instituto creatoris, mundas vero eas quae primo cibo contentae fuerunt, nempe herbis, oleribus et seminibus, ut oves, boves, caprae, columbae, anseres et similes'.

185. Campanella, *Delle virtù e dei vizi*, III, 44: 'Deus autem prohibuit sanguinem, non solum ne crudum edamus, sed quoniam *anima* (ait) *est in sanguine*, et brutorum affectibus noluit communicare, ut dixi in Magia. Sed coctum sumere nil prohibet, cum spiritus totus abscedat'. The biblical passage to which Campanella is referring is Leviticus 17: 14.

186. Campanella, *Delle virtù e dei vizi*, III, 44: 'Habemus a Deo declarationem iuris naturae in Gen. I et 9, ubi olera prius, deinde omne quod movetur dat nobis in cibum'.

187. Tommaso Campanella, *Ethica — Quaestiones super ethicam*, ed by Germana Ernst in collaboration with Olivia Catanorchi (Pisa: Scuola Normale Superiore, 2011), pp. 188–89.

188. I am considering here only the specific issue of killing for food. Campanella is careful to underline that 'ius naturale' is not equivalent to animal justice, and that therefore humans and animals are not to be considered on the same level in this respect: for instance, incest is against 'natural right', but not against 'animal justice' ('iustum animale'). See Campanella, *Delle virtù e dei vizi*, III, 34.

189. Campanella, *Metaphysica*, Part 3, p. 131^{a-b} (Book XIV.2). On this understanding of human dominion see Giglioni, 'Life and its Animal Boundaries', p. 127.

190. Campanella, *Delle virtù e dei vizi*, III, 52: 'Nec etiam animalia, quia non est factor eorum, sed tantum iuxta Dei concessionem ad cibum et defensam, et ne sibi noceant'.

191. Campanella, *Del senso delle cose*, p. 93: 'l'uomo fra poco tempo tutti gli animali vince, e si veste de loro pelli e magna le loro carni, e li doma e cavalca, e s'arma delle loro armi, usa la lor forza come sua'; *De sensu rerum*, pp. 89–90.

192. See on this see Jean-Louis Fournel, 'Nuovo Mondo', in *Enciclopedia Bruniana & Campanelliana*, ed. by Eugenio Canone & Germana Ernst (Pisa & Rome: Serra, 2006–), I, 291–303. See also Miriam Eliav-Feldon's definition of 'utopia' as 'an invitation to perceive the distance between things as they are and things as they should be': *Realistic Utopias: The Ideal Imaginary Societies of the Renaissance 1516–1630* (Oxford: Clarendon Press, 1982), p. 1.

193. Campanella, *De sensu rerum*, 'Epistola dedicatoria', sig. aiii^{v}: 'Civitas Solis, per me delineata, ac per Te aedificanda'.

194. See Tommaso Campanella, *Secunda delineatio defensionum*, in Luigi Firpo, *I processi di Tommaso Campanella*, ed. by E. Canone (Rome: Salerno Editrice, 1998), p. 178: 'Poëtae scripserunt de saeculo aureo, quod concupierunt; philosophi de statu optimae reipublicae, quem videre desiderantes non potuerunt; prophetae de reaedificata Ierusalem in tranquillitate et pace et gloria, quorum promissa non sunt visa'. The *Secunda delineatio* formed the first sketch of the later *Articuli prophetales*.

195. Ibid., p. 180: ' "Leo comedet paleam" [...] "Pascentur lupi cum agnis" '.

196. See Firpo's introduction in Tommaso Campanella, *La città del Sole*, ed. by Luigi Firpo, new ed. by Germana Ernst & Laura Salvetti Firpo (Rome & Bari: Laterza, 1997), pp. xxxv–xxxvi. See also Campanella's answer to art. 1.6 in the *Quaestio quarta de optima republica*, in *Philosophia realis* (Paris: Houssaye, 1637), p. 103 ('Pars secunda, epilogistica'): 'Dico hanc Rempublicam et seculum aureum ab omnibus desiderari, et peti a Deo, ut fiat voluntas eius in terra sicut in caelo'. See also Jean-Louis Fournel, 'Pensare la comunità di Campanella: utopia, politica e filologia', *Bruniana & Campanelliana*, 23.2 (2017), 619–27.

197. Tommaso Campanella, *Le Poesie*, ed. by Francesco Giancotti (Milan: Bompiani, 2013), p. 432: 'nec timeant agnive lupum, aut armenta leonem'.

198. Campanella, *Quaestio quarta de optima republica*, p. 102: 'si ad tam exactam reipublicae ideam pervenire non possumus, haud propterea superflui sumus, dum exemplum ponimus imitandum quantum possumus'. Quoted also in Jean-Louis Fournel, 'Dalla *Città del Sole* ai territori degli uomini: utopia e universalismo imperiale', in *Laboratorio Campanella: biografia, contesti, iniziative in corso*, ed. by Germana Ernst & Caterina Fiorani (Rome: 'L'Erma' di Bretschneider, 2007), pp. 163–76 (p. 163).

199. See Muratori, 'Real Animals in Ideal Cities', pp. 227–29. Campanella praises More's *Utopia* in *Quaestio quarta de optima republica*, p. 101.

200. Thomas More, *Utopia*, in *The Complete Works of St. Thomas More*, 15 vols (New Haven, CT, & London: Yale University Press, 1963–97), IV (ed. by Edward Surtz & J. H. Hexter), 139.

201. Ibid.: 'Ex pecudum laniena didicimus et homines iugulare'.

202. On the lack of slaves see Campanella, *La città del Sole*, p. 23. On sparing the useful animals see ibid., p. 37: 'Non però uccidono volentieri l'animali fruttuosi, come bovi e cavalli'.

203. Campanella, *Delle virtù e dei vizi in particolare*, I, 60: 'At sunt et aliae artes, quae speciem mali habent, non tamen sunt malae, sicut carnificum, venatorum et histrionum'.

204. Ibid.: 'nec pisces mactantur semper nisi sola extractione ab aqua'.

205. Campanella, *La città del Sole*, p. 32.

206. More, *Utopia*, p. 171 (original Latin text, p. 170: 'Utopienses totum hoc venandi exercitium, ut rem liberis indignam, in lanios [...] reiecerunt. [...] quam spectandae neci libidinem in ipsis etiam bestiis, aut ab animi crudelis affectu censent exoriri, aut in crudelitatem denique, assiduo tam efferae voluptatis usu defluere').

207. Campanella, *La città del Sole*, p. 37.

208. Campanella, *Del senso delle cose*, pp. 105–06: 'Parlai con un dotto fiorentino che credeva, come pur Macometto par che senta, le belve dover risuscitare a gloria con l'uomo. [...] Poi dicendo io ch'era bestialità credere che le mosche e pulici e zanzare avessero a risuscitare in gloria [...] et egli cominciò a discredere quella sentenza bestiale in favore delle bestie'; *De sensu rerum*, p. 102: 'Asserebat Florentinus vir consumptus in Theologicis, quo cum disserui olim, bestias omnes in fine seculi, sicut homines resuscitatum iri ad praemium, vel poenam. [...] Cumque replicarem, stultum esse putare muscas, cimices, ostreas, resuscitatum iri [...]. Tunc Florentinus a sua belluina sententia in favorem belluarum recedere coepit'. Writing to Sozzini, Pucci claimed that, since the animals followed Adam in his fall (even if they had not sinned themselves), they will also partake in his salvation: Pucci and Sozzini, *Disputatio*, p. 45 (Pucci: 'Confutatio dogmatis de mortalitate rerum'). With reference to St Paul, Pucci claims that there will be a 'liberation of all creatures in the final restitution of all things' ('liberatio[] omnium creaturarum in ultima restitutione omnium', ibid., p. 44). For the identification of Pucci as the 'dotto fiorentino' see Ernst, 'L'analogia e la differenza', p. 216.

209. Campanella, *La città del Sole*, p. 37.

210. On the formal structure of an early modern *disputatio*, and the subdivision of roles it implied, see Hanspeter Marti, 'Disputation', in *Historisches Wörterbuch der Rhetorik*, ed. by Gert Ueding, 12 vols (Tübingen: Niemeyer, 1994), II, cols. 866–80.

211. Anton Günther Heshusius ['Praeses'] and Michael Bohn ['Respondens'], *Dogma pythagoricum de abstinentia carnium* (Leipzig: Hahnius, 1668), § 43 (unpaginated): 'Quo enim modo bruta dici possunt rationalia? *At*, inquiunt, *unus est spiritus, qui instar animae totum mundum pervadit, nosque brutis unit*. Nego vero et hoc suppositum. Id enim si verum esset, qua ratione herbis aut oleribus ipsi vescerentur impune?'. The reference here is to the view presented in the Preface by Adam Olearius (1603–71) to Johann Albrecht von Mandelslo (1616–44), *Voyages celebres et remarquables faits de Perse aux Indes Orientales*, 2 vols (Leiden: Pierre Van der Aa, 1719), I, sig. ³★2v: 'Mais ces bons Philosophes n'étoient fondez que sur ce faux principe, *Est unus spiritus, qui instar animae totum mundum pervadit, et nos brutis unit* [...]. Mais si ce dogme est recevable, il s'ensuivra aussi qu'ils n'oseront manger ni plantes, ni herbes, ni aucune sorte de fruits, parce que cet esprit universel nous unit aussi-bien à eux qu'aux bêtes'. For an overview of seventeenth-century *disputationes* on the topic of the animal soul see Reimund B. Sdzuj, 'Zum Cartesianismus am Bremer *Gymnasium illustre*: Johann Eberhard Schwelings Dissertation *De anima brutorum* (1676)', in *Frühneuzeitliche Disputationen: polyvalente Produktionsapparate gelehrten Wissens*, ed. by Marion Gindhart, Hanspeter Marti, & Robert Seidel (Cologne, Weimar, & Vienna: Böhlau, 2016), pp. 179–98.

212. Heshusius and Bohn, *Dogma pythagoricum de abstinentia carnium*, §§ 47 & 51.

213. Campanella, *Delle virtù e vizi*, III, 12–14. See also *Quaestio quarta de optima republica*, p. 102, on choosing a 'via media'.

214. Campanella, *Ethica*, p. 62: 'Ex hoc vitio orta est anthropophagia et indifferens usus ciborum, cum natura nulla in similem prorsus agat, ut nec calor in calorem, nec ex dissimilibus nutriatur'.

215. Campanella, *Canzone seconda della medesima salmodia, Madrigale v*, in *Le Poesie*, p. 205: 'come d'erbe e di bruti uccisi per mia cena | non curo il mal, né a supplicanti vermi dentro a me nati do farvor, ma pena | [...] così Dio non sol pare che s'affermi | che del mal nostro pietade nol punga / ma ch'egli sembri il tutto'. Translations are my own, but cf. Tommaso Campanella,

Selected Philosophical Poems, ed. by Sherry Roush (Chicago & London: University of Chicago Press, 2011), p. 157. On the metaphor of the worms in the cheese, or in the belly, see Cecilia Muratori, 'Come vermi nel formaggio: la distinzione tra uomo e animali in una metafora Campanelliana', *Bruniana & Campanelliana*, 21.2 (2015), 381–94.

216. Campanella, *Le Poesie*, p. 205: 'E che Dio sia tutto, e gode che dentro a lui si mutino senza annullarsi le cose'.

217. Campanella, *La città del Sole*, p. 36: 'Essi dicono che prima bisogna mirar la vita del tutto e poi delle parti'.

218. Ibid., p. 37: 'una fiata mangiano carne, una pesce e una erbe, e poi tornano alla carne per circolo, per non gravare né estenuare la natura'.

219. Campanella, *Ethica*, p. 62: 'ergo animalium mobilium et immobilium partes meliores sunt nobis esca, non ‹autem humanae carnes nostrae speciei, nec› tellus et fimus, nec oppositae naturae plantae et bestiae, quae propterea vel veneno vel difficultate et depravatione nos afficiunt, ut in *Medicina* docebimus'. On this aspect see the discussion of the principle that 'like nourishes like' in Chapter 2, sections 2 & 3, above.

220. See Campanella, *Delle virtù e vizi*, III, 44, where Campanella leaves the possibility open for a special juridical justification ('epichéia') of the anthropophagic practice attributed to the Americans.

221. Ibid., p. 38: 'et sic potest praelatus et subditus interpretari, ut si iubet lex non manducare carnem in sabbato, et tu non habes alium cibum, non tenet lex, alioquin fame perires, quod est eius fini contrarium'.

222. Campanella, *Ethica*, p. 62: 'cibos praescribit solidiores illis, qui corpus exercent; tenuiores iis, qui ingenium'.

223. Ibid., p. 61: 'Quoniam cibo ac potu, tamquam naturalibus remediis contra mortem, vita humana stat primum, non eorum fruitio, sed usus medicinalis requiritur'.

224. Tommaso Campanella, *Lettere [1591–1639]*, ed. by Germana Ernst on the basis of unpublished preparatory materials by Luigi Firpo, in collaboration with Laura Salvetti Firpo & Matteo Salvetti (Florence: Olschki, 2010), p. 336 (n. 90): 'Gaudeo iterum quod nebulas Aristotelis excusseris, sed quod Epicureas veluti caecias ad te traxeris, non satis placet'.

225. Ibid., p. 338 (n. 91): 'Praeterea mundi constructio et animalium et plantarum, et partium usus et vis et notio satis superque declarant Virtutem hanc primam, quam vocamus Deum. Et nulla res est, quae non maxime ipsam manifestet'.

226. See Pierre Gassendi, *Epistolae*, in *Opera omnia in sex tomos divisa*, 6 vols (Lyon: Anisson, 1658), VI, 48[a], 54[a-b], 56[a]–57[a], 75[b]. Campanella, *Lettere*, pp. 335–39. See also Joseph Bourgerel, *Vie de Pierre Gassendi* (Paris: Vincent, 1737), pp. 104, 111, & 157; and on Gassendi's meeting Campanella at the house of Nicolas-Claude Fabri de Peiresc see pp. 144–45. Gassendi was invited to Peiresc's home in Aix to meet Campanella: Ernst, *Tommaso Campanella: The Book and the Body of Nature*, p. 242. On the correspondence between Campanella and Gassendi, see Germana Ernst, 'Atomes, Providence, signes célestes: le dialogue épistolaire entre Campanella et Gassendi', in *Gassendi et la modernité*, ed. by Sylvie Taussig (Turnhout: Brepols, 2008), pp. 61–82.

227. Gassendi, *Exercitationes paradoxicae adversus Aristoteleos* (Amsterdam: Elzevir, 1649), sig. [2]*4r: 'Brutis rationem restituo: Intellectum, Fantasiamque nullo discerno discrimine'. On Gassendi's anti-Aristotelianism see Barry Brundell, *Pierre Gassendi: From Aristotelianism to a New Natural Philosophy* (Dordrecht & Boston: Reidel, 1987), esp. pp. 98–99 on the *Exercitationes*. See also José R. Maia Neto, *Academic Skepticism in Seventeenth-century French Philosophy: The Charronian Legacy 1601–1662* (Berlin: Springer, 2014), p. 46 ff. On Gassendi's conception of the animal soul see Sylvia Murr, 'L'Âme des bêtes chez Gassendi', *Corpus — Revue de Philosophie*, 16–17 (1991), 37–63.

228. See Lisa Sarasohn, *Gassendi's Ethics: Freedom in a Mechanistic Universe* (Ithaca, NY, & London: Cornell University Press, 1996), p. 51, and also pp. 13–14. On his reasons for abandoning this project see Saul Fisher, *Pierre Gassendi's Philosophy and Science: Atomism for Empiricists* (Leiden: Brill, 2005), p. 5.

229. Gassendi, *Syntagma philosophicum*, Part 2, in *Opera omnia*, II, 522[b]–523[a].

230. Gassendi neither used Feliciano's translation (Porphyry, *De abstinentia ab esu animalium* (1547), pp. 22r–24v), nor Ficino's paraphrase.

231. Gassendi, *Syntagma philosophicum*, Part 3, in *Opera omnia*, II, pp. 725^a–735^b: 'Quae virtus et quanta boni sit vivere parvo'. This is a quotation from Horace, *Satires* II.2. See this section also in Pierre Gassendi, *Animadversiones in decimum librum Diogenis Laertii: qui est De vita, moribus, placitisque Epicuri*, 2 vols (Lyon: Guillaume Barbier, 1649), II, part 3 (*Ethics*), 1399–1420. With the exception of the incipit, the end, and the occasional Greek reference, the text was reprinted in the posthumously published *Syntagma philosophicum*. The actual quotation from Porphyry embraces pp. 730^a–732^b in the *Syntagma philosophicum* in the 1658 *Opera omnia* edition, vol. II. For a comment on this section of Gassendi's *Ethics* see Sarasohn, *Gassendi's Ethics*, p. 66, who points out that 'the striving for happiness or pleasure, even if it temporarily brings pain, raises man above the other animate beings, who lack the capacity of forethought'.

232. Gassendi, *Syntagma philosophicum*, Part 3, p. 733^a, states that diseases often derive from excess of food, or from bad food.

233. Gassendi, *Philosophiae Epicuri syntagma* (in *Opera omnia*, III, p. 75^b): 'quo minus probari carnium usus potest, qui sane potius officit sanitati, quam ad illam profit'. See *OA*, 1.52.1. See also Gassendi, *Syntagma philosophicum*, Part 3, p. 731^b: 'Ad haec vero neque ad sanitatem carnium usus confert; quin potius illi officit'.

234. See *OA*, 1.48.4. Gassendi, *Syntagma philosophicum*, Part 3, p. 730^b: 'Heinc illi quidem, qui carnibus vescitur, opus etiam est inanimis rebus, at illi, cui sunt res inanimae satis, dimidio solum opus est, ac ipso quidem tum facile parabili, tum ad apparandum modicis sumptibus egente'. Cf. *Philosophiae Epicuri Syntagma*, p. 75^b.

235. Gassendi, *Philosophiae Epicuri Syntagma*, p. 76^b: 'Ego certe, ut de me ipso, verecunde licet, pergam dicere, ipsis hortulorum plantaribus contentus, et laetus iis sum'.

236. The work was completed in 1634, but published only in 1647: Brundell, *Pierre Gassendi*, p. 48.

237. Pierre Gassendi, *De vita et moribus Epicuri libri octo* (Lyon: Barbier, 1647), p. 154. See Diogenes Laertius, *Lives of Eminent Philosophers*, X.11. The quotation from Porphyry is taken from *OA*, 1.48.3.

238. Pierre Gassendi, letter to Jan Baptist van Helmont (10 July 1629), in *Epistolae*, pp. 22^b-23^b.

239. See the story of a meat-eating sheep recounted by Gassendi in ibid., p. 23^a. Giglioni discusses this letter to van Helmont, and this argument in particular, in 'Life and its Animal Boundaries', pp. 114–23 (this chapter includes translations of key passages). On Gassendi and vegetarianism see also Stuart, *The Bloodless Revolution*, pp. 138–50.

240. Gassendi, letter to Jan Baptist van Helmont (10 July 1629), in *Epistolae* p. 20^{a-b}. See Plutarch, *On the Eating of Flesh* I, 995a (*Moralia*, XII, 550–51).

241. Gassendi, letter to Jan Baptist van Helmont (10 July 1629), in *Epistolae*, p. 21^a.

242. Ibid., p. 23^b.

243. Bourgerel, *Vie de Gassendi*, p. 431. Bourgerel devotes a substantial section (pp. 45–57) to the discussion of Gassendi's letter to van Helmont, including large extracts in translation.

244. On Sorbière see Lorenzo Bianchi, 'Sorbière's Scepticism'.

245. Samuel Sorbière, *Dissertatio de vita ac moribus Petri Gassendi*, in Pierre Gassendi, *Syntagma philosophiae Epicuri* (Amsterdam: Jansson-Waesberge, 1684), sigs. ^{2}★1r–^{6}★2v (sig. ^{4}★1r-v).

246. Emily Michael instead believes that 'Gassendi, who was influenced in the development of his moral theory by Epicurus, was, as was Epicurus, a vegetarian' ('Vegetarianism and Virtue: On Gassendi's Epicurean Defense', *Between the Species*, 7 (1991), 61–72 (p. 61)). I think the evidence from Gassendi's own work and from the biographies does not support this statement.

247. Porphyry's presentation of Epicureanism is discussed by Osborne, *Dumb Beasts and Dead Philosophers*, pp. 228–29.

EPILOGUE

❖

Abstinence: Veganism, Vegetarianism, or Moderation

In 1548, Ortensio Lando published a collection of letters by women.[1] One deals with the issue of abstinence from eating meat, and almost appears to be the reversal of Porphyry's address to Firmus. While Porphyry's composition of *On Abstinence* was prompted by hearing that his friend Firmus had reverted to carnivorism, the author of this letter, Camilla Pallavicini, writes to her addressee, Lucia, because she had heard that the latter reproached her for having turned to what Camilla calls 'a Carthusian life'.[2] The intent of Camilla's letter is thus that of a defence from accusations that the meatless diet, such as the one adopted by the Carthusians, is unsuitable to sustain human life.

Against Lucia's opinion 'that without that food [i.e. meat]' she could not keep herself alive, Camilla briefly summarizes a long series of arguments. Most of these have been discussed in this book.[3] The most important aspect of this text, however, and the reason for turning to it here in the Epilogue, is that it exemplifies the blurred contours of Renaissance abstinence. Whereas modern vocabulary carefully distinguishes between different diets that exclude consumption of animals — veganism (where all animal products, including milk, eggs, and honey, are avoided), vegetarianism (abstinence from meat and fish), or the pescatorian diet (meat is excluded, but fish is not) — Renaissance debates show a certain fluidity.[4] 'Abstinence' (*abstinentia*) can be used to label any of these dietetic strands. Camilla's first example is the Golden Age, 'when nobody ate meat, and yet they lived long and healthier lives'.[5] She then mentions the classical example of ancient veganism: the account of the diet of the Egyptian priests by the Stoic Chaeremon (1st century AD). As reported by Jerome, Chaeremon had claimed: 'What should I say [...] about birds, since they [i.e. the ancient priests of Egypt] abstain from egg, too, as if it were meat, and from milk? They claimed that the former was liquid meat, the latter blood with a changed colour'.[6] Camilla explains that the Egyptian priests refused all these foods as part of their dedication to the cult of the divine.[7] The next example is that of the Indian Brahmans, who abstained from meat (the source here is Eusebius's *Praeparatio evangelica*, as discussed in Chapter 3).[8] As a final piece of evidence in favour of the 'Carthusian life', Camilla mentions Herodotus's description of tribes of Babylonians that abstained from meat, but not from fish.[9] Camilla's position thus centres on the exclusion of meat, with the vegan and pescatorian options also belonging on the same spectrum. In her final appeal to Lucia, Camilla encourages her to turn herself to the diet that excludes meat, too, 'at least in imitation of the wise Fathers who refrained from it [i.e. meat] as something of little benefit (if not damaging)'.[10]

In another letter of the same collection, Margherita Zaffarda recommends to Leonora Vertema that she should not eat meat every day, to recover from her illness. Margherita's authority here is Porphyry, who, in line with Pythagoras and other 'ancient philosophers', 'detested eating animals'.[11] In this case, it is not complete abstinence that is endorsed, but moderation in the consumption of this food, and the selection of only certain types of meat.

The principle of moderation is frequently key in Renaissance discussions of vegetarianism. If there is one leitmotif in the vast material that forms the contours of Renaissance vegetarianism, it is that moderation in meat-eating is very often preferred to absolute abstinence. The most outspoken advocate of vegetarianism in the period, Gassendi, is no exception, in that he practiced moderation, while at the same time approving Porphyry's advocacy of a meat-less diet.[12] Even in the case of the Carthusians, selected by Camilla Pallavicini as the model of a vegetarian life, abstinence had blurred contours (fish at least was included), as was discussed in Chapter 2.

The stark opposition between carnivores and vegetarians often fades in Renaissance philosophical debates for and against vegetarianism, especially when the philosophers' own dietary practices are taken into account. Scrutinizing the plate of a philosopher is more than just a gossipy pleasure in this case, as Porphyry was perhaps the first to state in unequivocal terms: it is a touchstone for testing the translation of philosophical convictions into practice. A philosopher eats (or at least should eat) according to his or her view of the universe, and of the human being's position in it. Among the philosophers who engaged with Porphyry's appeal in detail, as for instance some of the prominent figures in this book — Ficino, Cardano, Campanella, and Gassendi — moderation prevailed over embracing vegetarianism. Together with Leonardo's and Zorzi's rejection of meat-eating, one of the clearest professions of vegetarianism comes not from a philosopher, but is spoken through the persona of a woman in Lando's collection of letters: she does not seek to convince with philosophical arguments, but simply lists a variety of sources and asks her interlocutor to side with authority, rather than engage in philosophical discussion.

For Porphyry, the diet of the philosopher required complete abstinence, not just moderation. Despite attracting widespread sympathy, Porphyry's *On Abstinence*, which remains the most comprehensive philosophical treatment of vegetarianism even today, seems not to have been particularly successful in convincing Renaissance philosophers to become vegetarian. The case of Gassendi is exemplary of the ambivalence of Porphyry's legacy in the Renaissance: assent to Porphyry's arguments is rarely accompanied by adherence to his dietetic guidelines.[13]

The total effect of Porphyry's claim appears to be fragmented in the reception. Porphyry refused to separate the health-benefits he saw in vegetarianism from a holistic vision of the vegetarian diet as a means of care for the body and the soul at the same time. He conceived his arguments as deeply interrelated, whether he addressed bloodshed during sacrifice, or the dangers of meat for physical health, or again the proofs of animal rationality. In the Renaissance reception, on the other hand, these strands are often considered separately, or in selected combinations.[14] A linked factor is the advance in various fields of knowledge since Porphyry's time. The intersection of different orders of arguments — drawn from psychology, medicine, anatomy, and religion — further contributed to blur the contours of what 'vegetarianism' meant. And finally, the emergence of new questions, such as regarding the sustainability of human civilization (as addressed in utopian literature, including *The City of the Sun*), further contribute to change the setting in which Porphyry's appeal is echoed, contested, and debated.

What is at stake in the Renaissance afterlives of *On Abstinence* that this book has explored is the meaning of vegetarianism, specifically as a philosophical diet. The role of the philosopher, too, changed, between Porphyry's time and the Renaissance: for Porphyry, the ascetic aspect of abstinence, and its practical realization, played a more central role than for his Renaissance sympathizers, such as Cardano or Gassendi. As Pierre Hadot has remarked, for a Platonist like Poprhyry, 'abstract theory is not considered to be true knowledge'.[15] With reference to *On Abstinence* (1.29.1–2), Hadot shows that for Porphyry contemplation needs to be fulfilled in life:

> We must, [Porphyry] tells us, undertake two exercises (*meletai*): in the first place, we must turn our thought away from all that is mortal and material. Secondly, we must return toward the activity of the Intellect. The first stage of these Neoplatonic exercises includes aspects which are highly ascetic, in the modern sense of the word: a vegetarian diet, among other things.[16]

Practical changes to one's own life, such as adherence to vegetarianism, support the philosopher's turn towards contemplation by providing philosophical discipline for contact with the outer world. It is logical that it was in religion, and specifically in the Carthusian order, that the vegetarian appeal found a fertile soil — that is to say, in a context in which the ascetic ideal was still prominent. This is shown exemplarily by Camilla's letter, in which she labels as the 'Carthusian life' what ancient philosophers and sages had called abstinence from eating animals. But it is worth noting that in the *Commentario delle più notabili et mostruose cose d'Italia e altri luoghi* [Commentary on the Most Notable and Marvellous Things in Italy and Other Places], Lando challenges the portrait of the Carthusian monks as embodying perfection: they might abstain from meat, but they also seem to live in an enclosed, comfortable bubble, enjoying refined vegeterian foods.[17]

It is possible that Porphyry's appeal to Firmus Castricius was successful, since in Porphyry's *The Life of Plotinus*, written around thirty years after *On Abstinence*, the portrait of Firmus is very favourable: Porphyry writes that, 'of all our contemporaries' Firmus was 'the greatest lover of beauty' and also a 'true brother'.[18] Renaissance philosophers, on the other hand, often remained torn between admiration for *On Abstinence* and the modulation of the vegetarian ideal on a varied argumentative terrain, between philosophical theory and philosophical practice, between the elaboration of new medical approaches and the appeal of ancient philosophical and hygienic discipline. As Gassendi puts it in his letter to Helmont, the vegetarian ideal still awaits realization in the future.

Notes to the Epilogue

1. The collection was published anonymously. On the identification of Lando as the author see Meredith K. Ray, *Writing Gender in Women's Letter Collections of the Italian Renaissance* (Toronto: University of Toronto Press, 2009), Chapter 2. Some of the women are historical figures, others are possibly invented by Lando. Ray calls the collection a case of 'epistolary ventriloquism', as the stylistic uniformity of the collection suggests, among other elements, that he was indeed the author (p. 45).

2. On Camilla Pallavicini see Francine Daenens, 'Donne valorose, eretiche, finte sante: note sull'antologia giolitiana del 1548', in *Per lettera: la scrittura epistolare femminile tra archivio e tipografia: secoli XV–XVII*, ed. by Gabriella Zarri (Rome: Viella, 1999), pp. 181–207 (p. 186). A translation of Boccaccio's *De mulieribus claris* was dedicated to Camilla Pallavicini in 1545.

3. Ortensio Lando, *Lettere di molte valorose donne* (Venice: Giolito, 1548), f. 158v: 'Ho inteso che mi biasimate molto ovunque vi ritrovate, per essermi posta a far la vita Ciartosina e al tutto rifiutare di mangiare la carne, e a voi pare che senza tal vivanda mantener in vita non mi possa'.

4. The word 'vegan' was coined in the mid-twentieth century (*OED*). It derives from the contraction of the term 'vegetarian'. Scaliger calls the eaters of fish 'piscivora', and in classifying birds according to their food, he uses the following terms: 'Carnivorae, piscivorae, frugivorae, herbivorae, vermivorae' (*Exotericae exercitationes*, f. 299v).

5. Lando, *Lettere di molte valorose donne*, f. 158v: 'nell'età dell'oro al tempo di Saturno non si mangiava da veruno carne, e pur vivevasi longamente e con maggior sanità'.

6. Chaeremon, 'Fragment 11' (Jerome, 'Adversus Iovinianum II.13') in *Chaeremon, Egyptian Priest and Stoic Philosopher. The Fragments Collected and Translated with Explanatory Notes*, ed. and trans. by Pieter Willem van der Horst (Brill: Leiden, 1984), pp. 22–23 (translation modified): ' "quid loquar", inquit, "de volatilibus, cum ovum quoque pro carnibus vitaverint et lac? quorum alterum carnes liquidas, alterum sanguinem esse dicebant colore mutato" '. All works by Chaeremon are now lost, and Porphyry is one of the main sources for reconstructing his thought (see ibid., pp. 12–23).

7. Lando, *Lettere di molte valorose donne*, f. 158v.

8. Lando discusses the vegetarian diets of the Egyptian priests and the Indian gymnosophists in *Sette libri de cathaloghi a varie cose appartenenti, non solo antiche ma anche moderne* (Giolito: Venice, 1552), f. 192v. See also f. 204r on Apollonius of Tyana, who abstained from wine and meat, and considered meat-eating to be brutish: meat might strengthen the body, but impedes the activity of the mind ('affermando esser cosa più tosto ferina che humana, e che la carne impediva le attioni dell'animo, quantunque desse forza al corpo').

9. Herodotus, *Histories*, trans. by David Grene (Chicago & London: University of Chicago Press, 1987), pp. 124–25 (Book 1.200): 'There are among them three tribes that eat nothing but fish. These fish, when caught, they dry in the sun and then throw them into a mortar, where they bray them with pestles and finally strain the result through muslin. Some of them who like it so make a kind of cake of this; others bake it like bread'.

10. Lando, *Lettere di molte valorose donne*, f. 159r: 'almeno per imitar i savi Padri che se ne guardavano come da cosa (se non dannosa) almeno poco giovevole'.

11. Ibid., f. 142v: 'Porphirio, mosso dalla Reverenda autorità de Pithagorici, e d'altri Antichi philosophanti, detestò il mangiare de gli animali'.

12. For a reflection on the historiographical and chronological borders of the 'Renaissance' see Muratori and Paganini, 'Renaissance and Early Modern Philosophy'.

13. On the gap between 'dietary advice' and 'actual consumption', see Gentilcore, *Food and Health in Early Modern Europe*, pp. 116–20.

14. Porphyry proceeds in *On Abstinence* by accumulating arguments, rather than constructing one linear chain of thought: see Clark in *OA*, p. 13.

15. Hadot, *Philosophy as a Way of Life*, p. 60.

16. Ibid., p. 100. See also Bidez, *Vie de Porphyre*, p. 99: 'Le vrai philosophe — dit Porphyre — , celui qui travaille à dégager son âme des liens de la matière, doit s'imposer l'abstinence de la viande; sinon, alourdissant son corps, stimulant ses appétits, il nuira à l'émancipation de son âme et à son

salut'. Catherine Osborne has pointed out that through vegetarianism the philosopher practices as strong a detachment from food as possible, *Dumb Beasts and Dead Philosophers*, p. 227: 'In a perfect world, philosophers would abstain from all food. This is not a perfect world, however, and vegetarianism is therefore merely a realistic second best: not an ideal, but a poor substitute for total detachment'.

17. Ortensio Lando, *Commentario delle più notabili et mostruose cose d'Italia e altri luoghi* (Venice: [n. pub.], 1548), ff. 33r–34r. See f. 33v: 'io non vedeva (lor dissi) qual cosa m'havesse a muovere a rendermi ciartosino, conciosia fusse che non ci vedessi quella perfettione qual mi dicevano, né vi conosceva sembianza alcuna della primitiva chiesa, voi habitate li dico agiatamente, a tal che molti principi vi portano invidia. [...] mangiate un pane che par fatto in paradiso, e quantunque (che si sappia) non gustiate carne, mancanvi però i saporiti intingoli, e i gratiosi manicaretti?'

18. *Neoplatonic Saints: The Lives of Plotinus and Proclus by their Students*, ed. and with an introduction by Mark Edwards (Liverpool: Liverpool University Press, 2000), p. 15. See also Bouffartigue and Patillon, 'Introduction', p. xx.

BIBLIOGRAPHY

❖

Primary Sources

ACOSTA, JOSÉ DE, *De natura novi orbis libri duo. Et de promulgatione Evangelii apud barbaros, sive de procuranda indorum salute, libri sex* (Cologne: Mylius, 1596)

AGRIPPA, HEINRICH CORNELIUS VON NETTESHEIM, *De occulta philosophia libri tres*, ed. by Vittoria Perrone Compagni (Leiden: Brill, 1992)

AMBROSE OF MILAN, *The Brahman Episode: St. Ambrose's Version of the Colloquy between Alexander the Great and the Brahmans of India, Edited from a Vatican Manuscript*, trans. by S. V. Yankowski (Ansbach: Wiedfeld & Mehl, 1962)

ANGHIERA, PETER MARTYR OF, *De orbe novo Decades 1: Oceana Decas*, ed. by Brigitte Gauvin (Paris: Les Belles Lettres, 2003)

ARISTOTLE, *The Complete Works*, trans. by Jonathan Barnes, 2 vols (Princeton: Princeton University Press, 1984)

AUGUSTINE OF HIPPO, *The City of God Against the Pagans*, ed. by Robert W. Dyson (Cambridge: Cambridge University Press, 1997)

——*Contra Adimantum*, in *Corpus scriptorum ecclesiasticorum latinorum*, ed. by Joseph Zycha (Prague, Vienna, & Leipzig: Tempsky & Freytag, 1891), XXV.I, 113–90

——*Contra Faustum*, in *Corpus scriptorum ecclesiasticorum latinorum*, ed. by Joseph Zycha (Prague, Vienna, & Leipzig: Tempsky & Freytag, 1891), XXV.I, 249–797

——*De civitate Dei*, in *Corpus scriptorum ecclesiasticorum latinorum*, ed. by Emanuel Hoffman (Prague, Vienna, & Leipzig: Tempsky & Freytag, 1899–1900), XL.I–2

——*Epistulae*, in *Corpus scriptorum ecclesiasticorum latinorum*, ed. by Alois Goldbacher (Prague, Vienna, & Leipzig: Tempsky & Freytag, 1898), XXXIV.2

Avisi particolari delle Indie di Portugallo ricevuti in questi doi anni del 1551 & 1552 (Rome: Dorico & Bressani, 1552)

BAILLET, ADRIEN, *La Vie de Monsieur Des-Cartes*, 2 vols (Paris: Horthemels, 1691)

BARROS, JOÃO DE, *Decada primeira da Asia* (Lisbon: Rodriguez, 1628)

BAYLE, PIERRE, *Dictionaire historique et critique*, 5th edn, 4 vols (Amsterdam: Brunel and others, 1740)

BENTHAM, JEREMY, *An Introduction to the Principles of Morals and Legislation* [1970], ed. by J. H. Burns & H. J. A. Hart (Oxford & New York: Oxford University Press, 1996)

BESSARION, BASIL, *De sacramento Eucharistiae*, in *Kardinal Bessarion als Theologe, Humanist und Staatsmann*, ed. by Ludwig Mohler, 3 vols (Paderborn: Schöningh, 1927; repr. 1967), III, 1–69

——*In calumniatorem Platonis*, in *Kardinal Bessarion als Theologe, Humanist und Staatsman*, ed. by Ludwig Mohler, 3 vols (Paderborn: Schöningh, 1927; repr. 1967), II

The Bible: Authorized King James Version, ed. by Robert Carroll and Stephen Prickett (Oxford & New York: Oxford University Press, 1998)

BÖHM, JOHANN, *Gli costumi, le leggi et l'usanze di tutte le genti, raccolte qui insieme da molti illustri scrittori*, trans. by Lucio Fauno (Venice: Tramezzino, 1542)

BOTERO, GIOVANNI, *Le relationi universali* (Venice: Angelieri, 1596)

BOULDUC, JACQUES, *De ecclesia ante legem libri tres, in quibus indicatur quis a mundi principio usque ad Moysen fuerit ordo Ecclesiae* (Lyon: Landry, 1626)

—— *De ecclesia post legem: liber analogicus nondum in lucem editus, in quo ostenditur quanta sit similitudo inter legem naturalem et legem evangelicam* (Paris: Cottereau, 1630)

—— *De oggio Christiano* (Lyon: Boissat & Anisson, 1640)

BOURGEREL, JOSEPH, *Vie de Pierre Gassendi* (Paris: Vincent, 1737)

BROCKIE, MARIANUS ['Praeses'], and FRIEDRICH B. STELLE ['Respondens'], *Tractatus philosophicus de anima brutorum quo asseritur illam esse materialem, sensu et perceptione contra cartesianos praeditam; cogitatione vero et ratiocinio adversus quosdam neotericos, destitutam* [...] (Erfurt: Werther, 1715)

BURTON, ROBERT, *The Anatomy of Melancholy*, ed. by J. N. Bamborough, 6 vols (Oxford: Clarendon Press, 2000)

CAMPANELLA, TOMMASO, *Atheismus triumphatus* (Rome: Zannetti, 1631)

—— *La città del Sole*, ed. by Luigi Firpo, new ed. by Germana Ernst and Laura Salvetti Firpo (Rome & Bari: Laterza, 1997)

—— *De homine* (*Inediti theologicorum liber IV*), ed. by Romano Amerio, 2 vols (Rome: Centro internazionale di studi umanistici, 1960–61)

—— *Del senso delle cose e della magia*, ed. by Germana Ernst (Rome & Bari: Laterza, 2002)

—— *De sensu rerum et magia* (Paris: Bechet, 1637)

—— *Delle virtù e dei vizi in particolare* (*Inediti theologicorum liber X*), ed. by Romano Amerio, 4 vols (Rome: Centro internazionale di studi umanistici, 1976–88)

—— *Epilogo magno (1598)*, ed. by Carmelo Ottaviano (Rome: Reale Accademia d'Italia, 1939)

—— *Ethica — Quaestiones super ethicam*, ed. by Germana Ernst in collaboration with Olivia Catanorchi (Pisa: Scuola Normale Superiore, 2011)

—— *Lettere [1591–1639]*, ed. by Germana Ernst on the basis of unpublished preparatory materials by Luigi Firpo, in collaboration with Laura Salvetti Firpo and Matteo Salvetti (Florence: Olschki, 2010)

—— *Philosophia realis* (Paris: Houssaye, 1637)

—— *Le Poesie*, ed. by Francesco Giancotti (Milan: Bompiani, 2013)

—— *Selected Philosophical Poems*, ed. and trans by Sherry Roush (Chicago & London: University of Chicago Press, 2011)

—— *Sintagma dei miei libri e sul corretto metodo di apprendere*, ed. by Germana Ernst (Pisa & Rome: Fabrizio Serra, 2007)

—— *Universalis philosophiae seu metaphysicarum rerum* [...] *libri 18* (Paris: D. Langlois, 1638)

CARDANO, GIROLAMO, *The Book of My Life*, trans. by Jean Stoner (New York: Dutton, 1930; repr. 2002)

—— *De libris propriis: The Editions of 1544, 1550, 1557, 1562 with Supplementary Material*, ed. by Ian Maclean (Milan: FrancoAngeli, 2004)

—— *De sanitate tuenda* (Rome: Zanetti, 1580)

—— *De sapientia*, ed. by Marco Bracali (Florence: Olschki, 2008)

—— *The 'De subtilitate'*, trans. by John M. Forrester, 2 vols (Tempe: Arizona Center for Medieval and Renaissance Studies, 2013)

—— *De uno / Sobre lo uno*, ed. by José Manuel García Valverde (Florence: Olschki, 2009)

—— *Opera omnia*, ed. by Charles Spon, 10 vols (Lyon: Jean-Antoine Huguetan & Marc-Antoine Ravaud, 1663; repr. 1966); in particular: *De vita propria* (I, 1–54); *De uno* (I, 277–83); *Hyperchen* (I, 284–92); *Proxeneta seu de prudentia civili* (I, 355–474); *De consolatione* (I, 588–636); *De utilitate ex adversis capienda* (II, 1–282); *Theonoston* I (II, 299–371); *Theonoston* II (II, 373–402); *Problemata naturalia* (II, 621–67); *De rerum varietate* (III, 1–351); *De subtilitate* (III, 353–672); *De sanitate tuenda* (VI, 8–294); *Contradicentia medicorum* (VI, 295–923); *In librum Hippocratis de alimento commentaria* (VII, 356–515); *In librum Hippocratis de aere, aquis, et locis commentarii* (VIII, 1–212); *Consilia medica* (IX, 47–236)

CASE, JOHN, *Speculum quaestionum moralium* (Frankfurt am Main: Basse, 1589)

CELSUS, *De la médecine*, ed. by Guy Serbat, 2nd edn (Paris: Les Belles Lettres, 2003)

CHAEREMON, *Chaeremon, Egyptian Priest and Stoic Philosopher: The Fragments Collected and Translated with Explanatory Notes*, ed. and trans. by Pieter Willem van der Horst (Leiden: Brill, 1984)

CICERO, *De officiis*, ed. and trans. by Walter Miller (Cambridge, MA, & London: Harvard University Press, 1913)

COLOMBO, CRISTOFORO, *Diario di bordo: libro della prima navigazione e scoperta delle Indie*, ed. by Gaetano Ferro (Milan: Mursia, 1985)

COLOMBO, CRISTOFORO, and OTHERS, *Prime relazioni di navigatori italiani sulla scoperta dell'America. Colombo — Vespucci — Verazzano*, ed. by Luigi Firpo (Turin: UTET, 1966)

Commentarii Collegii Conimbricensis Societatis Iesu, in octo libros Physicorum Aristotelis Stagiritae, 2 vols (Lyon: Buysson, 1594)

CORNARO, ALVISE, *Trattato della vita sobria* (Padua: Percacino, 1558)

——*Writings on the Sober Life: The Art and Grace of Living Long*, ed. and trans. by Hiroko Fudemoto (Toronto, Buffalo, & London: University of Toronto Press, 2014)

CORSALI, ANDREA, *Lettera di Andrea Corsali allo Illustrissimo Signore Duca Iuliano de Medici, Venuta Dell'India del Mese di Octobre Nel MDXVI* (Florence: Stefano di Carlo da Pavia, 1516)

DELLA PORTA, GIOVAN BATTISTA, *De humana physiognomonia libri sex / Della fisionomia dell'uomo*, ed. by Alfonso Paolella, 2 vols (Naples: Edizioni scientifiche italiane, 2011–13)

DESCARTES, RENÉ, *Œuvres*, ed. by Charles Adam & Paul Tannery, 12 vols (Paris: Cerf, 1897–1913)

DIOGENES LAERTIUS, *Lives of Eminent Philosophers*, trans. by R. D. Hicks, 2 vols (Cambridge, MA, & London: Harvard University Press & Heinemann, 1925)

——*Lives of Eminent Philosophers*, ed. by Tiziano Dorandi (Cambridge: Cambridge University Press, 2013)

DONI, ANTON FRANCESCO, *La Zucca, espurgata e corretta da Girolamo Giovannini da Capugnano* (Venice: Zanetti and Presegni, 1595)

EPICURUS, *Epicurea*, ed. by Hermann Usener (Leipzig: Teubner, 1887)

ERASMUS OF ROTTERDAM, *The Collected Works of Erasmus*, 89 vols (Toronto, Buffalo, & London: University of Toronto Press, 1974–)

——*Colloquies*, in *The Collected Works of Erasmus*, vols 39–40, trans. and annotated by Craig R. Thompson (Toronto, Buffalo, & London: University of Toronto Press, 1997)

——*Controversies*, in *The Collected Works of Erasmus*, vol. 73, ed. and trans. by Denis L. Drysdall (Toronto, Buffalo, & London: University of Toronto Press, 2015)

——*The Correspondence of Erasmus: Letters 1252 to 1355*, in *The Collected Works of Erasmus*, vol. 9, trans. by R. A. B. Mynors, annotated by James M. Estes (Toronto, Buffalo, & London: University of Toronto Press, 1989)

——*Epistola de delectu ciborum, cum scholiis per ipsum autorem recens additis* (Basel: Froben, 1532)

——*Opera omnia Desiderii Erasmi Roterodami*, ed. by C. Augustijn, 9 vols (Amsterdam: Brill, 1982)

EUSEBIUS OF CAESAREA, *De evangelica praeparatione*, trans. by George of Trebizond (Venice: Jenson, 1470)

FABRICI D'ACQUAPENDENTE, GIROLAMO, *De locutione / De brutorum loquela*, ed. by Stefano Gensini & Michela Tardella (Pisa: ETS, 2016)

FICINO, MARSILIO, *Commentaries on Plato*, ed. and trans. by Michael J. B. Allen, 2 vols (Cambridge, MA: Harvard University Press, 2008)

——*Commentarium in Convivium Platonis De Amore*, ed. by Pierre Laurens (Paris: Les Belles Lettres, 2002)

——*Commentarium in Epistolas Pauli*, ed. by Daniele Conti (Turin: Aragno, 2018)

——*De le tre vite*, trans. by Lucio Fauno (Venice: Michele Tramezzino, 1548)

—— *The Letters of Marsilio Ficino*, ed. and trans. by the Language Department of the School of Economic Science, 10 vols (London: Shepheard-Walwyn, 1975–)

——*Opera omnia*, 2 vols (Basel: Petri, 1576; reprint Turin: Bottega d'Erasmo, 1959)

——*Platonic Theology*, Latin text ed. by James Hankins & William Bowen and trans. by Michael J. B. Allen & John Warden, 6 vols (Cambridge, MA: Harvard University Press, 2001–06)

——*Predicationes*, ed. by Daniele Conti (Turin, Aragno, 2014)

——*Supplementum Ficinianum: Marsilii Ficini Florentini philosophi Platonici opuscula inedita et dispersa*, ed. by Paul Oskar Kristeller, 2 vols (Florence: L. S. Olschki, 1937)

——*Three Books on Life*, ed. by Carol V. Kaske & John R. Clark (Tempe: Arizona Center for Medieval and Renaissance Studies, 2002)

FRACANZIANO, ANTONIO, *In librum Hippocratis de alimento commentarius* (Venice: ex officina Marci de Maria Salernitani, 1566)

FRACASTORO, GIROLAMO, *Syphilis sive morbus gallicus* (Basel: Bebel, 1536)

FRANCK, SEBASTIAN, *Weltbuch: Spiegel und Bildtnis des gantzen Erdtbodens* (Ulm: Varnier, 1542)

FRANCO, NICCOLÒ, *Dialoghi piacevolissimi* (Venice: Salicato, 1590)

GALEN, *La dieta dimagrante*, ed. and trans. by Nino Marinone (Turin: Paravia, 1973)

——*On the Properties of Foodstuffs*, ed. and trans. by Owen Powell (Cambridge: Cambridge University Press, 2003)

——*Opera omnia*, ed. by Karl Gottlob Kühn, 20 vols (Leipzig: Cnobloch, 1821–33; repr. 2011)

——*Selected Works*, trans. by Peter N. Singer (Oxford & New York: Oxford University Press, 1997)

GASSENDI, PIERRE, *Animadversiones in decimum librum Diogenis Laertii: qui est De vita, moribus, placitisque Epicuri*, 2 vols (Lyon: Guillaume Barbier, 1649)

——*Exercitationes paradoxicae adversus Aristoteleos* (Amsterdam: Elzevir, 1649)

——*Opera omnia in sex tomos divisa*, 6 vols (Lyon: Anisson, 1658)

——*Syntagma philosophiae Epicuri* (Amsterdam: Jansson-Waesberge, 1684)

GELLI, GIOVAN BATTISTA, *La Circe* (Venice: Bonibelli, 1595)

GERSON, JEAN CHARLIER DE, *De non esu carnium apud Carthusienses*, in *Œuvres complètes*, ed. by Palémon Glorieux, 5 vols (Paris & New York: Desclée, 1960–73), III, 77–95

——*Opera omnia*, 5 vols in 4 (Antwerp: Sumptibus Societatis, 1706)

GIOVANNINI DA CAPUGNANO, GIROLAMO, *Discorso sopra tutti li parlari* [1604] (Venice: Barezzi, 1622)

GUIGUES IER PRIEUR DE CHARTREUSE, *Coutumes de Chartreuse, introduction, texte critique, traduction et notes par un Chartreux* (Paris: Éditions du Cerf, 1984)

HENNINGS, CHRISTIAN, *Geschichte von den Seelen der Menschen und Thiere* (Halle: Gebauer 1774)

HERMES TRISMEGISTOS, *Hermetica: The Greek Corpus Hermeticum and the Latin Asclepius in a New English Translation, with Notes and Introduction*, ed. by Brian Copenhaver (Cambridge: Cambridge University Press, 1992)

——*Il Pimandro di Mercurio Trismegisto*, trans. of Ficino's Latin text by Tommaso Benci (Florence: [Torrentino], 1549)

——*Pimander sive de potestate et sapientia Dei*, ed. by Maurizio Campanelli (Turin: Aragno, 2011)

HERODOTUS, *Histories*, trans. by David Grene (Chicago & London: University of Chicago Press, 1987)

HESHUSIUS, ANTON GÜNTHER ['Praeses'] and MICHAEL BOHN ['Respondens'], *Dogma pythagoricum de abstinentia carnium* (Leipzig: Hahnius, 1668)

HIPPOCRATES, *On Ancient Medicine*, ed. by Mark J. Schiefsky (Leiden: Brill, 2005)

HOSIUS, STANISLAV, *Opera omnia hactenus edita* (Venice: Nicolini, 1573)

IAMBLICHUS, *De mysteriis*, with an introduction by Stéphane Toussaint (Enghien-Les-Bains: Les Éditions du Miraval, 2006; facsimile edn of Venice: Aldus Manutius, 1497)

——*I misteri egiziani*, ed. by Angelo R. Sodano (Milan: Rusconi, 1984)

——*On the Mysteries*, ed. by Emma C. Clarke and others (Atlanta: Society of Biblical Literature, 2003)

——*On the Pythagorean Life*, ed. by Gillian Clark (Liverpool: Liverpool University Press, 1989)

——*Réponse à Porphyre (De mysteriis)*, ed. by Henri Dominique Saffrey & Alain-Philippe Segonds (Paris: Les Belles Lettres, 2013)

LANDO, ORTENSIO, *Commentario delle più notabili et mostruose cose d'Italia e altri luoghi* (Venice: [n. pub.], 1548)

——*Lettere di molte valorose donne* (Venice: Giolito, 1548)

——*Sette libri de cathaloghi a varie cose appartenenti, non solo antiche ma anche moderne* (Venice: Giolito, 1552)

[LANE, CHARLES], 'Flesh Diet (The Editor's Answer to Barbara's Letter)', Part 1: *The Healthian*, 5.1 (April 1842), 33–35; Part 2: *The Healthian*, 6.1 (May 1842), 42–44

LEONARDO DA VINCI, *Quaderni d'Anatomia*, ed. by Ove C. L. Vangensten, A. Fonahn, & H. Hopstock, 6 vols (Christiania: Jacob Dybwad, 1911–16)

——*The Notebooks*, ed. by Jean Paul Richter, 2 vols (New York: Dover Publications, 1970)

Libretto de tutta la navigatione de re de Spagna de le isole et terreni novamente trovati, ed. by Angelo Trevisan (Venice: [n. pub.], 1504; facsimile repr. with an introduction by Lawrence C. Wrote, 1929)

LICETI, FORTUNIO, *De feriis altricis animae nemeseticae disputationes* (Padua: Varisco, 1631)

'The Life of Plants' [anonymous], *British Quarterly Review*, 11.22 (February–May 1850), 336–55

'The Life of Plants' [anonymous], *The Vegetarian Messenger*, 3.41 (March 1853), 20–22

MANDELSLO, JOHANN ALBRECHT VON, *Voyages celebres et remarquables, faits de Perse aux Indes Orientales*, trans. by A. de Wicqufort, 2 vols (Leiden: Pierre Van der Aa, 1719)

MANDEVILLE, SIR JOHN, *The Book of Marvels and Travels*, trans. by Anthony Bale (Oxford & New York: Oxford University Press, 2012)

MANFREDI, GIROLAMO, *Liber de homine* (Bologna: Ruggeri & Bertocchi, 1474)

——*Liber de homine / Il Perché*, ed. by Fabio Foresti, Anna Maria Nada Patrone, & Anna Laura Trombetti Budriesi (Bologna: Luigi Parma, 1988)

MERSENNE, MARIN, *Harmonie universelle* (Paris: Cramoisy, 1636)

MEXÍA, PEDRO, *Della selva di varia lettione, di Pietro Messia, ampliate e di nuovo rivedute per Francesco Sansovino* (Venice: Polo, 1574)

——*Selva di varia lettione di Pietro Messia Spagnuolo, da lui divisa in tre parti, alle quali s'è aggiunta la quarta di Francesco Sansovino* (Venice: de' Cavalli, 1564)

MONTAIGNE, MICHEL DE, *Essais*, ed. by André Tournon, 3 vols (Paris: Imprimerie nationale, 1998)

MORE, THOMAS, *Utopia*, in *The Complete Works of St. Thomas More*, 15 vols (New Haven, CT, & London: Yale University Press, 1963–1997), IV (ed. by Edward Surtz & J. H. Hexter)

NAUDÉ, GABRIEL, and GUY PATIN, *Naudaeana et Patiniana* (Amsterdam: van der Plaats, 1703)

'Old Battles Fought Over Again' [anonymous], *The Vegetarian Messenger*, 3.41 (March 1853), 15–20

OVID, *Metamorphoses*, trans. by Frank Justus Miller, revised by G. P. Goold, 6 vols (Cambridge, MA: Harvard University Press, 1916)

PEREIRA, BENEDICTUS, *Commentariorum et disputationum in Genesim tomi quatuor*, 4 vols (Lyon: Iunta, 1594–1600)

PEREIRA, GÓMEZ, *Gómez Pereira's 'Antoniana Margarita': A Work on Natural Philosophy, Medicine and Theology*, ed. by José Manuel García-Valverde & Peter Maxwell-Stuart (Leiden: Brill, 2019)

PERSIO, ANTONIO, *Trattato dell'ingegno dell'huomo*, ed. by Luciano Artese, *Bruniana & Campanelliana*, Supplementi, Testi, 2 (Pisa & Rome: Serra, 1999)

PETIT, PIERRE, *De natura et moribus anthropophagorum dissertatio* (Utrecht: Rudolph Zyll, 1688)

PICO DELLA MIRANDOLA, GIOVANNI, *Conclusiones nongentae: le novecento tesi dell'anno 1486*, ed. by Albano Biondi (Florence: Olschki, 1995)

—— *Conclusioni cabalistiche*, ed. by Paolo Edoardo Fornaciari (Milan: Mimesis, 1994)

—— *De hominis dignitate, Heptaplus, De ente et uno, e scritti vari*, ed. by Eugenio Garin (Florence: Vallecchi, 1942)

PICO DELLA MIRANDOLA, GIOVANNI, and ARCANGELO DA BORGONOVO, *Cabalistarum selectiora obscurioraque dogmata, a Ioanne Pico ex eorum commentationibus pridem excerpta, et ab Archangelo Burgonovensi Minoritano nunc primum luculentissimis interpretationibus illustrata* (Venice: Franceschi, 1569)

PICTORIUS, GEORG [GEORG MAHLER], *Dialogi [...] del modo di conservare la sanità: nuovamente dalla lingua latina nella volgar italiana tradotto* (Venice: Bottega d'Erasmo di Vincenzo Valgrisi, 1550)

—— *Opera nova* (Basel: Petri, 1569)

PLATO, *Dialogues of Plato*, trans. by Benjamin Jowett, 4 vols (London & Oxford: Macmillan & Clarendon, 1871; repr. 2011)

PLEMP, VOPISCUS FORTUNATUS, *De togatorum valetudine tuenda commentatio* (Brussels: Foppens 1670)

PLETHON, GEORGIUS GEMISTHUS, *Peri on Aristoteles pros Platona diapheretai* (Venice: Scotus, 1540)

PLINY, *Natural history*, 10 vols, trans. by William H. S. Jones, Harris Rackham, & E. H. Warmington (Cambridge, MA: Harvard University Press; London: Heinemann, 1938–62)

PLOTINUS, *Enneads*, trans. by Stephen MacKenna, abridged with an Introduction and Notes by John Dillon (New York: Penguin, 1991)

PLUTARCH, *Moralia*, trans. by Frank Cole Babbitt and others, 15 vols (Cambridge, MA: Harvard University Press; London: Heinemann, 1928–2004)

POLIZIANO, ANGELO, *Lamia*, ed. by Ari Wesseling (Leiden: Brill, 1986)

POLO, MARCO, *Il milione: edizione del testo toscano ('Ottimo')*, ed. by Ruggero M. Ruggieri (Florence: Olschki, 1986)

PORPHYRY, *Against the Christians*, ed. by Robert M. Berchman (Leiden: Brill, 2005)

—— *De abstinentia ab esu animalium*, trans. by Giovanni Bernardo Feliciano (Venice: Gryphius, 1547)

—— *De l'abstinence*, ed. by Jean Bouffartigue and others, 3 vols (Paris: Les Belles Lettres, 1977–95)

—— *Lettre à Anébon l'Égyptien*, ed. by Henri Dominique Saffrey & Alain Segonds (Paris: Les Belles Lettres, 2012)

—— *The Life of Plotinus and the Order of His Books*, in Plotinus, *Enneads*, vol. 1, ed. by A. H. Armstrong (Cambridge, MA: Harvard University Press, 1969), pp. 1–87

—— *On Abstinence*, ed. by Gillian Clark (London & New York: Bloomsbury, 2000)

—— *Select Works of Porphyry, Containing His Four Books on Abstinence from Animal Food [...]*, trans. by Thomas Taylor (London: Thomas Rodd, 1823)

—— *Vie de Plotin: travaux préliminaires et index grec complet*, ed. by Luc Brisson and others, 2 vols (Paris: Vrin, 1982)

—— *Vie de Pythagore. Lettre à Marcella*, ed. by Edouard des Places (Paris: Les Belles Lettres, 1982)

——*Vita di Pitagora*, ed. by Angelo R. Sodano & Giuseppe Girgenti (Milan: Rusconi, 1998)

PORPHYRY, and OTHERS, *Neoplatonic Saints: The Lives of Plotinus and Proclus by their Students*, ed. by Mark Edwards (Liverpool: Liverpool University Press, 2000)

PUCCI, FRANCESCO, and FAUSTO SOZZINI, *De statu primi hominis ante lapsum disputatio*, ed. by Mario Biagioni (Rome: Edizioni di storia e letteratura, 2010)

RAMUSIO, GIOVANNI BATTISTA, *Navigazioni e viaggi*, ed. by Marica Milanesi, 6 vols (Turin: Einaudi, 1978–88)

RANGONI, TOMMASO, *De vita hominis ultra CXX annos protrahenda* (Venice: [Comin da Trino?], 1550)

RENZI, SALVATORE DE, ed., *Collectio Salernitana ossia documenti inediti, e trattati di medicina appartenenti alla scuola medica Salernitana*, 5 vols (Naples: Filiatre-Sebezio, 1852–59)

RORARIO, GIROLAMO, *Quod animalia bruta ratione utantur melius homine* (Paris: Cramoisy, 1648)

SCALIGER, JULIUS CAESAR, *Commentarii et animadversiones in sex libros de causis plantarum Theophrasti* (Lyon: Apud Ioannem Crispinum, 1566)

——*Exotericarum exercitationum liber XV de subtilitate, ad Hieronymum Cardanum* (Paris: Vascosan, 1557)

——*In libros de plantis Aristoteli inscriptos commentarii* (Lyon: Rovillius, 1566)

SENECA, *Ad Lucilium Epistulae Morales*, ed. by L. D. Reynolds, 2 vols (Oxford: Oxford University Press, 1965)

——*Selected Letters*, ed. by Elaine Fantham (Oxford & New York: Oxford University Press, 2010)

SENNERT, DANIEL, *Practica medicina*, 6 vols (Wittemberg: Mevius, 1648–54)

SHELLEY, PERCY BYSSHE, 'A Vindication of Natural Diet', in *Selected Poetry, Prose and Letters*, ed. by A. S. B. Glover (London: Nonesuch Press, 1951), pp. 900–14

SORBIÈRE, SAMUEL, *Dissertatio de vita ac moribus Petri Gassendi*, in Pierre Gassendi, *Syntagma philosophiae Epicuri* (Amsterdam: Jansson-Waesberge, 1684), sigs. ²★1r–⁶★2v

SOTO, DOMINGO DE, *De iustitia et iure libri decem* (Antwerp: Nutium, 1569)

STADEN, HANS, *Hans Staden's True History: An Account of Cannibal Captivity in Brazil*, ed. and trans. by Neil L. Whitehead & Michael Harbsmeier (Durham, NC: Duke University Press, 2008)

TELESIO, BERNARDINO, *De rerum natura iuxta propria principia*, ed. by Luigi De Franco, 3 vols (Cosenza: Casa del libro; Florence: La Nuova Italia, 1965–76)

——*De rerum natura iuxta propria principia, liber primus, et secundus, denuo editi (Naples 1570) / Opuscula (Naples 1570)*, anastatic copy of the exemplar in the Biblioteca nazionale di Napoli, with an introduction and index by Roberto Bondì (Rome: Carocci, 2013)

——*De rerum natura iuxta propria principia libri ix (Naples 1586)*, anastatic copy with an introduction and index by Guido Giglioni (Rome: Carocci, 2013)

—— *Varii de naturalibus rebus libelli*, ed. by Luigi De Franco (Florence: La Nuova Italia, 1981)

TERTULLIAN, *Apology*, trans. by Gerald H. Rendall (Cambridge, MA: Harvard University Press; London: Heinemann, 1931)

THEOPHRASTUS OF ERESUS, *Commentary 5: Sources on Biology (Human Physiology, Living Creatures, Botany: Texts 328–435)*, ed. by Robert W. Sharples (Leiden: Brill, 1995)

——*Commentary 6. 1: Sources on Ethics*, ed. by William W. Fortenbaugh, with Contributions on the Arabic Material by Dimitri Gutas (Leiden: Brill, 2011)

THOMAS AQUINAS, *Summa contra gentiles*, in *Opera omnia iussu edita Leonis XIII P.M.*, vol. 14 (Rome: Garroni, 1926)

——*Summa contra gentiles*, trans. by Vernon J. Burke and others (New York: Hanover House, 1955–57)

TREBIZOND, GEORGE OF, *Comparatio philosophorum Platonis et Aristotelis* (Venice: Penzio, 1523; facsimile edn Frankfurt am Main: Minerva, 1975)

Valla, Lorenzo, *Le postille all''Institutio Oratoria' di Quintiliano*, ed. by Lucia Cesarini Martinelli & Alessandro Perosa (Padua: Antenore, 1996)

Vanini, Giulio Cesare, *Tutte le opere*, ed. by Francesco Paolo Raimondi, Luigi Crudo, & Mario Carparelli (Milan: Bompiani, 2010)

Vasari, Giorgio, *Lives of the Artists*, trans. by Julia Conaway Bondanella & Peter Bondanella (Oxford & New York: Oxford University Press, 2008)

'Vegetarian Intelligence' [anonymous], *The Vegetarian Advocate*, 5 (December 1848), 60–64

Vergil, Polydore [Polidoro Virgili], *On Discovery*, ed. by Brian P. Copenhaver (Cambridge, MA: Harvard University Press, 2002)

Vespucci, Amerigo, *Il mondo nuovo di Amerigo Vespucci: Vespucci autentico e apocrifo*, ed. by Marco Pozzi (Milan: Serra e Riva, 1984)

Vettori, Piero, *Variarum lectionum libri xxv* (Florence: Torrentino, 1553)

Villanova, Arnau de, *De esu carnium*, in *Opera medica omnia*, 16 vols (Granada & Barcelona: Publicacions de la Universitat de Barcelona, 1975–), xi, ed. by Dianne M. Bazell

—— *Opera utilissima di Arnaldo di Villanuova* (Venice: Michele Tramezzino, 1549)

Vincent of Beauvais, *Speculum maius*, 4 vols (Venice: Nicolini, 1591)

Voltaire, *Les Œuvres complètes* (Oxford: Voltaire Foundation, 1968–)

Vossius, Gerardus Joannes, *De origine ac progressu idolatriae* (Frankfurt: Wächtler, 1668)

Willis, Thomas, *De anima brutorum quae hominis vitalis ac sensitiva est, exercitationes duae* (London: Wells & Scott, 1672)

Zorzi, Francesco, *L'armonia del mondo / De harmonia mundi*, ed. by Saverio Campanini (Milan: Bompiani, 2010)

—— *L'elegante poema e commento sopra il poema*, ed. by Jean-François Maillard (Milan: Archè, 1991)

Secondary Sources

Abbattista, Guido, 'Trophying Human "Otherness": From Christopher Columbus to Contemporary Ethno-ecology (Fifteenth–Twenty First Centuries)', in *Encountering Otherness: Diversities and Transcultural Experiences in Early Modern European Culture*, ed. by Guido Abbattista (Trieste: Edizioni Università di Trieste, 2011), pp. 19–41

Addey, Crystal, *Divination and Theurgy in Neoplatonism* (Farnham: Ashgate, 2014)

Agrimi, Jole, *Poteri carismatici e informali: chiesa e società medioevale* (Palermo: Sellerio, 1992)

Albala, Ken, *Eating Right in the Renaissance* (Berkeley, Los Angeles, & London: University of California Press, 2002)

Alden, John, ed., *European Americana: A Chronological Guide to Works Printed in Europe Relating to the Americas 1493–1776*, 6 vols (New York: Readex Books, 1980–88)

Allen, Michael J. B., 'Marsilio Ficino', in *Interpreting Proclus From Antiquity to the Renaissance*, ed. by Stephen Gersh (Cambridge: Cambridge University Press, 2014), pp. 353–79

—— *Plato's Third Eye: Studies in Marsilio Ficino's Metaphysics and its Sources* (Farnham: Ashgate, 1995)

—— 'Pythagoras in the Early Renaissance', in *A History of Pythagoreanism*, ed. by Carl A. Huffman (Cambridge: Cambridge University Press 2014), pp. 532–43

—— 'Summoning Plotinus: Ficino, Smoke and the Strangled Chickens,' in *Reconsidering the Renaissance: Papers from the Twenty-first Annual Conference of the Center for Medieval and Early Renaissance Studies*, ed. by Mario A. Di Cesare (Binghamton, NY: Medieval and Renaissance Texts and Studies, 1992), pp. 63–88

Armstrong, Susan J., and Richard G. Botzler, eds, *The Animal Ethics Reader*, 3rd edn (Abingdon: Routledge, 2017)

Avramescu, Cătălin, *An Intellectual History of Cannibalism*, trans. by Alistair Ian Blyth (Princeton: Princeton University Press, 2009; originally published as *Filozoful Crud: O Istorie a Canibalismului* (Bucharest: Humanitas, 2003))

BANDRÉS, JAVIER, and RAFAEL LLAVONA, 'Minds and Machines in Renaissance Spain: Gómez Pereira's Theory of Animal Behavior', *Journal of the History of Behavioral Sciences*, 28 (1992), 158–68

BANNER, NICHOLAS, *Philosophic Silence and the 'One' in Plotinus* (Cambridge: Cambridge University Press, 2018)

BARNES, JONATHAN, *The Presocratic Philosophers* (London & New York: Routledge, 1979)

BARTOLUCCI, GUIDO, 'Marsilio Ficino, Eusebio di Cesarea e un trattato sulle religioni degli Antichi', *Accademia*, 9 (2007), 37–55

BIANCHI, LORENZO, 'Rorario tra Naudé e Bayle', in *Bruniana & Campanelliana*, 17.1 (2011), 175–84

—— 'Sorbière's Scepticism: Between Naturalism and Absolutism', in *The Return of Scepticism: From Hobbes and Descartes to Bayle*, ed. by Gianni Paganini (Berlin: Springer, 2003), pp. 267–82

BIDEZ, JOSEPH, *Vie de Porphyre, le philosophe néo-platonicien* (Ghent & Leipzig: van Goethe & Teuber, 1913)

BIRNBACHER, DIETER, *Naturalness: Is the 'Natural' Preferable to the 'Artificial'?*, trans. by David Carus (Lanham, MD: University Press of America, 2014; originally published as *Natürlichkeit* (Berlin: De Gruyter, 2006))

BLACK, CROFTON, *Pico's 'Heptaplus' and Biblical Hermeneutics* (Leiden: Brill, 2006)

BOLZONI, LINA, 'Conoscenza e piacere: l'influenza di Telesio su teorie e pratiche letterarie tra cinque e seicento', in *Bernardino Telesio e la cultura napoletana*, ed. by Raffaele Sirri & Maurizio Torrini (Naples: Guida, 1992), pp. 203–39

BONDÌ, ROBERTO, *Introduzione a Telesio* (Rome & Bari: Laterza, 1997)

BORLIK, TODD A., *Ecocriticism and Early Modern English Literature: Green Pastures* (London & New York: Routledge, 2011)

BOTTIGLIERI, NICOLA, *Nel verde mare delle tenebre: viaggi reali e immaginari nei secoli XIV e XV* (Rome: Edizioni Associate, 1994)

BOUFFARTIGUE, JEAN, and MICHEL PATILLON, 'Introduction', in Porphyry, *De l'abstinence*, ed. by Jean Bouffartigue and others, 3 vols (Paris: Les Belles Lettres, 1977–95), I, xi–lxxxiv

BRUNDELL, BARRY, *Pierre Gassendi: From Aristotelianism to a New Natural Philosophy* (Dordrecht & Boston: Reidel, 1987)

BURKERT, WALTER, *Homo necans: Interpretationen altgriechischer Opferriten und Mythen* (Berlin: De Gruyter, 1972)

BYNUM, CAROLINE WALKER, *Holy Feast and Holy Fast: The Religious Significance of Food to Medieval Women* (Berkeley: University of California Press, 1987)

CABRAS, PIER LUIGI, DONATELLA LIPPI, and FRANCESCA LOVARI, *Due millenni di melancholia: una storia della depressione* (Bologna: CLUEB, 2005)

CAMPANELLI, MAURIZIO, 'Marsilio Ficino's Portrait of Hermes Trismegistus and its Afterlife', *Intellectual History Review*, 29.1 (2019), 53–71

CAMPANINI, SAVERIO, 'Francesco Giorgio's Criticism of the *Vulgata*: Hebraica Veritas or Mendosa Traductio?', in *Hebrew to Latin, Latin to Hebrew: The Mirroring of Two Cultures in the Age of Humanism*, ed. by Giulio Busi (Turin: Aragno, 2006), pp. 206–31

—— 'Pici Mirandulensis bibliotheca cabbalistica Latina: sulle traduzioni latine di opere cabbalistiche eseguite da Flavio Mitridate per Pico della Mirandola', *Materia Giudaica*, 7.1 (2002), 90–96

—— 'A Sefirotic Tree from a Miscellany of Christian Kabbalistic Texts', *Manuscripts hébreux et arabes*, 38 (2014), 387–401

—— 'Ein unbekannter Kommentar zum "Hohelied" aus der kabbalistischen Schule von Francesco Zorzi: Edition und Kommentar', in *Erzählende Vernunft*, ed. by Günter Frank, Anja Hallacker, & Sebastian Lalla (Berlin: Akademie Verlag, 2006), pp. 265–81

CAMPORESI, PIERO, *Bread of Dreams: Food and Fantasy in Early Modern Europe*, trans. by David Gentilcore (Cambridge: Polity Press; Chicago: University of Chicago Press, 1989; originally published as *Il pane selvaggio* (Bologna: Il Mulino, 1980))

CANZIANI, GUIDO, ' "Nihil est quod sapientia ipsa efficere nequeat": Cardano e la magia', *Bruniana & Campanelliana*, 16.2 (2010), 439–50

CARPENTER, AMBER, 'Eating Your Own: Exploring Conceptual Space for Moral Restraint', in *Ethical Perspectives on Animals in the Renaissance and Early Modern Period*, ed. by Burkhard Dohm & Cecilia Muratori, Micrologus' Library, 55 (Florence: SISMEL, Edizioni del Galluzzo, 2013), pp. 21–45

CARRÉ, ANTÒNIA, and LLUÍS CIFUENTES, 'Girolamo Manfredi's *Il Perché*: I. The *Problemata* and its Medieval Tradition', *Medicina & Storia*, 10.19–20 (2010), 13–38

CAVALLINI, CONCETTA, 'La Description de l'animal sauvage dans les *Navigationi e Viaggi* de Giovanni Battista Ramusio', in *L'Animal sauvage à la Renaissance (Colloque international organisé par la Société française d'étude du XVIe siècle et Cambridge French Colloquia, Cambridge, 3–6 septembre 2004)*, ed. by Philip Ford (Cambridge: Cambridge French Colloquia, 2007), pp. 345–56

CAVALLO, SANDRA, and TESSA STOREY, *Healthy Living in Late Renaissance Italy* (Oxford & New York: Oxford University Press, 2013)

CAVARERO, ADRIANA, *A più voci: filosofia dell'espressione vocale* (Milan: Feltrinelli, 2003)

CELENZA, CHRISTOPHER S., ed., *Angelo Poliziano's 'Lamia': Text, Translation, and Introductory Studies* (Leiden: Brill, 2010)

——'Late Antiquity and Florentine Platonism: The "Post-Plotinian" Ficino', in *Marsilio Ficino: His Theology, His Philosophy, His Legacy*, ed. by Michael J. B. Allen & Valery Rees with Martin Davies (Leiden: Brill, 2002), pp. 71–97

——*Piety and Pythagoras in Renaissance Florence: The 'Symbolum Nesianum'* (Leiden: Brill, 2001)

——'Temi neopitagorici nel pensiero di Marsilio Ficino', in *Marsile Ficin ou les mystères platoniciens: Actes du XLIIe Colloque International d'Études Humanistes. Centre d'Études supérieures de la Renaissance. Tours, 7–10 juillet 1999*, ed. by Stéphane Toussaint, Les Cahiers de l'humanisme, 2 (Paris: Les Belles Lettres, 2002), pp. 57–70

CHERCHI, PAOLO, *Polimatia di riuso: mezzo secolo di plagio (1539–1589)* (Rome: Bulzoni, 1998)

CICALA, ROBERTO, and ANGELO L. STOPPA, eds, *L'umanista aronese Pietro martire d'Anghiera primo storico del 'nuovo mondo': Atti del convegno Arona 28 Ottobre 1990* (Novara: Interlinea edizioni, 1992)

CLARK, GILLIAN, 'Augustine's Porphyry and the Universal Way of Salvation', in *Studies on Porphyry*, ed. by George Karamanolis & Anne Sheppard (London: Institute of Classical Studies, University of London, 2007), pp. 127–40

——'The Fathers and the Animals: The Rule of Reason?', in *Animals on the Agenda*, ed. by Andrew Linzey & Dorothy Yamamoto (London: SCM Press, 1998), pp. 67–79

——'Fattening the Soul: Christian Asceticism and Porphyry's *On Abstinence*', *Studia Patristica*, 35 (2001), 41–51

——'Introduction', in *On Abstinence*, ed. by Gillian Clark (London & New York: Bloomsbury, 2000), pp. 1–28

——'Philosophic Lives and the Philosophic Life', in *Greek Biography and Panegyric in Late Antiquity*, ed. by Tomas Hägg & Philip Rousseau (Berkeley: University of California Press, 2000), pp. 29–51

CLARK, STUART, *Thinking with Demons: The Idea of Witchcraft in Early Modern Europe* (Oxford & New York: Oxford University Press, 1997)

CLARKE, EMMA, *Iamblichus' 'De Mysteriis': A Manifesto of the Miraculous* (Aldershot: Ashgate, 2011)

COPENHAVER, BRIAN, 'Giovanni Pico della Mirandola', in *The Stanford Encyclopedia of Philosophy* (Fall 2016 edition), ed. by Edward N. Zalta, <https://plato.stanford.edu/archives/fall2016/entries/pico-della-mirandola/>

CORRIGAN, KEVIN, 'Humans, Other Animals, Plants and the Question of the Good: The Platonic and Neoplatonic traditions', in *The Routledge Handbook of Neoplatonism*, ed. by Pauliina Remes & Svetla Slaveva-Griffin (Abingdon: Routledge, 2014), pp. 372–90

CORVAGLIA, LUIGI, *Le opere di Giulio Cesare Vanini e le loro fonti*, 2 vols (Milan: Società Editrice Dante Alighieri, 1933–34)

COTTINGHAM, JOHN, '"A Brute to the Brutes?": Descartes' Treatment of Animals', *Philosophy*, 53.206 (1978), 551–59

COUDERT, ALISON, 'The Ultimate Crime: Cannibalism in Early Modern Minds and Imaginations', in *Crime and Punishment in the Middle Ages and Early Modern Ages: Mental-historical Investigations of Basic Human Problems and Social Responses*, ed. by Albrecht Classen & Connie Scarborough (Berlin & Boston: De Gruyter, 2012), pp. 521–54

CRISCIANI, CHIARA, 'Premesse e promesse di lunga vita: tra teologia e pratica terapetica (secolo XIII)', in *Vita longa. Vecchiaia e durata della vita nella tradizione medica e aristotelica antica e medievale*, ed. by Chiara Crisciani, Luciana Repici, & Pietro B. Rossi, Micrologus' Library, 3 (Florence: SISMEL, Edizioni del Galluzzo, 2009), pp. 61–86

CRISCIANI, CHIARA, and GABRIELLA ZUCCOLIN, eds, *Michele Savonarola: medicina e cultura di corte* (Florence: SISMEL Edizioni del Galluzzo, 2011)

CRO, STELIO, 'Antiquity, America and the Noble Savage', in *The Classical Tradition and the Americas: European Images of the Americas*, ed. by Wolfgang Haase & Reinhold Meyer (Berlin: De Gruyter, 1994–), I.1, 379–418

—— *The Noble Savage: Allegory of Freedom* (Waterloo, ON: Wilfrid Laurier University Press, 1990)

CUNNINGHAM, ANDREW, 'Fabricius and the "Aristotle Project" in Anatomical Teaching and Resarch at Padua', in *The Medical Renaissance of the Sixteenth Century*, ed. by A. Wear, R. K. French, & I. M. Lonie (Cambridge: Cambridge University Press, 1985), pp. 195–222

CURTO, DIOGO RAMADA, ANGELO CATTANEO, and ANDRÉ FERRAND ALMEIDA, eds, *La cartografia europea tra primo Rinascimento e fine dell'Illuminismo: atti del convegno internazionale 'The Making of European Cartography'* (Florence: L. S. Olschki, 2003)

DAENENS, FRANCINE, 'Donne valorose, eretiche, finte sante: note sull'antologia giolitiana del 1548', in *Per lettera: la scrittura epistolare femminile tra archivio e tipografia: secoli XV–XVII*, ed. by Gabriella Zarri (Rome: Viella, 1999), pp. 181–207

DAVIES, SUREKHA, *Renaissance Ethnography and the Invention of the Human: New Worlds, Maps and Monsters* (Cambridge: Cambridge University Press, 2016)

DEL SOLDATO, EVA, 'Bramani e colori tra Ficino e Campanella', *Rinascimento*, 41 (2001), 315–25

DES CHENE, DENNIS, *Life's Form: Late Aristotelian Conceptions of the Soul* (New York: Cornell University Press, 2000)

—— *Physiologia: Natural Philosophy in Late Aristotelianism and Cartesian Thought* (Ithaca, NY, & London: Cornell University Press, 1996)

—— *Spirits and Clocks: Machine and Organism in Descartes* (Ithaca, NY: Cornell University Press, 2001)

DESAN, PHILIPPE, 'Le Simulacre du Nouveau Monde: à propos de la rencontre de Montaigne avec les Cannibales', *Montaigne Studies*, 22 (2010), 101–18

DIERAUER, URS, *Mensch und Tier im Denken der Antike: Studien zur Tierpsychologie, Anthropologie und Ethik* (Amsterdam: B. R. Grüner, 1977)

DOHM, BURKHARD, & CECILIA MURATORI, eds, *Ethical Perspectives on Animals in the Renaissance and Early Modern Period*, Micrologus' Library, 55 (Florence: SISMEL, Edizioni del Galluzzo, 2013)

——'Introduction', in *Ethical Perspectives on Animals in the Renaissance and Early Modern Period*, ed. by Burkhard Dohm & Cecilia Muratori, Micrologus' Library, 55 (Florence: SISMEL, Edizioni del Galluzzo, 2013), pp. 3–19

DOLS, MICHAEL W., 'Galen and Islamic Psychiatry', in *Le opere psicologiche di Galeno: Atti del terzo colloquio galenico internazionale, Pavia, 10–12 settembre 1986*, ed. by Paola Manuli & Mario Vegetti (Naples: Bibliopolis, 1988), pp. 243–80

DOMBROWSKI, DANIEL, *The Philosophy of Vegetarianism* (Amherst: University of Massachusetts Press, 1984)

DÖRRIE, HEINRICH, 'Kontroversen um die Seelenwanderung im kaiserzeitlichen Platonismus', *Hermes*, 85 (1957), 414–38

DURANTI, TOMMASO, *Mai sotto Saturno: Girolamo Manfredi, medico e astrologo* (Bologna: Clueb, 2008)

DURLING, RICHARD J., 'Galen in the Renaissance: A Chronological Census of Renaissance Editions and Translations of Galen,' *Journal of the Warburg and Courtauld Institutes*, 24.3–4 (1961), 230–305

EDWARDS, G. FAY, 'Irrational Animals in Porphyry's Logical Works: A Problem for the Consensus Interpretation of *On Abstinence*', *Phronesis*, 59.1 (2014), 22–43

——'The Purpose of Porphyry's Rational Animals: A Dialectical Attack on the Stoics in *On Abstinence from Animal Food*', in *Aristotle Re-Interpreted: New Findings on Seven Hundred Years of the Ancient Commentators*, ed. by Richard Sorabji (London & New York: Bloomsbury, 2016), pp. 263–89

——'The Puzzle of Porphyry's Rational Animals' (unpublished PhD thesis, King's College London, 2013)

——'Reincarnation, Rationality, and Temperance: Platonists on Not Eating Animals', in *Animals: A History*, ed. by Peter Adamson & G. Fay Edwards (Oxford & New York: Oxford University Press, 2018), pp. 27–55

EDWARDS, MARK J., 'Two Images of Pythagoras: Iamblichus and Porphyry', in *The Divine Iamblichus: Philosopher and Man of Gods*, ed. by Henry J. Blumenthal & E. Gillian Clark (Bristol: Bristol Classical Press, 1993), pp. 159–72

ELIAV-FELDON, MIRIAM, *Realistic Utopias: The Ideal Imaginary Societies of the Renaissance 1516–1630* (Oxford: Clarendon Press, 1982)

ERNST, GERMANA, 'L'analogia e la differenza: uomo e animali in Campanella', in *The Animal Soul and the Human Mind: Renaissance Debates*, ed. by Cecilia Muratori (Pisa & Rome: Serra, 2013), pp. 209–25

——'Atomes, Providence, signes célestes: le dialogue épistolaire entre Campanella et Gassendi', in *Gassendi et la modernité*, ed. by Sylvie Taussig (Turnhout: Brepols, 2008), pp. 61–82

——'"Nascosto in ciclopea caverna": natura e condizione umana in Campanella', in *Il neoplatonismo nel rinascimento*, ed. by Pietro Prini (Rome: Istituto della enciclopedia italiana, 1993), pp. 65–81

——'Sol libertà può farci forti, sagaci e lieti: comunità e libertà in Campanella', *MORUS — Utopia e Renascimento*, 8 (2012), 175–91

——'Tommaso Campanella', in *The Stanford Encyclopedia of Philosophy* (Fall 2014 edition), ed. by Edward N. Zalta, <https://plato.stanford.edu/archives/fall2014/entries/campanella/>

—— *Tommaso Campanella: The Book and the Body of Nature*, trans. by David L. Marshall (Berlin: Springer, 2010; originally published as *Tommaso Campanella: il libro e il corpo della natura* (Rome & Bari: Laterza, 2002))

FESTUGIÈRE, ANDRÉ-JEAN, *La Révélation d'Hermès Trismégiste*, 4 vols in 3 (Paris: Les Belles Lettres, 1981)

——'Sur une nouvelle édition du *De vita pythagorica* de Jamblique', *Revue des Études Grecques*, 50 (1937), 470–94

—— 'Une source hermétique de Porphyre: l'"Egyptien" du *De Abstinentia* (II, 47)', *Revue des Études Grecques*, 49 (1936), 586–95

FIRPO, LUIGI, *I processi di Tommaso Campanella*, ed. by E. Canone (Rome: Salerno Editrice, 1998)

FISHER, SAUL, *Pierre Gassendi's Philosophy and Science: Atomism for Empiricists* (Leiden: Brill, 2005)

FITZPATRICK, JOAN, ed., *Renaissance Food from Rabelais to Shakespeare: Culinary Readings and Culinary Histories* (London & New York: Routledge, 2016)

FLORIDI, LUCIANO, 'Scepticism and Animal Rationality: The Fortune of Chrysippus' Dog in the History of Western Thought', *Archiv für Geschichte der Philosophie*, 97.1 (1997), 27–57

FOER, JONATHAN SAFRAN, *Eating Animals* (New York: Little, Brown & Co., 2009)

FOURNEL, JEAN-LOUIS, 'Dalla *Città del Sole* ai territori degli uomini: utopia e universalismo imperiale', in *Laboratorio Campanella: biografia, contesti, iniziative in corso*, ed. by Germana Ernst & Caterina Fiorani (Rome: 'L'Erma' di Bretschneider, 2007), pp. 163–76

—— 'Nuovo Mondo', in *Enciclopedia Bruniana & Campanelliana*, ed. by Eugenio Canone & Germana Ernst (Pisa & Rome: Serra, 2006–), I, 291–303

—— 'Pensare la comunità di Campanella: utopia, politica e filologia', *Bruniana & Campanelliana*, 23.2 (2017), 619–27

FUDGE, ERICA, *Perceiving Animals: Humans and Beasts in Early Modern Culture* (Urbana & Chicago: University of Illinois Press, 2002)

FUMAGALLI BEONIO BROCCHIERI, MARIATERESA, *Pico della Mirandola* (Casale Monferrato, Alessandria: Piemme, 1999)

FUSCO, MARIA, 'Il linguaggio degli animali nel pensiero antico: una sintesi storica', *Studi filosofici*, 30 (2007), 17–44

GARIN, EUGENIO, *Giovanni Pico della Mirandola: vita e dottrina* (Florence: Le Monnier, 1937)

GARNSEY, PETER, *Food and Society in Classical Antiquity* (Cambridge: Cambridge University Press, 1999)

GARROD, RAPHAËLE, and OTHERS, *Logodaedalus: World Histories of Ingenuity in Early Modern Europe* (Pittsburgh, PA: Pittsburgh University Press, 2018)

GEMELLI MARCIANO, M. LAURA, 'The Pythagorean Way of Life and Pythagorean Ethics', in *A History of Pythagoreanism*, ed. by Carl A. Huffman (Cambridge: Cambridge University Press 2014), pp. 131–48

GENSINI, STEFANO, 'Il *De brutorum loquela* di Fabrici d'Acquapendente', *Bruniana & Campanelliana*, 17.1 (2011), 163–74

—— '"E io in Napoli vidi un cane polacco...": ancora sui linguaggi animali, da Gesner a Campanella', *Bruniana & Campanelliana*, 23.2 (2017), 639–49

—— 'Locutio in hominis fabrica: il contributo di Girolamo Fabrici d'Acquapendente', in *Traguardi e prospettive nelle scienze del linguaggio: riflessioni con Federico Albano Leoni*, ed. by Francesca M. Dovetto, Valeria Micillo, & Elda Morlicchio (Rome: Aracne, 2012), pp. 165–96

GENSINI, STEFANO, and MICHELA TARDELLA, 'Language in Humans and in Other Animals: Fabrici d'Acquapendente Between Medicine and Philosophy', *Theoria et Historia Scientiarum*, 13 (2016), 17–33

GENTILCORE, DAVID, *Food and Health in Early Modern Europe: Diet, Medicine and Society, 1450–1800* (London & New York: Bloomsbury, 2016)

GENTILE, SEBASTIANO, 'Sulle prime traduzioni dal greco di Marsilio Ficino', *Rinascimento*, 2nd ser., 40 (1990), 57–104

GENTILE, SEBASTIANO, SANDRA NICCOLI, and PAOLO VITI, eds, *Marsilio Ficino e il ritorno di Platone: mostra di manoscritti, stampe e documenti, 17 maggio-16 giugno 1984*, exhibition catalogue (Florence: Le Lettere, 1984)

GERBI, ANTONELLO, *Nature in the New World: From Christopher Columbus to Gonzalo Fernández de Oviedo*, trans. by Jeremy Moyle (Pittsburgh, PA: University of Pittsburgh

Press, 1985; originally published as *La natura delle Indie Nove: da Cristoforo Colombo a Gonzalo Fernández de Oviedo* (Milan: Riccardo Ricciardi, 1975))

GERSH, STEPHEN, 'Marsilio Ficino as Commentator on Plotinus: Some Case Studies', in *Plotinus' Legacy: The Transformation of Platonism from the Renaissance to the Modern Era*, ed. by Stephen Gersh (Cambridge: Cambridge University Press, 2019), pp. 19–43

GIELIS, MARCEL, 'Leuven Theologians as Opponents of Erasmus and of Humanistic Theology', in *Biblical Humanism and Scholasticism in the Age of Erasmus*, ed. by Erika Rummel (Leiden: Brill, 2008), pp. 197–214

GIGLIONI, GUIDO, 'The First of the Moderns or the Last of the Ancients? Bernardino Telesio and Sentience', *Bruniana & Campanelliana*, 16.1 (2010), 69–87

——'Girolamo [Geronimo] Cardano', in *The Stanford Encyclopedia of Philosophy* (Summer 2019 edition), ed. by Edward N. Zalta, <https://plato.stanford.edu/archives/sum2019/entries/cardano/>

——'Girolamo Cardano e Giulio Cesare Scaligero: il dibattito sul ruolo dell'anima vegetativa', in *Girolamo Cardano: le opere, le fonti, la vita*, ed. by Marialuisa Baldi & Guido Canziani (Milan: FrancoAngeli, 1999), pp. 313–39

——'Health in the Renaissance', in *Health: A History*, ed. by Peter Adamson (Oxford & New York: Oxford University Press, 2019), pp. 141–73

——'Humans, Elephants, Diamonds and Gold: Patterns of Intentional Design in Girolamo Cardano's Natural Philosophy', *Gesnerus*, 71.2 (2014), 237–57

——'Life and its Animal Boundaries: Ethical Implications in Early Modern Theories of Human Animation', in *Ethical Perspectives on Animals in the Renaissance and Early Modern Period*, ed. by Burkhard Dohm & Cecilia Muratori, Micrologus' Library, 55 (Florence: SISMEL, Edizioni del Galluzzo, 2013), pp. 110–37

——'La magia e i poteri dell'immaginazione', in *I vincoli della natura: magia e stregoneria nel Rinascimento*, ed. by Germana Ernst & Guido Giglioni (Rome: Carocci, 2012), pp. 63–78

——'Man's Mortality, Conjectural Knowledge, and the Redefinition of the Divinatory Practice in Cardano's Philosophy', in *Cardano e la tradizione dei saperi*, ed. by Marialuisa Baldi & Guido Canziani (Milan: FrancoAngeli, 2003), pp. 43–65

——'Medicina e metafisica della vita animale in Cardano', *Bruniana & Campanelliana*, 8.1 (2002), 113–58

——'Medicine', in *Brill's Encyclopaedia of the Neo-Latin World*, ed. by Philip Ford, Jan Bloemendal, & Charles E. Fantazzi, 2 vols (Leiden: Brill, 2014), I, 679–90

——'Scaliger versus Cardano versus Scaliger', in *Forms of Conflict and Rivalries in Early Modern Europe*, ed. by David A. Lines, Jill Kraye, & Marc Laureys, Veröffentlichungen der Bonn University Press (Göttingen: Vandenhoeck & Ruprecht, 2015), pp. 109–30

——'Spirito e coscienza nella medicina di Bernardino Telesio', in *'Virtù ascosta e negletta': la Calabria nella modernità*, ed. by Germana Ernst & Rosa M. Calcaterra (Milan: Franco Angeli, 2011), pp. 154–68

——'Theurgy and Philosophy in Marsilio Ficino's Paraphrase of Iamblichus's De mysteriis Aegyptiorum', *Rinascimento*, 52 (2012), 3–36

GINZBURG, CARLO, *The Cheese and the Worms: The Cosmos of a Sixteenth-century Miller*, trans. by John & Anne C. Tedeschi (Baltimore: Johns Hopkins University Press, 1980; originally published as *Il formaggio e i vermi: il cosmo di un mugnaio del '500* (Turin: Einaudi, 1976))

GLIOZZI, GIULIANO, *Differenze e uguaglianza nella cultura europea moderna*, ed. by Anna Strumia (Naples: Vivarium, 1993)

GLORIEUX, PALÉMON, 'Gerson et les chartreux', *Recherches de théologie ancienne et médiévale*, 28 (1961), 115–53

GONTIER, THIERRY, *De l'homme à l'animal. Paradoxes sur la nature des animaux: Montaigne et Descartes* (Paris: Vrin, 1998)

GRAFTON, ANTHONY, *Cardano's Cosmos: The Worlds and Works of a Renaissance Astrologer* (Cambridge, MA: Harvard University Press, 1999)

GRAFTON, ANTHONY, and NANCY SIRAISI, 'Between the Election and My Hopes: Girolamo Cardano and Medical Astrology', in *Secrets of Nature: Astrology and Alchemy in Early Modern Europe*, ed. by William R. Newman & Anthony Grafton (Cambridge, MA: MIT Press, 2002), pp. 69–113

GRANADA, MIGUEL ÁNGEL, ' "Spiritus" and "anima a Deo immissa" in Telesio', in *Bernardino Telesio and the Natural Sciences in the Renaissance*, ed. by Pietro Daniel Omodeo (Leiden: Brill, 2019), pp. 33–50

GRANT, ROBERT M., 'Dietary Laws among Pythagoreans, Jews, and Christians', *The Harvard Theological Review*, 73.1–2 (1980), 299–310

GREENBLATT, STEPHEN, ed., *New World Encounters* (Berkeley, Los Angeles, & Oxford: University of California Press, 1993)

GREGORY, JAMES, *Of Victorians and Vegetarians: The Vegetarian Movement in Nineteenth-century Britain* (London & New York: Tauris Academic Studies, 2007)

GROTTANELLI, CRISTIANO, 'Uccidere, donare, mangiare: problematiche attuali nel sacrificio antico', in *Sacrificio e società nel mondo antico*, ed. by Cristiano Grottanelli & Nicola F. Parise (Pisa: Laterza, 1988), pp. 3–53

GRUMETT, DAVID, and RACHEL MUERS, *Theology on the Menu: Asceticism, Meat and Christian Diet* (Abingdon & New York: Routledge, 2010)

GUICHET, JEAN-LUC, ed., *De l'animal-machine à l'âme des machine: querelles biomécaniques de l'âme (XVIIe–XXIe siècle)* (Paris: Publications de la Sorbonne, 2010)

HADOT, PIERRE, *La Philosophie comme manière de vivre: entretiens avec Jeannie Carlier et Arnold I. Davidson* (Paris: Albin Michel, 2001)

——*Philosophy as a Way of Life: Spiritual Exercises from Socrates to Foucault*, ed. by Arnold I. Davidson, trans. by Michael Chase (Oxford: Blackwell, 1995; originally published as *Exercices spirituels et philosophie antique* (Paris: Études augustiniennes, 1993))

HAHN, THOMAS, 'The Indian Tradition in Western Medieval Intellectual History', *Viator*, 9 (1978), 213–34

HALBERTAL, MOSHE, *On Sacrifice* (Princeton & Oxford: Princeton University Press, 2012)

HALL, ROBERT E., 'Intellect, Soul and Body in Ibn Sīnā: Systematic Synthesis and Development of the Aristotelian, Neoplatonic and Galenic Theories', in *Interpreting Avicenna: Science and Philosophy in Medieval Islam. Proceedings of the Second Conference of the Avicenna Study Group*, ed. by Jon McGinnis (Leiden: Brill, 2004), pp. 62–86

HANKINS, JAMES, *Plato in the Italian Renaissance*, 2 vols (Leiden: Brill, 1990)

HARTOG, FRANÇOIS, *The Mirror of Herodotus: The Representation of the Other in the Writing of History*, trans. by Janet Lloyd (Berkeley, Los Angeles, & London: University of California Press, 1988; originally published as *Le Miroir d'Hérodote: essai sur la représentation de l'autre* (Paris: Gallimard, 1980))

HASSE, DAG NIKOLAUS, *Avicenna's 'De anima' in the Latin West: The Formation of a Peripatetic Philosophy of the Soul 1160–1300* (London & Turin: The Warburg Institute & Nino Aragno Editore, 2000)

HAUSSLEITER, JOHANNES, *Der Vegetarismus in der Antike* (Berlin: Töpelmann, 1935)

HEDLEY, DOUGLAS, *Sacrifice Imagined: Violence, Atonement, and the Sacred* (London: Bloomsbury, 2011)

HELDUSER, URTE, and BURKHARD DOHM, eds, *Imaginationen des Ungeborenen / Imaginations of the Unborn: Kulturelle Konzepte pränataler Prägung von der Frühen Neuzeit zur Moderne / Cultural Concepts of Prenatal Imprinting from the Early Modern Period to the Present* (Heidelberg: Winter, 2018)

HENDERSON, JOHN, 'Public Health, Pollution and the Problem of Waste Disposal in Early Modern Tuscany', in *Interazioni fra economia e ambiente biologico nell'europa preindustriale secc.*

XIII–XVIII, ed. by Simonetta Cavaciocchi (Atti della Quarantunesima Settimana di Studi 26–30 aprile 2009) (Florence: Firenze University Press, 2010), pp. 373–82

HENRY, DEVIN, 'Aristotle on Animals', in *Animals: A History*, ed. by Peter Adamson & G. Fay Edwards (Oxford & New York: Oxford University Press, 2018), pp. 9–26

HILTNER, KEN, ed., *Renaissance Ecology: Imagining Eden in Milton's England* (Pittsburgh, PA: Duquesne University Press, 2008)

HODGEN, MARGARET T., *Early Anthropology in the Sixteenth and Seventeenth Centuries* (Philadelphia: University of Pennsylvania Press, 1964)

HOGG, JAMES, 'Carthusian Abstinence', in *Analecta cartusiana: Spiritualität heute und gestern*, 35.14, ed. by James Hogg (New York & Salzburg: Edwin Mellen & Institut für Anglistik und Amerikanistik, 1991), pp. 5–15

JAYNE, SEARS REYNOLDS, *Plato in Renaissance England* (Dordrecht: Kluwer, 1995)

JOOST-GAUGIER, CHRISTIANE L., *Pythagoras and Renaissance Europe: Finding Heaven* (Cambridge: Cambridge University Press, 2009)

JOUANNA, JACQUES, 'Dietetics in Hippocratic Medicine: Definition, Main Problems, Discussion', in *Greek Medicine from Hippocrates to Galen: Selected Papers* (Leiden: Brill, 2012), pp. 137–53

JOY, MELANIE, *Why We Love Dogs, Eat Pigs, and Wear Cows: An Introduction to Carnism* (San Francisco: Conari Press, 2010)

KAISER, CHRISTIAN, *Das Leben der Anderen im Gemenge der Weisheitswege: Diogenes Laertios und der Diskurs um die philosophische Lebensform zwischen Spätantike und Früher Neuzeit* (Berlin: De Gruyter, 2013)

KATINIS, TEODORO, *Medicina e filosofia in Marsilio Ficino: il 'Consilio contro la pestilenza'* (Rome: Edizioni di Storia e Letteratura, 2007)

KESSLER, ECKHARD, '*Alles ist eines wie der Mensch und das Pferd*: zu Cardanos Naturbegriff', in *Girolamo Cardano: Philosoph, Naturforscher, Artz*, ed. by Eckhard Kessler (Wiesbaden: Harrassowitz, 1994), pp. 91–114

KLEIN, JOEL A., 'Daniel Sennert and the Chymico-atomical Reform of Medicine', in *Medicine, Natural Philosophy and Religion in Post-Reformation Scandinavia*, ed. by Ole Peter Grell & Andrew Cunningham (Abingdon & New York: Routledge, 2017), pp. 20–37

KLIBANSKI, RAIMOND, ERWIN PANOFSKI, and FRITZ SAXL, *Saturn and Melancholy: Studies in the History of Natural Philosophy, Religion and Art* (London: Nelson, 1964)

KLUBERTANZ, GEORGE, *The Discoursive Power: Sources and Doctrine of the 'Vis Cogitativa' According to St. Thomas Aquinas* (Carthagena: Messenger Press, 1952)

KLUTSTEIN, ILANA, 'Marsile Ficin et Hermès Trismégiste: quelques notes sur la traduction du Pimandre dans la Vulgata de Ficin', *Renaissance and Reformation / Renaissance et Réforme*, n.s., 14.3 (1990), 213–22

——*Marsilio Ficino et la théologie ancienne: oracles chaldaïques, hymnes orphiques — hymnes de Proclus* (Florence: Olschki, 1987)

KRISTELLER, PAUL OSKAR, 'Between the Italian Renaissance and the French Enlightenment: Gabriel Naudé as an Editor', *Renaissance Quarterly*, 32.1 (April 1979), 41–72

——*Die Philosophie des Marsilio Ficino* (Frankfurt am Main: Klostermann, 1972)

——*Studies in Renaissance Thought and Letters*, 4 vols (Rome: Edizioni di Storia e Letteratura, 1956–96)

KUHN, BARBARA, *Mythos und Metapher: Metamorphosen des Kirke-Mythos in der Literatur der italienischen Renaissance* (Munich: Fink, 2003)

KUPPERMAN, KAREN ORDAHL, ed., *America in European Consciousness 1493–1750* (Chapel Hill: University of North Carolina Press, 1995)

LARUE, RENAN, *Le Végétarisme des Lumières: l'abstinence de viande dans la France du XVIIIe siècle* (Paris: Garnier, 2019)

LASPIA, PATRIZIA, 'Aristotele e gli animali' in *Bestie, filosofi e altri animali*, ed. by Felice Cimatti, Stefano Gensini & Sandra Plastina (Milan: Mimesis, 2016), pp. 17–35

LEITGEB, MARIA-CHRISTINE, 'Marsilio Ficino — der Philosoph der Tierseelen?', in *The Animal Soul and the Human Mind: Renaissance Debates*, ed. by Cecilia Muratori (Pisa & Rome: Serra, 2013)

LESTRINGANT, FRANK, *Mapping the Renaissance World: The Geographical Imagination in the Age of Discovery* (Cambridge: Polity Press, 1994; originally published as *L'Atelier du cosmographe* (Paris: Albin Michel, 1991))

—— 'Le Nom des "Cannibales" de Christophe Colomb à Michel de Montaigne', *Bulletin de la Société des Amis de Montaigne*, 17–18 (1984), 51–74

—— 'The Philosopher's Breviary: Jean de Léry in the Enlightenment', *The New World*, special issue of *Representations*, 33 (Winter, 1991), 200–11

LÉVI-STRAUSS, CLAUDE, *We Are All Cannibals, and Other Essays*, trans. by Jane Marie Todd (New York: Columbia University Press, 2016; originally published as *Nous sommes tous des cannibales* (Paris: Éditions du Seuil, 2013))

LINES, DAVID A., 'When is a Translation not a Translation? Girolamo Manfredi's *De homine* (1474)', *Rivista di storia della filosofia*, 74.2 (2019), 287–307

MACK, BURTON, 'Introduction: Religion and Ritual', in *Violent Origins: Walter Burkert, René Girard, and Jonathan Z. Smith on Ritual Killing and Cultural Formation*, ed. by Robert G. Hamerton-Kelly (Stanford, CA: Stanford University Press, 1987), pp. 1–70

MACLEAN, IAN, 'Cardano's Eclectic Psychology and its Critique by Julius Caesar Scaliger', in *Transformations of the Soul: Aristotelean Psychology 1250–1650*, ed. by Dominik Perler (Leiden: Brill, 2009), offprint of *Vivarium*, 46.3 (2008), 170–95

MAGGI, ARMANDO, *In the Company of Demons: Unnatural Beings, Love, and Identity in the Italian Renaissance* (Chicago: University of Chicago Press, 2006)

MANNUCCI, ERICA JOY, *La cena di Pitagora: storia del vegetarianesimo dall'antica Grecia a internet* (Rome: Carocci, 2008)

MARCIALIS, MARIA TERESA, *Filosofia e psicologia animale: da Rorario a Leroy* (Cagliari: STEF, 1982)

—— 'La questione dell'anima delle bestie ovvero la razionalità senza soggetto', *Rivista di Storia della Filosofia*, 48.1 (1993), 83–100

MARTI, HANSPETER, 'Disputation', in *Historisches Wörterbuch der Rhetorik*, ed. by Gert Ueding, 12 vols (Tübingen: Niemeyer, 1994), II, cols. 866–80

MARVIN, JULIA, 'Cannibalism as an Aspect of Famine in Two English Chronicles', in *Food and Eating in Medieval Europe*, ed. by Martha Carlin & Joel T. Rosenthal (London: Hambledon Press, 1998), pp. 73–86

MASAI, FRANÇOIS, *Pléthon et le platonism de Mistra* (Paris: Les Belles Lettres, 1956)

MENNINGER, ANNEROSE, *Die Macht der Augenzeugen: Neue Welt und Kannibalen-Mythos, 1492–1600* (Stuttgart: Steiner, 1995)

MICHAEL, EMILY, 'Vegetarianism and Virtue: On Gassendi's Epicurean Defense', *Between the Species*, 7 (1991), 61–72

MIGLIETTI, SARA, and JOHN E. MORGAN, eds, *Governing the Environment in the Early Modern World: Theory and Practice* (Abingdon & New York: Routledge, 2017)

MILANESI, MARICA, 'Arsarot o Anian? Identità e separazione tra Asia e Nuovo Mondo nella cartografia del Cinquecento (1500–1570)', in *Il nuovo mondo nella coscienza italiana e tedesca nel Cinquecento*, ed. by Adriano Prosperi & Wolfgang Reinhard (Bologna: Il Mulino, 1992), pp. 19–78

MONFASANI, JOHN, 'George Gemistos Pletho and the West: Greek Émigrés, Latin Scholasticism and Renaissance Humanism', in *Renaissance Encounters: Greek East and Latin West*, ed. by Marina S. Brownlee & Dimitri H. Gondicas (Leiden: Brill, 2013), pp. 19–34

—— *George of Trebizond: A Biography and a Study of His Rhetoric and Logic* (Leiden: Brill, 1976)

——'Marsilio Ficino and Eusebius of Caesarea's *Praeparatio Evangelica*', *Rinascimento*, 49 (2009), 3–13

——'Platonic Paganism in the Fifteenth Century', in *Reconsidering the Renaissance: Papers from the Twenty-first Annual Conference of the Center for Medieval and Early Renaissance Studies*, ed. by Mario A. Di Cesare (Binghamton, NY: Medieval and Renaissance Texts and Studies, 1992), pp. 45–61

——'The Pre- and Post-History of Cardinal Bessarion's 1469 *In Calumniatorem Platonis*', in '*Inter graecos latinissimus, inter latinos graecissimus': Bessarion zwischen den Kulturen*, ed. by Christian Kaiser, Claudia Märtl, & Thomas Ricklin (Berlin: De Gruyter, 2013), pp. 347–66

——'*Prisca theologia* in the Plato-Aristotle Controversy Before Ficino', in *The Rebirth of Platonic Theology: Proceedings of a Conference Held at The Harvard University Center for Italian Renaissance Studies (Villa I Tatti) and the Istituto Nazionale di Studi sul Rinascimento (Florence, 26–27 April 2007), for Michael J. B. Allen*, ed. by James Hankins & Fabrizio Meroi (Florence: Olschki, 2013), pp. 47–59

——'A Tale of Two Books: Bessarion's *In Calumniatorem Platonis* and George of Trebizond's *Comparatio Philosophorum Platonis et Aristotelis*', *Renaissance Studies*, 22.1 (2008), 1–15

MONTAGUE, CHRISTOPHER, *George Gemistos Plethon: The Last of the Hellenes* (Oxford: Clarendon Press, 1986)

MONTANARI, MASSIMO, *Alimentazione e cultura nel Medioevo* (Rome & Bari: Laterza, 1988)

——*The Culture of Food*, trans. by Carl Ipsen (Oxford: Blackwell, 1994; originally published as *La fame e l'abbondanza: storia dell'alimentazione in Europa* (Rome & Bari: Laterza, 1994))

MORRIS, KATHERINE, 'Bêtes-machines', in *Descartes' Natural Philosophy*, ed. by Stephen Gaukroger and others (London & New York: Routledge, 2000), pp. 401–19

MOTOLESE, MATTEO, *Lo male rotundo: il lessico della fisiologia e della patologia nei trattati di pesti fra Quattro e Cinquecento* (Rome: Aracne, 2004)

MURATORI CECILIA, ed., *The Animal Soul and the Human Mind: Renaissance Debates* (Pisa & Rome: Serra, 2013)

——'Animali automatici precartesiani: due argomenti a partire da Aristotele', in *La voce e il logos. Filosofie dell'animalità nella storia delle idee*, ed. by Stefano Gensini (Pisa: ETS, 2020), pp. 111–37

——'Animals in the Renaissance: You Eat What You Are', in *Animals: A History*, ed. by Peter Adamson & G. Fay Edwards (Oxford & New York: Oxford University Press), pp. 163–86 & 371–76

——'The Aristotelian Carnivore: The Ethical Afterlives of Aristotle's Theory of Animal Irrationality', *Revue des sciences religieuses*, 93.3 (2019), 257–79

——'Better Animal than Human: The Happy Animal and the Human Animal in the Renaissance Reception of Aristotle', in *Die nackte Wahrheit und ihre Schleier. Weisheit und Philosophie im Mittelalter und früher Neuzeit. Studien zum Gedenken an Thomas Ricklin*, ed. by Christian Kaiser, Leonhard Maier, & Oliver Schrader, Dokimion 42 (Münster: Aschendorff, 2019), 477–97

——'La caduta dell'uomo e la sofferenza degli animali nella Disputatio tra Francesco Pucci e Fausto Sozzini', *Bruniana & Campanelliana*, 17.1 (2011), 139–49

——'Come vermi nel formaggio: la distinzione tra uomo e animali in una metafora Campanelliana', *Bruniana & Campanelliana*, 21.2 (2015), 381–94

——'The Earth's Perilous Fertility: Telesio on Spontaneous Generation and the Continuity of Living Beings', in *The Animal Soul and the Human Mind: Renaissance Debates*, ed. by Cecilia Muratori (Pisa & Rome: Serra, 2013), pp. 131–51

——'From Animal Bodies to Human Souls: Animals in Della Porta's Physiognomics', *Early Science and Medicine*, 22.1 (2017), 1–23

——'From Animal Happiness to Human Unhappiness: Cardano, Vanini, *Theophrastus redivivus* (1659)', in *Early Modern Philosophers and the Renaissance Legacy*, ed. by Cecilia Muratori & Gianni Paganini (Berlin: Springer, 2016), pp. 185–200

——'Henry More on Human Passions and Animal Souls', in *Emotional Minds*, ed. by Sabrina Ebbersmeyer (Berlin: De Gruyter, 2012), pp. 209–26

——'"In Human Shape to Become the Very Beast!" Henry More on Animals', *Cambridge Platonism*, ed. by Sarah Hutton, special issue of *British Journal for the History of Philosophy*, 25.5 (2017), 897–915

——'"Inter hominem & bruta nulla est similitudo": die Bestimmung der Grenze zwischen Mensch und Tier in *De statu primi hominis ante lapsum disputatio*', in *Religiöser Nonkonformismus und Frühneuzeitliche Gelehrtenkultur: akademische Netzwerke und Formen praktizierter Toleranz*, ed. by Friedrich Vollhardt (Berlin: Akademie Verlag, 2013), pp. 127–47

——'Medical and Ethical Aspects of Vegetarianism: On the Reception of Porphyry's *De abstinentia* in the Renaissance', in *Medical Ethics: Premodern Negotiations between Medicine and Philosophy*, ed. by Mariacarla Gadebusch Bondio (Stuttgart: Steiner, 2014), pp. 143–60

——'Of Rivers Changing their Course and of Animals Born in Foundries: Paradoxes in Telesio's Natural Philosophy', in *Sense, Affect and Self-preservation in Bernardino Telesio (1509–1588)*, ed. by Guido Giglioni & Jill Kraye (Berlin: Springer, forthcoming)

——'Pitagora tra i cannibali: dieta e ordine dei viventi a partire dalla letteratura rinascimentale sul nuovo mondo', in *Bestie, filosofi e altri animali*, ed. by Felice Cimatti, Stefano Gensini, & Sandra Plastina (Milan: Mimesis, 2016), pp. 143–60

——'Real Animals in Ideal Cities: The Place and Use of Animals in Renaissance Utopian Literature', special issue of *Renaissance Studies* dedicated to *The Animal in Renaissance Italy*, edited by Stephen Bowd & Sarah Cockram, 31.2 (2017), 223–39

MURATORI, CECILIA, ed., *The Animal Soul and the Human Mind: Renaissance Debates* (Pisa & Rome: Serra, 2013)

MURATORI, CECILIA, and GIANNI PAGANINI, eds, *Early Modern Philosophers and the Renaissance Legacy* (Berlin: Springer, 2016)

——'Renaissance and Early Modern Philosophy: Mobile Frontiers and Established Outposts', in *Early Modern Philosophers and the Renaissance Legacy*, ed. by Cecilia Muratori & Gianni Paganini (Berlin: Springer, 2016), pp. 1–18

MURR, SYLVIA, 'L'Âme des bêtes chez Gassendi', *Corpus — Revue de Philosophie*, 16–17 (1991), 37–63

NASEMANN, BEATE, *Theurgie und Philosophie in Jamblichs 'De mysteriis'* (Stuttgart: Teubner, 1991)

NAUTA, LODI, 'From an Outsider's Point of View: Lorenzo Valla on the Soul', *Vivarium*, 46.3 (2008), 368–91

NETO, JOSÉ R. MAIA, *Academic Skepticism in Seventeenth-century French Philosophy: The Charronian Legacy 1601–1662* (Berlin: Springer, 2014)

NEWMYER, STEPHEN T., *Animals, Rights and Reason in Plutarch and Modern Ethics* (New York: Routledge, 2006)

NUTTON, VIVIAN, *Ancient Medicine* (Abingdon & New York: Routledge, 2004)

O'DOHERTY, MARIANNE, *The Indies and the Medieval West* (Turnhout: Brepols, 2003)

OSBORNE, CATHERINE, *Dumb Beasts and Dead Philosophers: Humanity and the Humane in Ancient Philosophy and Literature* (Oxford & New York: Oxford University Press, 2007)

PADE, MARIANNE, 'The Reception of Plutarch from Antiquity to the Italian Renaissance', in *A Companion to Plutarch*, ed. by Mark Beck (Oxford: Blackwell, 2014), pp. 531–43

PAINTER, CORINNE M., 'The Vegetarian Polis: Just Diet in Plato's Republic and in Ours', *Journal of Animal Ethics*, 3.2 (2013), 121–32

PALUMBO, MARGHERITA, 'Maineri, Maino', in *Dizionario Biografico degli Italiani*, ed. by Alberto M. Ghisalberti and others, 85 vols (Rome: Istituto della Enciclopedia Italiana, 1960–2016), LXVII (2006), 595–97

PARASECOLI, FABIO, and PETER SCHOLLIERS, eds, *A Cultural History of Food*, 6 vols (Oxford: Berg, 2012)

PÉLICIER, YVES, 'Les Nourritures à la Renaissance: essai de typologie', in *Practiques et discours alimentaires à la Renaissance*, ed. by Jean-Claude Margolin & Robert Sauzet (Paris: Maisonneuve et Larose, 1982)

PETRUS, KLAUS, and MARKUS WILD, eds, *Animal Minds and Animal Ethics: Connecting Two Separate Fields* (Bielefeld: Transkript Verlag, 2014)

PFISTERER, ULRICH, 'Animal Art/Human Art: Imagined Borderlines in the Renaissance', in *Humankinds: The Renaissance and its Anthropologies*, ed. by Andreas Höfele & Stephan Laqué (Berlin: de Gruyter, 2011), pp. 217–43

PIERAZZO, ELENA, 'Un intellettuale a servizio della Chiesa: Girolamo Giovannini da Capugnano', *Filologia & critica*, 23 (1998), 206–48

PIRILLO, DIEGO, 'Relativismo culturale e "armonia del mondo": l'enciclopedia etnografica di Johannes Boemus', in *L'Europa divisa e i nuovi mondi: per Adriano Prosperi*, ed. by Massimo Donattini, Giuseppe Marcocci e Stefania Pastore, 3 vols (Pisa: Edizioni della Normale, 2011), II, 67–77

POHLENZ, MAX, *Die Stoa: Geschichte einer geistigen Bewegung* (Göttingen: Vandenhoeck & Ruprecht, 1992)

PRICE, MERRALL L., *Consuming Passions: The Uses of Cannibalism in Late Medieval and Early Modern Europe* (London & New York: Routledge, 2003)

PURNELL, FREDERICK, JR., 'Hermes and the Sibyl: A Note on Ficino's *Pimander*', *Renaissance Quarterly*, 30.3 (1977), 305–10

QUINT, DAVID, 'A Reconsideration of Montaigne's *Des cannibales*', in *America in European Consciousness 1493–1750*, ed. by Karen Ordahl Kupperman (Chapel Hill: University of North Carolina Press, 1995), pp. 166–91

——*Montaigne and the Quality of Mercy: Ethical and Political Themes in the Essais* (Princeton: Princeton University Press, 1998)

RACHELS, JAMES, 'The Basic Argument for Vegetarianism', in *The Animal Ethics Reader*, ed. by Susan J. Armstrong, & Richard G. Botzler, 3rd edn (Abingdon: Routledge, 2017), pp. 274–79

RADDEN, JENNIFER, ed., *The Nature of Melancholy: From Aristotle to Kristeva* (Oxford & New York: Oxford University Press, 2000)

RAY, MEREDITH K., *Writing Gender in Women's Letter Collections of the Italian Renaissance* (Toronto: University of Toronto Press, 2009)

REISS, TIMOTHY J., 'Montaigne, the New World, and Precolonialisms', in *The Oxford Handbook of Montaigne*, ed. by Philippe Desan (Oxford & New York: Oxford University Press, 2016), pp. 196–214

RICE, TAMARA TALBOT, *The Scythians* (London: Thames & Hudson, 1957)

RICHARDS, JENNIFER, 'Useful Books: Reading Vernacular Regimens in Sixteenth-century England', *Journal of the History of Ideas*, 73.2 (2012), 247–71

RIEDWEG, CHRISTOPH, *Pythagoras. Leben — Lehre — Nachwirkung: eine Einführung* (Munich: Beck, 2007)

ROBICHAUD, DENIS J.-J., 'Ficino on Force, Magic, and Prayers: Neoplatonic and Hermetic Influences in Ficino's *Three Books on Life*', *Renaissance Quarterly*, 70 (2017), 44–87

——*Plato's Persona: Marsilio Ficino, Renaissance Humanism, and Platonic Traditions* (Philadelphia: University of Pennsylvania Press, 2018)

ROMANO, FRANCESCO, 'Il vocabolario della "natura" nel *De Mysteriis* di Giamblico', in *The Divine Iamblichus: Philosopher and Man of Gods*, ed. by Henry J. Blumenthal & E. Gillian Clark (Bristol: Bristol Classical Press, 1993), pp. 159–72

ROTZOLL, MAIKE, *Pierleone da Spoleto: vita e opere di un medico del Rinascimento* (Florence: Olschki, 2000)

ROZZO, UGO, 'Italian Literature on the Index', in *Church, Censorship and Culture in Early Modern Italy*, ed. by Gigliola Fragnito, trans. by Adrian Belton (Cambridge: Cambridge

University Press, 2001), pp. 194–222

—— *La letteratura italiana negli 'Indici' del Cinquecento* (Udine: Forum, 2005)

RUBIÉS, JOAN-PAU, *Travel and Ethnology in the Renaissance: South-India through European Eyes, 1250–1625* (Cambridge: Cambridge University Press, 2000)

SAFFREY, HENRI DOMINIQUE, 'Analyse de la réponse de Jamblique à Porphyre, connue sous le titre *De mysteriis*', *Revue des Sciences philosophiques et théologiques*, 84.3 (July 2000), 489–511; reprinted in Saffrey, *Le Néoplatonisme après Plotin* (Paris: Vrin, 2000), pp. 77–99

—— 'Les Livres IV à VII du *De mysteriis* de Jamblique relus avec la *Lettre de Porphyry à Anébon*, in *The Divine Iamblichus: Philosopher and Man of Gods*, ed. by Henry J. Blumenthal & E. Gillian Clark (Bristol: Bristol Classical Press, 1993), pp. 144–58

SAKAMOTO, KUNI, *Julius Caesar Scaliger, Renaissance Reformer of Aristotelianism: A Study of 'Exotericae Exercitationes'* (Leiden: Brill, 2016)

SARASOHN, LISA, *Gassendi's Ethics: Freedom in a Mechanistic Universe* (Ithaca, NY, & London: Cornell University Press, 1996)

SCAFI, ALESSANDRO, *Maps of Paradise* (London: British Library, 2013)

SCALA, AIDÉE, *Girolamo Rorario: un umanista diplomatico del Cinquecento* (Florence: Olschki, 2004)

SCATTOLA, MERIO, 'Naturrecht als Rechtstheorie: die Systematisierung der "res scholastica" in der Naturrechtslehre des Domingo de Soto', in *Die Ordnung der Praxis: neue Studien zur Spanischen Spätscholastik*, ed. by Frank Grunert & Kurt Seelmann (Tübingen: Max Niemeyer Verlag, 2001), pp. 21–47

SCHÄFER, DANIEL, *Old Age and Disease in Early Modern Medicine* (London: Pickering & Chatto, 2011)

SCHIESARI, JULIANA, *The Gendering of Melancholia: Feminism, Psychoanalysis and the Symbolics of Loss in Renaissance Literature* (Ithaca, NY, & London: Cornell University Press, 1992)

SCHMITT, CHARLES B., *John Case and Aristotelianism in Renaissance England* (Kingston & Montreal: McGill-Queen's University Press, 1983)

SCILLACIO, NICOLA, *Delle isole del mare meridiano e indiano recentemente scoperte*, ed. by Osvaldo Baldacci (Florence: Olschki, 1992)

SDZUJ, REIMUND B., 'Zum Cartesianismus am Bremer *Gymnasium illustre*: Johann Eberhard Schwelings Dissertation *De anima britorum* (1676)', in *Frühneuzeitliche Disputationen: polyvalente Produktionsapparate gehlerten Wissens*, ed. by Marion Gindhart, Hanspeter Marti, & Robert Seidel (Cologne, Weimar, & Vienna: Böhlau, 2016), pp. 179–98

SECRET, FRANÇOIS, 'Notes sur quelques kabbalistes chrétiens', *Bibliothèque d'Humanism et Renaissance*, 36.1 (1974), 67–82

SFAMENI, GIULIA GASPARRO, 'Critica del sacrificio cruento e antropologia in Grecia: da Pitagora a Porfirio. II. Il *De abstinentia* porfiriano', in *Sangue e antropologia nella teologia: Atti della VI Settimana, Roma, 23–28 nov. 1987*, ed. by Francesco Vattioni (Rome: Edizioni Pia Unione Preziosissimo Sangue, 1989), pp. 461–505

SHEHADI, FADLOU, *Philosophies of Music in Medieval Islam* (Leiden: Brill, 1995)

SICHERL, MARTIN, *Die Handschriften, Ausgaben und Übersetzungen von Iamblichos 'De mysteriis': eine kritisch-historische Studie* (Berlin: Akademie Verlag, 1957)

SIMMONS, MICHAEL B., *Universal Salvation in Late Antiquity: Porphyry of Tyre and the Pagan-Christian Debate* (Oxford & New York: Oxford University Press, 2015)

SINGER, ISAAC B., *Come mai Dio non è vegetariano? Intervista di Matteo Bellinelli* (Bellinzona: Edizioni Casagrande, 2005)

SINIOSSOGLOU, NIKETAS, *Radical Platonism in Byzantium: Illumination and Utopia in Gemistos Plethon* (Cambridge: Cambridge University Press, 2011)

SIRAISI, NANCY, *The Clock and the Mirror: Girolamo Cardano and Renaissance Medicine* (Princeton: Princeton University Press, 1997)

—— *Medieval and Early Renaissance Medicine: An Introduction to Knowledge and Practice* (Chicago: University of Chicago Press, 1990)

SKENAZI, CYNTHIA, *Aging Gracefully in the Renaissance: Stories of Later Life from Petrarch to Montaigne* (Leiden: Brill, 2013)

SMITH, PAUL J., 'Montaigne in the World', in *The Oxford Handbook of Montaigne*, ed. by Philippe Desan (Oxford & New York: Oxford University Press, 2016), pp. 287–305

SOLMI, EDMONDO, *Scritti vinciani* (Florence: La Nuova Italia, 1976)

SORABJI, RICHARD, *Animal Minds and Human Morals: The Origins of the Western Debate* (Ithaca, NY: Cornell University Press, 1995)

—— *The Philosophy of the Commentators, 200–600 AD: Physics* (Ithaca, NY: Cornell University Press, 2005)

SPENCER, COLIN, *Vegetarianism: A History* (London: Grub Street, 2000)

STANCATI, CLAUDIA, 'Oltre Descartes: linguaggio e pensiero degli animali tra XVII e XVIII secolo', in *Macchine e vita nel XVII e XVIII secolo*, ed. by Francesca Bonicalzi (Florence: Le Monnier, 2006), pp. 113–40

STEINER, GARY, *Anthropomorphism and its Discontents: The Moral Status of Animals in the History of Western Philosophy* (Pittsburgh, PA: University of Pittsburgh Press, 2005)

—— 'Descartes on the Moral Status of Animals', *Archiv für Geschichte der Philosophie*, 80.3 (1998), 268–91

STEINMANN, MARC, *Alexander der Große und die 'nackten Weisen' Indiens: der fiktive Briefwechsel zwischen Alexander und dem Brahmanenkönig Dindimus* (Berlin: Frank & Timme, 2012)

STEPHENS, WALTER, 'Habeas Corpus: Demonic Bodies in Ficino, Psellus and *Malleus maleficarum*', in *The Body in Early Modern Italy*, ed. by Julia L. Hairston & Walter Stephens (Baltimore: The Johns Hopkins University Press, 2010), pp. 74–91

STRAWSON, GALEN, 'Realistic Monism: Why Physicalism Entails Panpsychism', in *Consciousness and Its Place in Nature: Does Physicalism Entail Panpsychism?*, ed. by Anthony Freeman (Exeter: Imprint Academic, 2006)

STUART, TRISTRAM, *The Bloodless Revolution: Radical Vegetarians and the Discovery of India* (London: Harper Collins, 2006)

TAORMINA, DANIELA PATRIZIA, *Jamblique: critique de Plotin et de Porphyre. Quatre études* (Paris: Vrin, 1999)

TARTABINI, ANGELO, *Cannibalismo e antropofagia: uomini e animali, vittime e carnefici* (Milan: Mursia, 1997)

TEMKIN, OWSEI, *Galenism: Rise and Decline of a Medical Philosophy* (Ithaca, NY: Cornell University Press, 1973)

THOMAS, ROSALIND, *Herodotus in Context: Ethnography, Science and the Art of Persuasion* (Cambridge: Cambridge University Press, 2000)

TIELEMAN, TEUN, 'Galen's Psychology', in *Galien et la philosophie: huit exposés suivis de discussions*, ed. by Jonathan Barnes & Jacques Jouanna (Geneva: Librairie Droz, 2003), pp. 131–61

TIMOTIN, ANDRÉI, *La Démonologie platonicienne* (Leiden: Brill, 2012)

TOBIAS, MICHAEL CHARLES, and JANE GRAY MORRISON, *Why Life Matters: Fifty Ecosystems of the Heart and Mind* (Berlin: Springer, 2014)

TOURNON, ANDRÉ, *Montaigne: la glose et l'essai* (Lyon: Presses universitaires de Lyon, 1983)

TOUSSAINT, STÉPHANE, 'L'individuo estatico: tecniche profetiche in Marsilio Ficino e Giovanni Pico della Mirandola', *Bruniana & Campanelliana*, 6.2 (2000), 251–379

ULLUCCI, DANIEL C., *The Christian Rejection of Animal Sacrifice* (Oxford & New York: Oxford University Press, 2012)

VAN GROESEN, MICHIEL, *The Representations of the Overseas World in the De Bry Collection of Voyages (1590–1634)* (Leiden: Brill, 2008)

VANHAELEN, MAUDE, 'L'Enterprise de traduction et d'exégèse de Ficin dans les années 1486–1489: démons et prophétie à l'aube de l'ère savonarolienne', *Humanistica*, 1 (2010), 125–36

—— 'Ficino's Commentary on St Paul's First Epistle to the Romans (1497): An Anti-savonarolan Reading of Vision and Prophecy', in *The Rebirth of Platonic Theology:*

Proceedings of a Conference Held at The Harvard University Center for Italian Renaissance Studies (Villa I Tatti) and the Istituto Nazionale di Studi sul Rinascimento (Florence, 26–27 April 2007), for Michael J. B. Allen, ed. by James Hankins & Fabrizio Meroi (Florence: Olschki, 2013), pp. 205–33

VASOLI, CESARE, 'Il *De christiana religione* di Marsilio Ficino. Parole chiave: religione, sapienza, profezia, vita civile, ebrei', *Bruniana & Campanelliana*, 13.2 (2007), 403–28

—— *Filosofia e religione nella cultura del Rinascimento* (Naples: Guida, 1988)

—— 'Pitagora in monastero', *Interpres*, 1 (1978), 256–72

—— *Quod sit Deus: studi su Marsilio Ficino* (Lecce: Conte, 1999)

VECCE, CARLO, 'In margine alla prima lettera di Andrea Corsali (Leonardo in India)', in *Ai confini della letteratura. Atti della giornata in onore di Mario Pozzi, Morgex, 4 maggio 2012*, ed. by Jean-Louis Fournel, Rosanna Gorris Camos, & Enrico Mattioda (Turin: Aragno, 2014), pp. 67–81

VEGETTI, MARIO, *Il coltello e lo stilo* (Milan: Il Saggiatore, 1996)

VERNANT, JEAN-PIERRE, and MARCEL DETIENNE, *The Cuisine of Sacrifice Among the Greeks*, trans. by Paula Wissing (Chicago: University of Chicago Press, 1989; originally published as *La Cuisine du sacrifice en pays grec* (Paris: Gallimard, 1979))

VESCOVINI, GRAZIELLA FEDERICI, *'Arti' e filosofia nel secolo XIV: studi sulla tradizione aristotelica e i 'moderni'* (Florence: Vallecchi, 1983)

VIGUS, JAMES, 'Adapting Rights: Thomas Taylor's *A Vindication of the Rights of Brutes*', in *Romantic Adaptations*, ed. by Cian Duffy, Peter Howell, & Caroline Ruddell (Farnham: Ashgate, 2013), pp. 41–56

VILLING, ALEXANDRA, 'Don't Kill the Goose that Lays the Golden Egg? Some Thoughts on Bird Sacrifices in Ancient Greece', in *Animal Sacrifice in the Ancient Greek World*, ed. by Sarah Hitch & Ian Rutherford (Cambridge: Cambridge University Press, 2017), pp. 63–101

VOGT, KATJA MARIA, *Law, Reason and the Cosmic City: Political Philosophy in the Early Stoa* (Oxford & New York: Oxford University Press, 2008)

WALKER, DANIEL P., 'Orpheus the Theologian and Renaissance Platonists', *Journal of the Warburg and Courtauld Institutes*, 16.1–2 (1953), 100–20

—— *Spiritual and Demonic Magic from Ficino to Campanella* [1958], 2nd edn (University Park: Pennsylvania State University Press, 2000)

WALTERS, KERRY S., and LISA PORTMESS, eds, *Ethical Vegetarianism: From Pythagoras to Peter Singer* (Albany: State University of New York Press, 1999)

WATSON, KELLY L., *Insatiable Appetites: Imperial Encounters with Cannibals in the North Atlantic World* (New York & London: New York University Press, 2015)

WERTZ, TILLMANN, *Georgius Pictorius (1500–1569/73): Leben und Werk eines oberrheinischen Arztes und Humanisten* (Heidelberg: Palatina Verlag, 2006)

WHITEHEAD, NEIL L., 'Sacred Cannibals and Golden Kings: Travelling the Borders of the New World with Hans Staden and Walter Ralegh', in *Borders and Travellers in Early Modern Europe*, ed. by Thomas Betteridge (Abingdon: Routledge, 2017), pp. 169–85

WILKINS, JOHN, 'The Contribution of Galen, *De subtiliante diaeta (On the Thinning Diet)*', in *The Unknown Galen*, ed. by Vivian Nutton, supplement 77 of the *Bulletin of the Institute of Classical Studies* (2002), 47–55

WIRSZUBSKI, CHAIM, 'Francesco Giorgio's Commentary on Giovanni Pico's Kabbalistic Theses', *Journal of the Warburg and Courtauld Institutes*, 37 (1974), 145–56

—— *Pico della Mirandola's Encounter with Jewish Mysticism* (Cambridge, MA: Harvard University Press, 1989)

WOJCIEHOWSKI, HANNAH CHAPELLE, *Group Identity in the Renaissance World* (Cambridge: Cambridge University Press, 2011)

ZAMBELLI, PAOLA, *L'apprendista stregone: astrologia, cabala e arte lulliana in Pico della Mirandola e seguaci* (Venice: Marsilio, 1995)

ZAMBON, FRANCESCO, *La cena segreta: trattati e rituali catari* (Milan: Adelphi, 1997)

ZIEGLER, JOSEPH, *Medicine and Religion c. 1300: The Case of Arnau de Vilanova* (Oxford: Clarendon Press, 1998)

Manuscript

FORLÌ, BIBLIOTECA COMUNALE 'Saffi', Ms. O.VII.57 (fondo Piancastelli)

Online Source

Archivio dei filosofi del Rinascimento: <http://www.iliesi.cnr.it/atc>

INDEX

❖

www.ingramcontent.com/pod-product-compliance
Lightning Source LLC
Chambersburg PA
CBHW081424090426
42740CB00017B/3167